John James Raven

The Church Bells of Suffolk, a Chronicle in Nine Chapters

with a complete list of the inscriptions on the bells, and historical notes

John James Raven

The Church Bells of Suffolk, a Chronicle in Nine Chapters
with a complete list of the inscriptions on the bells, and historical notes

ISBN/EAN: 9783744768078

Printed in Europe, USA, Canada, Australia, Japan

Cover: Foto ©Andreas Hilbeck / pixelio.de

More available books at **www.hansebooks.com**

The Church Bells of Suffolk.

THE

Church Bells of Suffolk,

A CHRONICLE IN NINE CHAPTERS,

With a Complete List of the Inscriptions on the Bells,
and Historical Notes.

BY

JOHN JAMES RAVEN, D.D.,

Of Emmanuel College, Cambridge;
Vicar of Fressingfield with Withersdale; and Honorary Canon of
Norwich Cathedral;
President of the Norwich Diocesan Association of Ringers;

AUTHOR OF "CHURCH BELLS OF CAMBRIDGESHIRE," ETC., ETC.

LONDON:
JARROLD AND SONS, 3, PATERNOSTER BUILDINGS.
1890.

DEDICATED,

BY PERMISSION,

TO THE

HONOURABLE AND RIGHT REVEREND

THE

Lord Bishop of Norwich.

PREFACE.

As this, the latest contribution to English Campanology, is in one sense the earliest, a few words seem necessary to explain the history of a book which has been forty-two years in hand, and to account for its imperfections.

In the days of my boyhood at Mildenhall, where my father was curate, I took great delight in the sound of the bells, and raised a five-pound note for the repair of the gear of the fine old tenor. The bell-hanger, one Flanders Green, an enthusiastic ringer, asked me to read for him two of the inscriptions, of which I made a transcript in a copy-book on August 28th, 1848, and proceeded to the investigation of other bells in the neighbourhood. In the course of two years I had made a considerable collection from Norfolk, Suffolk, Cambridgeshire, and South Lincolnshire. Wherever I went I carried on the work; but undergraduate life and residence in Dorset and Kent prevented the county of Suffolk receiving very much attention till my college presented me to the Mastership of Bungay Grammar School in 1859, when I attacked at once the north-east of the county. During these eleven years I had become acquainted with Messrs. Ellacombe, Tyssen, Sperling, Lukis, and L'Estrange; and our comparison of discoveries was throwing much light on the history and interpretation of bell-marks. I was enabled to finish and publish the *Church Bells of Cambridgeshire*, after my removal to Yarmouth in 1866, and by the kindness of the Cambridge Antiquarian Society to put forth a second and improved edition in 1885. Other counties seemed to pass by me at a gallop while poor Suffolk was slowly hobbling on. Mr. Tyssen's Sussex, Mr. Ellacombe's Devon, and Mr. L'Estrange's Norfolk were things of the far past. Mr. Ellacombe added Somerset and Gloucester, Mr. Dunkin Cornwall, Mr. North swept clear the wide area embraced by Leicester, Northampton, Rutland, Lincoln, and Bedford, leaving at his lamented death Hertford to be completed by Mr. Stahlschmidt, who by himself gave us Surrey and Kent, and, in his turn summoned to rest, has placed Essex within the reach of a third hand.

When my college presented me to the Vicarage of Fressingfield in 1885, the end of my labours seemed not far distant; but it receded, and had it not been for the energy of my good friends in other corners of the County, I should have made but little progress.

Mr. Sperling's collection, chiefly from North-west Suffolk, communicated to the *East Anglian* some thirty years ago, has supplied the inscriptions from many towers; and his letters to me about the same time added many useful notes. Messrs. J. L. Biddell, Herbert W. Birch, Charles Candler, E. M. Dewing, R. S. Dewing, C. H. Hawkins, W. C. Pearson, Percy Scott, Shaw, E. J. Wells, Freeman Wright, F. D. Young, and many others among the clergy and laity have been helpers in various parts of the county; among whom the name of Cecil Deedes, late Rector of Wickham S. Paul's, Essex, demands especial mention. To him we are indebted for the bulk of the south-west corner of our county.

Mr. Amherst D. Tyssen has kindly allowed me the use of the wood blocks cut for his lamented father; and a like favour has been granted to me by the representatives of our departed friends, North and Stahlschmidt. The Cambridge Antiquarian Society, too, has permitted me to illustrate the Bury lettering, and other marks, with the cuts made for my *Church Bells of Cambridgeshire.*

To Messrs. Wertheimer I am greatly obliged for the cut of the effigy of Robert Brasyer, fig. 53.

Mr. Tyssen has supplied the translation of the Year Book record of the great bell Lawsuit, on pp. 40, etc.

The music of *Requiem Eternam* has been sent to me by the courtesy of Mr. W. J. Birkbeck.

The weights and notes of the bells are to be regarded only as approximations, in many cases. The former are generally determined by tradition, with a tendency to magnification. The latter vary with notions of pitch, and the actual note is frequently between two received semitones. When I began my work I had no ambition beyond a registration of inscriptions, and took little account of anything else.

During the period that the work has been preparing for the press many changes have come about through recasting. Some of these have not been noticed; and in other instances, additions to rings have swelled up the list of errata.

The lists of bells cast by the various founders are not exhaustive; and at the last moment information keeps coming in. I may take occasion in the *East Anglian* to give additional short notes from time to time; and perhaps to write at greater length in the Journal of the Suffolk Institute of Archæology and Natural History.

Had not the work possessed for me special attractions, it could not have come forth in any form. As it now stands before me I recognize, more fully perhaps than any one else, its errors and shortcomings. I ask the indulgent judgment of those of my subscribers who have not undergone a labour of the kind. From my fellow-labourers I expect it. Those who know what the toil is will say that, with all its faults, it is better that this contribution to the Campanology of England should have come forth than that the heap of material collected should remain without an attempt to reduce it to order.

J. J. RAVEN.

Fressingfield Vicarage, Harleston,
August 28th, 1890.

TABLE OF CONTENTS.

CHAPTER I.

Introduction—The origin of large bells probably Oriental—General absence of bells of the Saxon and Norman periods—Mediæval instructions for bell-founding—Walter of Odyngton's—Those appended to the treatise of Gerbertus Scholasticus on Music—Castings from wax models very rare—Existing Ante-Conquestal towers—Scanty notices of the Norman and Early English periods—A solitary bell from the Lynn foundry c. 1300, in Suffolk—Early Aldgate founders, from Robert Rider to Henry Derby, and their works in Suffolk ... ... 1—12.

CHAPTER II.

Transition from Longobardic to black-letter—"William ffoundor," shown to be William Dawe—His Suffolk bells—His gun-founding for Dover Castle in 1385—His will—John Danyell's bells—Richard Hille's—Henry Jordan, Fishmonger and Founder—His works at King's College, Cambridge, and at East Bergholt—His will—Bequest remaining to this day—His obit—His son, Dan Henry ... ... 13—32.

CHAPTER III.

Two bells probably by Thomas Bullisdon—The "moon and stars" shield—Two bells by William Culverden—His rebus—History of the use of the word *Emmanuel*—Culverden's rebus interpreted—His will—Westminster School—Boston Merchant Guild—The Norwich Foundry—A nameless group—Fressingfield tenor—The Brasyers—A Mediæval Law-suit—Richard Brasyer in the Court of Common Pleas—Ingenious argument of Serjeant Genney—The large group of the Brasyers' bells—The Burlingham group ... ... 33—63.

CHAPTER IV.

Suffolk founders—Bury S. Edmund's—A joke on S. Barbara's name—H. S.—The Chirches—Reginald Chirche at Bishop's Stortford—His will—Redenhall tenor the greatest remaining work from Bury—Thomas Chirche—Roger Reve—The Seventh at All Saints', Sudbury—Gun-founding at Bury—Waifs—A Venlo bell at Whitton—A Mechlin bell at Bromeswell—Some account of the Mechlin foundry—Gregory Pascal of Capel—The Tonne family—Sproughton tenor ... ... 64—80.

CHAPTER V.

Sance and Sacring bells—Funeral uses—Angelus bell—Curfew—Chime-barrels—Jack o' th' Clock ... ... 81—89.

CHAPTER VI.

The Reformation—Number of Church bells then in Suffolk Spoliation—Restoration—Stephen Tonni of Bury, and his man William Land—Their work at Long Melford—Death of Julian Tonney the weaver—Bury foundry goes to Thetford—Founders dining at Wattisfield—Thomas Draper, Mayor of Thetford—The Brends of Norwich—Dier's bell at Clare—Topsel's at Cratfield—Richard Bowler—The Thorington bell and a reminiscence of Kett's rebellion—Aldgate gun-founding again 90—107.

CHAPTER VII.

John Clarke, an itinerant, in Suffolk—Joseph Carter—Peter Hawkes—The Bury founders in the days of the Stuarts—John Draper of Thetford—The later Brends of Norwich—"Colchester Graye" and his works, including the Lavenham tenor—The siege of Colchester—Miles Graye's foundry burnt—The Puritan *régime*—Bunyan—Milton—Compulsory ringing—John Darbie of Ipswich ... ... 108—125.

CHAPTER VIII.

Dick Whittington—Call changes—Early peals—The "Twenty all over," or "Christmas Eve"—7,360 Oxford Treble Bob at Bungay, in 1860 ... ... 126—130.

CHAPTER IX.

Later bells—Robard Gurney of Bury—Christopher Hodson of S. Mary Cray—Miles Graye the younger—A solitary bell of Christopher Graye's at Thrandeston—His difficulties in Cambridgeshire—Is succeeded by Charles Newman, and the foundry taken to Lynn—Thomas Newman at Bracondale and Bury—John Stephens—Sudbury and its founders—Henry Pleasant—Thomas Gardiner—His critic at Edwardstone—John Goldsmith of Redgrave—Ransomes and Sims—London founders—Newton and Peele—Catlin—The Whitechapel men—Phelps and his record of Dr. Sacheverell at Charsfield—His eight at Bury S. Mary's—Lester—Pack—A failure at Beccles—Chapman—The Mears family—Benefactions of the Suffolk nobility and others—The Warners of Cripplegate—A ship's bell from Stockholm at Lavenheath—John Briant of Exning—The St. Neot's men and their successors—Joseph Eayre—Arnold—The Taylors of Loughborough—Osborn and Dobson of Downham Market—Birmingham founders—Blews at Lowestoft—Carr at Newbourne—The Redenhall foundry—Recommendation to Southwold—Jubilee bells at Mildenhall—Conclusion ... ... 131—155.

INSCRIPTIONS ... ... 156—259.

LIST OF ILLUSTRATIONS.

I.—PLATES.
I. Lettering and Cross used by Richard Wymbish on Bell
at Great Bradley ... ... *Opposite p.* 10
II. Cross and Capitals on Bell at Sudbury S. Peter ,, 35
III. London Marks ... ... ,, 37
IV. Norwich Lettering ... ... ,, 45
V. Lettering, Cross, and Stop of the Burlingham Type 60
VI. The Flight into Egypt, The Annunciation, and a
Piece of Border from a Mechlin Bell at
Bromeswell ... . ,, 75
VII (*a*) Trefoil from Whitton. (*b*) The Presentation
in the Temple, from a Mechlin Bell at
Bromeswell. Border and Medallion of S.
Michael and the Dragon, from a Mechlin
Bell at Bromeswell ... ... ,, 76
VIII. "Requiem Æternam" ... ,, 86

II.—CUTS INSERTED IN THE LETTER-PRESS.

Figure   *Page*
1. Cross of John Godynge of Lynn, from Worlington   7
2. Early London Cross, from Barnardiston ...   8
3. Stop, from Barnardiston   9
4. Capital A, from Barnardiston   9
5. Capital G ,, ,, ...   9
6. Head of King Edward III., from Ampton ... 12
7. Initial Cross, from Ampton ... 12
8. The larger Laver Shield 13
9. The smaller Laver Shield 13

Figure		Page
10.	Seal of Sandre de Gloucetre, with laver	14
11.	The Trefoils Shield	15
12.	Larger Initial Cross, in Octagon, used by William Dawe and others	15
13.	Smaller ditto, ditto	16
14, 15.	Smaller Crosses in Lozenges, used by William Dawe and others	16
16.	Rebus of William Dawe	16
17.	Medallion from Clare ...	17
18.	Octagon with six fleur-de-lys ...	18
19.	Arms of France and England, crowned	21
20.	,, ,, ,, uncrowned	21
21.	Mark, of a somewhat French type, used by London Founders	21
22.	iþu . merci . laði . þelp	22
23.	Cross and ring shield	23
24.	Cross on Bell formerly at Wangford S. Denis	23
25, 26.	Henry Jordan's Shields	24
27.	Clochard formerly at King's College, Cambridge ...	27
28.	,, at East Bergholt	28
29.	Shield of T. B., from Kesgrave and Iken	33
30.	Cross sometimes used by T. B. ...	34
31.	Moon and Stars Shield	35
32—35.	Emblems of the Evangelists, from Bradfield Combust and Saxmundham ...	35, 36
36, 37.	Crosses sometimes found with them ...	36
(38—44.	London Marks, on Plate III.)	
45.	Culverden's Rebus, from Stratford S. Mary and Ubbeston	37
46.	Pot of Thomas Potter of Norwich, from Market Weston	42
47.	Cross from Cratfield Clock-bell, in the early part of the fifteenth century	42
48.	The earlier Norwich Lion's Head	42
49.	Fine Initial Cross, Norwich, from Fressingfield	43
50.	Brasyer's larger Ermine Shield ,,	44
51.	,, Sprigged Shield ,, ...	44
52.	,, smaller Ermine Shield ,, ...	44
53.	Effigy of Robert Brasyer, from S. Stephen's, Norwich ...	45
(54—60.	The letters D, H, A, L, C, M, and N, used by the Brasyers, on Plate IV.)	

LIST OF ILLUSTRATIONS. xv

Figure		Page
61.	Brasyer's Later Initial Cross	46
62.	,, ,, Lion's Head	46
63.	Shield used in Kent, with letters of the Burlingham type, see Plate V.	61
64.	Shield of Abbot of St. Edmundsbury	62
65.	Larger Bury Shield, with Cannon	64
66.	Smaller ,, ,,	64
67.	Cross used at the Bury Foundry, about two-thirds real size	65
68.	Stop ,, ,, ,, ,,	65
69—71.	Bury Lettering	65, 66
72.	Venlo Trefoil, from Whitton	74
73.	Large Cross of John Tonne, from Stanstead	78
74—76.	Stops ,, ,,	79
77.	Small Cross ,, from Stoke-by-Clare	80
78.	Sance-bell on Hawstead Rood-screen, from the east	82
79.	Sance-bell Cot. from Fressingfield	83
80.	Jack o' th' Clock, from Southwold	89
81.	Stephen Tonni's Crown and Arms ⎫ used at Bury, in the ⎫	95
82.	,, Fleur-de-lys ⎭ reign of Q. Elizabeth ⎬	
83.	Clipped Crown and Arrows, probably used at Thetford	98
84.	Fleur-de-lys, probably used at Thetford	99
85.	Thomas Draper's Fleur-de-lys, from Ashbocking	100
86.	Arms of Norwich City, used by William Brend	115
87.	A Mark used by Miles Graye, sen., of Colchester, from Stradbroke	116
88.	Mark of James Bartlett of London, from Somerleyton	147
89.	Old London Initial Cross, from Hadleigh	197
90.	Laxfield Tower	213
91.	Cross from All Saints, Sudbury	240

ERRATA.

Read on page 24, last line but one, "third" for "treble."
,, ,, 39, line 11, "Noah's" for "Noah."
,, ,, 54, ,, 2, "second" for "fourth."
,, ,, 54, ,, 11, "Earl" for "East."
,, ,, 56, last line but one, "second" for "tenor."
,, ,, 57, line 25, omit "Eye second."
,, ,, 64, ,, 5, "Bromeswell" for "Bromenville."
,, ,, 69, ,, 9, "treble" for "third."
,, ,, 78, ,, 12, "possibly" for "probably."
,, ,, 86, ,, 10, add "and third" to "second."
,, ,, 109, ,, 23, "tenor" for "second."
,, ,, 109, ,, 31, "fifth" for "tenor."
,, ,, 111, ,, 26, "second" for "treble."
,, ,, 112, ,, 2, "Little" for "Great."
,, ,, 112, four lines from bottom, "third" for "second."
,, ,, 113, line 35, "Marlesford" for "Marlingford."
,, ,, 114, ,, 4, "third" for "treble."
,, ,, 114, ,, 17, *Ilketshall S. Andrew* should be under 1623.
,, ,, 114, four lines from bottom, "second" for "fourth."
,, ,, 117, last line but one, "second" for "third."
,, ,, 119, line 6, "Barham" for "Parham."
,, ,, 123, eight lines from bottom, Ipswich, S. Mary-at-Elms, should be under 1660.
,, ,, 124, line 2, omit "second."
,, ,, 124, ,, 4, "seventh" for "fifth."
,, ,, 124, ,, 22, "second" for "treble."
,, ,, 124, ,, 25, "treble" for "second," "tenor" for "fourth."
,, ,, 125, ,, 12, "tenor" for "fifth."
,, ,, 113, ,, 22, "fourth" for "third."
,, ,, 134, ,, 11, "first, fourth, and fifth" for "first three."
,, ,, 138, ,, 1, "treble" for "tenor."
,, ,, 139, ,, 25, "Hawkedon" for "Hawkendon."
,, ,, 139, ,, 31, "third" for "fourth."
,, ,, 140, ,, 23, Westhorpe under 1702.
,, ,, 140, ,, 33, "Earl" for "East."
,, ,, 141, ,, 12, "Mr." for "Dr."
,, ,, 143, ,, 27, Mickfield under 1716.
,, ,, 144, ,, 7, "treble and second" for "third and fourth."
,, ,, 144, ,, 17, "second" for "bell."
,, ,, 145, ,, 8, "treble, second, and third" for "fourth."
,, ,, 145, ,, 15, "tenor" for "second."
,, ,, 146, after line 2, add Syleham second, *Margaret*.
,, ,, 148, line 9, Bruisyard under 1732.
,, ,, 148, ,, 11, Little Stonham under 1729.
,, ,, 148, ,, 20, the Helmingham bell went to Henley.
,, ,, 151, ,, 7, omit "Norton and."
,, ,, 151, ,, 8, "work" for "works."
,, ,, 166, ,, 8, "Greyse" for "Greyfe."
,, ,, 179, ,, CORNARD, LITTLE, 4 "1591" for "1597."
,, ,, 183, DENNINGTON, 1, "66" for "52."
,, ,, 189, EYKE, 3, "65" for "55."
,, ,, 205, ICKLINGHAM ALL SAINTS, 1, "51" for "8."
,, ,, 222, OFFTON, "2, 5" for "2, 4."
,, ,, 225, PETISTREE, 6, "50" for "8."

Fig. 34, on p. 36, is on its side.

The Church Bells of Suffolk.

CHAPTER I.

Introduction—The origin of large bells probably Oriental—General absence of bells of the Saxon and Norman periods—Mediæval instructions for bell-founding—Walter of Odyngton's—Those appended to the treatise of Gerbertus Scholasticus on Music—Castings from wax models very rare—Existing Ante-Conquestal towers—Scanty notices of the Norman and Early English periods—A solitary bell from the Lynn foundry c. 1300, in Suffolk—Early Aldgate founders, from Robert Rider to Henry Derby, and their works in Suffolk.

THE sweet voices of our Church Bells contribute to our lives a certain inexpressible charm, yet few realize the fact that bells have a history. They will be found to be no exception to the general rule that on whatever matter man has worked, traces will be sure to remain of the times, places, and methods of workmanship. Such traces often have an important bearing on the general history of a people, and record names of individuals gone long ago, and events of local, or even of national importance; so that a history of the Church Bells of any County might be expanded without difficulty into a County history. In dealing with those of Suffolk, it will be my endeavour to keep Campanology and Topography abreast of each other, as far as possible. Yet, first of all, a few words must be said about the origin of the kind of bell which we now use, as distinguished from those of more remote days, whether Etruscan, Roman, Greek, Keltic, or any other.

A

There can be little doubt that the idea of casting bells of the size which now hang in our towers came from the East, and possibly reached England about the sixth century. The absence of any traces of such things in the Roman period precludes a much earlier date. The Roman *æs thermarum*, which sounded to announce the hour for admission to the public baths, seems to have been of a smaller size, and fabricated rather than cast. And the mention of large bells during the Saxon period[*] leads us to infer that the date of their introduction is not much later than that which I have ventured to assign to it. But there are no bells which may be reasonably supposed to be of this high antiquity.

We may be sure that such bells existed. The regulation by which the estate of a Thane was reached, necessitated the erection of a bell-tower;[†] and it could not have remained inoperative in a well-settled district.

It may be remarked in passing from this period, that at the venerable "Old Minster," in the Rural Deanery of Southelmham, assigned by tradition to S. Felix the Burgundian, there are no signs of a tower, that there was once a round church at Bury S. Edmund's, the foundations of which were discovered in 1274,[‡] that the church of Flixton S. Mary had a Saxon tower, pulled down within the memory of man, and that the round towers of Southelmham All Saints, Bungay Holy Trinity, and others, which were apparently adapted for the reception of a bell or bells, are Ante-Conquestal in their character.

The wildness of note in early bells led to free use of the hard chisel and file, always fatal to quality of tone, and sometimes even to existence. This may help to account for the absence of any which may be safely ascribed to the Saxon and Norman times.

Such a specimen as that at Wordwell may possibly be the

---

[*] E. g. The direction in Wulfred's Canons (A.D. 816) for the sounding of the *Signum* in every church upon the death of a Bishop. See Johnson's *English Canons*, part I., p. 306.

[†] Churton's *Early English Church*, p. 230.

[‡] Chronicle of John of Oxenedes (Rolls Series), p. 246.

original bell of the little Norman church, and scattered up and down the county are a few of narrow make and sloping crown, which seem old, but may have come from a local hand later on.

The county of Suffolk is sparsely supplied with specimens of Norman work, mostly doorways, but at Bury S. Edmund's is a grand tower, built in 1095, as a gateway to the Abbey, and admirably adapted for a campanile, though according to Mr. Gage Rokewode, it did not serve that purpose till 1630.

One of the towers of the Abbey fell in 1210, and another, certainly a campanile, in 1430. In one of the two, we may suppose hung some of those bells of which Jocelin de Brakelond tells us as greeting the newly-appointed Abbot, Sampson de Tottington,* which also were among the Suffolk bells, which rang without human help, at the great earthquake in Ely, Norfolk and Suffolk, on the six and twentieth day of January, in the eleventh year of King Henry II.†

The earliest instructions for making bells, known to me, are found in a treatise by Walter of Odyngton, a monk of Evesham, in the time of Henry III.‡

This manuscript, which through Archbishop Parker's care escaped the destruction attending on the Dissolution of the Monasteries, is No. 410 in his collection at Corpus Christi College, Cambridge. Mr. Lewis considers the copy to have been made in the fifteenth century. The chapter on bells, headed in red ink, *De symbalis faciendis*, contains only eleven lines of text, and is to the following effect (recto of f. 17):

"Ad simbola facienda tota vis et difficultas extat in appensione ceræ ex qua formantur et primo sciendi quod quanto densius est tintinnabulum tanto acutius sonat tenuius vero gravius. Unam appensam ceram quantamlibet ex qua formandum primum cimbalum divides in octo partes et octavam partem addes tantæ ceræ sicut integra fuit, et fiet tibi cera secundi simbali. Et cetera facies ad eundem modum a gravioribus inchoando. Sed cave ne

---

* "Sonantibus campanis in choro et extra." Cron. Joc. de Brakelonda, p. 18.

† "Eodemque anno terræmotus factus est septimo Kalendas Februarii in Ely et Norlfolc et Sufoc, ita quod stantes prostravit, et campanas pulsavit."—Matth. Paris, *Chronica Majora*, A.D. 1165.

‡ *Summus fratris Walteri monachi Eveshamie musici de speculatione musica.*

forma interior argillæ cui aptanda est cera alio mutetur, ne etiam aliquid de cera appensa addat ad spiramina, proinde et ut quinta vel sexta pars metalli sit stannum purificatum a plumbo, reliquum de cupro similiter mundato propter sonoritatem. Si autem in aliquo defeceris, cum cote vel lima potest rectificari."

He begins by saying that for making bells, the whole difficulty consists in estimating the models from which they are formed, and first in understanding that the thicker a bell is, the higher is its note, and the reverse. From the use of the word "cera" for a model, some might be inclined to infer that the bells of that time were cast in moulds formed by wax models, but no such instances are known to exist in England. When a bell is to be made, a core or central block is first formed, to which is fitted a model, or "thickness" of the bell that is to be. Outside the model comes the cope. These models seem to have been made at one time from wax. When complete, the outer earth, forming a cope, was rammed tightly round them. A fire was lighted, and the melted wax allowed to escape, the cavity being afterwards filled by the metal from the furnace. There was an easy way of ornamenting the outer earth, or cope, by laying on the model extra strips of wax in the form of letters, &c., which would leave their impression on the cope. We have lighted on no instances of this kind in England, nor does there seem any probability of such a discovery. Mr. Lynam, in his *Church Bells of Staffordshire* (plates 3a and 3b), gives an interesting and well-executed drawing of what appears to be an inscription thus formed, from a bell at Fontenailles in Normandy, dated 1211, but he tells us nothing more about it. He also mentions similar lettering at Moissac, with the date 1273, recorded by Viollet le Duc. Our earliest inscriptions are set in separate letters, each in its own patera; and this would be impracticable, save by stamping the cope itself. In castings from wax models the cope is inaccessible. Hence we conclude that loam models were used in England while these instructions remained in the letter.

Walter of Odyngton then proceeds to expound the estimation of the wax models of a ring of bells.

Starting with any given "model" for the first bell, you take nine-eighths of it as a "model" for the second bell, and so on. If you start from the heavier bells and work on to the lighter ones, you must use a like method, i.e., let each "model" be eight-ninths of the previous one. *But take care lest the core to which the "model" is to be fitted be changed in a different proportion. Take care also that none of your allotted "model" get itself into the breathing holes.* Then he gives directions about the metal—*a fifth or sixth part of the metal to be tin, purified from lead, and the rest copper similarly cleansed.* Lastly, contemplating the abominable noise which would be sure to arise from these handiworks, he says that *if you fail in any point it can be set right with a whetstone or a file,* of which the former would be used for sharpening purposes, grinding away the rim of the bell, and the latter for flattening, filing off the inner surface of the soundbow.

Let us then imagine Walter of Odyngton attending to his own instructions. He starts by allotting a certain amount of wax for his first bell, makes his core by rule of thumb answerable to it, and then weighs both. By weight he gets his wax for the other bells, on the nine-eighths system. The whole method is so obviously empiric that there is no ground for wonder at the necessity for burine, whetstone, hard chisel, file, or any other tuning apparatus. Indeed, the free use of these instruments may account for the almost total disappearance of bells of the Saxon and Norman periods.

We are next to consider an improved method. Unfortunately no date can be assigned to it. It is a little prose tract (c. ii.), appended to an early poem, called *Ars Musica.* The poem itself is attributed to Gerbertus Scholasticus, afterwards Pope Sylvester II.; and if this be right, we are carried, as far as the poem is concerned, beyond the Norman Conquest. But the chapter in which we are interested belongs to a much later time. It seems as though the unknown writer had known of Walter of Odyngton's method, had seen that his nine-eighths made no difference between tones and semitones, and to have thus supplied a more workable plan:—

Should anyone wish to regulate the sound of bells, like that of organ pipes, he should know that thicker bells, like shorter pipes, have a higher note. But one must be careful in the weighing of the wax from which they are formed. He then proceeds to designate the various bells in a ring by letters :—

The first, A,
The second, B,
The third, C,
The fourth, D,
The fifth, E,
The sixth, F, and
The eighth, G.

It is needless to say that the absence of the mention of a seventh is very perplexing, and not at all to be accounted for by the first and eighth being in unison. Perhaps some master of mediæval music can solve the mystery. I am content to record the instruction as I find it.

B is formed from A, and C from B on Walter of Odyngton's nine-eighths system. But to get D, which is a "semitonium" from C, you take four-thirds of A. Then E is formed from D, and F from E on the nine-eighths system; but G from D (there being a "semitonium" between G and F), by taking four-thirds. It may be that the text requires emendation, but I am not bold enough to touch it. The MS. is Rawlinson, c. 720, in the Bodleian Library, and the passage, as follows, occurs on f. 13 recto and verso :—

"Sonitum tintinnabulorum si quis rationabiliter juxta modum fistularum organicarum facere voluerit scire debet quia sicut fistulæ breviores altiorem sonum habent quam longiores, ita et unumquodque tintinnabulum quantum superat densitate alterum tantum excellit et sono. Quod caute providendum est in appensione ceræ qua formantur. Ad primum autem quod est A littera quali volueris pondere ceram appende, dividesque illam ipsam ceram æque in octo partes, ac recipiat sequens, B, videlicet, ejusdem appensionis iterum octo partes alias, addita insuper nona parte. Illasque novem partes in unum collige dividesque in octo, recipiat tercium quod est C, eadem appensione octo alias partes, addita etiam parte nona ejusdem ponderis. Tunc primi appensionem divide in tres partes, supereturque a quarto quod est D quarta parte, hoc est semitonium. Item divides quartum in octo, supereturque a quinto quod est E, nona parte, dividesque similiter quintum in octo et recipiat sextum quod est F nonam partem amplius. Quartum nichilominus in tres partes æque appensum ab octavo quod est G superetur quarta parte, hoc est semitonium."

According to my calculation the models of the seven bells would be in this ratio :—

A . 8
B . 9
C . 10·125
D . 10·6
E . 12
F . 13·5
G . 14·2

Early English remains are few comparatively. Mildenhall seems to have had a tower in this style, to judge from the dog-tooth work buried in the buttresses of the present tower, and Rumburgh still has the lower stage of a large square structure with three single lights ; but the record of the bells begins much about the time to which most of the earlier bell-chambers may be referred ; and first we break ground with a solitary specimen from the King's Lynn foundry.

Fig. 1.

This is the tenor at Worlington, inscribed + JOHANNES : GODYNGE : DE : LENNE : ME : FECIT, with a plain initial cross on four steps given here (fig. 1). The Tallage Roll, Lynn Bishop, 27 Edward I., mentions a Master John, founder of bells, as paying half a mark as his share to the County Subsidy in 1299, and as the same sum was paid in 1333, by Thomas Belleyettir, the business probably went on in the same place. The former is thus mentioned, "Mag'r Joh'nes fundator Campanar' solvit die ven'is p'x ante festum Ste Margar' in subsidiū Co'itatis dj m're sterl."* The latter (or his successor, Edmundus Billeyettir) may be the person from whom Cok, the emissary of Alan de Walsingham, purchased copper and tin in 1346.† The examination of lettering will, I think, identify Magister Johannes Riston, at Bexwell, Norfolk, Jhoannes de Guddine, at Wendling in the same county, and Johannes Godynge de Lenne at Worlington, and the time points to the Subsidy payer of 1299 as combining these designations. The location of this one Lynn bell in Suffolk is not without significance. The old hythe, or staithe, still exists at Worlington, and the bell was no doubt brought by water, showing that the Lark was navigable six hundred years ago. The neglect of the last few years has blocked it, but I see that a company is just formed to open the little river up again.

In preparing the *Church Bells of Cambridgeshire* I was picking my way timidly under the uncertain light of lettering and marks into the history of a little group of bells, bearing a cross (fig. 2);

Fig. 2.

"Quale per incertam lunam sub luce maligna
Est iter in silvis."

but in the last seven years the labours of Mr. Stahlschmidt have shown that I was on the right lines. The cross is found in Suffolk, on the tenor at Barnardiston, inscribed + OMNES SANCTI DEI ORATE PRO NOBIS, with three roundlets in

* L'Estrange's *Church Bells of Norfolk*, p. 22.
† *Church Bells of Cambridgeshire*, p. 5.

a vertical line by way of stop (fig. 3), and lettering closely resembling that used by Robert Rider, whose will, dealing with his real estate only, is dated 1386. His third wife's name was Cristina, and he left her, inter alia, his claim on John and Walter, his apprentices, for their unfinished term of apprenticeship. His body was to be buried in the churchyard of S. Andrew over Cornhill (Undershaft), and he had a son, Sir John Rider, a chaplain; but his business cannot be traced into other hands, though the cross appears on bells after his date, e.g., the

Fig. 3.

fine tenor in Carlisle Cathedral, which belongs to the time of Bishop Strickland, 1400—1419, and the fifth and sixth at Christchurch, Hampshire. I place this Barnardiston bell at the head of the Londoners, as being very possibly, from the character of the lettering, earlier than Rider's time, going back perhaps to one of the three Suffolk founders exhumed by Mr. Stahlschmidt, from the City Records, William de Suffolck, potter, 1276, Philip de Ufford,* potter, 1294—1316, and Alan de Suffolk, potter, 1330—1331. I would venture to suggest that John Aleyn, who uses the same cross, was a son of this Alan, "Johannes filius Alani."

The accompanying A (fig. 4) is a specimen of the lettering on the Barnardiston tenor. The G (fig. 5), of a slightly smaller

Fig. 4.   Fig. 5.

* It seems probable that Ufford, near Woodbridge, is intended.

size, occurs with the Barnardiston lettering on the second bell at Cherry Hinton, Cambridgeshire.

In the same part of the county lie the third at Assington, and the fifth at Monks Eleigh, bearing the cross and lettering, which is shown to have been used by Peter de Weston, 1330—1348, and William Revel, c. 1356.

An unquestionably early date may be assigned to the tenor at Great Bradley, which bears the name of Richard de Wimbis. This man's name first occurs in 1303, as one of a jury for appraising the value of pledges for debt in the custody of Nicholas Pycot, Chamberlain of the Guildhall. His delivery of a bell, weighing 2,820 pounds, "every hundredweight thereof containing 112 pounds," to the Priory of the Church of the Holy Trinity in Aldgate, in 1312, has been mentioned in the Cambridgeshire book; but an additional fact has now come out, that one Richard de Wymbish was Prior of the Convent from 1316 to 1325. Mr. Stahlschmidt suggests that relationship or fellow-townmanship may account for the employment of one Richard, when another was probably sub-prior.

Only five of his bells are known to remain, and Suffolk is most fortunate in possessing one of them. Here and at Goring, Oxon., he styles himself "Ricard"; at Burham, Kent, and Slapton, Northamptonshire, " Richard "; at Rawreth, Essex, his name is not given; but at Berechurch (now re-cast), was the full Latin " Ricardvs." The Goring third has the Norman-French "fist," and asks prayers for Peter Quivil, Bishop of Exeter, without mention of his soul, whence we may infer that the date is earlier than 1291, when the Bishop died. Three other founders bore the same surname, Michael de Wymbish, 1297—1310, Ralph Wymbish, 1303—1315, and Walter Wymbish, in 1325.

This lettering is also now rare. It remains on the third at Fairstead, Essex, and the third at S. Laurence, Norwich, both inscribed

+ VOCOR : JOHANNES, the first bearing also + PETRVS : DE : WESTON : ME : FECIT, and the other + WILELMVS : REVEL : ME : FECIT, and on the third at Heckfield, Hampshire, which bears a charming little piece of old English:

PLATE I.

LETTERING & CROSS USED BY RICHARD WYMBISH ON BELL AT GREAT BRADLEY.

here. The former mentions Mary, the wife of Henry Derby, whom we shall next name, and as a matter of general historical interest, refers to a tenement purchased by him of Alice Perrers, the favourite of Edward III. in his last years. This woman seems to have had considerable possessions in the city. Twenty shillings left for poor prisoners in Newgate, and ten for those in Ludgate, bespeak the humanity of the testator, and there are the usual religious and charitable bequests.

The last of the Londoners of this period who appears in Suffolk is Derby, who made the tenor at Ampton. He is mentioned in the Cambridgeshire book,* as the founder of the third and fourth bells at Chippenham.

My conjecture as to his being a resident in Derby seems to vanish in face of Mr. Stahlschmidt's evidence connecting him with Henry Derby, ironmonger; and though the union of trades may seem somewhat irregular, and against guild law, there is no more reason *in rerum natura* to object to a bell-founder being called an ironmonger, if he did ironmonger's work, than to his being called *ollarius*. Some of us have seen in this last quarter of the nineteenth century an ironfounder's appliances utilised for casting a ring of bells. Henry Derby's time seems to have been from 1362 to 1390. The Ampton bell bears the heads of King Edward III. (fig. 6), and an initial cross well known in other counties (fig. 7).

Fig. 6.   Fig. 7.

Of Norfolk bells, those at New Houghton and Burnham Deepdale, record Derby's name, and the treble at Wimbotsham and the bell at West Lynn are presumably his.

* P. 16.

CHAPTER II.

Transition from Longobardic to black-letter—" William ffoundor," shown to be William Dawe—His Suffolk bells—His gun-founding for Dover Castle in 1385—His will—John Danyell's bells—Richard Hille's—Henry Jordan, Fishmonger and Founder—His works at King's College, Cambridge, and at East Bergholt—His will—Bequest remaining to this day—His obit—His son, Dan Henry.

SUFFOLK is remarkably rich in bells bearing those London marks which come next in order of time, and form a connecting link between the Longobardic and black-letter periods. There are twenty-two of them against ten in Kent, six in Norfolk and Lincolnshire respectively, and five in Cornwall, which are the only counties at present known to possess more than two or three. The principal shields (figs. 8 and 9) bear a chevron between three lavers, or ewers, and they show the importance

Fig. 8.   Fig. 9.

of these common articles of domestic use. Sandre (Alexander) of Gloucester, an ecclesiastic, before this time, used a laver in his seal (fig. 10), and the word AVE on it has a double force, being the part of the inscription, VENEZ LAVEZ, which the

Fig. 10.

seal-sinker chose to exhibit. Now, to what peculiar circumstance are we to attribute the pre-eminence of Suffolk in this respect? It seems to me that there had been a succession of Suffolk men engaged in the founder's craft in Aldgate. Close following on William de Suffolck, already mentioned, come John le Rous, potter, 1281, and William le Rous, potter, 1286, a name strongly suggestive of the county. After a short interval we have Roger le Rous, potter, 1311, and Nicholas le Rous, potter, 1315.

A longer break intervenes, and then appear Robert Russe, brazier, 1356—1397; Roger Rous, or Rose, de Bury, 1358—1392; and Alan Rous, potter, 1361. Peter de Blithe, potter, 1335—1353, and Robert de Blithe, brazier, 1356, very likely hail from Blythburgh,* and Philip de Ufford (who is called in his will both Philip de Ufford and Philip de Rafford) is regarded by Mr. Stahlschmidt as possibly the father of one William Rofforde, who made the fourth bell at West Mill, Hertfordshire, using the same lettering and cross as Henry Derby, of whom we have lately spoken. The connection is a little strengthened by the mention of the soul of John Rufford, and of a legatee, Mary, the wife of Henry Derby, in the will of William Burford, citizen of London and Belzeter, proved 1390.

* *East Anglian*, I., 203.

After the lapse of five centuries, it is out of all reason to expect evidence to be clear and coherent. All that can be done is to use care in putting the precious fragments together, and to leave them to tell their tale as to the irrecoverable past.

These indications, at any rate, prepare our mind for a connection between the county of Suffolk and that which was pre-eminently the founder's parish, S. Botolph, Aldgate, and may help to account for the large number of bells of the "Laver" group, which we are discussing.

Besides the laver shields, larger and smaller, these bells bear sometimes a shield with a chevron between three trefoils slipped, the arms of Rufford, Underhill, Fitz-Lewes, and other families,

Fig. 11.

(fig. 11), two crosses, larger and smaller (figs. 12, 13), which generally go with the larger and smaller lavers, other crosses

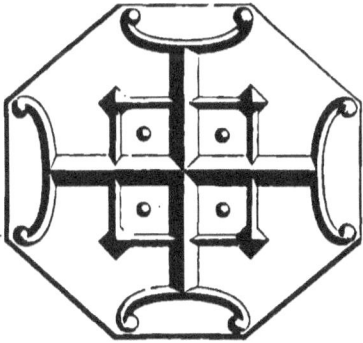

Fig. 12.

Fig. 13.

(figs. 14, 15), and most notable of all a certain medallion (fig. 16), bearing two birds, and the words, 𝔚illiam ffounder me fecit.

Fig. 14.   Fig. 15.

Fig. 16.

I will not inflict on my readers the endless variety in which these marks occur, being convinced from careful tabulation that no theory can be based on their aberrations. The group of bells on which they are found is :—

Barking, fourth and tenor,
Butley bell,
Clare, seventh,
Cornard, Great, fourth,
Elmham, South, S. Peter, the three bells,
Hawstead, treble,
Ilketshall, S. Margaret, treble and second (poor bells, the former now split).
Ipswich, S. Stephen, treble and second,
Nedging, second,
Oakley, Great, fourth,
Peasenhall, tenor,
Petistree, fourth and fifth,
Sibton, third,
Ufford, fourth,
Westerfield, treble and second.

To these, before 1860, might have been added the Ingham bell. On every one of this group, with one exception, occur figs. 8, 9, 11, or 16. That exception is the Clare seventh, marked with a handsome medallion (fig. 17); but this must go with the

Fig. 17.

others, as on the South Lopham fifth this mark occurs with fig. 9, and with an octagon (fig. 18) which we find in con-

Fig. 18.

junction with fig. 12, on the Pebmarsh tenor. Mr. Stahlschmidt* says that the trefoils never appear with the birds. The second at South Elmham S. Peter upsets this, bearing the trefoils four times on the shoulder, and the birds six times between the words of the inscription. To add to our perplexity, the three at South Elmham S. Peter, with all their variety, are nearly certainly of one casting, and the treble, which has a band in the place of an inscription, is nearly the counterpart of the treble at Brent Tor, on Dartmoor, which has for its fellow another (also almost certainly co-eval with it), bearing Longobardic letters, and thus likely to date further back than the little black-letter ring at South Elmham S. Peter. This is a specimen of our difficulties in sorting out bells. On one point I am disposed to agree with Mr. Stahlschmidt, in attributing all that bear William Founder's name to one William Dawe, the birds being presumably a rebus on his name. In addition to the Southelmhamites, this mark is found at Nedging, Great Oakley, and Ufford only. Certainly the mark survived William Dawe, for it appears on the seventh at Magdalen College, Oxford, the year of that foundation being 1456,† and on a bell at Radcliff, Bucks, bearing indications of a still later date. However, so far as Suffolk is concerned, I think we may stick

---

* *Surrey Bells and London Bell-founders*, p. 46.
† Bishop Waynflete may have placed a second-hand bell in Magdalen Tower.

to William Dawe. He is worth the trouble taken about him, bringing us for the first time into the stream of general history. Mr. Stahlschmidt is justly proud of having solved the mystery. Through the kindness of Mr. Walter Rye he was allowed to examine some deeds about East-end property belonging to the Cornwallis family. He found two, bearing date 1392 and 1395 respectively, relating to the same premises, executed in the presence of the same four witnesses, of whom one stands described in the earlier deed as "William Dawe Found^r," and in the later one, as "William Found^r." Subsequently it was discovered that in the same ward, and at the same time, there was another William Dawe, by trade a "white tawyer," or dresser of white leather. This is a sufficient reason for William Dawe persistently describing himself as William Founder. Possibly the founder was a son of the "white tawyer," who appears on the Hustings Rolls for 1371.*

But how does this man, whose name has to be ferreted out through musty parchments, and bells known to the birds, namesakes of William Dawe, in obscure village towers, belong to the general history of the nation? We must come to the year 1385, to see his services and the scanty trace of them yet remaining. That year, though little noted in school books, was a busy and anxious year in England. A short truce with the French had terminated, and the advisers of the young King Charles VI. were bent on executing a general assault on English territory. There was such a scare throughout the kingdom that if the chroniclers are to be credited, Richard II. was soon at the head of 300,000 men, the greater part of which he reserved for the defence of the south coast. The ports must be defended, and guns must be had for Dover. They had, as it appears, already been mounted at Calais, under the governour, Sir Hugh Calverley. "William the founder," doubtless this William Dawe, is the man employed. In the issue rolls of the year (1st May) is the following payment:—"To Sir Simon de Burley, Knight, Constable of Dover Castle, for the price of 12

---

* Stahlschmidt's *Church Bells of Kent*, pp. 24, &c. ; Preface, p. xii.

guns, 2 iron 'patella,' 120 stones for the guns, 100 lbs. of powder, and 4 stocks of wood purchased of William the founder, of London and delivered to the said Simon by the hands of William Hanney, Clerk, for fortifying and strengthening Dover Castle, £97 10s."* I would suggest for the consideration of artillerists whether this does not point to an earlier date for cast guns than that which is commonly received. Now I think that the county of Kent contains some traces of the handiwork of this same year. There are four bells only in that county which bear the "birds" medallion (fig. 16), and of these two at Downe are on the road from London to Dover; one at Upper Hardres is about four miles off the road, and one at Otham is close by Maidstone.

Thus a group of Suffolk bells seems to be connected with the foundry which caused the Frenchmen's ears to tingle with the roar of Dover Castle; and another group of Kent bells possibly first sounded for service about the time when William Dawe was completing his Dover job.

One more little glimpse, and we bid good-bye to William Founder. Richard II. is now some years dead, poor hapless man, and the first usurping Lancastrian is on the throne. The business of the nation goes on much the same. There are marryings and givings in marriage, births, deaths, probate of wills in due course. In 1408, one John Plot, or Rouwenhale, Citizen and Maltman, of London, dies, a widower and probably childless. He leaves his money for divers purposes, charitable, pious, beneficial. Among legacies for Mass of Requiem and repair of "fowle weys," is this:—" Also my wyll ys that John Walgrave, seruaunt of Wyllyam fondour haue of my gode iijs. iiijd."† Although we know nothing of John Walgrave in Suffolk, he has left his mark in other counties.

We turn to another group, dating plainly after 1413, for in that year Henry V., not to be behindhand in the fashion, changed the semée of fleur-de-lis in the French shield to three, following the example of his rival Charles VI. This shield

* Stahlschmidt's *Surrey Bells and London Founders*, p. 45.
† *Fifty Earliest English Wills*, p. 15.

(figs. 19, 20), sometimes crowned and sometimes uncrowned,* is usual on bells of this group, which consists of
Bildeston, treble,
Brockley, three bells,
Lakenheath, second and third,
Mildenhall, sixth.
Stowmarket, fourth.

Fig. 19.

Fig. 20.

Before 1860 there was the old fourth at Mildenhall, from which the present fifth was made, and the largest of the three bells which used to stand in the north aisle of S. James's Church, Bury St. Edmund's, formerly the clock bell there.

The readers of my *Church Bells of Cambridgeshire* will remember a mark (fig. 21) used by this founder. It occurs on

Fig. 21.

* No theory can be based on the absence of the crown.

all of the group, except at Bildeston and Stowmarket. The initials J D are plain enough on the Bildeston treble. There is some difficulty about the letters on the treble at S. Botolph's, Cambridge; but I think that Blomefield is right in taking them also for J D, and the pencil sketch (still remaining in the Muniment Room of King's College) of the inscriptions on the grand five bells which that Society unfortunately sold in 1754, records also J D on the treble, though the ink sketch gives J E. These seem undoubtedly to be the initials of John Danyell, bell-founder and vintner. We only know his surname, but J at that time is pretty sure to stand for John.* Now we have a certain date for him, for the Bursar at King's College paid in 1460, £3 13s. 4d. to one Coke for bringing a bell of "Danyell fonder's" from London to Cambridge. Again, the tenor in Crowland Abbey, which is mark for mark like the Brockley second and the Mildenhall late fourth, and inscribed, In Multis Annis Resonet Campana Johannis, is certainly later than 1465, when it was cast in London, and apparently bore the name of Michael, if we may give credence to the continuation of Ingulph's chronicle. So much for his date. That he did not confine himself to metallurgy we know from these same King's College accounts, where it is recorded that he received 53s. 4d.

Fig. 22.

* There were John Danyells in London in 1435. Stahlschmidt's *Church Bells of Kent*, p. 54.

for half the cost of a tun (dolium) of wine. Among his marks, though only once occurring with his royal shields in Suffolk, on the Brockley second, is a beautiful cross bearing the words, i𝔥𝔲 𝔪𝔢𝔯𝔠𝔦 𝔩𝔫𝔡𝔦 𝔥𝔢𝔩𝔭 round it (fig. 22), which we know to have been used largely by Henry Jordan, or Jurden, who overlapped Danyell, and possibly had some trade connection with him.

To keep in order of time, however, we must first take another group, assigned by Mr. Stahlschmidt to Richard Hille.* For this the principal mark is a shield divided by a bend, with a cross above and a ring below (fig. 23).

Fig. 23.

The number is very limited, viz.,
Glemham, Great, fifth,
Higham, S. Mary, fifth,
Ipswich, S. Mary-at-Elms, second,
Ringshall, second,
Washbrook bell.

Fig. 24.

* Stahlschmidt's *Surrey Bells and London Founders*, p. 35.

These all belong to South-east Suffolk, but there was another, now recast, in the opposite corner of the county, the old second at Wangford S. Denis, which bore also the cross (fig. 24), elsewhere known in connection with the "ring and cross" shield.

That Richard Hille died in 1440, that his wife Joan

"resigned to Heaven's will,
carried on the business still,"

and in the end survived her second husband, Sturdy, and carried on further business in 1459 with the town of Faversham, is to be read in the annals of London bell-founders, to which we have so often referred; but the widow's works did not apparently extend into our county.

We must now turn to the marks which generally accompany the iḥu merci laḋi ḥelp cross, already mentioned as on the Brockley second. These are an elaborate shield divided saltireways by two keys, with a fish above, a laver below, a garb (wheatsheaf) on the right, and a bell on the left (fig. 25), and a shield bearing a merchant's mark (fig. 26), which are so united, the one with

Fig. 25.   Fig. 26.

the other, and with fig. 22, that they and they alone occur on nine of the twelve bells of this group. These bells are of a superior character, and the marks are known in almost every county. They are

Barnardiston, treble,
Bergholt, East, second,

Boxford, second,
Bramfield, third, fourth, and fifth,
Groton, third,
Iken, treble and third,
Ipswich, S. Laurence, second,
Stradbroke, tenor, a fine bell, with a somewhat hard tone.
Wixoe bell.

North-west Suffolk, be it observed, is entirely unrepresented in this group, and the Stradbroke tenor is the only bell in North Suffolk. This, however, is a grand specimen, in E, weighing by repute 21 cwt. All these are ascribed to Henry Jordan, or Jurdeyn, already mentioned. His overlapping Danyell in time has been referred to, and in one instance (Wixoe) the use of his personal shield (fig. 25) with a certain elegant octagon (fig. 18), which I have mentioned as found at Pebmarsh, Essex, in conjunction with an earlier one (fig. 12), shows some connection even with Dawe.

But let us look at that same personal shield, which would be a horror to heralds, past or present, and see if it will not tell us its story. Certainly it does seem rather a strange jumble, not quite so excruciating as the arms of the Oddfellows, but enough to make Rouge Dragon and Portcullis stare and gasp. Heraldic language seems thrown away upon it, and it shall be described in unadorned prose. A dolphin above, and S. Peter's cross-keys seem to speak of fishery, a bell and a laver of foundry, and a wheatsheaf of farming. The last interpretation we must abandon. The wheatsheaf (in heraldic language, *garb*), turns out to be part of the arms of the family of Harleton, from which Henry Jordan was descended.

· Now in Henry Jordan (one spelling must suffice for his name) we have this strange union of Fishmonger and Founder. But after all what does the strangeness amount to? I remember two shoemakers in Blandford, Dorset, who announced themselves as qualified to bleed, and to extract teeth, and many tradesmen at the present day trench on other business than their own. Besides, have we not seen "Danyell fonder" vending half a dolium of wine to King's College, Cambridge? Let us then fearlessly gaze on this hybrid tradesman of the Middle Ages.

We have read of Richard Hille, and of his widow Joan. He had also a daughter Joan, to whom he left the substantial sum of two hundred marks. Far be it from me, after the lapse of these ages, to deny to the young lady the possession of many estimable qualities and personal charms, besides this "tocher"; but it did not make her the less desirable in the eyes of Henry Jordan, himself a "citizen of credit and renown," and a member of the Fishmongers' Company, if not actually engaged in that avocation.

The Jordans appear to have come from Loughborough, where in All Saints' Church a battered remnant of a monumental brass records the burial of Giles Jordan and Margaret his wife, apparently in 1455. Henry Jordan's father and mother, as we read in his will, were named Giles and Margaret, but in that document he speaks of them as buried in the Church of S. Botolph, Aldgate, directing that "ij tapers of wex" should burn beside his own tomb and his wife's, and one should "stand upon the middes of the stone there as the bodies of my father and mod^r there lien buried", and in like manner another, for Richard Hille and his wife Joan, the second husband, Sturdy, being left in darkness.

Some clever man may arise to read the riddle of this seemingly double burial. On the Loughborough stone were formerly arms, Jordan and Harleton quarterly, *ar*. three mullets, *gu*. and *sa*. a chevron between three garbs *ar*. A mullet, by the way, is not a fish, but a five-pointed star, and we shall come across it again before long.

We have a very important notice of Henry Jordan at Cambridge, in 1465—6. The visitor to King's College Chapel may notice in dry summer weather a peculiarly arid spot occupying some space on the lawn to the west of that noble building. This is the site of an ancient "Clochard," or bell-house (fig. 27), dating from the time just named. The building at the back of it in the engraving is Clare College.

In 1466 one "Cartare" was paid for the hanging of the bells,

Fig. 27.

the intention being, as it seems, that the bells should remain there till a tower was ready for them. But King's College is an uncompleted building, and the Clochard had to be propped up before 1660. Eighty years more brought it to the last stage of "calm decay," and the bells were removed to the ante-chapel, whence in 1754 they went to another chapel, to wit, Whitechapel bell-foundry, where Messrs. Lester and Pack boiled them down, and none can say where the metal now gives forth its tuneful sound.

Between the extracts made by Mr. J. Willis Clark from the College "Mundum" book, and a drawing found among the College archives, the largest bell of the five and possibly the smallest (though this was more probably a remanent from older work of our vintner friend "Danyell fonder") may be traced to Henry Jurden, whose heavy bill of forty pounds was paid by the College in instalments of ten pounds. The former was a magnificent bell, weighing 2 tons 6 cwt. 2 qrs. 7 lbs.—about 5 cwt. more than the noble tenor at S. Peter Mancroft, Norwich, and thus the largest bell that East Anglia has ever seen. Alas! that it should have perished. I have said that the Stradbroke tenor is the largest extant work of Henry Jordan's in Suffolk. The East Bergholt second is remarkable in its way as being one of the tenants of a mediæval Clochard (fig. 28) co-eval with that

Fig. 28.

which used to exist at King's, but more tenacious of life. A very picturesque object is this antique bell-house, well-known to all that frequent the villages which touch on the Stour valley. Here, as at King's, the structure was only intended as a stopgap, for the base of a western tower may yet be seen. I think it quite possible that the foundations on the south side of Mildenhall Church are those of a Campanile intended for the reception of the bells, while the present tower was building. The dimensions are 33 feet by 21.

To revert to Henry Jordan's shields, no one as yet has read the meaning of the device on the "banner shield" (fig. 26).

As is commonly the case, we know most of the man's history from his will, dated October 15th, 1468, with a codicil annexed, printed *in extenso* in the *Surrey Bells and London Bell-founders*.* It is a most curious and interesting document in many respects, giving us derivations of present local names, and insight into the life of our forefathers. After the usual pious commendation of his soul to his Maker he directs that his body should be buried in "the Chapell of our lady in the Northeside of the p'yshe Churche of Seynt Botulphes w'oute Aldgate of London that is to say in the place where as the body of Johanne my Wiffe there resteth buried." He had a son and as it seems an only one, who is not mentioned in the will, cut off with less than a shilling; for the " Wardeyns of the Comynaltie of the mistery or crafte of ffyshemong^{rs} of the said Citie of London," to wit William Turke, Robert Derlyngton, Edmond Newman, Lawrence Ffyncham, William Hayes and John Stanesby are his universal legatees. The will is preserved by the Fishmongers' Company, who still pay annually to the Founders' Company one of Jordan's bequests, "to twenty of the poverest people of the Crafte of Ffounders of London to ev^ryche of them eight pence (s^ume) thirtene shillyngs and foure pence." The lands bequeathed, with gardens, &c., are described (1) as "lien togeder" in the lane called Billiter Llane in the p'yshe of Seynt Katheryn Crechurche w^tin Aldgate of London, and (2) as "in the p'yshe of Seynt Brigide in Fleete Street in the subberbes of London as they be sett and lien betwene the Tenement belonging unto the ffraternytie of our blessed lady Seynt Mary the Virgyne in the said Church of Seynt Brigide on the p'tie of the Este and the Water of the Fleete on the p'tie of the West wherof th' one hed abutteth upon the gardeyn of the Gaile or Pryson of the Ffleete towards the North, and th' other heed abutteth upon the Kyngs way of Fflete Streete towards the South." "Billiter Llane," now Billiter Street is spelt in the Guildhall copy of the will "Bellezeterslane," and thus we have the derivation of a well-known place of business at the present day. The site of Jordan's shop and dwelling-house is supposed

* Pp. 60, &c.

to be at the north-west corner of Billiter Street, fronting on Leadenhall Street, and the foundry on the west side of Billiter Street, on a space partially occupied by the East and West India Dock-house.

This property still belongs to the Fishmongers' Company. It was confiscated in the "regular way of business" by Parliament for the Crown, in the days of young Edward VI., as being devoted to superstitious uses, but the Wardens of that mystical "crafte" of Fishmongers repurchased it.

The second property, lying to the North of Fleet Street recalls three very various pictures of the past, the Fleet Prison, the Guild of S. Mary in S. Bride's Church, with its masses and festivities, and the Fleet Ditch. But these are not in Suffolk, and we must not linger over them. The trusts for which the property is left are sundry and manifold. Among them of course stands prominently the "Obite or anniv'sarye of Placebo and Dirige," which terms require explanation. These are the first words in Antiphons of the office "Placebo Domino in regione vivorum," Ps. cxiv. (Vulg. our cxvi.) 9, "I will walk before the Lord in the land of the living," and "Dirige in conspectu tuo viam meam" (Ps. v. 9).

This obite is to be "with ryngyng of Bells (S. Botolph, Aldgate, being especially mentioned) for my soule and the soules aboverehersed openly to be named." We shall give instances of this custom from Suffolk before long. Works of piety (including xiij*s*. and iv*d*. for brede, ale, chese, and spices) being thus considered, those of charity follow, of which the bequest to the poor people of the craft of Founders, already mentioned, may serve as a specimen. Many shivering souls dwelling around Temple Bar had occasion to bless the memory of the good citizen Henry Jordan, from whose will flowed a long black stream of quarters of coals. Even the "sea coal fire," sitting by which Falstaff promised to make hostess Quickly a lady, may have blazed at that moment from some bequest analogous to Henry Jordan's.

But while all this magnificent array of works of piety and charity was being committed to parchment, natural affection seemed to slumber. The son, a scholar in his way, able to plead his "benefit of clergy," a Bachelor of Arts of Oxford or Cambridge, "Dan* Henry Jordon," a monk professed in the house of Horley in Barkeshire, receives no mention in the will. He must be regarded, we fear, as a "ne'er do well," but his father remembered him in a Codicil "annexed to the Testamente in Ptechement undre Seale." The Wardens of the "Comynaltie of the Mysterye of Ffyshemongers" were required to help Dan Henry in time of his neede, at their discretion, as often as such occasion might occur. There was reason to anticipate that occasion might occur, and that the periods of recurrence might not be separated by very long intervals. To carry out this intention a brother fishmonger, Thomas Wydm'pole, is appointed as a sub-almoner under the Wardens of the Fishmongers' Company. Clearly Dan Henry is not to be trusted with current coin of the realm. He is truly a monk professed at Hurley, but all is not bliss within those sacred walls. The Prior's discipline is likely to be too strict for Dan Henry, or Dan Henry is likely to be too lax for the discipline. "My coat is too short, or else I'm too tall," as the pauper said when he found himself "decently habited" after the fashion of the Union Workhouse. The need of Wydm'pole's appointment is thus rehearsed in the codicil. "And for this cause that if the Pryo' and Covent of the said house of Horley for the tyme beyng kepe hym to streightly or otherwise entrete hym than he ought of very right and duetie to be doone to or els that they wolle putte awey from hym his abite and living of a Monke there whiche he hath chosen to him." It may have been a case of corody,† complicated by misconduct. It is a sad picture, but if we would know the past, we must take it as it stands, the bitter with the sweet. Here we see the intelligent, successful, benevolent citizen, whose works in more senses than one survive to this day, who has sent his son to the University, and might

* *Dan* is short for *Dominus*, the term still applied in the Universities to Bachelors of Arts.

† Corody, *corodium*, the right of nominating a person to be sustained in a Religious House.

have looked to see him an Archdeacon or even a Bishop, obliged to make these humiliating arrangements for the young man, and even by anticipation blaming the Prior and Convent of Hurley for kicking the luckless scapegrace out of their doors. Thus we part from the story of Henry Jordan.

CHAPTER III.

Two bells probably by Thomas Bullisdon.—The "moon and stars" shield—Two bells by William Culverden—His rebus—History of the use of the word *Emmanuel*—Culverden's rebus interpreted—His will—Westminster School—Boston Merchant Guild—The Norwich Foundry—A nameless group—Fressingfield tenor—The Brasyers—A Mediæval Law-suit—Richard Brasyer in the Court of Common Pleas—Ingenious argument of Serjeant Genney—The large group of the Brasyers' bells—The Burlingham group.

A PAIR of bells now claim our attention,
Kesgrave bell,
Iken, fourth.
These bear a shield with the initials T. B. (fig. 29) well-known

Fig. 29.

in many counties, though rare in Suffolk. I found it on the second at Cudham, Kent, in 1857. It is also known at Little Gransden, and Rampton, Cambridgeshire, at Llandewednack, the parish in which the Lizard is situated, at S. Mary's, Bedford, Anstey, Hertfordshire, East Dean, Sussex, Paulerspury, Northamptonshire, and other places—most notably of all at the

E

grand old church of S. Bartholomew-the-Great, Smithfield, where there is a complete and melodious little ring of five of this make, which has happily survived the Great Fire of London.

The best instance of all for our purpose is the fifth at Weeley in Essex, with a prayer for the souls of William and Agnes Brooke. There seems to be only one Agnes Brooke of this district, to whose will a reference can be found at Somerset House. The wills themselves are lost, but the indexes remain, and from them it may be computed that Agnes Brooke died in 1506 or 1507. This tallies well with the Bullisdon, whom Mr. Amherst Tyssen records as casting bells in London in 1510.* The arms of Robert Billesdon, who was Lord Mayor of London in 1483, are no help to us. There was a Thomas Bullisdon, who represented the city in Parliament in 1492. T. in the middle ages is almost sure to stand for Thomas, and very possibly the founder of the Kesgrave bell and the Iken fourth was Thomas Bullisdon, son of this Thomas. But we know nothing more about him, and can tell no interesting stories as in the case of Henry Jordan. Sometimes his bells bear the fancy cross (fig. 30), which suggests connection with Danyell and Jurden.

Fig. 30.

The following eleven bells :—
Boxford, seventh,
Bradfield Combust, second,

* *Church Bells of Sussex*, p. 15.

CROSS AND CAPITALS ON BELL AT SUDBURY S. PETER.

Groton, fourth,
Hadleigh, fourth,
Levington, treble,
Saxmundham, third, fourth, and fifth,
Sudbury, S. Peter, fifth, sixth, and tenor,[*]
present in their location a marked exclusion of the north of the county. They are the handiwork of a man whose usual shield (fig. 31) bearing three mullets in chief, and a crescent in base,

Fig. 31.

below a chevron, is found in all the named towers, save Bradfield and Saxmundham. On the Bradfield bell and the Saxmundham fifth appear the emblems of the four evangelists (figs. 32, 33, 34, 35), which appear at Impington, Cambridgeshire, and

Fig. 32.   Fig. 33.

[*] This last is a good bell, weighing about 22 cwt.

Fig. 34.   Fig. 35.

elsewhere in conjunction with the shield just named. The initial crosses, of which figs. 36, 37 are examples, vary, as does the lettering, which at Sudbury is remarkably large and forcible. The resemblance between the shield and the arms of Sir Henry

Fig. 36.   Fig. 37.

Kebyll, citizen and grocer, Lord Mayor in 1510, leads Mr. Stahlschmidt to assign the bells "provisionally" to one of the Kebyll family, and he finds in the accounts of S. Stephen's, Walbrook, for 1480, payments amounting to £5 6s. 8d. for bell-hanging to John Kebyll, wheelwright. The arms of the Lord Mayor of 1510 are given in Wright's Heylin without the crescent, but variations in these points are very common in the *bourgeois* heraldry of that time. It is more than likely that evidence will turn up to confirm Mr. Stahlschmidt's conjecture.

These bells may be found in different parts of England, but in no great abundance. Like North Suffolk, Norfolk is destitute of them. I found two at Mumby, Lincolnshire, in 1855, and

PLATE III.

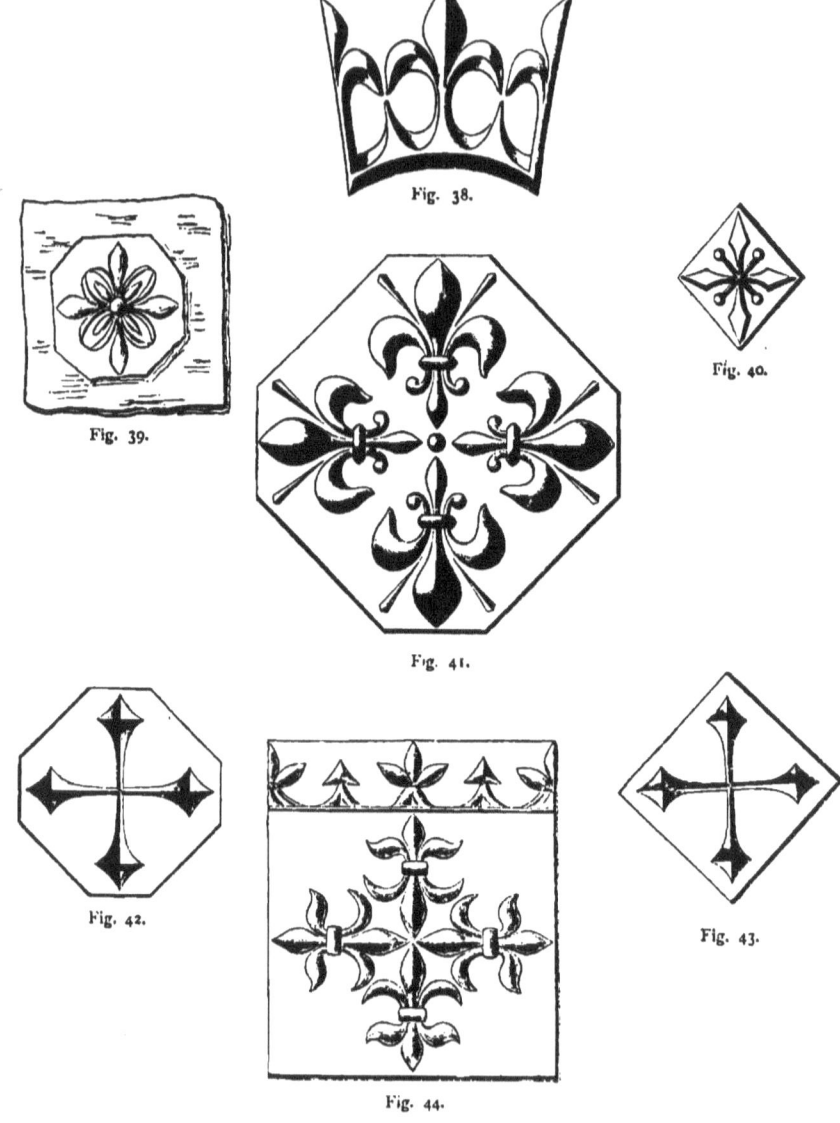

Fig. 38.

Fig. 39.

Fig. 40.

Fig. 41.

Fig. 42.

Fig. 43.

Fig. 44.

LONDON MARKS.

Mr. North records also one at Edworth, Bedfordshire, and one at Norton, Hertfordshire. Four are given in my *Church Bells of Cambridgeshire*, and five in Mr. Stahlschmidt's *Church Bells of Kent*, but so far as we know there are none in the western counties, and certainly there are none in the Diocese of Peterborough. Suffolk is as far above the average with these bells as it is with William Dawe's. We know as yet of no mediæval foundry in Essex, and the Londoners having there a "happy hunting-ground," readily crossed the Stour and did business against Norwich, penetrating, in the case of Henry Jordan, on one occasion quite to the north of that city. Other London marks are given opposite (figs. 38—44).

The most attractive of the London foundry-shields is that of our last ante-Reformation craftsman, William Culverden (fig. 45), a rebus which I guessed wrong. Further investigation by

Fig. 45.

Mr. Tyssen set me right. His bells are very rare, so rare that I give after the Suffolk pair,

Stratford, S. Mary, tenor,
Ubbeston, treble,

a complete list of towers containing those known to exist.
Cambridgeshire, Landbeach.
Dorset, Steeple.

Essex, Elsenham, Takely, Wicken Breaux.
Hertfordshire, Furneaux Pelham.
Kent, Boughton Aluph, Gravency.
Middlesex, Brentford.
Staffordshire, Kingstone.
Surrey, Chobham, Wimbledon.

A few more may perhaps turn up in the home counties and the Midlands. The Dorset bell is at present the sole contribution of the west. He was at work only from 1510 to 1523, which probably accounts for the paucity of his specimens. The shield is in many ways a great curiosity, and the ingenuity of my readers may be put to a test, as the meanings of the trefoil and monogram at the foot are not yet clear. Round the bell, which bears the word 𝔍𝔬𝔫𝔡 (Founder), are the opening words of Psalm xi., 𝔍𝔫 𝔡𝔫𝔬 𝔒𝔬𝔣𝔦𝔡𝔬 (In the Lord put I my trust), which were often used by our forefathers as a motto, especially at the outset of any business. Though I cannot recall the instance, I feel sure that at the beginning of one of the MSS. of a mediæval Chronicle these words occur, coupled with

𝔄𝔰𝔰𝔦𝔱 𝔓𝔯𝔦𝔫𝔠𝔦𝔭𝔦𝔬 𝔖𝔞𝔫𝔠𝔱𝔞 𝔐𝔞𝔯𝔦𝔞 𝔐𝔢𝔬.

Now this very pentameter occurs on one of William Culverden's bells, viz., that at Takely, Essex, which I therefore feel justified in regarding as his earliest. When the Reformation came in, this pentameter went out, but its place was taken by the word *Emmanuel*, which used to be written at the head of letters. I may be excused for enlarging on this, as it illustrates a place otherwise obscure in Shakespeare's *Henry VI.* That the fact is as I have stated is shown by a letter of Mr. William Carnsewe to "Customer Smyth" (purchaser of metals to Queen Elizabeth), dated 15 January, 1583, which is headed

" In te dñe, in te dñe
  speram' nos   Emanuell. In dño Confido."*

Now for the Shakespearian illustration. The "clerk" of Chatham is brought before Jack Cade, charged with the crime

---

* *The Smelting of Copper in South Wales*, by Col. Grant-Francis. See also "In the Old Muniment of Wollaton Hall," Part II., *New Review*, December, 1889.

of being able to read and write and cast accompt. The enormity of these charges was further enhanced by his name.

"*Cade.* What is thy name, sirrah?
Clerk. Emanuel.
Cade (reflecting). They use to write it at the head of letters. 'Twill go hard with you."

Having thus treated of the use of Psalm xi. i., we turn to the essence of the rebus, the bird with b̃e (den) over it. Now those versed in ornithology may scrutinize the feathered biped diligently. It rather resembles the little birds in a child's "Noah Ark," but it is meant for a culver, or pigeon, and thus the riddle of the rebus was read.

A rebus is a picture-riddle, such as an Ash-tree on a Tun for Ashton, a Mill on a Tun for Milton, &c. The difficulty of producing a "den" must be the composer's excuse for not completing his rebus.

The word "culver" for a wood-pigeon or dove is no doubt a corruption from *columba*, and was apparently not extinct in the west of England at the end of the last century. I must linger a little over this delicious old English word. We find it in the *Blickling Homilies*,* not later than A.D. 971, where our Lord addresses the Virgin Mary as "min culufre." In a Bestiary of the thirteenth century† we have a lesson drawn from the nature of the bird.

"Natura columbe et significacio
Dᵉ culuer haueth costes gode
alle we.s ogen to hauen in mode."
"The dove has habits good,
All we-them ought to have in manner."

Dan Michel in his *Ayenbite of Inwyt*‡ (Remorse of Conscience) speaks of our Lord as "that coluerhous," wherein the mild-hearted may rest, about a century afterwards. The rustic glossaries know the word. They are referred to in my *Church Bells of Cambridgeshire*‖, with the old Kentish word *culverkeys*.

* E. E. T. S, p. 157.
† *Old English Miscellany*, by Dr. R. Morris, E. E. T, S., p. 25.
‡ Reprint (1888), E. E. T. S., p. 162.
‖ P. 43.

for cowslips, and that it is "quite classical" (as Andrews encouragingly backs up a seemingly dubious word in his Latin dictionary) will be acknowledged by all who reverence Edmund Spenser as the poets' poet." The word occurs in the *Faerie Queene*, in Sonnet 38, and in *Teares of the Muses*, l. 245. William Culverden's will is given at length in my *Church Bells of Cambridgeshire*.* He describes himself as "citezen and brasier of London, and parishoner of the parishe of Sanct Botulph without Algate of London," the old foundry parish. He seems to have been a lone man, there being no mention of father or mother, wife or children. The guild-brethren of the brotherhood of Jesu within the church of S. Botolph, Aldgate, and of the guild of our blessed lady of Boston are to be paid up for the year, and if his assets suffice for the purpose, 33*s.* 8*d.* is bequeathed to the Abbey of Westminster "where I was brought upp in my youth."

From the special mention of the Boston guild it may be conjectured that Culverden (like the author of this book) was born "under the Stump." The Guild of the Blessed Mary was the *Gilda Mercatoria* of Boston, and the earliest mention of it is in 1393, when a Patent grant was issued to it. The present Hall used by the Boston Corporation is the Hall of this Guild. It was no small matter to belong to this Guild, considering the "jolly pardons," which according to Foxe were renewed to it by Pope Julius II. through Thomas Cromwell, in 1510.

The strange story of Cromwell's "gelly junkets" and their effect on Julius II. may be read in Foxe's *Acts and Monuments*, or in Pishey Thompson's *History of Boston.*†

Culverden's leasehold property in "Houndisdich," and his "belmolds and implements w^t all other stuffe w^{t}in the said house, grounde, and shedds necessarye and belonging to the crafte or science of Belfounders or brasiers," were to be sold to Thomas Lawrence, the lease for x marcs a year, the goods for £120, but no arrangement could be come to, the executors renounced the will, and letters of administration were granted to two of them, Sir Roger Preston, clerk, and John Ryon,

* Pp. 44, &c.   † Pp. 74, &c.

fruiterer. Thomas Lawrence was one of the witnesses to the will, and another was John Tynny. I wish we had a bell of Lawrence's in Suffolk, but though he is known at Margaretting, Essex, and at Kingston, Cambridgeshire, his gridiron does not appear within our borders. He died in Norwich in 1545. It is probable that John Tynny is identical with John Tonne, about whom a good deal has to be said hereafter.

I have now brought the Metropolitan founders whose bells occur in Suffolk down to the time of the Reformation, when there comes such a vast break-up of ideas and general cleavage in English life that I purpose to turn back and again follow the stream of time. I took King's Lynn (Bishop's Lynn, it was more commonly called at that time of day) first, because Suffolk has only one Lynn bell, and that a very early one. Now, having exhausted my London list, I will return to Norfolk, and discuss the very large company of bells from the Norwich mediæval foundries. After that I will come to the solitary Suffolk centre of that time, Bury S. Edmund's, and then having picked up some very remarkable waifs in the county, our threads will all be joined in one loop, and we can start fair for our post-Reformation annals.

The lion's share in Suffolk mediæval bells is taken by the city of Norwich, from which we have more than a hundred bells, about two-thirds of the number in Norfolk. Outside the two counties they are very rare. I cannot trace anything in Suffolk to the William "Brasiere de Notyngham," admitted to the freedom of Norwich in 1376, and mentioned in the Cambridgeshire book*, nor to John Sutton "Belleyeter," admitted in 1404; but Thomas Potter of the same year, or his successor, Richard Baxter, may claim the Clock-bell, probably the Sance-bell, at Cratfield,† the third at Somerleyton, the second at Ampton, and the fifth at Market Weston. The latter cast two bells for Mettingham College in 1416-17. The pot (fig. 46) on the Market Weston bell seems appropriate to Potter, but the initial

* P. 13.
† This was discovered by my young friends, E. St. Lo Malet and W. W. Channell.

cross (fig. 47), and lion's head (fig. 48), do not seem exclusively his.

Fig. 46.

Fig. 47.

Fig. 48.

The Cratfield Clock-bell, with its dedication to the Virgin + 𝔙irginis 𝔈gregie + 𝔙ocor 𝔙ampana 𝔐arie, bears also the words, 𝔓rey for 𝔗he 𝔖ole 𝔒f 𝔚illiam 𝔄leys. No will under this name appears in the Ipswich Registry, which begins in 1444; and we may safely assume this bell to be of an earlier date.

There are certain points of union between these men and the Brasyers, but before we can touch on the latter great family a curious little group comes across our way, which from the locality of the bells can hardly be assigned to any place but Norwich.

It consists of the Frostenden and Ellough trebles, and the third at Southelmham S. James, to which might have been added the old second at Gorleston. The maker of these bells, whoever he was, seems to have lived about the middle of the fifteenth century. He is only found in North-east Suffolk and East Norfolk (Caister by Norwich, Gillingham, Lessingham,

Mundham, Rockland All Saints, and Wramplingham), and gives sometimes the name of the donor, as JOHAᴎᴎES BᴙOVᴎ at Southelmham S. James, and EDᴍVᴎDVS ᴎOᴙᴍAᴎ at Lessingham. The latter seems identical with a certain Edmund Norman, lord of Filby, who died in 1444, though his name is only connected with the parish through one John Norman, a son of Henry Norman, a villain of the manor of Lessingham, who had a royal license to be presented to any ecclesiastical benefice, notwithstanding his villanage, in 1435. On the Gorleston second was a good piece of old English,

+ I Aᴍ ⋮ ᴍAD ⋮ Iᴎ ⋮ ᴛHE WOᴙDCHEPE ⋮ OH ᴛHE ⋮ CᴙOS

This bell was also naturally dedicated to S. Nicholas, hanging as it did in so prominent a sea-mark as Gorleston tower. Now, to revert to the connection between Potter and Baxter on the one part, and the Brasyers on the other, we have a connecting link in the Fressingfield tenor, the largest "Norwicher" in the county, though hard pressed in size by the Eye seventh. This fine old bell bears for initial cross fig. 49, and the lion's head,

Fig. 49.

fig. 48, which seem to belong to the earlier men, but withal the shield, fig. 50, which has a later appearance, being more strictly heraldic than fig. 51. When earlier and later signs are combined the later of course wins the day, and thus I dare not

Fig. 50.   Fig. 51.

Fig. 52.

ascribe to my own tenor a date earlier than c. 1460, which makes it somewhat earlier than magnificent carving on the benches, one of the bench-ends bearing the initials a p. apparently for Alicia de la Pole, Countess of Suffolk, widow of the beheaded Duke William, and grand-daughter of the poet Chaucer. It seems certain, from the evidence of the Paston Letters, that she was in residence at Wingfield Castle at this time. But whatever may be the exact date of the Fressingfield tenor, the connection of the marks is obvious. The inscription is unique : + 𝔖corum 𝔐eritis. 𝔓angamus 𝔒antica 𝔏audis.

The bells of the Brasyers swarm all over the county, from Bradwell to Stanningfield, from Icklingham to Wherstead, and being as remarkable for beauty as for number, I am going somewhat minutely into their history

PLATE IV.

Fig. 54.

Fig. 55.

Fig. 56.

Fig. 57.

Fig. 58.

Fig. 59.

Fig. 60.

NORWICH LETTERING.

The brass of Robert Brasyer, the first known of the name, is in St. Stephen's, Norwich, and the accompanying engraving (fig. 53) gives his effigy. The following is the inscription on the brass, which is a double one:—

☉ bos omes picturas istas intuentes deuotas ad deū ffudite preces p' (alabı) Koberti Brasyer istī ciuitatus quonda Aldermani et maions et cristiane br eius. Quibs requie eternam donet deus. Amen.

Fig. 53.

He combined the business of a mercer with that of a founder; and his son, Richard Brasyer, is entered as a goldsmith as well as a founder. The will of the latter was proved in 1482, by his son, also Richard Brasyer, who died childless in 1513. Of these men, Robert Brasyer was Mayor in 1410, Richard Brasyer the elder in 1456 and 1463, and Richard Brasyer the younger in 1510. No one can see the lettering of the Norwich bells, of which I give examples (figs. 54—60), without being struck by its great beauty. The inscriptions are generally in hexameters with an initial cross (fig. 61) and a lion's head (fig. 62), for stop at the place of the rhyming word.

Fig. 61. Fig. 62.

A more unexpected quarter for light to arise from in the history of a mediæval foundry than an Appeal Case in the House of Lords in 1881 can hardly be imagined. Yet so it has come about, and the relations of Richard Brasyer the elder to the town of Mildenhall in Suffolk have received illumination from the case of *Mackay v. Dick*, through the black-letter lore of Lord Blackburn.

Dick and Stevenson were engineers who invented a "steam navvy." Mackay, a contractor, purchased it conditionally, and alleged that it proved a failure. They for their part declared that it had not been tried fairly according to agreement. After divers appeals, the case came before the House of Lords, who decided for the respondents, Dick and Stevenson. Lord Blackburn, in delivering his opinion, quoted the case of the men of Mildenhall against this Norwich founder, Richard Brasyer the elder, in 1469. Let us look into the matter, as we have in existence one Mildenhall bell, anterior to the time, and other collateral matter.

The little town of Mildenhall had an abundant share in the prosperity of East Anglia in the early part of the fifteenth century, and the north-west corner parish of Suffolk was united closely to London by the twofold Mayoralty of Sir Henry Barton, citizen and skinner, the father of the public lighting of the metropolis. Barton, a native of Mildenhall, or perhaps of the adjoining village of Barton Mills, which yet contains a beautiful specimen of domestic architecture of that time, was

Lord Mayor in 1416 and 1430. His tomb still remains in Mildenhall Church, as well as a Font, bearing his arms and those of the City of London.

Great improvements appear to have taken place in Mildenhall in these days. A market-cross was erected, as well as the fine tower of the parish church, which was surmounted by a leaden spire, of somewhat the same character as those at Brandon and East Harling, making it a grand land-mark for many miles in the open heaths and fens of the district. The bell-frame, a great portion of which still remains, with the windlass for getting the bells into position, is rather earlier than the tower. This may be a surprise to some, but the fact that these frames are bolted together by wooden pins, so long that they could not have been driven in after the walls were built, is conclusive. It seems to have been the usual procedure.

There were five bells, if we may judge from the construction of the frame. Of these one remains, the original second, I believe, dedicated to S. John the Baptist, and another, the original treble, dedicated to S. Mary Magdalene, was recast in 1860. They have been already mentioned in the list of John Danyell's bells, though at one time, with less complete information than that which we now have, we were inclined to attribute them to Richard Hille. Though they must have been large, heavy bells, I do not think that they were remarkable for good tone. That recast in 1860 had a very "panny" sound, and the ringers forty or fifty years ago had such a hatred to their old fifth (the original second, as I think, and now the sixth) that they tried to split it by ringing it with a rope strained round the sound-bow. It resisted their kindly intentions, but possibly they would have succeeded with a chain instead of a rope.

Good or bad, by 1469 not only were their makers dead, but also the successful Henry Jurden. Another Mildenhall Lord Mayor, Sir Thomas Gregory (1451), if living must have been advanced in life, and the London connection was weakened. Meanwhile the Norwichers are carrying matters with a high hand in East Anglia, and in some way or other the great bell of Mildenhall was broken as early as 1464, when William Chapman of that parish bequeathed ten marks for its repair.

Who shall do the work? Norwich influence prevails, and the men of Mildenhall make an agreement with Richard Brasyer to bring him "le graund bell de Mildenhall," which was to be weighed in their presence and recast "de ce faire un tenor pour accorder in tono et sono a les auters belles de Mildenhall." But somehow there was a failure, and they went to law.

The scene is worth dwelling upon. Danby, C. J.,[*] is presiding in the Court of Common Pleas, his puisne brethren being Choke, Lyttleton,[†] Moyle, and Needham. Two eminent Serjeants are retained, Genney for the plaintiffs and Pigot for the defendant. They are both well known in the Paston Letters, where[‡] there is a bill of costs in the case of Calle v. Huggan with "wyne and perys," quite in the style of Solomon Pell; and Genney became a Judge of the King's Bench in 1481. The men of Mildenhall and Richard Brasyer must have found their purses lighter at the end of the performance.

The defendant is sued on his obligation. He does not deny that the bell was brought to his house, but he says that it was not weighed nor put into the furnace according to the indenture. Thereupon Serjeant Genney says that it is not a good plea, because defendant ought to have weighed it and put it in the furnace. The indenture certainly, he added, did not specify who was to weigh it, but it was clear that this was part of the occupation of the founder, and it might be understood that he was to carry it out. The learned Serjeant then drew a parallel case of a tailor and his customer. Suppose a tailor is under bond to me, on condition that if I bring to his shop three ells of cloth it shall be cut out and he shall make me a gown, then it is not for him to plead that the cloth was not cut out, for it is his business to cut it out. To this Choke, Lyttleton, and Moile agreed, Choke adding that the indenture expresses that it is to be weighed and put in the furnace in the presence of the men of Mildenhall, which showed that they were not to do it. Needham, however, held that they could have as well weighed it as

[*] Appointed 1461.
[†] Appointed 1466. Author of the Treatise on Tenures.
[‡] III., 25.

the defendant could have weighed it, that part of the affair requiring no special skill, and he also called up an imaginary tailor, the counterpart of Serjeant Genney's.

The truer parallel, said Justice Needham, would be the measuring and making up the cloth, not the cutting it out and making it up, and if the bond did not specify who was to measure it, the party to whom the bond was given ought to do so. However, as to the casting, he agreed with the other judges. Then uprises Serjeant Pigot for the defendant, reasoning on the bond somewhat in the style of the proceedings in the well-known case of *Shylock v. Antonio*. A bond, says he, means what it says. The weighing comes first, and the casting afterwards. Brasyer could not recast the bell till it had been weighed. The bond says that it is to be weighed in the presence of the men of Mildenhall, and they might have made other men weigh it. Chief Justice Danby's common sense puts all this aside. The substance of the bond was the casting of the tenor, the weighing being a mere accident. It is not in accordance with our ideas to find the counsel for the plaintiffs speaking after the Chief Justice, but Genney being a Serjeant was a brother, and he adds another case in point.

Suppose, says he, that a bond said that my son should walk to a certain church to marry your daughter, and that instead of walking he rode (*chavaucha*) or was carried in a litter (*en braces*), this accidental deviation would not forfeit the bond, the substance of it, the marriage, having been completed.*

* I regret that in my Supplemental paper on the *Church Bells of Norfolk* I was misled by the published report of this case, which differs materially from that in the Year Books, as here supplied to me through the kindness of Mr. Amherst D. Tyssen.

YEAR BOOK, EDW. IV. ANNO. IX. E T case 13.

En det sur obligaē le def. pled' un endenture, s. q̄ le
In debt on a bond the defendant pleads an Indenture according to which grand bell de *Mildenhall* sera cary al meason le defend' en *Norwich*, *the great bell of Mildenhall shall be carried to the house of the defendant in Norwich* al costes des hommes de *Mildenhall* x la serra wey x mis en few *at the costs of the men of Mildenhall and there shall be weighed and put in the furnace* in *praesentia hominum de Mildenhal*, x donq3 le def. de c̄ doit faire un *in the presence of the men of Mildenhal and then the defendant if it should make a*

G

Thus the Mildenhall folk won the day, but the tower long remained tenor-less. Henry Pope, whose family had for many years possessed the manor of "Twamil," now Wamill, in 1530 bequeathed £3 10s. "towarde the makyng of the gret belle...to be payde by the hands of...Thomas Larke whansoever the town doo go abowght the making thereof."

tenor p accordeȝ *in tono & sono* a les auters belles de *Mildenhal*, &c., *quod tenor to agree in note and sound with the other bells of Mildenhall, etc., that then tunc obligatio, p nullo habeatur &c.* x dit q le dit bell' ne fuit pas weye *the obligation should be deemed void, etc., and says that the said bell was not weighed* ni mise en few accordant al endenture, xc judgȝ si *or put in the furnace according to the indenture, etc. (prays) judgment if the* action.
action will lie.

¶ *Genney.* Ceo n'est plée, car le def. duist (*Plaintiff's Counsel*). *That is not a (good) plea, because the defendant ought* aver wey c̄ x mis en few, car il n'est pas mis en certein en *to have weighed it and put it in the furnace, because it is not made certain by* l'endenture q̄ doit weyer, donqȝ il sȝra entend' q̄ cesty q̄ ad le *the indenture who ought to weigh it, then it shall be understood that he who had the* conningȝ de c faire, ou a q̄ occupation appent de c̄ faire, doit c̄ faire, xc. x icy *skill to do it, or whose business it is to do it ought to do it, and here* appiert q̄ le defend. est le Brasier q̄ duist faire le bell' issint il *it appears that the defendant is the Brasier who ought to make the bell, therefore it* appertient a son occupation de c̄ faire, xc. come si un Tailour soit obligȝ a moy sur *appertains to his business to do it as if a tailor is bound to me on* condic̄ q̄ jeo port a son shoppe ill. ulnes de cloth le quel sȝra shape, x *condition that I bring to his shop 3 elles of cloth which shall be cut out, and* si le Tailour fait a moy un gown de c̄ q̄ adonqȝ obligȝ sȝra avoid, x sir ore *if the tailor makes me a gown of it that then the bond shall be void, and* il n'est mis en certein q̄ doit shape le cloth, x p c̄ il sȝra *it is not rendered certain who ought to cut out the cloth, and for this reason it shall be* entend' q̄ le Tailour c̄ doit faire car il ad le conning de c̄ faire, issint icy, *held that the tailor should do it, because he had the skill to do it, therefore here* quod *Choke, Littleton, & Moile concesser, & Choke* dit auxi, l'endenture voiet, *which (three of the judges) agreed and Choke said also, the indenture expresses* in præsentia hominum de *Mildenhal* sȝra wey x mis en few, x *in the presence of the Men of M. it shall be weighed and put in the furnace, and* c̄ sȝra entend p auters quant il voet q̄ sȝra fait en lour presence, *that shall be held by others when it expresses that it shall be done in their presence,* x il ne poit · estre entend p nul auȝ forsqȝ p def. p que, xc. *and it cannot be understood to mean by any others than the defendant, wherefore, etc.*

¶ *Neddam.* Le pl. poet auxbien weier le bell' come poit le def. (*One of the judges*). *The plaintiff can as well weigh the bell as can the defendant*

It seems impossible to refer either to the elder Richard
Brasyer, or to his successors, Richard Brasyer the younger, and
Thomas Barker, any special bells, unless we have better evi-
dence than marks and lettering to support our classification.
No doubt the sprigged shield is less heraldic in its character
than that with an ermine feld, but the ermine shield is found

x auxi grand conning ad, donqʒ qñt chose est reherse en le condition
and had as great skill   then when a thing is stated in the condition (of the bond)
d'estre fait, le quel poet auxibñ estre fait p l'un com͞ p l'auter,   l'un   ad auxi
to be done   which can as well be done by one   as by the other, and the one has as
bon conning come l'auī   x n'est pas mis en certein   q̄   duist č faire, cesty n
good   skill   as the other, and it is not rendered certain who ought to do it, he   to
q̄ l'obligʒ est fait doit   le faire.   Come si un soit oblige a moy sur condie
whom the bond is made ought to do it.   As if one is bound to me on condition
q̄ si jeo porī draps a luy,   le q   sʒra   measure   la,   s'il   fait a moy
that if I take cloth to him which shall be measured there, and if he makes me
un gowne de č   q̄ adonqʒ l'obligʒ   sʒra   voide, xc. icy   n'est   mis en certein
a gown   of it that then the bond shall be void, etc., here it is not rendered certain
q̄   doit measure   les draps, x   p̄ č q̄ jeo say   auxbien   measureī come le
who ought to measure the cloth, and because I know as well how to measure as the
def.   en č   case il covient a moy de faire č, x   issint   icy, xc. mes a metī le
defendant, in that case it   lies on   me   to do it, and therefore here, etc.   but to put the
bell'   en few   č appertient   al artificer   per q̄   come ad   estre dit   il
bell in the furnace that belongs to the workman wherefore   as has been said he
duist faire č.
ought to do it.

¶   *Pigot.*   Un fait sʒra   pris p entendim͞t, eins p les parolx,
(*Counsel for defendant*).   *A deed shall be taken to   mean   what the words say*
x   icy p les parolx il   n'est   tendq que il soit wey,   car
and here by the words he is not bound to make the bell until   it is weighed because
les parolx sont &⁕ tunc   defend.   faū, xc.   Et auxi   com͞t   q̄ le fait
the words are " and then the defendant make," etc.   And also in as much as the deed
voit   in   *præsentia hominum de M.*   issint   puissent faire auters homes de
expresses in the presence of the men of M., therefore they may make other   men
weier č en lour presence.
weigh it in their presence.

¶   *Danby.*   S'il mist   tout   le bell'   en few
(*Chief Justice of the Common Pleas*).   *If he put the whole bell in the furnace*
sans   weier   č   x   ad fait un bell' disaccord'   a   les auters,   n'ad il
without weighing it, and had made a bell out of tune with the others, would he not
p   forfeite l'obligʒ ; il appiert   q̄   le cause   del fesans   de l'obligʒ fuist   p̄ č
have forfeited the bond ; it appears that the cause of the making of the bond was in order
q̄ il ferroit a eux   un suffič belle, xc.   x   č covient   il meinī, x nemy
that he should make them a sufficient bell, etc., and that lies on him now, and it is no

on the Fressingfield tenor with earlier stops, and portions of the alphabet, which seem to belong to the infancy of inscriptions, are found at Barsham with the sprigged shield, and at Bradwell (tenor) with the ermine. False classification is far worse than none. I will confine myself, therefore, to sorting out the inscriptions, and then deal with extraneous evidence which we may have about special bells.

The Salutation to the Virgin occurs only on
Honington, second,
Saxham, Little, treble, and
Stanningfield, second.

Bells bearing the Salutation were used for the *Angelus*, as also would be those thus inscribed :—

+ 𝕳ac 𝕴n 𝕮onclabe. 𝕲abriel 𝕹unc 𝕻ange 𝕾uabe.

travers, adire q̄ le belle fuist carī a luy a les costes d'un estrange home, x
traverse to say that the bell was brought to him at the cost of a stranger, and
nemy al costes des homes de M. xc. Car c̄ n'est pas le substance de
not at the cost of the men of M., etc. Because that is not the substance of the
bond'.
bond.

¶ Genney. Si jeo soy oblige de amesner mon fits a tiel lieu, x
(*Plaintiff's counsel.*) *If I am bound to take my son to a specified place, and*
q̄ il illonq3 alera a tiel Esglise p̄ espous3 vr̄e file, en cel case
that he thence shall walk to a specified church to marry your daughter, in such a case
s'il espousa \F₂ file la, comt q̄ il chavaucha al Esglise, ou fuit
if he marries your daughter there, although he rode to the church, or was
port en braces, unc̄ c̄ ne forfeit mon oblig3 x unc̄ l'oblig3 voet
carried in braces,* yet that does not forfeit my bond, and yet the bond expresses
qu'il alera al Esglise, xc. mes c̄ n'est le substance del bond' eins q
that he shall walk to the church, etc., but that is not the substance of the bond as that
il espousera vr̄e file, c̄ est le substance, xc. (Case Fogassa, Com' 15.)†
he shall marry your daughter that is the substance.

¶ Choke, Lyttleton, Moyle, Needham, and Danby were the judges of the Common Pleas in 1469, Danby being chief justice. There were no judges named Genney or Pigott, so they must be counsel, and it is clear which was on which side.

* Braces, according to Johnson's Dictionary, may mean stout leathern bands put under a carriage on wheels—evidently to answer the purpose of springs. It may also mean arms, or armfulls.

† The reference Case Fogassa, Com' 15, is to p. 15 of the Commentaries or reports of Plowden, where the Mildenhall case is cited with approval, and very fully stated in a case of Reniger *v.* Fogossa, argued on Feb. 8, 4 Edw. VI.

(In this chamber, Gabriel, now sound sweetly), viz. :—
Bradwell, treble,
Fornham, All Saints, third,
Homersfield, tenor,
Melton, second,
Ottley, fourth,
Playford, treble,
Reydon bell,
Somerleyton, fifth,
Uggeshall bell, to which might have been added
Brandon, treble,
Bruisyard, tenor,
Weston, Coney, an old bell,
Herringswell, tenor ;
Also two inscribed :—
+ 𝔐𝔦𝔰𝔰𝔲𝔰 𝔡𝔢 𝔠𝔢𝔩𝔦𝔰. 𝔋𝔞𝔟𝔯𝔬 𝔑𝔬𝔪𝔢𝔫 𝔊𝔞𝔟𝔯𝔦𝔢𝔩𝔦𝔰. (I have the name of Gabriel sent from heaven. The proper form, as occurring in the Midlands, is *Missi*, not *Missus*), viz. :—
Martlesham, treble,
Saxham, Little, second ;
and the old treble at Flixton, and second at Pettaugh, bearing an inscription which belongs largely to the Western counties,
+ 𝔐𝔦𝔰𝔰𝔲𝔰 𝔙𝔢𝔯𝔬 𝔓𝔦𝔢. 𝔊𝔞𝔟𝔯𝔦𝔢𝔩 𝔣𝔢𝔯𝔱 𝔏𝔢𝔱𝔞 𝔐𝔞𝔯𝔦𝔢.* (Now Gabriel, being sent, bears joyful tidings to Holy Mary) where "vero" corresponds to "autem" in the Vulgate, S. Luke ii. 26. Perhaps an illiterate reference to the same text may have produced the error in the previous inscription. Stonemasons at the present day do not always deal skilfully with the Authorised Version. We will speak of the *Angelus* bell under mediæval usages.

Other inscriptions relating to the Virgin Mary are + 𝔠𝔢𝔩𝔢𝔰𝔱𝔦 𝔐𝔞𝔫𝔫𝔞. 𝔗𝔲𝔞 𝔓𝔯𝔬𝔩𝔢𝔰 𝔑𝔬𝔰 𝔠𝔦𝔟𝔢𝔱 𝔄𝔫𝔫𝔞. (May thy offspring, Anna, feed us with celestial manna) which is found on
Blakenham, Great, treble,
Cotton, fourth,

---

* The sixth at S. Giles', Norwich, bears this inscription.

Cretingham, fourth,
Rishangles, fourth.

+ **Virginis Egregie. Vocor Campana Marie.** (I am called the bell of the Glorious Virgin Mary) seems pretty well an exclusively Norwich inscription, occurring on

Finningham, second,
Icklingham, All Saints, second,
Linstead, Great, bell,
Risby, treble,
Somerleyton, fourth,
Stonham, East, fourth, to which in former days might have been added Saxstead tenor; and finally,

+ **Sum Rosa Pulsata. Mundi Maria Vocata.** (I am, when rung, called Mary, the Rose of the world), on the tenors at

Covehithe,
Dalham,
Ipswich S. Laurence.

This appears to have been an epigraph peculiarly applicable to tenors, from the local pronunciation "Roose," but it is recorded as on the old second at Brandon.

The whole company of the Faithful we find commemorated in a somewhat common-place hexameter:—

+ **Hec Fit Sanctorum. Campana Laude Bonorum.** (This bell is made in the praise of good saints), which is on

Charsfield, second,
Cransford, second,
Glemham, Great, treble,
Rishangles, treble, and was on
Herringswell, second.

A line of more force and more dubious theology is on the Fressingfield tenor,

+ **Sanctorum Meritis. Pangamus Cantica Laudis.** (Let us sound songs of praise by the merits of the saints. It may be "to the merits." Bold is he who dogmatises on mediæval Latinity).

The Archangel Michael we might expect to find on bells used as "soul-bells," answering to our "death bell," rung, however, before the latest travail of man on earth. The hexameter,

+ **Dulcis Sisto Melis. Campana Vocor Michaelis** is on
Brundish, second,
Charsfield, fourth,
Hacheston, third,
Kirkley bell,
Mendlesham, second,
Soham, Monk, third,
Spexhall bell, and formerly on
Campsey Ash, second, and
Herringfleet, third.

I am much exercised as to the true meaning of this line. *Sisto* is in some cases *Cisto*, perhaps a mistake for *Cista*, and *Melis*, an utterly abnormal form, may have lost a letter. Thus the line would read *Dulcis Cista Mellis Campana Vocor Michaelis.* (Box of sweet honey, I am called Michael's bell), with an allusion to the shape of a bell, and what Mr. Haweis calls a "combination hum." I am bound to admit that I can find no such mediæval use of *Cista*, but in the Eighth-century Epinal Glossary the word is explained by *corbes grandes*, a country term for a large basket, and not inapplicable to a hive.

The favourite saint of the Norwich founders is that turbulent patriot martyr, Thomas à Becket. The Apostle of the same name shrinks into insignificance in comparison with S. Thomas of Canterbury, as may be understood by any who will examine the dedications of Churches to S. Thomas ; and the merits of him of Canterbury are those referred to in

+ **Pos Thome Meritis. Mereamur Gaudia Lucis:** (May we merit the joys of Light by the merits of Thomas!) Here follows a round dozen of instances :—
Cotton, tenor,
Elmham, South, S. George, fourth,
Hinderclay, tenor,
Hoxne, fourth,
Ipswich, S. Laurence, fourth,
Ixworth, fifth,
Melton, third,
Ottley, fifth,

Sapiston, fourth,
Sylcham, tenor,
Thornham, Great, tenor,
Wherstead, tenor, and formerly
Bungay, S. Mary, fifth, and
Wissett, tenor.

No one can fail to notice that this is eminently (like Rose, pronounced Roose), an inscription for tenors, on account of the booming sound of large bells resembling the word "Tom." Thus we have Tom of Oxford and Tom of Lincoln, and there is an inscription somewhere on paper, which none of us have ever found on metal, " In Thome Laude Resono Bim Bom sine fraude," translated " In praise of Thomas I repeat,

My Dong Ding Dong without deceit."

S. Peter, with the line,

+ Petrus Ad Eterne. Ducat Nos Gaudia Vite (May Peter lead us to the joys of Eternal Life!) claims the following list:—

Bradwell, second,
Bredfield, tenor,
Cove, South, bell,
Covehithe, fourth,
Dallinghoo, third,
Hepworth, tenor,
Mendlesham, third,
Sibton, fourth,
Soham, Earl, fourth
Soham, Monk, fourth,
Wyverstone, third.

To S. Andrew (Petrus ante Petrum), with the line + Quesumus Andrea. Famulorum Suscipe Vota, (We pray thee, Andrew, receive the vows of thy servants,) belong

Barningham, treble,
Bedingfield bell,
Brundish, tenor,
Friston, second,
Icklingham, All Saints, tenor,
Peasenhall, third,

Pettaugh bell,
Soham, Earl, second,
Stonham, Earl, third,
Wenhaston, tenor, and formerly
Flixton, second, and
Herringfleet, second.

S. Margaret, the mediæval *Lucina*, has the following, bearing
+ 𝔉𝔞𝔠 𝔐𝔞𝔯𝔤𝔞𝔯𝔢𝔱𝔞. 𝔑𝔬𝔟𝔦𝔰 𝔚𝔢𝔠 𝔐𝔲𝔫𝔢𝔯𝔞* 𝔏𝔢𝔱𝔞. (Make, Margaret, these offices joyful to us).

Bungay, Holy Trinity, bell,†
Dennington, second,
Homersfield, second,
Hoxne, fifth,
Martlesham, second
Thrandeston, second,
Ufford, second, and formerly
Herringswell, treble.

The history of S. Katherine, and her torture on the wheel, appears to have suggested the appropriateness of dedications of bells to her. The line,

+ 𝔖𝔲𝔟𝔟𝔢𝔫𝔦𝔞𝔱 𝔇𝔦𝔤𝔫𝔞. 𝔇𝔬𝔫𝔞𝔫𝔱𝔦𝔟𝔲𝔰 𝔥𝔞𝔫𝔠 𝔎𝔞𝔱𝔢𝔯𝔦𝔫𝔞, (May worthy Katherine help the givers of this bell) may be read on

Bildeston, fourth,
Cretingham, tenor,
Eye, second,
Southwold, seventh,
Stowlangtoft, third, and formerly on
Troston, second. This inscription has a philological value, as showing the pronunciation of *digna*, rhyming with *Katerina*, which yet survives in our *condign*.

The name of S. Mary Magdalen was given with the same reference to benefactors:—

+ 𝔇𝔬𝔫𝔞 𝔑𝔢𝔭𝔢𝔫𝔡𝔢 𝔓𝔦𝔞. 𝔑𝔬𝔤𝔬 𝔐𝔞𝔤𝔡𝔞𝔩𝔢𝔫𝔞 𝔐𝔞𝔯𝔦𝔞.

It remains still on
Eye, seventh, a good bell,

---
* Nescio an hic versus rectius ad campanas an ad obstetrices referatur. J. J. R.
† Brought from some other church.

Kelsale, seventh,
Layham, bell,
Melton, tenor, and was on
Barningham, treble,
Felsham, fifth,
Fressingfield, fifth,
Troston, tenor.

S. Nicholas, as the patron Saint of sailors, we should have expected to find near the sea. Such, however, was not the will of the Norwich men.

+ 𝔍𝔲𝔫𝔤𝔢𝔯𝔢 𝔑𝔬𝔰 𝔈𝔥𝔯𝔦𝔰𝔱𝔬. 𝔖𝔱𝔲𝔡𝔢𝔞𝔱 𝔑𝔦𝔠𝔥𝔬𝔩𝔞𝔲𝔰 𝔈𝔫 𝔄𝔩𝔱𝔬 (May Nicholas strive to join us with Christ on high !) is on
Petistree, tenor, and
Playford, second ; and a better-known line,

+ 𝔑𝔬𝔰 𝔖𝔬𝔠𝔦𝔢𝔱 𝔖𝔞𝔫𝔠𝔱𝔦𝔰. 𝔖𝔢𝔪𝔭𝔢𝔯 𝔑𝔦𝔠𝔥𝔬𝔩𝔞𝔲𝔰 𝔈𝔫 𝔍𝔩𝔩𝔦𝔰, on two hanging within earshot of each other :—
Barningham, second,
Market Weston, third.

S. Edmund, especially a Patron of East Anglia, is mentioned on
Cretingham, third,
Rishangles, tenor,
Semer, second, with an inscription,

+ 𝔐𝔢𝔯𝔦𝔱𝔦𝔰 𝔈𝔡𝔪𝔲𝔫𝔡𝔦. 𝔖𝔦𝔪𝔲𝔰 𝔄 𝔈𝔯𝔦𝔪𝔦𝔫𝔢 𝔐𝔲𝔫𝔡𝔦, which we know as used also at the Bury foundry.

There are three inscriptions to S. John Baptist,
(a) + 𝔍𝔫 𝔐𝔲𝔩𝔱𝔦𝔰 𝔄𝔫𝔫𝔦𝔰. 𝔑𝔢𝔰𝔬𝔫𝔢𝔱 𝔈𝔞𝔪𝔭𝔞𝔫𝔞 𝔍𝔬𝔥𝔞𝔫𝔫𝔦𝔰.
(May the bell of S. John resound for many years!)
(b) + 𝔐𝔲𝔫𝔢𝔯𝔢 𝔅𝔞𝔭𝔱𝔦𝔰𝔱𝔢. 𝔅𝔢𝔫𝔢𝔡𝔦𝔠𝔱𝔲𝔰 𝔖𝔦𝔱 𝔈𝔥𝔬𝔯𝔲𝔰 𝔈𝔰𝔱𝔢.
(May this ring be blessed, by the function of the Baptist!)
(c) 𝔑𝔬𝔰 𝔓𝔯𝔢𝔠𝔢 𝔅𝔞𝔭𝔱𝔦𝔰𝔱𝔢. 𝔖𝔞𝔩𝔲𝔢𝔫𝔱 𝔗𝔲𝔞 𝔙𝔲𝔩𝔫𝔢𝔯𝔞 𝔈𝔥𝔯𝔦𝔰𝔱𝔢.
(May Thy wounds, O Christ, save us, by the prayer of the Baptist !)

That the S. John mentioned in (a) is the Baptist is clear from the addition of the word 𝔅𝔞𝔭𝔱𝔦𝔰𝔱𝔢 at Buckhorn Weston, Dorset, and its insertion at Beddingham and Twineham, Sussex. The old London founder Dawe commenced his inscription with the word 𝕰𝖙𝖊𝖗𝖓𝖎𝖘. Later, men weighed the transitory state of things sublunary, and adopted the more modest 𝕴𝖓 𝕸𝖚𝖑𝖙𝖎𝖘. If we had not (c) to compare with (b), we might think that there was only a reference in (b) to the baptism of bells. There probably is such a reference. The limits of space will prevent our entering on the subject.

(a) is on
  Barnby bell,
  Marlesford, treble
  Ufford, tenor, and formerly on
  Cransford, tenor.

(b) is on Glemham, Great, third, and the tenors at
  Ilketshall, St. Margaret,
  Marlesford,
  Metfield.

(c) is only found on the Combs second.

S. Giles is the patron Saint of Blacksmiths. His churches are generally in the outskirts of the town, where the smiths would be keeping a look-out for the wants of poor way-worn jades. His only Norwich bell, however, is in the midst of Ipswich town, the third at S. Laurence's, bearing + 𝕾𝖔𝖓𝖎𝖙𝖚𝖘 𝕰𝖌𝖎𝖉𝖎𝖎. 𝕬𝖘𝖈𝖊𝖓𝖉𝖎𝖙 𝕬𝖉 𝕮𝖚𝖑𝖒𝖎𝖓𝖆 𝕮𝖊𝖑𝖎. (The sound of Giles rises to the vaults of heaven.)

Two fine sentiments remain, without reference to any saint. + 𝕹𝖔𝖇𝖎𝖘 𝕾𝖔𝖑𝖆𝖒𝖊𝖓. 𝕮𝖊𝖑𝖎 𝕯𝖊𝖙 𝕯𝖊𝖚𝖘. 𝕬𝖒𝖊𝖓. Brampton tenor. (May God give us the solace of Heaven!) and one mixed from Latin and English.

+ 𝕴𝖓 𝖂𝖊𝖑𝖙𝖍 𝕬𝖓𝖉 𝕴𝖓 𝖂𝖔. 𝕷𝖆𝖚𝖉𝖊𝖘 𝕯𝖊𝖔. Southwold sixth, formerly, as it appears, the tenor at South Elmham All Saints, and Rushmere S. Michael treble, where the second word is 𝖂𝖎𝖑𝖊𝖙.

The variety of inscriptions on the Norwich bells is thus seen to be very large. And from its company we may suppose the double dedication of the old tenor at Brandon, recorded 𝕴𝖓 𝕳𝖔𝖓𝖔𝖗𝖊 𝕾𝖆𝖓𝖈𝖙𝖎 𝕸𝖆𝖗𝖎𝖊 𝖊𝖙 𝕾𝖆𝖓𝖈𝖙𝖎 𝕶𝖆𝖙𝖊𝖗𝖎𝖓𝖊 𝖁𝖎𝖗𝖌𝖎𝖓𝖊𝖘 to have a Norwich origin. The casting of all Syntax to the winds is here remarkable.

Three bells from the mediæval Norwich foundry bear the

names of benefactors, John Ripyng at Barnby, and John Samson at Hinderclay, probably alive at the time of casting, and Richard Smith, of Hoxne, deceased. That the bells were dedicated to the saint whose Christian name the benefactor bore is disproved by the second instance. That bell-dedications do not accord with Church-dedications will be plain to any one who will study the catalogue of inscriptions at the end of the book.

"The Brasyers lived," says Mr. L'Estrange,* "at the northeast corner of S. Stephen's parish, where, says Mackerell, 'now Mr. Nuthall's Brewing office is.' The triangular plot of ground bounded by Red Lion Street on the east and Rampant Horse Lane and Little Orford Street on the other two sides, in King's Map of Norwich, dated 1766, is marked 'Foundry'; in Blomefield's plan, 1741, it is numbered 66; and at p. 605 he says, 'on the triangular Peice at Wastelgate stands a Brewhouse, where anciently stood (66) a Work House.'"

The well-known shield with the three bells and the ducal coronet gave the name to this house in S. Stephen's, which Barker in his will (1538) calls "The Three Bells." The name was retained as late as 1670.

Further notices of the Norwich foundry, with extracts from wills, &c., may be found in Mr. L'Estrange's well-known *Church Bells of Norfolk*.

Before leaving Norwich we must treat of a group which seems to gravitate towards this city. As in Geology, so in Campanology, the circumstances of early observation determine names, and the bells in question first receiving notice at Burlingham S. Andrew, Norfolk, the "Burlingham" type, for want of a better, has become the designation of a group of bells with Longobardic or capital lettering, engraved in L'Estrange's *Church Bells of Norfolk*, opposite p. 80.

There appear to be thirty-eight specimens yet remaining in Norfolk, and fifteen in Suffolk. None are found in Cambridgeshire, or further west and north; and though Essex is nearly

---

* *Church Bells of Norfolk*, pp. 30, 31. He quotes from a MS. of B. Mackerell's on S. Stephen's Parish, p. 35.

PLATE V.

LETTERING, CROSS, AND STOP OF THE BURLINGHAM TYPE.

worked out none have been found there. But in Kent there is a considerable group, traced by Mr. Stahlschmidt to a Canterbury founder, c. 1325.

Willelmus le Belyetere, of that city, however, always uses a remarkable shield (ftg. 63) which is unknown in East Anglia;

Fig. 63.

and in his inscriptions he never ventures beyond the Salutation or *ora pro nobis*, whereas nothing can be more remarkable than the variety and comparative scholarship of the inscriptions in Norfolk and Suffolk.

Not that the Salutation is absent from the East Anglian group. We have it, more or less imperfectly, on five Norfolk bells, and on the Athelington treble and Swilland bell in Suffolk, but perfectly on the third at Southelmham S. George. *Ora pro nobis* is supplanted by some equivalent in the Suffolk specimens. Passages from the Vulgate appear, Psalm cl. 6, *Omnis Spiritus Laudet Dominum* at Sprowston in Norfolk, and Psalm xxvii. 7, *Dominus Sit Adjutor Meus* on the treble at Weston, Suffolk, and on the treble at Frettenham, Norfolk, is an apparent allusion to S. John xiv. 6.

Sit Cunctis Annis Nobis Via Vita Johannis.

Knowledge of Scansion is also made manifest from the cæsural syllable on the second at Thorpe-next-Haddiscoe, Norfolk.

Ora Mente Pia Pro Nobis Virgo Maria.

The lovers of metre probably know how rare it is to find attention paid to quantity in this class of composition.

These considerations would lead us to assign a later date for the East Anglian group than for that round Canterbury. The late Mr. J. R. Daniel Tyssen assigned the middle of the fifteenth century as their probable period, which is confirmed by documentary evidence giving the dates of some Norfolk towers containing these bells, and by the style of the fine tower of Laxfield, wherein is one inscribed,

Divinum Aunxilium (sic) *Maneat Semper Nobiscum.*

But there is one shield, fig. 64, which Kent and East Anglia

Fig. 64.

alike know. Mr. Stahlschmidt is puzzled by it, but it is ascribed to "King Edmond" in Harl. MS. 6163, quoted by himself, and indeed is tolerably well-known in all places which were connected with the Abbey of Bury S. Edmund's, as for instance, in the porch of Fressingfield Church. The rarity of these bells in West Suffolk, and the absence of the shield at Little Welnetham and Rickinghall Inferior, the nearest points to Bury, do not justify us in locating the foundry at that place. Moreover, that at Newton-next-Castleacre, Norfolk, bears a well-known Norwich shield (fig. 51), as well as a cross used by Austen Bracker, which also occurs on the Sotterley second, and the Sprowston third, Norfolk. This produces a marvellous complication which I must confess myself unable to solve. The old second at

Weybread, recast by Messrs. Moore, Holmes, and Mackenzie, another of this type, and bearing the Salutation, was a mere "whited sepulchre," very fair outside, but incredibly honey-combed within. *Per contra*, Athelington and Weston are pretty little rings "maiden," and in good tune. L'Estrange[*] notes one of the recast Stuston bells, either the third or fourth, as having been of the same type. And thus we pass from the "Burlingham" group.

[*] P. 80.

CHAPTER IV.

Suffolk founders—Bury S. Edmund's—A joke on S. Barbara's name—
H. S.—The Chirches—Reginald Chirche at Bishop's Stortford—His will—
Redenhall tenor the greatest remaining work from Bury—Thomas Chirche—
Roger Reve—The Seventh at All Saints', Sudbury—Gun-founding at
Bury—Waifs—A Venlo bell at Whitton—A Mechlin bell at Bromenville—
Some account of the Mechlin foundry—Gregory Pascal of Capel—The
Tonne family—Sproughton tenor.

AT last we get to an artificer working within the limits of the county. We have already seen how that not only Suffolk men generally, but a Bury man in particular, dwelt in the Founders' Parish, S. Botolph without Aldgate, London; but it is rather late in the day when we reach St. Edmund's Bury itself.

Fig. 65.   Fig. 66.

The Mediæval Bury St. Edmund's foundry has barely a hundred bells altogether now in existence, between fifty and sixty in Suffolk, eighteen in Norfolk, twelve in Cambridgeshire, two in Northamptonshire, one in Hertfordshire, and the rest (a number not as yet strictly determinable) in Essex. The shield (fig. 64) already mentioned, though belonging to the Abbey of St. Edmundsbury, does not appear to draw the bells which bear it to the old Suffolk capital, and our earliest certainty is the well-known pair (figs. 65 and 66) about which there need be no doubt. The greatest interest which attaches to this group of bells is in the evidence of gun-founding at Bury in the shield.

The inscriptions are not remarkable for erudition, and errors appear to have been freely propagated. In the three East Anglian counties the Invocation to the Trinity is incomplete,

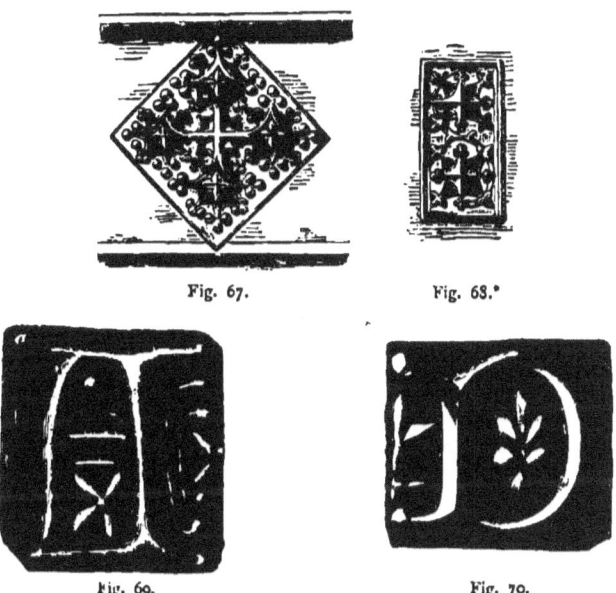

Fig. 67.   Fig. 68.*

Fig. 69.   Fig. 70.

Hemingstone third and Wickham Market fourth bearing 𝔒𝔢𝔩𝔦 𝔡𝔢𝔱 𝔐𝔲𝔫𝔲𝔰 + 𝔔𝔲𝔦 . 𝔑𝔢𝔤𝔫𝔞𝔱 . (𝔗𝔯𝔦𝔫𝔲𝔰) 𝔈𝔱 . 𝔘𝔫𝔲𝔰, just like Trumpington fourth and Garboldisham third, and more than three-fourths of all simply 𝔒𝔯𝔞 . 𝔓𝔯𝔬 . 𝔑𝔬𝔟𝔦𝔰, generally with the

* These are rather under the actual size.

Virgin's name. One lovely pentameter to gladden the heart of an old schoolmaster turns up on the Monks Eleigh fifth:—

𝔒𝔯𝔞 . 𝔏𝔞𝔲𝔯𝔢𝔫𝔱𝔦 . 𝔅𝔬𝔫𝔞 . 𝔈𝔞𝔪𝔭𝔞𝔫𝔞 . 𝔓𝔞𝔠𝔦

The initial cross (fig. 67) and stop (fig. 68) are far more elaborate than the lettering, of which specimens are given (figs. 69, 70, and 71). Another stop, not engraved, is frequently used on smaller bells. A very plain cross is not uncommon.

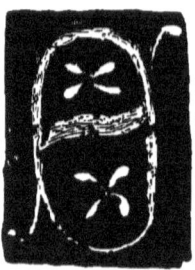

Fig. 71.

One remarkable piece of jocularity has fortunately been preserved. S. Barbara, unnoticed by the Norwichers, has a few Bury bells dedicated to her,

Barton Mills, treble,
Stanton All Saints, second,
Bealings, Little, old second, probably,
Stratford, S. Andrew, old tenor, certainly.

The last of these contained the "lytyll geste," such as it is, of the bell-founder or his counsellor. Barbara, be it known to those of my readers who have never studied Logic, is the name of one of the Figures in that Art, as well as the name of a Saint. These figures are arranged in two "premises," "major," and "minor," and a conclusion. The vowels a, e, i, o are used to show whether the statements are positive or negative, universal or special. Thus from

Aff Irmo, and
nEg O

we have a and i positive, e and o, negative, the first of each pair being universal, and the second special. So in the figure

B·Arb Ar A, both premises and the conclusion are universal and positive; and when an Act in the University was being kept, the figure was denoted by the side of the argument, thus :—
B Ar All animals can feel.
b Ar All cats are animals.
A *Ergo* all cats can feel.

Now some jocular genius has transferred Barbara on the old tenor at Stratford S. Andrew[*] from the saint to the logical syllogism,

+ Sancta . Bar . Bar . A . Ora . Pro . Nobis.

There are only two dedicated to S. Edmund,
Elmswell, third,
Risby, tenor,
which is rather surprising, and some of the inscriptions, such as

+ Virgo . Coronata . Duc . Nos . Ad . Regna . Beata.

(Lead us, crowned Virgin, to the blessed realms), on
Rendham, third,
Stonham, Little, third,
Wilby, tenor.

+ Johannes . Christi . Care . Dignare . pro . Nobis . orare, a dedication, rare in East Anglia, to S. John-the-Evangelist, on Halesworth sixth, and

+ Stella . Maria . Maris . Succurre . Piissima . Nobis

(Star of the sea, most holy Mary, succour us), on the seventh at Sudbury All Saints, are better known in Wessex than in East Anglia.

Though a large number of the East Suffolk bells from the Bury foundry cluster round the cell of the Abbey at Monk Soham, yet in that parish Norwich influence was the stronger.

It is a matter of great regret that we cannot find the name belonging to the initials, H. S., of the first founder who used the Bury shield. A good 'approximate date for his work is given by the third bell at Isleham, Cambridgeshire, which bears the arms of Bernard and Peyton, and a long intercessory prayer, addressed to the angel Gabriel, for the souls of John Bernard, who died in 1451, Thomas Peyton, who died in 1484, and their

[*] Fortunately preserved in a rubbing.

68   THE CHURCH BELLS OF SUFFOLK.

wives. The Registry of the Archdeaconry of Sudbury has been searched in vain for his will. A Henry Smyth of Bury indeed died in 1476, but his last will and testament* gives no indication whatever of metal. He left his son Galfridus (Geoffrey) ten shillings, and his daughter Constance ten sheep. There is a hiatus (valde deflendus) between the end of one book (Hawke), 1482, and the beginning of the next (Pye), 1491. Probably the missing document belongs to this period. But we must not despair. When the archives of the Bury Corporation emerge from their present chaos, the names of the fabricator of bells and guns may also come forth. I will now give as complete an alphabetical list as I can of the Bury mediævals now existing in Suffolk:—

Aldham, bell,
Barton Mills, treble,
——————— tenor,
Bealings, Little, second,
Bedfield, third,
Bradfield Combust, second,
Bradfield, S. Clare, treble,
Charsfield, tenor,
Chillesford bell,
Darsham, third,
Dennington, treble,
———— third,
Denston, treble,
———— second,
Depden, treble,
———— second,
Eleigh, Monks, fourth,
Elmswell, third,
Eyke, tenor,
Felsham, third,
Halesworth, fourth,
———— sixth,
Hemingstone, second,

* Lib. *Hawke*, 218 *verso*.

Hemingstone, tenor,
Henley, fourth,
——— tenor,
Hinderclay, third,
Hollesley, second,
Holton, S. Mary, treble,
——————— tenor,
Ipswich, S. Helen, second,
——— S. Laurence, third,
——— S. Matthew, third,
Ixworth, fourth,
Lakenheath, Clock bell,
Laxfield, third,
Offton, third,
Ottley, third,
Rendham, third,
Risby, tenor,
Shelley, third,
——— fourth,
Shottisham bell,
Stanton, All Saints, treble,
————— second,
————— third,
Stoke Ash, third,
——— fourth,
Stonham, Little, fourth,
Sudbury, All Saints, fifth,
——————— seventh,
Tuddenham, S. Mary, fourth,
Wattisham, second,
Weston Market, second,
Wickham Market, fourth,
Wilby, tenor.

All these bells seem to have been the work of H. S., Reignold Chirche, Thomas Chirche, or Roger Reve. The second died in 1498, the third late in 1527 or early in 1528, and the last was living in 1533. There are no means of classifying them, and I have already said a good deal about the dedications. As yet we have lighted on no documents in the county which relate to them; but something may be said about the operations of Reignold Chirche in Hertfordshire, of Thomas Chirche in Norfolk and Cambridgeshire, and of Roger Reve in Essex.

The reputation of the elder Chirche in 1489 induced the flourishing town of Bishop Stortford to trust them with the recasting of their five bells, and the accounts of the Churchwardens for that year record their costs and expenses "riding to Bury S. Edmund's in order to make the agreement with Reginald Chirche, 'bellfoundor,' for making the said bells within the time of the accounts this year, 4s. 8d. And paid for making the indenture and obligation concerning the aforesaid agreement, 22d."

We are gratified to find that no misadventure like that of the men of Mildenhall at Norwich seems to have befallen Bishop Stortford. "And in money paid about the carriage of the bells aforesaid from this town to the town of Bury S. Edmund's; and for costs and expenses about the re-carriage of the said bells from the town of Bury aforesaid to this town this year within the time of the account, 52s. And likewise in money paid to divers men being about the trussing of the said bells in carts at the same time and in 'trussing lyne' bought for the aforesaid carts, 3s. 4d." Business brings business. The Stortford men from employing a Bury founder go on to employ a Bury smith, who received 29s. for clappers. And, like founders of the present day, Reginald Chirche cast the brasses for the gudgeons to work in—at least seven out of the necessary ten, for which he received 19s. 8d. John Thurkill had 4s. 8d. for himself and six horses for the carriage of the bells, and the last item is for money paid for the sanctification of the bells, 17s. 4d. After this year come the instalments to Reginald Chirche, who seems to have turned out a respectable ring of five. The details may be read *verbatim* in Mr. Glasscock's *Records of S. Michael's Parish Church*, Bishop's Stortford.

The following extracts from the will of Reignold Chirche were given in my *Church Bells of Cambridgeshire*,[*] but they deserve rehearsal here:—

[* P. 35.]

"My body to be buryed in Seynt Mary chirche, in the Ele of Seynt Pet', vnder the marble ston thar be me leid. To the parysshe preest of the same chirche to p'y for my soule, and to reherse my name in the bede rolle eu'y Sunday be an hooll yeer vjs. viijd. Myn executors shall visite all the psones that lye sike and bedred, gevy'g eu'y pson iiijd., or more, as they thynke nede. My executors to kepe a sangrede and an erth tyde yeerly for my soule, etc., in the chirche of our lady. To the new worke wtin the Monast'y of Seynt Edm'nd, x m'rc. To the gilde of the holy name of Jhu', xs. To the gilde of Corpus, xpi. xijd. To the gilde of Seynt Petyr, xijd. To the gilde of the Purificac'on of our lady callyd Candelmesse gilde, xxs. To the gilde of Seynt Margerete, iijs. iiijd. To the gilde of the Decollac'on of Seynt John Baptist, xxd., and a cuppe of silu' called a peace.* My iij small ten'ntries set in Reyngate strete shall remayn to almesis housis for eu'. Itm. I will Avery Foppys have hir dwellyng in one of the same almesse housis duryng hir lyve. It'm. I will the seid Avery Foppe haue of my goods quarterly, xxd. as longe as she levyth, after the discresson of myn executo's. It'm. I will that Alis Power haue hir dwellyng in the hous that I bought of hir duryng hir lyffe, and aft' hir discease I will the seid hous shalbe leten eu' aft' to thentent that the seid almesse housis may be repared and susteyned vp wt the fferme of the same hous for eu'. I will that Thomas Chirche my sone do make clene the grete lectorn that I gave to Seynt Mary chirche quart'ly as longe as he levyth."

The greatest work now in existence which came from the Bury foundry is just outside the boundaries of our county, the tenor at Redenhall. A few words must be said about this magnificent bell. It must be Thomas Chirche's, bearing as it does the Bury marks, and dating from 1514 or thereabouts, when Thomas Bayly of Harleston willed 6s. 8d. "to the church of Rednall to the yotyng of the gret belle." It has been terribly mangled from chipping, at one time sharpened and at another flattened, so that from the former process its diameter has probably lost three-quarters of an inch. Its weight is about 24 cwt., and none that have heard it will fail to acknowledge the grandeur of its tone. The following dimensions are on the authority of my old friend, Captain A. P. Moore, of Weybread:—

* The readers of Shakespeare's Henry V. will remember the *pax* which Bardolph stole. A deal of needless ingenuity seems to have been spent on this passage. This was a "loving-cup" for the gilde.

Diameter . . 50·5 inches.
Height to crown . . 37·5 „
„ to top of cannons . 56 „
„ inside . . 37 „

We have notices of Thomas Chirche's operations at King's College, Cambridge, in 1500, when he supplied the College kitchen with sundry pots and ladles, and recast the second bell of their five, also at S. Mary-the-Great, Cambridge, in 1514. His will, dated July 12th, 1527, contains the following extracts, especially interesting to Bury people:—

> "My body to be buried in Seynt Mary chirche in the Ele of Seynt Petyr', vnd' the ston ther be me layd. A priest to synge for my soule at the Awter of Seynt Thom's, etc., for 5 years. To the seid chirche of o'r lady oon food' of led. To eu'y of the iiij priests that shall bere my body to chirche, xijd. To Margaret my wyfe, my ten't joynyng to the capitall ten't late my ffadres in the Southgate strete, su'tyme called Cobbold's. To Seynt Nicholas Gylde holdyn in the College w'thyn the seid Town of Bury a litil stondyng maser."*

Of Roger Reve we have but little to say. He recast the "meane belle" (the second of three, apparently) for the parish church of Debden, in Essex, in 1533, and gave the usual year-and-day bond to William West, gentleman, William Byrde and Richard Hamond, "yomen," of that parish. The amount was £40, which may suggest that the amount forfeited by Richard Brasyer in the matter of the Mildenhall tenor must have been at least £60, if anything like proportion was observed on account of the size of the bell. Reve did not guarantee his success at the first attempt. The Debden people were to carry the bell backwards and forwards as often as need should require, and to take it up into the steeple and set it down again "redy to the carte." This bond throws light on the weighing business, about which Serjeants Genney and Pigot argued before the judges of the Common Pleas *in banco*. Should the new bell weigh more than the old, the parish is to pay to the founder at the rate of 30s. the hundred of five score and twelve to the

* *Church Bells of Cambridgeshire*, pp. 36, 37.

hundred, but if the contrary, the founder was to pay the parish at the rate of 15*s.* the hundred.

Roger Reve is styled "clothear," at which by this time we need feel no surprise. Mr. L'Estrange* suggested that the transcriber had misread a contraction of some such word as "clochearius," but the word is unknown, and no explanation at all seems necessary. The bond is given in full in my *Church Bells of Cambridgeshire*† and in the *East Anglian.*‡

The largest bell in the county from the Bury foundry is the seventh at All Saints', Sudbury, inscribed :—+ 𝔖tella . 𝔐aria . 𝔐aris . 𝔖uccurre . 𝔓lissima . 𝔑obis. It is a fine bell, with a diameter of 48 inches, and weighing a ton, more or less. The fifth in the same tower is also from Bury, but the sixth, between them, is a London bell, tolerably co-eval. This is rather puzzling. Perhaps the London bell hung there by itself for a time, and then was joined by its two Suffolk companions, the effort for adding a big tenor not coming till 1576.

I regret much that as in the case of Dawe, no old bronze guns have been discovered with the Bury mark. The Woolwich collection is certainly destitute of them. No doubt they served their purpose, and then went to the melting pot. It can hardly be thought incredible that the guns which riddled the galleys and galleons of the Spanish Armada, did not number amongst them some old campaigners which first saw the light of day at Bury S. Edmund's, under the approving eye of H. S., one of the Chirches, or Roger Reve.

In the church of S. Mary, Bury S. Edmund's, there used to be a double brass, to a citizen and his wife, with bells; the figures had long been removed, but the incident remained. By this time the stone has possibly disappeared, in the course of "restoration." It is pretty sure to have commemorated one of the artificers of whom we have been treating.

And now having dealt with the masses we must look up the mediæval waifs and strays within our borders, some of which

* *Church Bells of Norfolk*, p. 63.
† P. 37. ‡ II., 25.

will turn out to be of peculiar importance. A Longobardic three first present themselves:—
Ellough, treble,
South Elmham, S. James, third,
Frostenden, treble.

The first bears the Salutation, the second records the name of the donor:—

+ JOHANNES : BROVN : ME : BECIT : BIERI, and the last is inscribed,

+ CAMPANA OMNIVM SANCTORVM, the dedication of the bell in this instance according with that of the church, not an every-day occurrence. Of the same make was the old second at Gorleston, appropriately dedicated to S. Nicholas, the patron Saint of fishermen, and with these words on the shoulder:—

+ I AM : MAD : IN : YE WORCHEPE : OF YE : CROS.

These seem to have been the work of some itinerant founder, roaming through East Norfolk and North-east Suffolk. There are seven in Norfolk, at Caister-by-Norwich, Gillingham, Lessingham, Mundham, Rockland All Saints, and Wramplingham. As we know nothing further about them we must leave them. The Whitton bell, inscribed abe . maria . gracia . āno . m . cccc . xli, is a thing quite by itself. Dates at that time of day are exceptional, in England, and the trefoil (fig. 72) which separates the words and lettering, as well as the general aspect of the bell, are Continental, possibly Low Country, possibly French.

Fig. 72.

PLATE VI.

THE FLIGHT INTO EGYPT, THE ANNUNCIATION, AND A PIECE OF BORDER FROM
A MECHLIN BELL AT BROMESWELL.

I incline to the former theory, and from the identity of the lettering with that on a bell at Baschurch, Salop, I feel disposed to ascribe it to Jan Van Venloe. The Baschurch bell is inscribed + maria . int . iner . ons . ḣeeren . m . cccc . ende . ɼlbii (In the year of our Lord 1400 and 47), with the name jan . ban . benloe. The marks at Baschurch and Whitton certainly differ, the former bearing an initial cross, with the Lion of S. Mark and the Eagle of S. John, and only a single stop between the words. But the lettering, the nearness of date, and the fact that the only other recorded bell of Jan Van Venloe's (now, alas! recast) at Vowchurch, Hertfordshire, bore the Salutation, turn the scale with me, in the absence of other evidence. The Baschurch bell is said to have been brought from Valle Crucis Abbey, but such stories are not reliable. Venlo has been the seat of important manufactures in metal for many centuries.

An enthusiastic Welshman, misreading the Baschurch inscription, and thinking it to be in his mother tongue, rendered it into English :—

"When cut off from life we become dead earth, the soul departs, and proceeds through the air to Eternal Glory."*

The county is most happy in possessing one indubitable foreigner of a high type of beauty, the smaller of the two bells hanging in Bromeswell tower. I mounted this dangerous place on January 13th, 1870, and certainly doubted my getting down again alive. However, I thankfully record the preservation of my life, and proceed to the inscription, in Flemish,

Jhesus ben ic ghegoten van Cornelis Waghevens int iaer ons Heeren MCCCCCXXX. (Jesus am I, cast by Cornelis Waghevens in the year of our Lord, 1530), with four medallions on the waist, of which facsimiles are given opposite, and a bold and deep arabesque border. There was formerly a bell smaller than this in the tower, but it fell down, was broken and sold. The note of this bell is C sharp, and of its companion B natural, so that the lost bell, if in tune, was in D sharp.

The larger bell belongs to a Longobardic group, and is a

* See Morris's MS. collection in the Shrewsbury Museum.

century or two older. Flemish bells are so rare, and the later specimens have received such high praise at the mouth of Mr. Haweis, that it is not out of place to say that this one is more remarkable for ornamentation than for tone.

The family of Waghevens is well known in the annals of the city of Mechlin, and through the kindness of the Reverend William van Caster, one of the Canons of the Cathedral, I am able to give a list of the founders bearing that name :—

Henry, who died shortly before 1483. He was twice married, and had issue by the first marriage a son Henry. His second wife (Margaret van Belle) bore him two sons, *Peter* and *George*, who carried on the paternal trade from 1483 to 1530, or thereabouts.

Simon is supposed to have been a younger brother. His range is from 1491 to 1516. From *Medard* (1524—1557), who is partly conterminous with our *Cornelis*, came a bell at Herendal, not far from Mechlin, which bears a legend comparable to some of the less elegant in Suffolk :—

+ Maria es meinen name
Mijn gheluit sij Gode bequame,
Also verre me mij horen sal
Wilt God beware overal.

Medardus Waghevens goet mi te Mechelen in stede als nien screfe.

MCCCCCXXXIII. wede.

i.e. Mary is my name,
May my sound be agreeable to God!
Also whoever shall hear me
May God preserve everywhere!

1530, the Bromeswell date, is the earliest for *Cornelis* known to Canon van Caster.

Jacop's earliest and latest dates are 1542 and 1554.

John, c. 1542, was possibly a cousin.

From Jacop Waghevens we have the tongueless bell in Glasgow Cathedral called the S. Catherine bell, on which the hours are struck, weighing about five cwt. It bears on one side

PLATE VII.

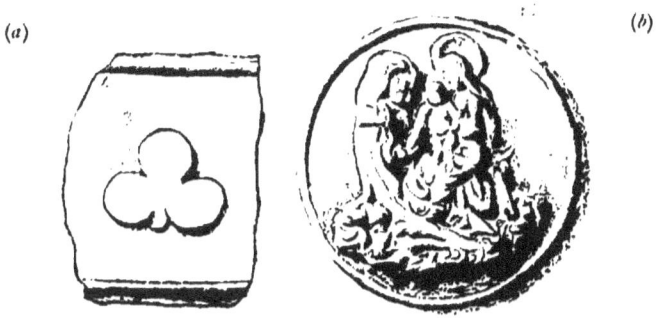

(a) TREFOIL FROM WHITTON.

(b) THE PRESENTATION IN THE TEMPLE, FROM A MECHLIN BELL AT BROMESWELL.

BORDER AND MEDALLION OF S. MICHAEL AND THE DRAGON, FROM A

the figure of S. Catherine, and on the other the arms of Mechlin, and is inscribed, Katherina ben ic, ghegoten van Jacop Vohaghevens int iaer ons Heeren, 1554, which the reader will by this time be able to translate for himself. A bell discovered by my friend, Mr. Justice Clarence of Colombo, Ceylon, in a bell-cot at Nicholaston, Glamorganshire, seems to have come from the hands of Peter or George Waghevens, or both. There is no dedication, but it is simply inscribed :—Ic ben ghegoten int iaer ons Heeren MCCCCCXVIII. Its tone is excellent, and it bears two medallions. Peter Waghevens (or Waghevents) cast an octave of bells for Louvain in 1525. There seems to have been a later Jacop or Jacques, c. 1590.

In 1861, Mr. A. D. Tyssen examined, with his father, the bells in Mechlin Cathedral. He found three inscribed thus :—

(1) MICHAEL VOCOR ET FACTA SUM PER GEORGIV̄ WAGHEVENS ANNO DŌI. MCCCCCXV,

(2) meester spmon waghuens ghaf mpn accoort meccerebiii sereefnen boort

(3) Henricus wagheuen me fecit anno domini m cccc lxxx.

These words are only portions of the inscriptions, and the bells are profusely ornamented.

Mr. Tyssen thinks that another Mechlin bell is lurking about somewhere in Middlesex.

Two bells present inscriptions in great confusion, with the same lettering or letterings :—

Capel, S. Mary, tenor,

Levington, second.

On the former some letters are upside down, and some face the wrong way, while others are afflicted with both these maladies, and there are three distinct types, unknown to me or to anyone to whom I have shown them. The general character of the lettering is early, but when at last deciphered the inscription brings the date down to the later days of Henry VIII.

OF YOUR CHERITE PRAY FOR THE WELFARE OF GREGORY PASCAL.

Whoever the man may have been who bore this highly ecclesiastical name, the rector of Capel, the Rev. A. Cecil Johnson, found his name early in the register :—

"Sepultura 32 Henrici Octavi. Sepultura Gregorii Pascall quarto die Februarii. A° p'dicto."

The Levington bell has its inscription (to the Virgin) backwards, but adds no further element of enigma. These I should attribute to some local hand.

We now come to the connecting link between the ante-Reformation and post-Reformation bells, the members of the Tonne family. And here I must cast a doubt on much written by me in the *Church Bells of Cambridgeshire* about two bells at Wood Ditton. I read 1588 as their date, but it is more likely to be 1544. There appear to have been two members of the house of Tonne, probably brothers, often using the same mark, casting

Fig. 73.

bells about the same time. John is the man whose name more frequently occurs on the whole, but we have three of Stephen's in East Anglia, the Wood Ditton bells just mentioned, and the fifth at Stanstead of the same date, which bears the large French cross (fig. 73), known elsewhere as John Tonne's, together with three other marks recognizable as used by him (figs. 74, 75, 76).

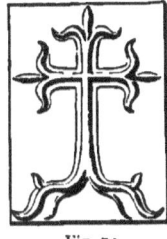  

Fig. 74.   Fig. 75.   Fig. 76.

I am not aware that any bell of John Tonne's is dated so late as 1544. Most are undated, but in Sussex, where they are chiefly found, we find 1522 at Sullington, and 1536 at Botolph's, and at Stanstead Mountfitchet, Essex, I read 1540, though I may be wrong, for the figures are very peculiar.

On the whole I think that Stephen was the son of John, and identical with the Stephen Tonni, whose works we shall consider in the Elizabethan period. Mr. Amherst Tyssen, who knows more about French bells than anybody, past or present, considers these specimens as decidedly French, and that the name *Tonne*, or *Tonni*, is a corruption of *Antoine*, like our own Tony.[*] I have already suggested that this John Tonne may be identical with the John Tynny named in Culverden's will. He has left us one little bell in Suffolk, the Clock-bell at Stoke-by-Clare, inscribed, + surge : mane : sarbire : deo. (Rise in the morning to serve God), with a cross (fig. 77) and stop, well known as his. It is a rare and good inscription, occurring only once besides, on the third at Down, Kent, dated 1511. Here, however, neither

[*] The surname, however, is known in Suffolk in the previous century. We have Johēs Tony instituted rector of Icklingham in 1453-4.

marks nor lettering are John Tonne's, and I adopt the theory of the Kentish historian, that the bell came from some one from whom our man learned his business. The ornamentation at Down is of a foreign character. We must remember this inscription, for an expansion of it will come from Stephen Tonni in the time of Queen Elizabeth.

Fig. 77.

I should be inclined to class Sproughton tenor among the mediævals. It has four coins, apparently the reverse of a shilling, and some letters which may stand for I. H. I found the third and the "ting-tang" at Great Amwell, Hertfordshire, to be of the same character, but so far as I know the universe contains no more of them. Thus my mediævals have gone all over the county. They began in the north-west, and they end in the south-east.

CHAPTER V.

Sance and Sacring bells—Funeral uses—Angelus bell—Curfew—Chime-barrels—Jack o' th' Clock.

THIS discussion of the bells themselves does not release us from the middle ages. The reader must now be carried in imagination to the usages of those distant days. We must devote a little time to *Sance* and *Sacring Bells, Burial uses*, the *Angelus Bell*, the *Curfew*, the use of *Chime-barrels* in *Trentals*, and *Jack o' th' Clock*.

First then, of the Sance bell, for which my readers have often noticed a bell-cot standing on the gable of a church nave.

By the Constitution of Archbishop Winchelsey all that is required of parishes, in the way of bells, is a Handbell to be carried before the Host at the Visitation of the Sick, and Bells with ropes, which latter seem to have been for the tower alone. About 1367 came the Constitutions of Archbishop Sudbury, wherein we find the first-mentioned, together with "Handbells and Bells in Belfry, with cords to the same."

By degrees the hand-bells were partly supplanted by bells hung in the rood-screen, of which instances remain (fig. 78) at Hawstead, and in Norfolk at Wiggenhall S. German's and Scarning, though for several purposes, of which we shall speak presently, the hand-bells were still required. The bell so hung appears to be that which is meant by a Sance, Sancts or Sanctus bell, for we never find this word in the plural number. The main use of it was to arrest attention at important parts of the service, and especially at the Celebration of the Eucharist, where it was rung at the *Ter Sanctus*, just before the Canon of the Mass.

It appears to have occurred to some mind that this use might

L

be extended for the benefit of those unable to come to church ; and thus in the Perpendicular period of architecture arose the practice of erecting a Sance-bell cot on the nave-gable. That belonging to my own church at Fressingfield is (fig. 79) as good

Fig. 78.

an example as I can find, the spout for the rope still remaining in the chancel-arch, and a groove for guiding the rope till it would reach the hand of one standing on the floor being still marked in the easternmost of the south arches of the nave. The will of John Colmar of Fressingfield, dated 1495, bequeathing one such bell, weighing 100 lbs., gives an approximate date for all this work, as it would have been impossible to have inserted the spout into the chancel-arch after it was built.

At Mildenhall, where there is an unusually fine Early English chancel-arch, there was never a sance-bell cot, but a turret on the north side of the arch was erected in the Perpendicular period for the purpose, and the mark of the rope is still plain below.

Fig. 79.

In some cases the Sanctus bell may have been hung in the tower, with the other bells.* The lawfulness or unlawfulness of such things is just the kind of question to rend a nation asunder, upset a throne, cause a frightful effusion of rage and finally of blood, and generally to do the devil's work in the world. There was certainly a time when they were not, so that it is a marvel why anyone should have been seriously injured for the want of them. And, on the other hand, they could have by no possibility propagated error, and their only function was that performed daily in every elementary school in the kingdom by the teacher's little dish-bell, the calling for silence and attention. A bell thus used at the Mass would be called a

* See *Church Bells of Cambridgeshire*, p. 53.

Sacring bell, whether sounded by hand or by rope; but the name of Sanctus bell appears to be restricted to the latter kind. The smaller hand-bells are called Rogation Bells in some of the Essex Inventories, and were doubtless used in the parochial perambulations on the Rogation Days.*

The use of the Handbell prescribed in the Winchelsey Constitutions was not the only one. When a funeral took place, a handbell was rung as the procession went from the abode of the deceased to the church. And this, which was observed at Oxford at the death of Dr. Radcliff,† Principal of Brasenose, in 1645, and is an everyday occurrence on the Continent, is a practice of immemorial antiquity.

Under the Levitical Law contact with a corpse produced ceremonial defilement.‡ The Roman Law was in some points more stringent still. The Flamen Dialis was not allowed to hear the sound of funeral pipes, and even the statues of gods by the roadside had their faces covered with a cloth before a funeral passed by.‖ We have it on good authority that bell-men in black preceded Roman funerals,§ to prevent persons in authority thus being contaminated, and the same plan was pursued in case of those who were being led forth to crucifixion or public scourging. Hence appears to have sprung the custom of ringing a handbell before a funeral; and no doubt one of those which we find in the parish inventories of the reign of Edward VI., was used for the purpose.

The other burial customs which we find prevalent seem to be of later origin, the Soul bell, and bells during Thirty-days and other commemorations, and at Earth-tides. The first requires no treatment from me, having received such abundant illustration in the histories of Bells of other countries.

The best instance for the latter in our county will be from the

---

* *Transactions of the Essex Archæological Society*, vol. ii., part iii., New Series, pp. 223, etc.
† N. and Q., III., 297.
‡ Lev. xxii. 4. Numb. xix. 11.
‖ Festus on Aulus Gellius, *Noctes Atticæ*, x. 15.
§ Suidas and Gul. Budæus, quoted by Hieronymus Magius, c. x.

will of John Baret of Bury S. Edmund's, who died in 1463, and is buried in S. Mary's Church in that town. I make no apology for inserting his epitaph, which has a noble ring in its sound, and serves to bring the man before us. The will may be read in full in Mr. Tymms's well-known *Wills and Inventories* from the Registers of the Commissary of Bury St. Edmund's and the Archdeaconry of Sudbury.*

	" He that will sadly behold me with his ie	
John	Maye see his own Merowr and lerne to die.	Baret
	Wrappid in a schete, as a full rewli wretche,	
	No mor of al my minde to me ward will streche,	
	From erthe I kam and on to earth I am brought,	
	This is my natur: for of erthe I was wrought,	
	Thus erthe on to erthe tendeth to knet,	
	So endeth ech creature : doeth John Baret.	

"Wherefore ye pepil in waye of charitie,
With your goode prayeres I pray ye help me.
For such as I am : right so shalle ye al bi
Now God on my sowle : have merci and pitie.
"Amen."

His directions are most ample. The two bellmen that went about the town at his death were to have gowns, and to be two of the five torch-holders, for which they were to have twopence and their meat, the Sexton receiving twelve pence and his bread, drink, and meat. At the "yeerday," the bellmen were to receive fourpence each for going about the town to call on the inhabitants to pray "for my soule and for my faderis and modrys."

The "Thirty day" (which may spring from the thirty days' mourning for Moses and Aaron,)† is well-known for its Trental of Masses, always of course thirty in number, but varying in detail from time to time. Our concern with them is limited to

---

* Pp. 17, &c.
† Deut. xxxiv 8. Numb. xx. 29.,

the use of bells. We find bellmen employed on the "Thirty day," which seems equivalent to another well-known expression, the "Month's Mind." All the good people of Bury, however, were not of the same opinion as John Baret. John Coote, for instance, "will neyther ryngyn nor belman goynge," but his almsgivings and dinners on his Thirty-day to be "don in secret manner."

Joan Mason, widow, of Bury, in 1510, directed the "bellemen to go abowte the paryssh," at her anniversary and earth-tide to "pray and reherse the sowles" of all the persons she recited.

Another remarkable custom was the sounding by means of a Chime-barrel the *Requiem Eternam*, which, as may be seen, ranged only over five notes. John Baret, of whom we have spoken, makes special arrangement for this music during his Thirty-day.

"Itm I wil that the Sexteyn of Seynt Marie chirche hawe at my yeenday xijd. so he rynge wil and fynde breed and ale to his ffelashippe, and eche yeer what tyme my yeerday fallyth that at twelve of the clokke at noon next be forn my dirige he do the chymes smythe Requiem eternam and so to contynue seven nyght aftir tyl the Vtas* of my yeerday be passyd and at eue' lenton Requiem eternam and in lykvyse such day as God disposith for me to passe I wil the seid chymes smyth forthwith Requiem eternam and so day and nyth to cotynwe with the same song tyl my xxx^u day be past for me and for my freends that holpe therto with any goods of here. Itm I wil geve and beqwethe yeerly to the Sexteyn of Seynt Marie chirche viijs. to kepe the clokke, take hede to the chymes, wynde vp the pegs and the plummys as ofte as nede is, so that the seid chymes fayle not to goo through the defawte of the seid sexteyn who so be for the tyme, and yif he wil not take it vpon hym the owner of my hefd place, the parish preest, and the Seynt Marie preest to chese oon of the parysh such as wyl do it for the same money, tyl such a sexteyn be in the office that wil undyrtake to do it and to contynwe, for I wolde the sexteyn hadde it be fore

---

* Octaves.

PLATE VIII.

Office or Introit, "REQUIEM ÆTERNAM" (Sarum Version).

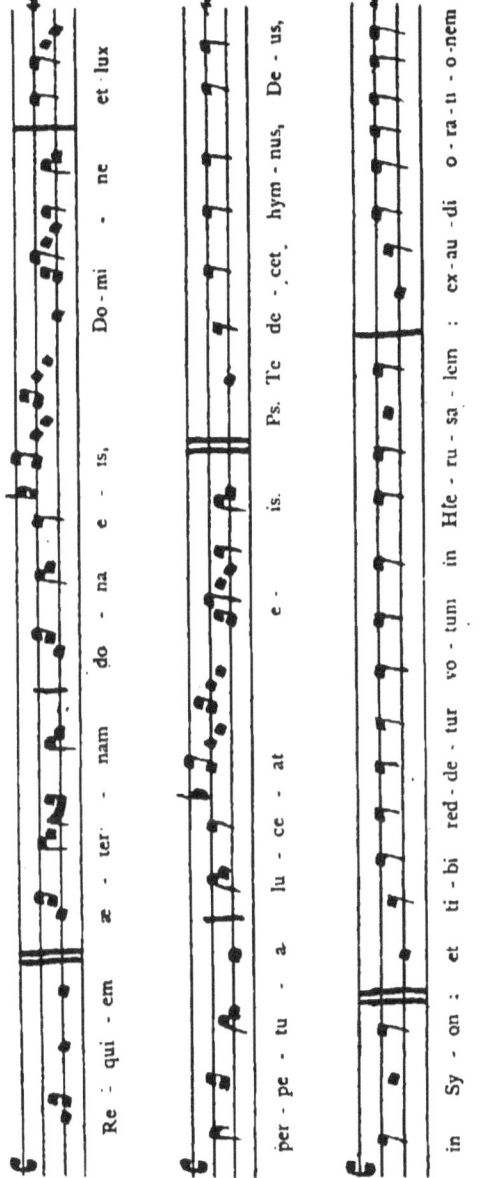

anothir, for his wagys be but smale, so he wil vndirtake to do it and not fayle." And having made provision for the repair of the chimes, he wills "the seid chymes to goo also at the avees, at the complyñ eche Satirday, Sunday and hooly day thowrghout the yeer."

These chime-barrels seem to have been no novelty in the middle of the fifteenth century.

The *Angelus* or *Gabriel* bell appears to have varied in use from time to time. Polydore Vergil, writing from Urbino in 1499, attributes its origin to Pope John XXII. (1316—34), who ordained that thrice every day at evening time bells should be rung, and that then each should thrice recite the Angelic Salutation to the Holy Virgin. He adds that the institution became so permanent that it was in use in every nation to his day, so that as soon as the sound of the bell was heard all forthwith bent the knee and prayed. Another name for it was the *Ave* bell, from the first word of the Salutation. In 1399 Archbishop Arundel issued a mandate that at early dawn one *Pater* and five *Aves* should be said. Thus arose the morning *Angelus*, distinguished in Italy at the present day as *Ave Maria dell' Aurora* from the older *Ave Maria della Sera*.

The well-known Jewish practice of the noon-tide prayer induced a *Meridian Angelus* on the Continent, but it does not seem to have come into England, though in some parts a midday bell is rung. At first any bell would be used, but the prevalence of the Salutation and of the name of Gabriel on some bells seems to indicate that the bell so inscribed was used for the special purpose. But that which we have treated of as the Sance bell, may have been also used. " A gabryell, weighing 100 lbs." is mentioned, as at Blickling, Norfolk, in the returns of 1553, and there would hardly have been two bells of this size in a church. Donors of such bells were desirous of having themselves remembered in prayer. Thus John Alcock, Bishop of Ely,[*] in 1490, consecrated one large bell at Gamlingay, in Cambridgeshire, and granted forty days' indul-

---

[*] Founder of Jesus College, Cambridge.

gence to all truly penitent, who at the sound of the great bell shall say five *Paternosters* and five *Salut. Angel.* for the good state of the Catholic Church, for the Bishop consecrating, the King, the Queen, and all the souls of the faithful departed this life ; and to all who, at the sound of the little bell, shall say five *Salut. Angel. ad claus. adjunct.* "God have mercy of John, Bishop of Ely, that hallowede the alters and bells aforesaid, either seting, standing, lyeing, or kneeling."*

Though the Curfew bell, of which there are traces before the Norman Conquest, ceased to have legal sanction in the reign of Henry I., there are abundant traces of it all along the years to the present time. It served some useful purpose, and so it survived. At Bury it saved the life of John Perfay, draper, who was not forgetful of the incident, as appears in his will, dated 1509. " I wole that my close which ys holdyn by copy off my lord abbot of Bury Seynt Edmund, and ye which I purchasyd of Thom^{a}s Russell gentylmā, my lord payde the residue, I gyve toward ye ryngers charge off the gret belle in Seynt Mary Churche, callyd corfew belle."

The original of this bequest is thus related by Mr. Gage Rokewode†:—" John Perfey, tenant of the manor of Fornham All Saints, is said to have lost his way in returning from the court to Bury, and to have recovered himself from a perilous situation by accident, by hearing the striking of the *clock* or *bell* at S. Mary's, Bury. This circumstance, if we are to believe a tale not uncommon, led to his devising certain pieces of land, which took the name of Bell Meadow, parcel of the manor of Fornham All Saints, to the churchwardens of S. Mary's, in order that the bell might be tolled in summer regularly at four o'clock in the morning and nine in the evening ; and in winter at six in the morning and eight at night."

Mr. Gage Rokewode is very likely right in thinking that one purpose of this endowment was to excite the people to repeat the *Angelus.*

Two instances known to me remain of the "Jack o' th'

---

* *Gent. Mag.*, vol. lxxiii., p. 174.
† *History of Hengrave*, p. 11.

Clock," at Southwold (fig. 80), and at Blythburgh. I conjecture that they date back to the earlier part of the sixteenth century. There are many others, of a later period, up and down the country.

Fig. 80.

By Shakespeare's time they were "household words," put by him into the mouth of Richard II., who says,

"My time
Runs posting on in Bolingbroke's proud joy,
While I stand fooling here, his Jack o' th' Clock."*

In Lacroix's *Les Arts du Moyen Age*† (Paris, 1869), is an account of the celebrated clock brought by one of the Dukes of Burgundy, from Courtray to Dijon, which has two figures, a man and a woman, who strike the hours from one to twenty-four. The name Jacquemart has been usually given to these figures, and a question has arisen as to the origin of the name, which has probably given rise to "Jack o' th' Clock." One derivation was *jacco marchiardus*, a Low-latin word for a coat of mail (*jacque de mailles*). But a more probable derivation is from a clock-maker, *Jacques Marck*, or *Jacquemart*. There was such a man at Lille in 1422, who seems to have been a grandson of one of the same name, living at Courtray in 1360.

* Shakespeare's *Richard II.*, Act v., Sc. 5. See also *Coriolanus*, Act. v., Sc. 2.
† Pp. 179, 180.

CHAPTER VI.

The Reformation—Number of Church bells then in Suffolk—Spoliation—Restoration—Stephen Tonni of Bury, and his man William Land—Their work at Long Melford—Death of Julian Tonney the weaver—Bury foundry goes to Thetford—Founders dining at Wattisfield—Thomas Draper, Mayor of Thetford—The Brends of Norwich—Dier's bell at Clare—Topsel's at Cratfield—Richard Bowler—The Thorington bell and a reminiscence of Kett's rebellion—Aldgate gun-founding again.

My last chapter will prepare the reader to expect some account of the fate of our Church bells during the Reformation. Under the court of Augmentation, established in 1536, in view of the Dissolution, Commissioners were appointed for the reception of the goods and chattels of the smaller priories. Inventories were taken, and those for S. Olave's, Flixton, Ipswich (Priory of the Holy Trinity), Redlingfield, Blythburgh, Letheringham, Leyston, Eye, Ixworth, and Campsey remain in the Record Office.* No bells occur in any of these. There must have been similar inventories for the larger houses afterwards, but I know nothing about them.

Early in the reign of Edward VI. enquiries were set on foot with respect to plate, jewels, bells, and other ornaments belonging to the parish churches, which in some parts of the country, especially in Kent, had been embezzled by the churchwardens and others. By whom certificates were demanded from the Suffolk churchwardens does not appear. The volume containing them is 510 of the "Miscellaneous Books" of the Augmentation office, containing 179 certificates from Essex and Suffolk.

* Bundle 1393, File 136, No. 1. The date of the earliest, S. Olave's, is 20 Aug., 1536, and the Commissioners were Sir Humphrey Wingfield, Richard Southwell, and Thomas Mildmay. William Dale was the Prior.

The Suffolk certificates are dated early in November, 1547, whereas the letter of the Privy Council to Cranmer, charging him to prohibit alienation, bears date the last day of April, 1548.*

The labours of Mr. J. J. Muskett, by which that most useful publication, the *East Anglian*, has been enriched with these records, have been used by me ; and I desire here to return my best thanks to him, and to another valued friend, the editor, the Rev. C. H. Evelyn White, whom the county would gladly welcome again.

Plate went wholesale, and that these prohibitions were needed as to bells, is clear from the sales which had taken place at Belstead, Chelmondiston, and Lound, while the men of Aldringham made return that "all ornamēts, playt, and belles belongyng to owʳ cherche ar fore to sell." Robert Thurston and Edmund ffcavyear, churchwardens of Rendham, strong in their honesty, fear neither Commissioners nor any one else, and stoutly reply, " For yᵉ ornaments and yᵉ Bells we haue solde non as we wull answere." "j peyer of hand bells" was sold at Darsham for ijs. iiijd. In the great majority of instances nothing is said about the bells. So far as one can judge from these relics of the certificates of 1547, and the state of things in 1553, there had been no general robbery of bells. In one parish, Ilketshall S. Andrew, the money from the chalices went to the bells.

On March 3rd, 1553, another Commission was issued, the Commissioners being Thomas Lord Darcye of Cheche, Thomas Lord Wentworth, John Jernegan, William Waldegrave, and Thomas Cornwaleys, Knights, Owen Hopton and Christopher Goldyngham. They did not ask for returns, but summoned the churchwardens of each parish before them. The original summons remains in Bedingfield Church chest, and runs thus :—

"These shal be by vertue of a precepte dyrected unto me and others ffrom the Ryght Wurshyfull Thomas lord Wentworthe Wyllyam Walgrave John Jernynghm̄ and Thomas Cornwaleys Knyghtes Owen hopton and cʳofer Goldynghm̄ Esquyers the Kynge Maties Comyssyoners To Wyll you and

* Strype's *Cranmer* (E. H. S.), II., 90.

neverthelesse in the Kynge Maties name straightely to charge and comaunde you That ye fayle not psonallye to appere before the Kynge ma^ties sayde Comyssyoners at Ypswych the secounde daye of maye next ensuenge before ix of the clocke. . And that ye brynge before them (All excuses sett ap'te) All and everye suche p'cell of plate Jewells metall or other ornamente (whatsoever they be) belongynge to y^or churche chapell Guylde Brotherheede ffraternytyes or cōpanyes as doe Remayne in y^r custodye or of eny other psonne or psonnes to y^r knowledge to the uses aforesayd as yow wyll answere upon othe The grete Belles and Saunce Belles in the Steples only excepte. ffrom Brundysshe in Suff the xxvijthe of Aprylle A° 1553

By me Roger Wade"

Endorsed

"To the Churchwardens of the townshyppe of Bedyngfelde
Geve these."*

The Commissioners' book is in a perfect condition. The entries show nothing but chalices and bells, one of the former generally remaining to each parish. There were 1,669 great bells, and 85 "Sancts" bells in the county, without Ipswich, which formed the subject of a separate report, and Thetford S. Mary's, which no doubt appeared in Norfolk. The Ipswich Inventories, which are very full, show a total of 52 large bells and 6 Sanctus.† The grand total for the county was therefore 1,812. At the present day, excluding the six at Thetford S. Mary's, and the metal of the recently melted four at Ilketshall S. Andrew's, there are 1,864 Church bells in Suffolk; and in weight of metal we have, of course, a great advantage. In the towns and larger villages there has been a gain which more than counterbalances the loss in cutting down the pretty little threes in the smaller villages.

But the Commissioners' 1,812 is rather under the mark for such a date as 1520, I should say, for though we can point to an increase in some places, there had been a decrease from depredation in others, and in one instance for certain the Commissioners did not receive a full report.

A very suggestive case of depredation is that in the parish of

* *East Anglian*, New Series, II., 345. Communicated by the Rev. J. W. Millard, Shimpling Rectory, Scole.

† The Commissioners' total is 51, but the figures give a total of 52.

Woolverstone. In the thirty-eight year of Henry VIII., Philip Wolferston, Esq., of that place, sold two bells and two vestments belonging to the parish church. When the Commissioners of 1553 were making their enquiries, this transaction came to light, and the loss to the parish was reported to be £20. Wolferston took the course of bringing in a certificate stating that the bells were not worth £5, that the vestments were of small value, and that he had taken them "supposing the sayd churche to be hys owne chapell."*

His name appears foremost in the catalogue of those who who were bound by their recognizances to appear and answer their several debts.

"philipp Wolverston, Gentilman, xx*li*.
Robt Wynkfeld of Branthm̄, Gentilman, xxx*li*.
ffrauncis Sone of Wantisden, gentilman,
                            iiij*li*. xiij*s*. iiij*d*.

[the xxith of June, ffrauncis Noone of Martlishm̄, v*li*.
1553, paid.]   Nicolas Bramston of Chelmeton, yeoman,
                            xiij*li*. vij*d*.
Jeffery Blower, Symond Maddocke, William Harrison, and William dennaunt of debbenh*m, yeomen, x*li*."

By the side is written...hath brought in a testimonyall seelyd and subscrybyd...to...payd the xxjth of June, 1553.

The seals and subscriptions are gone from the "testimonial" presented to Wolferston in recognition of his little mistake as to the ownership of the church, but the words just quoted appear to refer to that veracious document. As the Commissioners made remissions in the case of certain "pore men," which remissions were noted in a "p'ticulr boke" in the custody of Sir Richard Cotton, Comptroller of the Household, we cannot say whether these delinquents paid up in full, after the example of Noone of Martlesham. That parish, with Wantisden and Debenham, will appear not to have suffered in bell metal. Chelmondiston acknowledges to have sold an old broken bell to the value of xxj*s*. viij*d*.

* The certificate may be read in full in the *East Anglian*, New Series, III., 112.

Brantham seems a bad case. £30 is a lot of money, and there was only one bell there in 1553. Robert Wingfield (son of the Commissioner of 1536, Humphrey Wingfield), who had married the heiress of Sir John Pargeter, Lord Mayor of London, is absolutely without excuse. The parishes do not seem to have taken benefit from these fines.

I have said that in one instance certainly the Commissioners did not receive a full report. That instance is Brockley, which is returned as having one bell, whereas three of Jordan's hang now in the tower, without doubt the same which hung there in 1553.

Perhaps the men of Brockley feared that what had been done in the disturbances of 1549 might be attempted in Suffolk, and only one bell of the smallest size left for their church,* and for that reason concealed the true number, relying not vainly on their sequestered position.

It must not be supposed that Suffolk is peculiar in these respects. We will take an instance from Northamptonshire, in which county "the towneshipp of Soulgrave...sold before the fyrst Inventory was taken and maid by John Humfrey and John Mayo, Churchewardens there one bell unto Thomas Stuttesbury and Lawrence Wasshyngton,† gent' of the same towne for xvj*li.* whereof vj*li.* is delyvyd to the Inhÿtaunts of the same towne And is bestowed uppon the highe wayes and ford*.

"And their intent is to bestowe all the rest so," etc.‡

We have already heard of Stephen Tonni. A gap of fifteen years separates the name found at Stanstead, Suffolk, from that on the bell at Reepham, Norfolk, which first bears the name of Bury S. Edmund's:—

BEATI QUI HABITAT (sic) IN DOMO TUA DOMINE.

(Blessed are they who dwell in Thy house. Psalm lxxxiv. (lxxxiii. vulg.), 5).

DE BVRI SANTE EDMONDE STEFANVS TONNI ME BECIT. 1559.

---

* Froude, II. E., V. 186.

† Ancestor of the first American President. See Henry F. Waters's *Ancestry of Washington,* 1889.

‡ *North's C. B. of Northamptonshire,* p. 412.

I am not to decide on the identity of the two Stephens. The latest date of the name is 1587, which would give a range of forty-three years, a good long spell, but nothing incredible. This Reepham bell bears the seal of the cloth subsidy for the county of Suffolk, which may be applied to the history of Roger Reve, "clothear," and a representation of the Crucifixion. Neither of these occur again. His usual marks are the crown and arrows, indicative of the borough (fig. 81), and a fleur-de-lis, perhaps with reference to his French origin (fig. 82).

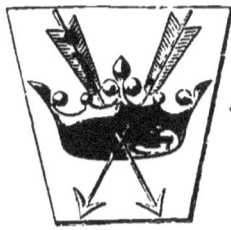
Fig. 81.

Fig. 82.

As his are the first bells which bear the name of a Suffolk town, I will take them in order of date. I know of none out of East Anglia. The Norfolk and Cambridgeshire bells are in italics, and those now recast have a dagger (†) prefixed to them :—

1560. Stanton, All Saints, fourth,
†1562. Helmingham, tenor,
†1564. Cockfield, tenor,
   „   *Stetchworth*, tenor.

The inscription on the Cockfield tenor was given me by Flanders Green, who set me bell-hunting more than forty years ago, an enthusiastic bell-hanger :—

MANE CITVS RECTVM BVGE, MOLLEM DISCVTE SOMNVM, TEMPLVM APPROPINQVES, ET VENERARE DEVM.

It may be compared with the short admonition to rise early, on the Stoke-by-Clare clock-bell.

1566. Hargrave, tenor,

1567. Kettlebaston, third,
    „   Stanningfield, third,
†   „   Troston, treble,
1570. Stradishall, third,
1572. Chediston, tenor,
    „   Fakenham, Great, second,
    „   Gedding, the two bells,
L „   Haughley, four lower bells,
L „   Letheringham bell,
1573. Somerton, second,
    „   Sternfield, tenor,
    „   Ubbeston, tenor,
1574. Glemham, Little, second,
1575. Mendlesham, tenor, a fine bell, reputed to weigh 24 cwt.,
L D. „   Whatfield, second,
L 1576. Bradley, Great, second,
L „   Kersey, third,
L „   Ottley, tenor,
† „   Petistree tenor,
† „   Sudbury, All Saints, tenor, the counterpart of the Mendlesham tenor,
    „   Walsham-le-Willows, fourth,
L „   *Cambridge, S. Edmund, fourth,*
L „   *Landbeach, third,*
    „   *Wilbraham, Little,* treble and second,
L „   *Winch, West,* treble,
L 1578. Rede, treble,
L „   Somerton, treble,
L 1580. Newmarket, S. Mary, second and third,
L 1581. Levington, tenor,
1582. Elmswell, second,
    „   *Oxburgh, third,*
    „   *Wicken, fourth,*
1586. Monewden, treble,
    „   Rede, second,
L 1587. Barham, tenor.

The bells on this list marked L bear the initials W. L., thought with great probability to be those of William Land, Stephen Tonni's foreman, of whom more hereafter. Whatfield second also bears those of Thomas Draper.

It is a strange thing that we cannot find the will of this active and successful bell-founder, but perhaps (like Briant of Hertford) his labours were more useful to others than profitable to himself. Beyond what is found on his bells, the only glimpses we gain of him are derived from the Long Melford and Wattisfield Parish Books, and from the will of his brother Julian. In the former document, 1582—1584, Hugh Isacke being then Churchwarden, may be read.

*" For takeinge downe the broken Belle   v*s*.
For carryinge the broken Belle to Burye   v*s*.
For helpe to loade it   ij*d*.
For layde out at Burye for wayinge the belle   viij*d*.
Two jorneys to Burye   xvj*d*.
For makinge the wrytinge between the Church-
    wardens and the Bell-founder   ij*d*.
To the Bell-founder for castinge of the belle
    and metalle   iij*li*. xiiij*s*. ij*d*.
For hangeinge the belle   xj*s*. viij*d*."

And now we stand by the death-bed of Julian Tonney, weaver. It is the 9th of February, 1583. "Julian Tonneye of Bury S*t* Edmonde in the countye of Suff., weaver, being of good and p'fect remembraunce (thankes be unto God) did speake theise words in manner as followeth, I geve and bequeath unto Stephen Tonney my brother all those my goods, chattells, moveables, and howsholde stuffe, under what manner of kynde soever they be, fownder to paye my debtes so far as they will extend unto, in the p'sence of these men underwritten, John Sterne, Robert Smyth, Willm Longe, John Barrett, John Beacher, Thomas Tonney."

Poor Julian did not regard his estate with much confidence. He must have died very soon after making this nuncupative

---

* Kindly sent me by Mr. Percy C. L. Scott, Hall Mills, Long Melford.

will, for on the 12th of February, Dr. Deye, Commissary and Official of the Archdeaconry of Sudbury, granted letters of administration to Stephen Tonni, as no executors had been named by the deceased. The Thomas Tonney here mentioned did not follow his father's trade, nor did William Land do much on his own account.

I cannot say how we first found the latter name, though it seems familiar enough to me. The original "Wylliam Lawnd," in 1548—9, appears in one of those dealings in old metal for which that remarkable time is eminent. The Churchwardens of the Parish of "Mary Maudelen in Barmondesey" note

"Item sold more by them a crose of copper and other olde mettyll of lattyn to Wylliam Lawnd weying xlvj pound pryce the pound iiij$d$. somme xvs. iiij$d$."*

Possibly he was father to the W. L., whose initials we have seen on Stephen Tonni's bells as early as 1572. This later W. L. cast the tenor at Brettenham in 1574. He made an excursion to Halstead in Essex in 1575, for which church, in conjunction with Thomas Draper, he cast the fine tenor now in that tower, a very grand bell, said to weigh 25 cwt. It is marked with a crown and clipped arrows (fig. 83), as though

Fig. 83.

to mark some past connection with Tonne, but its motto is also on the Whatfield tenor of the same year, which bears the initials of all three founders :—

Omnia Jovam laudant animantia.

We have this combination of W. L. and T. D. at Wiston in 1574, and at Wattisfield in 1584, where on the fourth appears the following quaint couplet, the words separated by a fleur-de-

* *Surrey Inventories*, by J. R. Daniel-Tyssen, p. 98.

lis in a lozenge, (fig. 84) to distinguish it from Tonni's fleur-de-lis in an oblong,

WL TD IN THE RAYNE
OF QVENE ELSEBETH BIS XIII.

Fig. 84.

The Wattisfield folk had foundry dealings with Bury in 1578, as we find from their book, but this job was carried out at Thetford. The detail is very graphic :—

" Itm. the belfounders dyd dyne, thre of them   xd."

Very suggestive of Tonni being with Land and Draper on this occasion. Perhaps as senior man he consumed the extra penn'orth. Perhaps also the poetry as above was post-prandial. It must have involved a great effort.

" Itm the belfounders hade for earnest for the bell   vs.
Itm layd out to the belfounders men when the
    bell was felt (sic.)   iiij$d$.
Itm. layd out to father Smyth for the bell hangen   xv$d$.
    and for the bell caryenge and recaryenge   iiij$s$.
    and for bordynge of four men one daye   ij$s$.
    and for bordynge of two men one daye   xij$d$.
    and for one man's wages one daye   iiij$d$.
    and for fetching of father Smyth's gear at Reck-
        ynghal to wynd up the bell   ij$d$.
Itm. layd out for eyornes for the bell   viiij$d$.
Itm. layd out at fetfor (Thetford) to the bel-
    founder at ōr ladyes day   xxxiij$s$. iiij$d$.
        ....

Itm. for caryenge of a lode of wode to fetfor to
  the belfounder   iijs.
and for fellyng and makyng of the wood   vd.
Itm. layd out for the bell clapper   vs.
Itm. The belfounders dyd dyne at Nycolas Lockes
  and thear dyner cam to   viijd.
Itm. Layd out to John Boulton for whyt lether to
  mend the belles   ijd.
Itm. layd out for half a hundred bord, and thear
  ar xiij to the half hundred lynge upon the
  steple to mend the belles wheeles   xxd."

Land's initials occur for the last time on a bell of Stephen Tonni's at Barham in 1587.

Another William Land, possibly his son, turns up at Crayford, Kent, 1615, Kirkoswald, Cumberland, 1619, and Wilmington, Kent, 1636. He was a Houndsditch man, and at Stapleford, Cambridgeshire (1622), his initials occur with those of Thomas Draper's son John. In 1624 he cast the "Silver Bell," at S. John's College, Cambridge, and probably in that town, as there is no charge for carriage.

Fig. 85.

Thomas Draper had moved on permanently to Thetford by 1588 at any rate, when he cast there the sixth for Redenhall, esteemed by some the finest bell of that grand eight. It is remarkable that in the same year he cast a small bell for Hutton-in-the-Forest, Cumberland. He has left us but five bells in Suffolk:—

1584. Ashbocking, second, with a peculiar fleur-de-lis (fig. 85),
1591. Tuddenham, S. Mary's, third,
  „   Sapiston, third,

1593. Stradishall, tenor,
1594. Yaxley, tenor.

His health was evidently failing by this time, and he died in 1595. Municipal honours in his case were accompanied with heavy cares. There was a turbulent burgess in Thetford named Roger Herbert, who had to be expelled from the "twentieship" for divers heinous offences, "first, he geveth not his money towards the maiors diet; he opposeth him selfe against the maior and his companie in repugninge against the constitunes and orders of the Towne made, etc., viz., made for hogges*, for making rescues against the Serjeant Harington in arestinge him, he cometh to no assemblie of longe tyme, he defraude men of their money and paye not his detts to the discredit of the towne, and for div'se and sondrie other causes, he misused the maior and burgesses in bad names, in calling ·Mr. Asteley splittershankes, and some other of the companie cadowes† and p'ticadowes‡ and Churles meaninge churle by Mr. Sheringe." This expulsion is signed   Rich. Asteley   John Buxton.

" Mr. Drap ƿ Maior his m'ke John Goldyngham
Anthonie Frere."

We can only trust that the newly-chosen member of the Thetford "twentie" refrained from reflecting on the slenderness of Mr. Richard Asteley's legs, and the loquacity with which Mr. John Goldyngham, Mr. Anthonie Frere, Mr. John Buxton, and even his Worship Mr. Thomas Draper may have been affected. Thomas Draper's last mark in the records of the borough is on May 8th, 1595, in a very trembling hand. His will, proved July 9th in that year, mentions his messuage in S. Cuthbert's parish, his wife Margaret, and his sons Thomas, Edmonde, John, Henrye, Richard, and William. Of these the first and third followed their father's calling. The eldest son was in business before his father's death, the old fourth at Hepworth, before being recast in 1825, having borne the inscription :—

Thomas Draper the younger made me 1593.‖

* No doubt analogous to those at Ipswich.
† Jackdaws.
‡ Magpies?
‖ MSS. Davy in loc.

No bell of his seems now to remain, the second at Cranworth, Norfolk, dated 1598, which I saw in 1850, having been recast in 1853. His domestic relations were not very happy, as he was returned in the Episcopal Visitation for Norwich Diocese in 1597 "for that he keepeth not with his wife, but remaineth wth his mother, and so have contynewed a quarter of a yeare nowe laste past."

I will postpone the larger subject of the third son, John, and leave for a time the Bury and Thetford work with the mention of Thomas Andrew, who used Stephen Tonni's well-known marks. From him we have

Carlton, S. Peter's, four bells,

Nedging, treble, all dated 1598; to which might have been added the Naughton second, now gone, dated 1599.

The Norwich Elizabethan bells, from members of the Brend family, form a considerable group :—

1567. I. B., Stradbroke sixth (the figure 6 is inverted),
1568. I. B., Metfield treble,
 „ No initials, Little Ashfield second, inscribed Charoli Framlingham Militis,
 „ No initials, Horham, tenor,
1581. I. B., Elmham, South, S. James's, tenor,
1582. No initials of founder, Hacheston, tenor.

As John Brend the elder died on the 29th or 30th of July, in that year, and was buried on the 31st of July, "greatly indetted to diu'se men in diu'se somes of money," these are the only Suffolkers in which he had a hand. The Horham bell was probably made by him in conjunction with a brother Robert. The works were in S. Stephen's parish, no doubt on the site of the great mediæval foundry. His lettering is large and clumsy, and the arabic numerals very misleading. William Brend, his son, removed the foundry into All Saints' parish. From him we have :—

1583. Framlingham, sixth,
1590. Farnham, treble,
1592. Dallinghoo, treble,
 „ Kettleburgh, tenor,

1592. Monewden, tenor,
1593. Cookley, tenor,
„ Cratfield, tenor,
1596. Elmham, South, S. Margaret, tenor,
1597. Ellough, tenor,
1598. Fritton bell,
1599. Glemham, Great, fourth,
with a large number of others, which we will treat of under the the next century. His 1592 bells are crowded with initials of subscribers or parishioners, notable by those who are reviving the records of their parishes.

One bell, the sixth at Clare, is by John Dier, an old acquaintance of mine, whom I unearthed at Maulden, Bedfordshire, in 1852, and subsequently at Much Hadham, Hertfordshire, in 1855. I am sorry to add that this prolonged intimacy has not resulted in knowledge of his locality or operations. This Clare bell, dated 1579, is his earliest known. In the following year he cast a bell for Broomfield, Essex, and in 1583, the bell for Arrington, Cambridgeshire. There are ten bells of his in Bedfordshire and eleven in Hertfordshire. His latest date is 1597, and he uses sometimes a pentacle in conjunction with other small trade-marks.

Another solitary bell, though hanging in good company, is the fourth at Cratfield, the work of Henry Topsel, in 1585, in which year he also made a bell for Hedenham, Norfolk. This the parish sold to Kirby Bedon, when the Hedenham four were run into six in 1838, and it still hangs in Kirby Bedon tower, bearing " Hednam " on it. This placing the name of the parish on a bell is unfortunately a very rare occurrence. " Cratfeld " is on that fourth, and let us hope that it will never show the name in any other tower. The initials R. T., for Roger, the son of Henry, are found on both these East Anglian bells. These artificers are elsewhere unknown save in Sussex, where they turn up, working at West Tarring, after an interval of fourteen years. The initials H. T. appear on the second at Bury, Sussex, in 1599, and the names of Henry and Roger on the tenor at Felpham in the following year. " Henry Tapsell, the elder," was buried at West Tarring, October 5th, 1604. Roger went on with his Sussex work some thirty years afterwards. Their bells are of no surpassing excellence. The surname is curious, as denoting a nautical origin.

A far better artificer is Richard Bowler, whom all agree in placing at Colchester, though there is nothing but tradition for it. We have fourteen bells of his in Suffolk:—

1589. Stratford, S. Mary, fifth,
1591. Bergholt, East, priest's bell,
  „ Cornard, Little, fourth,
1592. Wenham, Great, tenor,
1598. Cookley, treble,
  „ *Ilketshall, S. Andrew, tenor* (melted in the fire of 1889),
1600. Creeting, S. Peter, treble,
  „ Depden, tenor,
  „ Freston bell,
1601. Bergholt, East, third,
  „ Campsey Ash, tenor,
  „ Wickham Market, fifth,
1603. Lavenham, fourth and sixth,
  „ Withersfield, second.

His lettering is generally of a bold Roman type, resembling that of the first Miles Graye, the prince of founders, who is supposed to have learned his business under Bowler. At Waltham, Essex, is a bell of his with Richard Holdfeld's mark, an unusual combination. There are two of his bells in Cambridgeshire, but none in Norfolk, or further north, west or south, to the best of my knowledge. An Augustine Bowler turns up in Lincolnshire twenty or thirty years later than our Richard, but we know little about him.

And now, for the last time I regret to say, we are brought into touch with the gun-founders. The bell at Thorington bears in shallow black letter, with a pentacle at the beginning, a stop, and consisting of one lozenge over another, *à la* John Dier and the Clarkes, the inscription,

𝕾amwell 𝕺wen 𝕸ade 𝕸e for wansted. 1598.

The Owens of Houndsditch were a great gun-making family,

and some idea of John Owen, the first known of the name, and his relations to two who bore the name of Samuel, may be gleaned from his will. We all remember Shakespeare's fop, and his objection to gunpowder. This fabricator of the King's ordnance does not seem to have loved it too well. He is called to a disagreeable service. Kett and his fellows have exchanged their camp on Mousehold heath, around the oak of Reformation, for an occupation of Norwich. Lord Sheffield is killed, and Norwich knows the place of his death to this day. Sir Thomas Cornwallis is a prisoner. Parr, Marquis of Northampton, late in command, has fallen back on Cambridge, and John Dudley, then Earl of Warwick, better known as the Duke of Northumberland, Lady Jane Grey's father-in-law, is summoned to take his place. The rebels have guns, and Owen, called to Warwick's side, makes his will :—

"In the name of God, Amen. The xijth daye of August Anno dm MVXLIX. I John Owyn of London (and one of the kinge's founders of his ordynance) hole in bodye and in p'fte memorie, being sent into Norfolke ageynst the Rebles at Norwich, make this my last will and testament in maner and forme following, that is to saye, I bequeathe my bodye and soule into the keping of the lyvinge god who sees all things.

"I give and bequeathe unto Anne Chainley als Rainse fyftie pounds that she owith me without specialtie, and for the fourscore pounds I will that after my death she have the occupying of the said iiij/li. for foure years, putting in suerties for the payment thereof withoute intereste.

"I give and bequeathe to my syster Alice twentie poundes, to the poore people and presoners fourtie poundes. And I bequeathe to a childe that is none of myne although yt is named of me (and as a bill of rekenyng hereto annexed more playnlye shall declare) the whiche is at norsse in sowth mēnīes, whose name is Samuell fourtie pounds, unto Samuell my brother Robert sonne I give twentie pounds, to Jones tenne pounds, to Susan fyve pounds.

"The rest of my goodes, cattell, moveables and immoveables,

O

debts, wt all other things I give and bequeathe to my brother Robert whom I make my soole exccutour, to Robert Eyer I bequeath fyve pounds. In the thirde yere of Edwarde the sixte by the grace of god Kinge of England, Fraunce, and Ireland, defender of the faith, and of the churche of England and Irelande the supreme head.

"Wrytten in hast with my owne hande the yere and daye above said by me, John Owen."*

I make no apology for transcribing this in full. It is worth record on historical and religious accounts, as well for its connection with our special subject.

John Owen, however, came back from Norwich, and lived to the following year, when his brother Robert made his renunciation of the executorship, and the widow Anne, unmentioned in the will, took out letters of administration on the 25th of August.

To which of the Samuels of 1549, the unhappy nurseling, or the acknowledged son of Robert, we may refer the Thorington bell of 1596, is uncertain. Among the Bronze Ordnance in the Rotunda, Woolwich, are three guns (nos. 4, 8, and 9 in the Official Catalogue) by members of this family. Of the three, one is by John and Robert, a brass saker, dated 1538, one by John alone, a cannon royal, undated, but recovered from the wreck of the *Mary Rose*, lost off Portsmouth in 1545, and a sakeret on which may be read "Tomas Owen made this pese for the YE'L of Garnse, vhan Sir Peter Mevtas vas Governor and Captayn, Anno Dm̄ 1550."

How this Wanstead bell, the only Owen specimen remaining this side of the county, came to Thorington, may be read in the following memorandum on the second page of the earliest Register:—

Memorandū yt ye Right worshipfull Edward Coke Esquier Attourny Generall to the Queenes most excellent maiestie and Bridgett his Wife did Giue unto the Towneshippe of Thorington in June 1598 one Bell alone vppon this condicion that neyther the Churchwardens nor any of the inhabitants of

---

* Compare Latimer's Sermons, Parker S., p. 265.

the said Towne should at any time after ye aforesaid Guift sell awaye the said Bell but continve and maintayne the same for the callinge together of the inhabitants of the said Towne to divine Service and other seemely vses. In witnes whereof I Robert Golde minister of the said Towne of Thorington have sett to my hand to this wrightinge the xxth day of September 1607.

Robert' Golde.*

* Kindly sent me by the Rev. T. S. Hill, Rector.

CHAPTER VII.

John Clarke, an itinerant, in Suffolk—Joseph Carter—Peter Hawkes—The Bury founders in the days of the Stuarts—John Draper of Thetford—The later Brends of Norwich—" Colchester Graye" and his works, including the Lavenham tenor—The siege of Colchester—Miles Graye's foundry burnt—The Puritan *régime*—Bunyan—Milton—Compulsory ringing—John Darbie of Ipswich.

BEFORE proceeding to the large blocks of bells which occupy that great campanarian period, the first half of the seventeenth century, there are three single specimens to be disposed of.

The second at Wrentham is the second earliest known (1606) of a few bells, scattered about here and there, by John Clarke (he spells his name at Wrentham without the "e"), who in his pentacle and shallow lettering resembles John Dier and Samuel Owen. In the following year he cast a tiny treble for Cold Brayfield, in the county of Buckingham. At Wormington, Gloucestershire, and Rumboldswyke, Sussex, he appears undated. I turned him up, pentacle and all, at Flitwick, Bedfordshire, with the date 1608. In 1609 he cast the second at Eastry, Kent, and in 1613 the bell at Welney, Cambridgeshire. The earliest known bell of his is the little tenor of three at Eastwick, Hertfordshire, dated 1601. This seems a genuine case of itinerancy, and the poorness of the bells may account for it. A George Clarke cast a small ring of bells for Duxford S. Peter, Cambridgeshire, in 1564, and a certificate (dated 1557) of the weight of a bell from Wymondley Priory* shows that a bellfounder named Clarke was living at Datchworth at the time.

* North and Stahlschmidt's *C. B. of Hertfordshire*, p. 32.

The parish register records the baptism of a John Clarke in 1575, probably the maker of the Wrentham bell. He is not our only specimen of a proverbial rolling stone.

In 1609 Joseph Carter made the small bell at Great Finborough. He originally started business at Reading, his earliest date being 1579. Many bells of his and of his son-in-law, William Yare, are found in Oxfordshire bearing the well-known Norwich shield (fig. 50), but his best work seems to have been three for Wittersham, Kent. He died in 1610, not unmindful of his poor neighbours in Whitechapel.*

I wish I could say something about Peter Hawkes, who cast the Poslingford tenor in 1613. He is known in Essex, but not elsewhere. At Birdbrook a bird, perhaps a hawk, is stamped on one of his bells.

We will now take up the Bury bells, but the palmy days of Tonni are over, and such as came forth from James Edbury, John Driver, and Thomas Cheese, are not generally of a high character. They bear for the most part Tonni's marks, and sometimes a bit of arabesque border. These men sometimes worked separately and sometimes together. To disentangle them would be alike impossible and unprofitable, and I give the list in order of time, putting recast bells in italics:—

1602. Rede, second (I. D.)
1603. Saxham, Little, tenor (T. C.)
  „   *Sturston, old tenor* (I. E.)
1604. Onehouse bell (I. E.)
1605. Sudbury, S. Peter, fourth (I. E.)
       This was probably Edbury's greatest effort.
1608. Blythburgh bell (I. E.)
  „   Charsfield, third (I. E.)
  „   Cockfield, tenor (I. E.)
  „   Shadingfield bell (I. E.)
1612. Eleigh, Brent, tenor (I. E.)
1614. Denham, S. John Baptist, bell (I. D.)
  „   Friston, treble (I. D.)
  „   Stowlangtoft, second (I. D.)

* Tyssen's *C. B. of Sussex*, p. 36. Stahlschmidt's *C. B. of Kent*, p. 92.

1614. *Theberton, treble and second* (I. E. I. D.)
" *Worlington, third* (I. E. I. D.)
1615. Wickham Skeith, third (I. E. I. D.)
B. B. with them, and a host of parochial initials.
1618. Crecting, S. Peter, tenor.
Naughton bell.
Semer, tenor.

{ John Driver died this year, *teste registro*, in S. Mary's parish.
" Sep. 1618. John Driver belfounder, Nov. 21st."
These last-named three bells bear his name, (save that at Semer, which omits DRIVERVS,) and the initials of Cheese.

In 1619, July 17, Arthur Hindes, bell-founder, was buried } at S. James's, Bury. He has left no works behind him.

1621. Semer, treble (T. C.)
1622. Hargrave, treble (T. C. I. E.)
1623. Brettenham, second (T. C. I. E.)
1629. Thorpe Morieux, second (T. C.)
1630. Bradfield Combust, tenor (T. C.)
1632. Thorpe Morieux, treble (T. C.)

Pressed hard by the Brends on the North-east, and John Draper of Thetford, who had an agent, Andrew Girne, at Bury on the North-west, with Stamford men at work in Cambridgeshire, and the great reputation of Miles Graye all round, it is no wonder that these small Bury men did but little. I remember the old Worlington third, which was cracked at the lip. Parochial ingenuity sawed out the cracked part, the metal showing clean and strong, but somewhat pale. It used to sound just like a piece of wood. Cheese, who seems to have been the survivor of the three, died in 1635, leaving "Thomas Andrews" —perhaps the Thomas Andrew, bell-founder, lately mentioned— the supervisor of his will. He appears to have contemplated the possible re-marriage of his wife Mary, and while making all provision for her during her life, settles small sums of money on his daughters Mary and Elizabeth, and his son Thomas, who takes the reversion of the parlour furniture, the greatest kettle, and the greatest brass pot. The See of Norwich was vacant at this time through the death of Bishop Corbet, and the will was proved before John Jewell, Surrogate of Thomas Eden, LL.D., Archbishop Laud's Commissary, which Surrogate was one of the witnesses to the will.

Whatever came from Andrew Gerne we shall now consider under the works of his master, John Draper, third son of Thomas Draper the elder, and for more than forty years a bellfounder in Thetford. His earliest date is 1600, and he died in 1644. The following list gives his Suffolk bells:—

1600. Honington, tenor.

In this year in conjunction with his mother, Margaret, he gave a bond to the churchwardens of North Lopham, for the recasting of their second bell, which was again recast in 1733. This was on the 29th of August. He had by himself given a bond on the 19th of February of that year to the churchwardens of Lakenheath for the recasting of their tenor, to which his brother Thomas was a witness. This bell was again recast in 1676. Others since recast are in italics:—

1603. *Thelnetham, fourth.*

This bell, like some others in East Anglia, bears the crown and clipped arrows (fig. 83), used by Thomas Draper the elder, and to my mind denoting a past connection with Bury.

1605. Horham, fifth.

1606. *Braiseworth bell.* In this year he was casting at Wells, May 22nd, "divers of the neighbours of the towne and Beeston-next-Mileham accompanyinge them thither merily together."*

1608. Ampton, treble,
  ,, Barton Mills, second,
  ,, Icklingham, All Saints, tenor,
1609. Knettishall, tenor,
1615. Thetford, S. Mary, second,
1616. Elmswell, tenor,
1617. Risby, second,
1619. Barton, Great, second, fourth, and tenor,
  ,, Newmarket, S. Mary, treble and fourth,
1620. Chevington, treble,

* L'Estrange *C. B. of Norfolk*, p. 99.

1621. Hinderclay, fourth (I. D. and A. G.),
," Thurlow, Great, treble, second, third, and fourth,
," Bergholt, East, *tenor* (I. D. and A. G.),
1623. Barnham, S. Gregory, tenor,
," Exning, treble, second, third, and fourth,
," Fornham, All Saints, treble and second,
," Freckenham, second and third,
1624. Burgate, third,
," Fornham, All Saints, tenor,
1625. Lidgate, treble, second, and fourth (I. D. and A. G.),
1626. Hopton, All Saints, tenor,
," Pakenham, second,
," Timworth, tenor,
1627. Beyton bell,
," Combs, fourth,
," Cotton, third,
," · Dalham, second and third,
," Sturston, second,
," Wickham Skeith, tenor,
1628. Knettishall, tenor,
," Sapiston, treble,
1629. Hopton, All Saints, second,
," Stow, West, third and fourth,
1630. Badwell Ash, treble, second, and fourth,
," Hopton, All Saints, third, fourth, and fifth (these were the second, third, and fourth to complete a ring of five),
," Rickinghall Inferior, second,
," Thurston, treble and second (I. D. and A. G.),
1631. Ashfield, Great, third,
," Stow, West, second and tenor,
," Stowlangtoft, treble,
1632. Buxhall, treble and second,
1635. Buxhall, third,
," Worlington, second,
1636. Wetheringsett, second,
," Rushbrooke, second. This alone by Andrew Gerne, without John Draper's name.

This list is almost exclusively from West Suffolk, and East Suffolk during the same period is largely supplied by Norwich, which may be explained by relationship, for as he speaks in his will of John Brend* of Norwich, as his brother, he presumably married a Brend, no daughter being mentioned in the will of his father, Thomas Draper. A little "ring" was thus formed by the brothers-in-law, which kept out Miles Graye of Colchester from the north of the county, and led to a "mighty pretty quarrel" at Wickham Market, the traces of which yet remain. An observation of the dates will show that John Draper's Suffolk business arose mainly from the collapse of the Bury foundry.

As with his death bell-founding died out at Thetford, we will turn to his Norwich relatives, and take up the bells made by William Brend, or his son John, or both, during the first half of the seventeenth century.

1602. Wingfield, fifth,
1603. Elmham, South, All Saints, bell,
1606. Brundish, treble,
,, Wilby, second and third,
1608. Carlton Colville, treble,
,, Worlingham, third,
1609. Saxmundham, second,
1610. *Bruisyard, second*,
,, Elmham, South, S. George's, second,
,, Ringsfield, second,
1611. Halesworth, seventh,
,, Herringfleet, second,
1612. Brampton, second, third, and fourth,
,, Mendlesham, treble,
,, Mettingham, treble,
1613. Wickham Market, tenor,
,, Wingfield, third, fourth, and tenor,
1615. Campsey Ash, treble,
,, Marlingford, second and third,
,, Mutford, second,

* L'Estrange's *C. B. of Norfolk*, p. 47, note.

P

1616. Covehithe, second,
„ Westhall, treble and fourth,
1617. Kessingland, treble,
1618. Cratfield, treble and fifth,
„ Oulton, third, fourth, and tenor,
„ Pakefield, second,
1619. Homersfield, treble,
„ Ilketshall, S. Laurence, two bells,
1620. Hollesley, treble and tenor,
1621. Bramfield, treble and second,
„ Pakefield, tenor,
1622. Aldeburgh, third,
„ Bawdsey bell,
„ Benacre bell,
„ Bradfield, second,
„ Framlingham, seventh,
„ *Ilketshall, S. Andrew, treble, second, and third* (melted in the fire of 1889),
„ Knoddishall bell,
„ Rendham, fourth,
„ Worlingham, treble,
1623. Mendham, fifth,
1624. Badingham, second, third and tenor,
„ Rumburgh, treble, second, and fourth,
„ Wangford, S. Peter, treble,
1625. „ „ fifth,
1626. *Corton bell,*
„ Covehithe, third,
„ Westhall, tenor,
1627. Bury, S. Mary, fourth,
„ Elmham, South, S. Margaret, fourth,
„ Gisleham, treble and second,
„ Halesworth, fifth and tenor,
1628. Cove, North, fourth,
„ Dennington, fourth,
„ Mendham, third,
1630. Badingham, treble,

1631. Farnham, second,
1634. Carlton Colville, third, fourth, and tenor (in this year William Brend died),
1636. Mutford, third,
1637. Carlton Colville, second,
1639. Benhall, fourth,
  „   Frostenden, second,
1640. Chediston, second,
  „   Shipmeadow bell,
and lastly, in all probability the second, at Metfield, made in 1647. To these may be added the smaller of the two bells at Withersdale, bearing simply the initials W. B.

Let the judicious reader compare the blank years in this list with those in the others of the same period, and he will not fail to note the results of the occupation of the " Associated Counties" by the Earl of Manchester. The commission was accepted by the Earl, August 10th, 1643.

William Brend's wife's name was Alice, and the monogram of the two, A B with a W below, is very common on his bells.

Fig. 86.

He often uses also the Norwich ermine shield (fig. 50) and the arms of the city (fig. 86). He died in 1634, leaving his possessions to his wife and his son John, who received respectively a silver spoon and a hammer at the signing of the will.* Much of the later work seems to have been done by John, whose name alone occurs as founder in the Dennington Parish book in 1628, "ould Brend" being restricted to the hanging business.

I do not regard John Draper or these Brends as very uniform in their work. With some excellent bells there are many of an inferior quality. The Thetford bells are apt to be weak, and the Norwich bells harsh.

And now comes the record of their great rival, Miles Graye, of Colchester.

The general idea is that he learned his business under Richard Bowler, and the slight overlapping of date need not trouble us. There is a great similarity in the strong Roman lettering often used by both, but Bowler's rough cross goes out, and several marks are occasionally used, of which one found at Stradbroke and elsewhere (fig. 87) may serve as a specimen. The name is

Fig. 87.

almost invariably given in full and in English. When he ventures into Latin he appears, like the half-Romanized Celts, to have confounded the subject with the object, varying between "Milo" and "Milonem" Graye me fecit.

However defective his grammar may have been, he was a

* L'Estrange's *C. B. of Norfolk*, pp. 36, 37.

prince among workmen. Of the eighty bells and more in Suffolk which yet bear his name most are of excellent quality, and several are said to equal in grandeur of tone that which ringers consider his masterpiece, the celebrated Lavenham tenor. There are a few of his bells in Norfolk, the bulk of those at Swaffham, etc., some seventeen in Cambridgeshire, one in Sussex (Chiddingly, treble), a good sprinkling in Hertfordshire and Bedfordshire, and of course very many in Essex. His most distant work is the tenor at Newcastle-upon-Tyne, which he cast at Colchester in 1615, said in *Archæologia Æliana** to be his earliest date. However, Suffolk can find earlier. Here is the catalogue :—

1605. Ipswich, S. Matthew, fourth,
1607. „ S. Mary-le-Tower, seventh,
1608. Thrandeston, third,
1610. Ipswich, S. Mary-le-Tower, eleventh, the old tenor, a very fine bell,
„ Soham, Earl, treble,
„ *Woolverstone bell*,
1611. Harkstead, third and fourth,
„ Wickhambrook, fourth,
1613. Ipswich, S. Mary-at-Elms, third,
„ „ S. Mary-at-Quay, fourth,
„ Kenton, treble,
„ Stradbroke, fourth,
1614. Copdock, treble and second,
1615. Ashbocking, treble,
„ Copdock, third,
„. Ipswich, S. Mary Stoke, second,
„ Wilby, fifth,
1617. Stonham, Little, third,
1618. *Bromeswell, treble,*
„ Melton, treble,
„ Nettlestead bell,
1619. Combs, third,
1621. Chattisham bell,

* New Series II., 19.

1621. Ipswich, S. Helen, treble,
,,   Newbourne bell,
1622. Stradbroke, fifth, a good bell,
,,   Stowmarket, tenor, a very fine bell,
,,   Wherstead, second,
1623. Bucklesham bell,
1624. Capel, S. Mary, fourth,
1625. Lavenham, tenor, already mentioned,
,,   Nacton, treble,
1626. Bealings, Great, treble and second,
,,   Somersham, second,
1627. Felixstowe bell,
1628. Hasketon, five bells, *the second recast in* 1825,
1629. Shelley, second,
1630. Ipswich, S. Margaret, six bells,
,,   ,,   S. Nicholas, second,
,,   ,,   S. Peter, sixth,
,,   ,,   S. Stephen, third,
,,   Kenton, second,
1631. Martlesham, tenor,
,,   Soham, Monk, treble,
1632. Bramford, five bells, a treble added in 1805,
1636. Baylham, second, third, and fourth,
1637. Bedfield, treble,
,,   Brandeston, third,
,,   Eleigh, Monks, third,
,,   *Hollesley, treble,*
,,   Monewden, second,
(In this year he was at Saffron Walden, where he made a bell for Ickleford, Herts, since recast.)
1638. Eleigh, Monks, second and fourth,
,,   Felsham, second and fourth,
,,   Kersey, tenor ("Colchester Graye"),
,,   Winston, third and fifth,
1639. Felsham, tenor,
,,   Orford, treble,
1640. Clare, third,

1640. Edwardstone, third,
" Eye, sixth and tenor, very good,
" Preston, fourth,
1641. Culpho bell,
" Edwardstone, fourth,
" Parham, second,
" Sudbury, S. Peter, seventh,
" Wickhambrook, treble,
1646. Stradishall, fourth,

Also Barnardiston treble and second, the dates of which I have not.

This list is the most important by far which has yet been recorded, for sequences as well as for weight of bells. Especially the work of the years 1610, 1622, 1625, 1640, and 1641 deserves to be remarked. The break of Suffolk work after 1641 is again suggestive, and business was equally slack for him elsewhere at the same time. But worse misfortunes than slackness of business were in store for this great founder. Those that blow up the flame of partisanship in matters of religion and politics may well ponder the lessons taught by these "portions and parcels of the dreadful past" which come under our notice, and be content to let what is valuable in their principles work itself naturally to the front. There are no signs of a Millennium, either Anglican or Puritan, at Colchester in the summer of 1648. The Cavaliers of Kent, Hertfordshire, and Essex entered the town, and Fairfax let them "stew in their own juice," not adopting, however, this course till he had failed in an attack upon Headgate. In this attack Miles Graye's "capitall messuage or tenement...scituate and being below Headgate in Colchester" was burned down, as we find from his will, and he himself having endured the horrors of the siege, "set his house in order" on the seventeenth day of May, 1649, "weak in body and crased with age, but yet in p'fect mind and memory," and was dead in a month. There is a not unusual gap in the Register of Burials at S. Mary-at-Walls, Colchester from 1642 to 1653, another phenomenon which may be pondered by admirers of Cromwell and the Puritans. But we note the baptisms of Christopher* the son of Myles Gray and Jane his wife, 29th January, 1625, and that of Myles, son of Myles Graye and ———— his wife, 19th September, 1628, and "Moyles" Gray certifies the Register at this time as Churchwarden.

Old Miles's second wife was named Dorothy, and he left her nearly everything. Christopher's name does not appear in the will. Miles and the daughters Ann Darbye and Mary Starlinge are cut off, severally, with a shilling, but James gets the remainder of some leasehold property "to him and to his heyres for ever." The registers of Colchester Holy Trinity, S. Botolph's, and S. Leonard's, and of Stanway give us no information worth recording about either Bowlers or Grayes; but in 1656 Margaret Graye was imprisoned in Colchester Castle, as a Quaker, for declaring the truth in "Peter's Steeple House." It would be curious if she were a member of this family. The Puritan liberty of opinion, whether for prophetic or other purposes, was strictly confined to themselves. "New Presbyter is but Old Priest writ large," and when the Independents came in, it was the old song again to a fresh tune. Quakers were clearly out of it, but if George Fox had got the upper hand he would most likely have taken to coercion like the rest.

About this time the names of John Hardy and Abraham Greene, of Bury S. Edmund's, bell-founders, brothers-in-law, appear among the Bury wills, but no bells from either are known to exist. The former, who died in January, 1657, left his house, which he had lately purchased of Simon Wray, baker, "adjoining to a certaine gate then called Risby Gate," to his widow Mary for her life, then to go to John, the son of his brother-in-law John Bixby of "Thorpe Morioux." Abraham Greene, who had married Hardy's sister Joan, is probably identical with the Abraham Greene of Lindsey, who died in 1662, leaving everything to his sister, Prudence Dyer.†

The ten years from 1650 are of course not very productive of

* This, I think must be Christopher Graye the bell-founder; but there is in the Register another Christopher, son of Edward, born 1618.
† *Lib. Heron*, 7.

bells. The younger Miles Graye cast the Brantham bell in 1651, and the five for Stansfield in the following year, quite a phenomenon, which the parochial history may explain. John Brend breaks ground in 1654 with the Thrandeston treble, following on with two fives, for Blaxhall and Yoxford, splicing in a mediæval at Darsham as a third in a ring of four. But in 1657 he evidently regarded himself as having made a great hit. This was at Wickham Market, where the treble and second bear his name, the latter thus girding at the memory of the late man of Colchester :—

> The monument of Graie
> Is past awaie.
> In place thereof doth stand
> The name of John Brend.

South Elmham S. Margaret's upper three belong to the same year and man, Bures fourth and Horham fourth to 1658. About that time Miles Graye the younger made the Aldeburgh tenor; also the Chilton bell, the old second at Newton-next-Sudbury, the second at Acton, the second and third at Glemsford, and the treble at Great Thurlow, all pretty much in the same neighbourhood. The bell at Brightwell (1657) bearing the name of the parish is probably John Hodson's.

John Darbie's star now rises on the horizon, but he must be reserved for a complete list.

To do justice to the Puritan régime there seems to have been little or no bell spoliation; and though Bunyan regarded his own ringing of bells as a sin, there is nevertheless a charming allusion to their sweet voices, when he describes the entrance of Christian into the Celestial City. Milton's magnificent lines :—

> "Oft on a plot of rising ground
> I hear the far-off Curfew sound,
> Over some wide-watered shore,
> Swinging slow with sullen roar,"

belong to his earlier career, with

> "Or let the merry bells ring round,
> And the jocund rebecks sound
> To many a youth and many a maid
> Dancing in the chequered shade."

Whether he changed his mind about all this we know not, but we know that it would have been summarily put down in the cheerful days of the Major-generals. One compulsory peal in 1650 is recorded in my *Church Bells of Cambridgeshire*,* and it is worth rehearsing here, as displaying the wariness of the parish authorities of S. Mary-the-Great, Cambridge, in whose book is this entry:—

"1650. Paid to Persyvall Sekole the clarke for the ringers, *by an order from the Maior*, on 30 Jan.,† being a day of thanksgiving...... 0 . 2.0."

The latter part of the seventeenth century was a mighty time for bells, and for several reasons we shall lead it off with John Darbie's list, as for some time he was working at Ipswich, some of his bells being of excellent tone, and the earliest eight in Suffolk, Horham, mainly coming from his hand. In 1657 he cast the fourth at Rodmersham, Kent. This is his earliest date The Suffolkers run thus:—

1658. Henley, second,
,, Horham, fourth,
,, Sproughton, treble, second, and fourth,
,, Woolpit, fourth and fifth,
1659. Barking, treble and second,
1660. Blakenham, Little, treble and second,
,, Wetheringsett, treble,
,, Witnesham, second, fourth, fifth, and tenor,
1661. Hartest, five bells,
,, Holbrook, fourth,
,, Rougham, treble and second,
,, Soham, Monk, fifth,
,, Tattingstone, first three,
1662. Barrow, treble, fourth, and tenor,
,, Combs, treble,
,, Haverhill, third,
,, Ipswich, S. Mary-at-Quay, second, third, and tenor,
,, Nacton, second,

* P. 108.
† The anniversary of the execution of Charles I

1662. Somersham, treble,
„ Sudbury, S. Peter, second,
„ Winston, treble and second,
1663. Burgh Castle, tenor,
„ Chelmondiston bell,
„ Higham, fourth,
„ Horham, sixth and seventh,
„ Kettlebaston, treble,
„ Newton, Old, treble, third, and fourth,
„ Shelley, treble,
„ Soham, Earl, third and tenor,
„ Wickhambrook, tenor,
1664. Barnham, S. Gregory, treble,
„ Belstead bell,
„ Belton bell,
„ Elvedon bell,
„ Thetford, S. Mary, fifth,
1665. Grundisburgh, second and fourth, remains of a complete five,
„ Ixworth, second and third,
1666. Battisford bell,
„ Dennington, tenor, 25 cwt. (?), very fine,
„ Falkenham, treble and second,
1667. Offton, fourth,
„ Thorndon, second, third, fourth, and fifth,
1668. Brampton, treble,
„ Southwold, fourth and fifth,
„ Wangford, S. Peter, third,
1669. Haverhill, treble,
„ Ipswich, S. Mary-at-Elms, treble, third, and tenor,
„ Mendlesham, fourth,
1670. Sibton, second (he was rather busy in Norfolk and Cambridgeshire this year),
1671. Gislingham, fifth and tenor, very good,
„ Ipswich, S. Mary-le-Tower, eighth and tenth,
„ Thorndon, tenor (these are among his best bells),
1672. Stowmarket, seventh,

1672. *Wickham Market, third,*
1673. Kedington, second, third, fourth, and tenor,
1674. Holton, S. Mary, second,
,, Leiston, fifth,
,, Stow, West, fifth,
,, Sudbourne bell,
1675. Higham, S. Mary, second and tenor,
,, Rushmere, S. Andrew, treble and second,
,, Timworth, treble and second,
,, Tuddenham, S. Mary, tenor,
1676. Cavenham, second and tenor,
,, Claydon bell,
,, Groton bell,
,, Hoxne, treble,
,, Lakenheath, tenor,
,, Mildenhall, third (cast for a treble, a singularly fine bell),
,, Syleham, treble,
1677. Bealings, Little, treble,
,, Copdock, fourth,
,, Elmswell, fourth,
,, Hintlesham, treble,
,, Southolt bell.
1678. Akenham bell,
,, Hintlesham, second, third, and fourth,
,, Rougham, fourth,
,, Saxstead bell,
,, *Westhall, second,*
1679. Boyton bell,
,, Orford, third and fourth,
,, Ramsholt bell,
1680. Ipswich, S. Clement, six bells,
,, Stanton, S. John-the-Baptist, treble, second, and fourth (in this year he cast the tenor at Isleham, Cambridgeshire, a magnificent bell, said to weigh 25 cwt.),
1681. Kelsale, third and tenor,

1681. *Sibton, treble,*
1682. Ipswich, S. Peter, treble,
 „ Ixworth, treble,
1683. Barham, treble,
 „ Capel, S. Mary, third,
 „ Hacheston, second and fourth,
 „ Ipswich, S. Peter, fourth,
 „ Stradbroke, seventh,
1685. *Haverhill, tenor,*
 „ Tuddenham, S. Martin, treble,
 „ Wattisfield, treble, second, third, and tenor,
 „ Yoxford, fifth,
1686. Shotley bell,
 „ Ufford, third,
1691. Stowmarket, third.

This catalogue far exceeds that of Miles Graye the elder, whose daughter Ann I suspect that he married.

CHAPTER VIII.

Dick Whittington—Call-changes—Early peals—The "Twenty all over," or "Christmas Eve"—7,360 Oxford Treble Bob at Bungay, in 1860.

SOME day modern critics will be down on the story of Dick Whittington. While as yet we are free from their "triumphant results," let us receive it, as it is fit. The first of his three Lord Mayoralties was in 1397; and it must have been in the reign of Edward III. that he heard the Bow bells calling to him, supposing the peal to have been in G :—

Turn a - gain, Whit-ting-ton. Thrice Lord Mayor of Lon-don.

At any rate this sequence is that which all have known as "Whittington" by tradition, and the tale is natural enough. It is an excellent specimen of what is termed a "call-change." Before bell-machinery had reached its present development, and while most bells only swung to and fro in chiming, it was impossible to change the sequence at every round. So after thirty or forty rounds of one change, the caller would give the signal for another, just as it is done in Sunday chiming at the present day in many a village church.

There are very few common subjects on which there are such wild ideas as on bell-ringing. Every Christmas in the illustrated newspapers you see the most grotesque views of ringers plentifully exerting themselves in a way which would ensure their own destruction and the ruin of the bell-gear. People think that ringing is a vulgar, low kind of thing, only practised by boors and a few partially-deranged gentlemen, who ought to be in a private lunatic asylum. Did they know anything of the history of the Art, they would find that amongst its votaries have been a nobleman, Lord Brereton; a great judge, Sir Matthew Hale; senators, as Sir Symonds d'Ewes; scholars, as Dawes, and many others, of whose company no honest man need be ashamed. Nor is the nature of change ringing contemptible, for no small mathematical skill is involved in the composition of a peal. These compositions appear to have been unknown till the beginning of the seventeenth century, though the allotment of one man to each bell in Udall's *Ralph Roister Doister* seems to indicate some system of call-changes. But for a change at every round it was necessary that the mere chiming should be supplanted by a method which should give to the performers a more complete mastery of their instruments; and that method is what is called "ringing," where the bell, which was resting mouth upwards, swings completely round and balances mouth upwards again; a contrivance called the "stay and slide" prevents the bell from falling over, should the balance be disturbed. A certain time then, has to elapse between two strokes of the same bell; and in arranging the sequence of changes it is well to keep the place of any particular bell as near as possible to its place in the preceding change. Thus, if the third bell were sounding fifth in one change, in the next it should be sounding fourth or sixth. The simpler peals which are given by Fabian Stedman in his *Tintinnalogia*, published in 1667, are recorded by him as having originated fifty or sixty years before his time.

His method for treating four-and-twenty changes on four bells amounts to "hunting" the treble only. A bell is said to be "hunted up" as she moves towards the tenor's or last place, and "hunted down" when she moves towards the treble's or first place. By observing the sequence of changes, the treble or first bell being printed in stronger type, this movement will be manifest, while it should be seen that the other bells stay twice in each of the middle places, and thrice in the treble's and tenor's. Each change is called a "single," *i.e.*, a change of place between two bells only, as though the composer had wished to produce as little variety as possible.

THE CHURCH BELLS OF SUFFOLK.

1_234 43_21
2_134 4_312
23_14 4_132
234_1 1_432
324_1 1_423
3_214 4_123
3_124 42_13
1_324 423_1
134_2 243_1
3_142 24_13
34_12 2_143
342_1 1_243

A curious method on five is inserted by Stedman for antiquity's sake. He calls it the "Twenty all over"; but I find that it is still well known in Fressingfield by the name of "Christmas Eve." It is extremely simple. First the treble hunts up, while the others change no more than to make room for it.

1_2345
21_345
23_145
234_15
2345_1

Now the second does the same thing.

3_2451
34_251
345_21
3451_2

The third now hunts.

4_3512
45_312
45_132
4512_3

Now the fourth.

5_4123
51_423
512_43
5123_4.

And lastly the tenor, which brings the bells round again.

1_5234
12_534
123_54
1234_5

PLAIN CHANGES ON FIVE. 129

Here every change is a "single." The twenty changes arise, of course, from there being *four* in each of the *five* hunts.

Another method called "Cambridge Eight-and-Forty" will be found in my *Church Bells of Cambridgeshire*.

But the *plain changes* on five bells are worthy of preservation.

12345	41235	51432	51324
21345	42135	54132	53124
23145	42315	54312	53214
23415	42351	54321	53241
23451	24351	54231	53421
32451	24315	54213	53412
32415	24135	54123	53142
32145	21435	51423	51342
31245	12435	15423	15342
13245	12453	15243	13542
13425	21453	51243	31542
31425	24153	52143	35142
34125	24513	52413	35412
34215	24531	52431	35421
34251	42531	25431	35241
34521	42513	25413	35214
34512	42153	25143	35124
34152	41253	21543	31524
31452	14253	12543	13524
13452	14523	12534	13254
14352	41523	21534	31254
41352	45123	25134	32154
43152	45213	25314	32514
43512	45231	25341	32541
43251	45321	52341	23541
43521	45312	52314	23514
43215	45132	52134	23154
43125	41532	51234	21354
41325	14532	15234	12354
14325	15423	15324	12345
14235			

If Dr. Burney could assure his readers that the *Tintinnalogia* is "not beneath the notice of musicians who wish to explore all the regions of natural melody: as in this little book they will see every possible change in the arrangement of Diatonic sounds, from 2 to 12, which being reduced to musical notes, would, in spite of all which has hitherto been written, point out innumerable passages, that would be new in melody and musical

R

composition,"* I may venture to claim at least as high a regard for the modern peals, in which the bells are more freely moved about amongst each other.

This method is easily applicable to any number of bells, One of the six bell methods based upon it, the tenor and fifth "hunted down," is called the "*Esquire's Twelve-score*," proving by its name that bell-ringing two centuries ago was a gentleman's amusement.

I do not, however, intend to enlarge further on the subject of change-ringing, on which there are plenty of good treatises, nor to attempt a record of the most remarkable peals rung in the county, this being a work undertaken by Mr. Slater of Glemsford. However, as I have now the honour to hold the post of President of the Diocesan Society of Change Ringers, it would have been unbecoming in me to pass the subject in silence, nor must I be guilty of ingratitude in forgetting a certain 7,360 of Oxford Treble Bob Major, rung to welcome my bride and myself thirty years ago,† when I was Master of Bungay Grammar School, and a member of that Society of Ringers.

The band consisted of
Benjamin Smith, treble, Benjamin Spilling, fifth,
William Sheldrake, second, Jarvis Crickmore, sixth,
George Adams, third, Thomas Spalding, seventh,
Peter Page, fourth, Captain A. P. Moore, tenor.

Of this company, Messrs. Smith and Sheldrake, on the previous Friday, had rung 10,080 of the same method at Redenhall, taking the treble and third respectively. The second was taken by John Ellis, who was sixty-eight years old at the time. The 7,360 took 4 hours 40 minutes, and the 10,080, 6 hours 25 minutes.

* Burney, *General History of Music*, iii., 413. He gives a sprightly "Five Bell Consorte" by John Jenkins, which he traces to Fabian Stedman's *Tintinnalogia*.
† Monday, March 26th, 1860.

CHAPTER IX.

Later bells—Robard Gurney of Bury—Christopher Hodson of S. Mary Cray—Miles Graye the younger—A solitary bell of Christopher Graye's at Thrandeston—His difficulties in Cambridgeshire—Is succeeded by Charles Newman, and the foundry taken to Lynn—Thomas Newman at Bracondale and Bury—John Stephens—Sudbury and its founders—Henry Pleasant—Thomas Gardiner—His critic at Edwardstone—John Goldsmith of Redgrave—Ransomes and Sims—London founders—Newton and Peele—Catlin—The Whitechapel men—Phelps and his record of Dr. Sacheverell at Charsfield—His eight at Bury S. Mary's—Lester—Pack—A failure at Beccles—Chapman—The Mears family—Benefactions of the Suffolk nobility and others—The Warners of Cripplegate—A ship's bell from Stockholm at Lavenheath—John Briant of Exning—The St. Neot's men and their successors—Joseph Eayre—Arnold—The Taylors of Loughborough—Osborn and Dobson of Downham Market—Birmingham founders—Blews at Lowestoft—Carr at Newbourne—The Redenhall foundry—Recommendation to Southwold—Jubilee bells at Mildenhall—Conclusion.

ROBARD GURNEY, of Bury S. Edmund's, a son of the Andrew Gurney already mentioned, first appears in his father's will, dated 1643. He had accommodated his father with the loan of 2 cwt. of metal, which kindness is requited with a legacy of 3 cwt., "with all my tooles and moulds for to worke with all, as to my trade belongeth."

In 1649, as I find from a communication from the Rev. A. F. Torry, late fellow and dean of S. John's College, Cambridge, he recast the bells for that college, the cost of recasting, for new metal, and to the Bury carrier being £4 18s. 9d.[*] His earliest existing date is 1652, both in Suffolk and Cambridgeshire (Impington third). The Suffolk list follows:—

1652. Bradley, Little, bell,

[*] In spite of this, the bell still bears the date 1624, and the initials W. I.

1663. Santon Downham bell,
1664. Stanningfield, treble,
1665. Worlington, second (a very good bell),
1666. Tuddenham, S. Mary, second,
1667. Alpheton, two bells,
1668. Bradfield, S. George, second and third,
    „   Felsham, treble,
    „   Poslingford, treble, second, and third,
    „   Wangford, S. Denis, bell,
1670. Elmswell, treble,
1671. Tostock, tenor,
    „   Welnetham, Little, tenor,
1672. Tuddenham, S. Mary, treble,
1673. Onehouse, treble.

I consider him as unusually variant in his work. Some of his bells are detestable. Mr. Deedes notices the curiously truncated character of their edges. The Andrew Gurney, whose wife's name was Mary, who had a son Robert baptized in 1667, and was a legatee to the extent of £3 by will of his spinster sister Mary, was almost certainly a brother. There was also a sister Alice, who married a Jennings of Wickhambrook, and a kinsman Thomas.

Had it not been for Lothingland there would not have been a single bell in the county made by Edward Tooke, of Norwich. As it is there are three :—

1675. Blundeston, the larger of the two,
1676. Oulton, treble,
1677.   „   second.

His operations lasted from 1671 to 1679, when he died, and was buried in All Saints' parish. He was the second son of William Tooke, Alderman of Norwich, and Sheriff in 1650. These little bells of his in Suffolk call for no remark.

The London founders could hardly get their noses into the county during the heyday of John Darbie. John Hodson cast the Kersey fifth and the Shelley tenor in 1662, and Christopher, his son presumably, the fourth for Ipswich S. Mary-le-Tower and the East Bergholt fourth in 1688, and the Kersey fourth in the following year. Their bells are more notable for the Stuart coins on them than for specially fine tone. The family, I think, was of Cambridge extraction, the name of Christopher Hodson, gentleman, appearing in the Corporation Lease-book in the year 1589.* The locality of the London foundry is not known. Christopher was in a kind of partnership with his father for four or five years before 1677, when he removed to S. Mary Cray, when his foundry was "in the High Street, on or about the spot where the blacksmith's forge now stands, under the chestnut tree at the foot of the hill on which the vicarage is built."† No doubt Christopher each day attempted and did something to earn a night's repose, but it could not well have been always at Cray.

The situation is too awkward. He probably itinerated, and as he cast Great Tom of Oxford in 1680, it would be worth while seeing whether the Christchurch *compoti* for that year throw any light on the point. That Great Tom is a poor bell considering its weight, 7 tons 12 cwt.

I return to Miles Graye the younger, whom we have already seen at Brantham and Stansfield. He was in Bedfordshire and Cambridgeshire from 1653 to 1656. These are also from him:—

1656. Cockfield, third,
1658. Chilton bell,
" *Newton-next-Sudbury*, second,
1659. Acton, second,
" Glemsford, second and third,
1660. Thurlow, Great, treble,
1661. Clare, fifth,
1662. Stanstead, third and fourth,
1663. Acton, third,
" Edwardstone, fifth,
1664. Cornard, Great, third,
" Newton-next-Sudbury, fifth,
" Wiston, second,
(He is in Cambridgeshire for the next three years.)

* *Church Bells of Cambridgeshire*, p. 88.
† Stahlschmidt's *Church Bells of Kent*, p. 97.

1671. Assington, treble,
1672. Melford, Long, S. Catherine's Mission Room bell, which used to hang on the tower of the Parish Church,
1678. Hadleigh, treble and second,
1679.   „   third,
1680.   „   tenor, a fine bell, estimated to weigh 28 cwt.,
1681. Somerton, third,
1683. Bildeston, third,
   „   Hawkedon, five, the fourth since recast,
1684. Stutton, first three,
1685. Acton, tenor.

Another storm of politics was then raging over England, and some zealous Abhorrer marks the Acton tenor with "God save the King." About the middle of June in the following year, when James's Irish policy was in full bud, Miles Graye died at Colchester, leaving a shilling each to his children Samuel, Francis, Myles, James, Francis and Jane, and the residue to his widow Elizabeth. The gifts of his father had not fully descended to him or to his elder brother Christopher, whom we have only at Thrandeston, for which church he cast the fifth in 1678.

In my Cambridgeshire book I traced him to Ampthill in 1659. There can be no doubt that in 1677 he was at Ipswich helping John Darbie, for Mr. L'Estrange* says that the former name is on the third, and the latter on the fourth at East Harling, both dated 1677, while in the churchwardens' accounts the item of 2s. 6d. appear "for writen the Artickells and the bond between John Darby and the Towen," £1 6s. 0d. for bell-clappers bought of John Hollwell of Ipswich, and £3 6s. 0d. "payed John Darby in money for tow new bells casting." As no bells of Christopher Graye's are known to bear date 1673, 1674, 1675, 1676, the probability is very strong that all this time he was helping Darbie, and that the Thrandeston tenor was made at Ipswich, like the East Harling third.

* *Church Bells of Norfolk.* p. 67.

Being at Haddenham in 1683, very likely he was the man about whom the Rev. J. M. Freeman of Haddenham relates the following local story :—" An old inhabitant recalls a tradition of his early youth, some fifty years since, to the effect that there lived a bell-founder in this place in the olden time ; and that on one memorable occasion, when the operation of melting the metal had reached a critical stage, it was found that there was a deficiency in the supply of materials ; a few moments more and the process would be endangered, if not spoilt. Acting at once on the maxim that 'the end justifies the means,' our traditional 'man of metal' rushed frantically from his foundry and made his way to a neighbouring inn—the present 'Rose and Crown,' so the story goes—making an unceremonious raid upon the establishment, 'whipping up' the pewter pots and measures, as well as the ordinary vessels available for the purpose. These were hurriedly conveyed home and cast into the furnace in time, let us hope, to meet the exigences of the case. Passing, however, to the present time, I may just add, that in digging for the foundation of the new tower, a cavity was found in the rock, containing cinder ashes, portions of bell-metal and mussel shells, from which circumstances it has been conjectured that the church bells were, for convenience sake, cast on the very spot over which they were destined to hang."[*]

From Haddenham records it is pretty plain that there was some connection between Christopher Graye and Charles Newman, who in 1684 seems to have moved on to Lynn from that village. Some of his bells are very good, and the county contains about thirty of them :—

1686. Glemsford, tenor,
„ Hemingstone bell,
1688. Boxford, fourth,
1691. *Redgrave, five bells,*
1692. Stutton, second,
1693. Clare, tenor,
1695. Wickhambrook, second,

[*] *Cambridge Chronicle*, February 5th, 1876.

1696. Bentley bell,
  „ Bury S. Edmund's, St. Mary's, tenor,
1697. Lakenheath, fourth,
  „ Livermere, Little, bell,
  „ Stradbroke, third,
1698. Buxhall, fourth,
  „ Lidgate, third,
  „ Occold, third,
  „ Timworth, third,
1699. Bacton, treble,
  „ Bradfield, S. Clare, tenor,
  „ Cockfield, third,
  „. Kettlebaston, second (?),
  „ Stowmarket, fifth,
  „ Thurston, fourth,
  „ Walsham-le-Willows, second and third,
1700. Cockfield, second,
  „ Erwarton bell,
  „ Walsham-le-Willows, treble,
1701. Hundon, second,
  „ Thornham, Great, treble, second, and fourth,
1702. Barham, third.

This number pretty nearly equals that in Norfolk. There are some eight in Cambridgeshire, and none elsewhere.

Comparing the Norfolk work with the Suffolk in 1699, his busiest year, I am inclined to think that he had returned to Lynn, after a ramble into West and South Suffolk. He seems to have made use of water-carriage both by river and sea. The bell at Blakeney was made by him in 1699, and two years afterwards the churchwardens of S. Laurence's, Norwich, fetched their tenor from the same little port, which is hardly possible to have been used as a business centre. Most of the contemporaneous Suffolk bells are within a fair distance of the river Lark; and Lakenheath Lode would have carried the bell for that parish from the Little Ouse very conveniently.

The arabesques on Charles Newman's bells are something like John Darbie's. His wife's christian name was Alice.

While they were living at Haddenham, in 1682, she bore him a son Thomas, whose Suffolk works we shall have occasion to mention.

The wanderings of Thomas Newman were more frequent than extensive. He was born at Haddenham, April 2nd, 1682, and baptized on the 13th of the same month. The presence of Charles Newman's ornament on his earlier bells is to be noted. He began work when he was only nineteen years of age, his earliest date being 1701. In the following year his head-quarters were at Norwich,* and after a few single casts, he adventured himself on a ring of five at Tunstead, Norfolk, casting them (according to tradition) in the churchyard, with no remarkable success. Two little fives of his in Cambridgeshire, Cambridge Holy Trinity and Foulmire, cast in 1705 and 1704, are of poor quality. His Suffolk list contains nothing very remarkable, the peculiarity of his bells, in my opinion, being their inability to make themselves heard among their fellows. Here it is:—

1704. Culford bell,
,, Walsham-le-Willows, fifth and tenor,
1706. Somerleyton, tenor,
1707. Elmham, South, S. James, second,
1711. Blythford bell,
,, Kessingland, second,
,, Rushbrooke, tenor,
1727. Thornham, Little, bell,
1728. Kessingland, third,
,, Pakefield, tenor, " at Norwich,"
1729. Haverhill, tenor,
1730. Lound, three bells,
,, Lowestoft, S. Margaret, bell,
,, Sapiston, second,
1732. Burgh Castle, treble and second,
,, Mildenhall, third and fourth,
1733. Bardwell, fourth,

* *Teste*, the bell at Howe, Norfolk.

1733. Rushbrooke, tenor,
1734. Cowlinge, treble and second,
1735. Ashfield, Great, treble,
  „   Kentford, three bells,
  „   Lackford bell,
  „   Lawshall, five bells,
  „   *Pakenham, fourth*, "at Bury,"
  „   Shimpling, first four,
1736. Redgrave, lower five out of six,
1737. Brome, five bells,
  „   Palgrave, six bells,
1738. Boxstead, second,
1741. Fressingfield, third, fourth, and *fifth*,
  „   *Herringswell, treble*,
  „   Rickinghall Superior, tenor,
1742. Wingfield, treble,
1744. *Mildenhall Clock bell* (a good bell),
1745. Ashfield, Great, second,
  „   Wrentham, fourth,

In 1719, in conjunction with Thomas Gardiner, he cast the tenor for Newmarket S. Mary. One thing is to be noticed in his favour, that where he cast once, he very often cast again. Between 1711 and 1727 he was very busy in Norfolk, and afterwards in Cambridgeshire, Cambridge being his headquarters in 1724, when he cast the tenor for Berden, Essex, and in the following year when he received money for the "brasses" (sockets for the gudgeons to turn in) for S. Benedict's, Cambridge. But a reference to the foregoing list will show that before long he was back in Norwich, his foundry occupying the spot in "Brakindel," where now the "Richmond Hill" public-house stands. All the 1735 bells were doubtless cast at Bury.

He was of a poetical turn, no "mute inglorious Milton." As early as 1706 his genius burst forth at Worstead in

"I tell all that doth me see,
That Newman in Brakindel did new cast mee."

In 1707 he married Susan Aspland of Haddenham, who

seems to have survived him, for the entry of his burial in S. John Sepulchre, April 20th, 1745, describes him as a married man.

But neither family cares nor business trials could quench his light, which culminated in a lambent flame in 1732, when

"Thomas Newman cast me new
In 1732 (tew),"

occurs at Burgh Castle, Mildenhall, and Winfarthing.

Metaphor as well as rhyme occurs at Great Ashfield—

"Pull on, brave boys, I am metal to the backbone, but will be hanged before I crack."

During his absence from Suffolk the Bracondale foundry was occupied by John Stephens, a very fair workman, from whom we have some twenty bells:—

1718. Burgh, S. Botolph, five bells (a treble afterwards added),
,, Framlingham, treble and second to complete the octave. This seems to have been the second or third eight in Suffolk, Bungay S. Mary trebles to the old eight bearing the same date.
1720. Bealings, Great, second,
,, Framlingham, third,
1721. Eye, treble, *second*, and third. This seems to have been the third eight in Suffolk.
,, Hawkendon, fourth,
,, *Tunstall, six bells*,
,, Wangford, S. Peter, fourth,
1722. Mettingham, second,
1723. Thorpe-by-Ixworth bell,
,, *Mildenhall, tenor*,
1724. Hessett, five bells (the fourth since recast),
1726. Ringsfield, treble,
1727. Bergholt, East, tenor (a fine bell),

This was about his last work. His burial at S. John Sepulchre was on October 12th of that year, "widower." After his death the Bracondale foundry was occupied for a short time by Thomas Gardiner, of whom we shall speak presently, and with whom the long chronicle of Norwich founding ends.

Gardiner forms a good connecting link between Norwich and Sudbury, to which latter town we will now turn, when Henry Pleasant, another poetaster, was at work, taking in the district the place of the younger Miles Graye. His list follows :—

1691. Peasenhall, second,
1692. Barnardiston, fourth,
1694. Orford, second,
  „   Sibton, tenor,
1695. Bradfield, S. George, treble,
  „   Drinkstone, tenor,
  „   Welnetham, Great, bell,
1696. Drinkstone, second and fourth, *third and fifth,*
  „   Hawstead, second and third,
1697. Hitcham, fourth,
1698. Nayland, second,
1699. Stoke-by-Nayland, fifth,
1700. Offton, second and fifth,
1701. Euston, first three,
  „   Sudbury, All Saints, third,
  „   Westhorpe, first two,
1702. *Haughley, treble,*
  „   Lavenham, third and *seventh,*
  „   Preston, fifth,
1703. Lavenham, fifth,
  „   Wetherden, tenor,
1704. Preston, tenor,
1706. Eyke, second,
  „   Framsden, tenor,
  „   Ipswich, S. Nicholas, five bells, save the second,
  „   Stonham, East, treble,
  „   Stutton, third,
1707. Cornard, Little, second and third ; and Brettenham treble, undated.

He was evidently proud of his name, and in the last year of his life celebrated it thus at Maldon :—

"When three this steeple long did hold,
We were the emblems of a scold.
No music then, but we shall see
What Pleasant music six will be."

At Thetford S. Cuthbert's he simply records:—

"Henry Pleasant did me run
In the year 1701."

and with sublime idiom at Ipswich S. Nicholas:—

"Henry Pleasant have at last
Made as good as can be cast."

Mr. L'Estrange* quotes a writer in the *Bury and Norwich Post*, probably the late Rev. Dr. Badham of Sudbury, to the effect that Pleasant succeeded the Grayes at Colchester about 1686, and afterwards removed his foundry to Sudbury. He also speaks of Pleasant as casting at Bracondale about 1705, and that he was in some way acting with Charles Newman about that time appears from the fact that while two bells at Blickling, dated 1703, bear the name of the latter, three years afterwards the parish recovered three pounds of the former.

His English will not allow of his being considered the author of the not faultless hexameter on the tenor at Ipswich S. Nicholas:—

"Marlburio duce castra cano vastata inimicis," which records that great general's victory over Villeroy at Ramilies.

He left behind him a widow, Milicent, to whom letters of administration were granted February 12th, 1708.

John Thornton, whose bells generally please me, followed him, casting in

1708, Cornard, Great, treble, second, and tenor,
1712, Cornard, Little, bell,
,, *Thurlow, Great, fourth,*
(both these in conjunction with John Waylett,)
1716, Acton, treble,

* *Church Bells of Norfolk*, p. 67.

1718, Boxford, tenor (his most important work),
" Burstall, three bells,
" Withersfield, fourth,
1719, Wiston, tenor,
1720, Hundon, tenor.

There are also nice tenors of his at Cheveley and West Wickham, and a neat little five at Newmarket All Saints, all given in my Cambridgeshire book, and three bells in Norfolk, at Pulham S. Mary-the-Virgin, and Shropham. Otherwise he is not found but in Suffolk and Essex. His "infrequent partner," Waylett, however, is known in Sussex (1715–1724), Hertfordshire (1716), Kent (1717–1727), and Surrey (1718).

Some of Waylett's work in the South was done for Samuel Knight of Reading. He appears to have been a good, though rough workman, but he hardly belongs to us, and we will pass to the last Sudbury founder, who has been already mentioned, Thomas Gardiner. He started just after Thornton, his earliest date being 1709, when like others of the craft, his first efforts were not fully appreciated. Edwardstone was the earliest scene of his labours, where he was entrusted with splicing in three Miles Grayes (two of the elder and one of the younger) as third, fourth, and fifth in a ring of six. No fault apparently was found with his treble; but a local genius, one William Culpeck, otherwise to fame unknown, disagreed with him about the note of the second, designated him as a "want-wit," then no uncommon term of reproach, as we know from the *Pilgrim's Progress*, and humbled him by compelling him to cast on that bell these words, "Tvned by W$^{m.}$ Culpeck, 1710." But a quarrel with a founder is like a quarrel with a newspaper editor, and Gardiner had his revenge of the last word on casting the tenor, which he inscribed :—

"About ty second Cvlpeck is wrett
Becavse the fovnder wanted wett
Thair jvdgments were bvt bad at last
Or elce this bell I never had cast.
Tho. Gardiner."

Etymologically this is valuable, "ty" being the representative of "the," well-known to all who talk the beloved East Anglian tongue, and "wett" for "wit," shows the local pronunciation at the beginning of the eighteenth century.

At Ickworth he writes—

"Tho. Gardiner he me did cast,
I'll sing his praise unto the last,"

but otherwise he is plain enough, save that he sometimes puts on his bells impressions of coins, as at Pakefield, where I found those of a coin of John V. of Portugal, dated 1745, and a halfpenny of our George II., and uses a small cross reduced from a mediæval one at S. Giles's, Norwich. His Suffolk list is a long one :—

1709, 1710. Edwardstone, treble, second, and tenor,
1710. Badingham, fourth,
1711. Ickworth bell,
1712. Weston, Market, treble,
1713. Rendlesham, second,
„ Snape, tenor,
1714. Boxford, treble,
„ Campsey Ash, second,
„ Hemley bell,
„ Rendlesham, treble,
„ Waldringfield bell,
„ Wenham, Little, bell,
„ Wrentham, third,
1715. Bredfield, third,
„ Mickfield, tenor,
1716. Hinderclay, second,
„ Kersey, treble, second, and clock bell,
„ Sternfield, third,
„ Sweffling, tenor,
1717. Witnesham, tenor,
1718. Bildeston, tenor,
„ Chediston, treble,
„ Sweffling, third,
„ Wissett, second, third, and tenor (at Benhall),
1719. Wattisham, treble,

1719. Wyverstone, second,
1720. Huntingfield, five (the treble recast),
  „   Knettishall, treble,
1721. Lidgate, tenor,
1722. Barningham, tenor,
  „   Glemham, Great, second,
  „   Harkstead, third, fourth, and tenor,
  „   Hintlesham, fourth,
  „   Holbrook, tenor,
  „   Huntingfield, treble,
1723. Wrentham, treble,
1725. Poslingford, fourth,
  „   Stoke-by-Nayland, treble,
  „   Thetford, S. Mary, fourth,
  „   Weston, Market, tenor,
1726. Clare, clock bell,
  „   Creeting, S. Peter, bell,
  „   Elmsett, treble,
  „   Hepworth, first three,
  „   Hundon, third,
1727. Creeting, S. Mary, bell,
  „   Stonham, Earl, second,
1728. Falkenham, third and fourth,
  „   Rumburgh, third,
1729. Campsey Ash, third,
  „   Thelnetham, tenor,
1730. Euston, fourth,
1731. Barton, Great, treble,
  „   Easton, treble,
1732. Burgate, tenor,
  „   Ipswich, S. Mary-at-Quay, treble,
1733. Ipswich, S. Peter, second,
1734. Hinderclay, fifth,
1735. Barnham, S. Gregory, second and tenor,
  „   Ipswich, S. Peter, fifth,
  „   Offton, treble,
1737. Winston, fourth,

1739. Orford, tenor,
1740. Alderton bell,
  „   Westhorpe, third,
1743. Eriswell, tenor,
  „   Kedington, second,
  „   Stradishall, treble,
1744. Hitcham, tenor,
  „   Preston, fourth,
1745. Stratford, S. Mary, second (in this year he removed to Norwich),
1746. Burgate, treble and second,
1747. Acton, fourth (surely from Sudbury),
1748. Mendham, treble, second, fourth, and tenor,
1749. Pakefield, treble,
1750. Cove, North, treble and second,
1751. *Mildenhall, tenor* ("Norwich," a fine bell),
  „   Ipswich, Holy Trinity, bell,
1754. Boxford, third
  „   Glemsford, fourth   (all of these two years at
  „   Rattlesden, first four   Sudbury).
1755. Dalham, treble

His latest known date is 1759, on two bells at Danbury, Essex. The writer in the *Bury Post*, already quoted, says that the Hospitallers' Yard, near Ballingdon Bridge, and Curds or Silkweaver's Lane were successively the sites of foundries. This is all that can be said about Gardiner, save that in poetry Dr. Johnson would have called him a "barren rascal," for he uses the same jingle in 1754 as at Ickworth in 1711. And now comes a man of some little local interest, John Goldsmith of Redgrave, no poet, but fortunately a preserver of ancient dedications, his bells being frequently inscribed "Maria," "Gabriel," etc. In tone his bells are rather sweet than powerful. About twenty of them remain in Norfolk and Suffolk, and none in any other county. I append a complete list, with N. before those from Norfolk.

1702. Badley, second, *Maria*.
  „   „   third, *Margaret*.

T

N. 1707. Frenze bell.
N. 1708. Pulham, S. Mary-the-Virgin, fifth, *Margaret.*
      1710. Darmsden bell, *Maria.*
      1711. Hoxne, third, *Gabriel.*
      „ Oakley, Great, treble, *Margaret.*
      „   „ second and fifth,
N. 1711. Shimpling, third (split).
      „ Thetford, S. Mary, tenor, *Maria.*
N.   „ Terrington, S. Clement, second, *Maria.*
      1712. Rickinghall Superior, second, third, fourth, and fifth (very small).
N.   „ Ellingham, Little, bell,
N.   „ Rushall bell.
N.   „ Thorpe Abbot's, second.
      1713. Wilby, treble,

We know from Tom Martin that the tenor at Thetford S. Mary was inscribed:—

+ 𝔇ona 𝔎epende 𝔓ia. 𝔎ogo 𝔐agdalena 𝔐aria,

from which it appears that Goldsmith's learning did not extend to deciphering the whole inscription, or he would have lettered his recast bell *Magdalen* instead of *Maria.*

His *Margarets* were probably Brasyer's, bearing

+ 𝔉ac 𝔐argareta. 𝔎obis 𝔓ee 𝔐unera 𝔏eta, or Londoners with

+ 𝔓ee 𝔉lora 𝔊ampana 𝔐argareta 𝔈st 𝔑ominata.

His *Gabriel*, the Hoxne third, was no doubt the Angelus bell of that parish, probably a Brasyer, with the well-known

+ 𝔓ac 𝔈n 𝔊onclabe. 𝔊abriel 𝔑unc 𝔓ange 𝔖uabe.

With the solitary exception of Tattington tenor, cast by the well-known firm of Ransomes and Sims, at Ipswich, in 1853, the record of bells cast in the county now closes.

Having now altogether disposed of the bells of East Anglian make in Suffolk, we will revert to the Metropolis.

There are two *sui generis* at Kelsale, and one at Crowfield. All the rest come from the great foundry of Whitechapel, from which as yet we have only had one specimen, the bell at Great Finborough, 1609.

The Kelsale bells in question are the second and the sixth,

both dated 1708, the former bearing the name of John Peele, the latter that of Samuel Newton also. The site of their foundry is denoted by a court called Founder's Court, in the parish of S. Giles, Cripplegate, marked in old Ward maps. Newton was the master, and Peele the apprentice. Though the former was Master of the Founders' Company in 1711, there are very few of his bells in existence. The same remark applies to the latter, son of Samuel Peele, "latt of Bishopsgatt silkman deceased," whose apprenticeship was out in 1704, and who died in reduced circumstances between 1752 and 1755.* The Crowfield bell was made in 1740 by Robert Catlin, who in that year was elected a "love brother" of the Founders' Company, and took up the business of Samuel Knight of Holborn.†

Fig. 88.

Nearly a century separates the two first Whitechapel bells. The Somerleyton second is by James Bartlett in 1700, and bears a well-known mark of his (fig. 88). The name of the donor, Sir Richard Allen, Bart., appears on it.

James Bartlett, the elder son of Anthony Bartlett, a "lone man," wrought for about a quarter of a century, doing more work in the home counties than in East Anglia, where there are

* Stahlschmidt's *C. B. of Kent*, pp. 103, 104.
† P. 108.

three small College-chapel bells in Cambridge, and three not very notable specimens in Norfolk, besides this Somerleyton second. He died in 1701 intestate, and letters of administration were granted to his sister, Elizabeth Bixon, widow. He was succeeded by a very able man, Robert Phelps, said to have been a native of Avebury in Wiltshire, from whom we have :—

1710. Charsfield, treble,
1711. Kettleburgh, treble,
1723. *Bruisyard, treble,*
1728. Ottley, second,
    „   Stonham, Little, tenor,
1729. Rendham, second,
1731. Bedfield, second,
1734. Bures, second and third,
    „   Bury, S. Mary's, eight bells, splicing in the present fourth, a William Brend. Weight of tenor, 24 cwt., in D sharp, very good,
    „   Soham, Monk, second,
1735. Bredfield, second,
1736. Helmingham, third,
    „   Trimley, S. Mary's, bell,
1737. Ringshall, treble.

The first on the list has a truly notable legend :—" Sic Sacheverellvs [ore melos] immortali olli [ecclesiæ defensori h] anc dicat [Gvlielmvs] Leman de Cher[sfield Eqves 1710. R. Phelps]."

This is restored from Carthew's MS., and though "constructio latet," as Porson would have said, there can be no doubt as to the political feeling which dictated it. But the immortality of Dr. Sacheverell is not very enviable, and though "Hoy for Hoy Church and Sachefrel" was the shout at many a harvest home,* it may be doubted whether the name would have got into history save for that zeal which prompted his impeachment.

However, Sir William Leman thought well of him, and he may stand in the same hagiology as Thomas of Canterbury, though only a star of an inferior order. Phelps, described as

* *Waverley*, ch. li.

"a man from ye High Street," was buried at Whitechapel in 1738.

Thomas Lester, then thirty-three years old, took up his work. His predecessor had given the county an almost complete eight at Bury S. Mary's. He followed with six at Coddenham in 1740, either wholly in great part the gift of Theodore Eccleston, Esq., of Crowfield Hall. But the tenor, of 15 cwt., had to be recast in 1742, and then two trebles were added. In the three following years the same generous donor and the same founder were concerned in the first ten that were ever heard in Suffolk, the Stonham Aspall bells, tenor 24 cwt.; and the brick tower at Long Melford delighted by its eight tuneful bells, tenor 16 cwt., the ears of many whose eyes it had outraged. Besides these he made the two smaller bells at Cotton and the three smaller at Thelnetham. Soon afterwards he took Thomas Pack into partnership, and lived on to 1769, when he died of convulsions.

I have now reached a period with which the antiquary is hardly concerned; and I shall only notice the principal works of later founders. A pleasant five at Ousden, tenor 14¼ cwt., came from Lester and Pack in 1758, the gift of Thomas Moody, Esq., and the Reverend Richard Bethell; then in 1761 followed the eight at Debenham, tenor 20 cwt., while in the next year Suffolk saw the smallest five then known, Great Livermere, tenor 5 cwt., and a mighty ten boomed over the Waveney valley, from the massive tower at Beccles, tenor 27¼ cwt.* But these were originally a bad casting, and it is rather a marvel how they have lasted so long. The third was recast in 1804, and the sixth and seventh in 1871, after having existed in a cracked condition for many years. The treble, second, fourth, and eighth have wooden crowns, the eighth having also a strong iron band round the shoulder, though I could not discover where the crack was. The ninth has a crack in the crown, which did not amount to much when I examined it in 1861. On a second visit, in 1869, I found that a piece of metal,

* So by weight, in 1871. Lester and Pack's list gives 28 cwt., and common repute 29 cwt.

weighing some 15 lbs., had fallen from the lip of the seventh, while the fourth chattered, and the vibration of the sixth was a minimum. In the section of the fracture of the seventh, I observed that the metal was quite clear and free from honeycomb, but there was an oval-shaped grain, like the grain of wood, the nucleus of it in the middle of the fracture. Under these circumstances the Beccles folk need not be surprised at further collapses.

I am informed by Mr. S. B. Goslin, of the Cripplegate foundry, where the sixth and seventh were recast, that the peculiarity noticed by me occurs when castings are poured, the metal flowing in having a chilled surface or cake, which may slip in unless sufficient care is exercised, or sometimes from a chill in the mould, which for some reason may be cooler in one part than another. In such cases the metal, not being lively enough with heat, flows sluggishly, hence such faults in the casting.

After Lester's death Chapman became Pack's partner. They made five for Gazeley, tenor 10 cwt., in 1775, and a similar ring for Cavendish in 1779. Pack died of decline in 1781, and Chapman of consumption in 1784. In the meantime a young man from Canterbury, William Mears, had been taken into the Whitechapel business. His name appears on the little five at Moulton, tenor 6 cwt. After Chapman's death William Mears brought in his brother Thomas (said to have been a brewer) from Canterbury, and the two brothers cast the six for Clopton in 1788. Nothing of note came from Whitechapel after this till 1804, when Thomas Mears made the sixth for Worlingworth. The Duchess of Chandos, then resident in the parish, Lord Henniker, Emily, Lady Henniker, and others were benefactors, as may be seen in the list of inscriptions. The Suffolk nobility have not been unmindful of the bells on their estates. The Earl of Dysart gave eight to Helmingham (by Thomas Mears the younger) in 1815.

In 1820 the inhabitants of Bungay cut down a fine peal of eight, the second or third oldest in the county, to the present set, losing some 2 cwt. in the weight of the tenor, though possibly gaining in equability. The present tenor is in F sharp, and further information will be found in the list of inscriptions. Seven for Sudbury S. Gregory's, with a tenor of Pack and Chapman's, gave that tower a complete Whitechapel eight in 1821, and Polstead exchanged a grand old five (probably with one or two cracked) for a lighter but tuneful six of Thomas Mears's in 1825. Norton and Nowton, his last considerable works in Suffolk, followed in 1829. Fornham S. Martin's six in 1844 were from his sons, Charles and George Mears, the latter of whom survived his brother, dying at Landport, Portsmouth, in 1873. From his hand we have the five at Ingham, "offered" (as we find from the bells themselves) "at the church at Ingham in memory of her Ancestors by Frances Wakeham, June, 1860."

My fellow-townsman, Mr. Robert Stainbank, took up the Whitechapel work some time before George Mears's death. From him we have two sixes, Troston (1868), and Gorleston (1873), both prompted by the same kindly natal feeling, the former also notable for the preservation, as far as possible, of the old inscription. The donors, respectively, were E. Stanley and Miss Miriam Chevallier Roberts.

The Whitechapel foundry has had of late a formidable rival in the Warners of Cripplegate. They did a mighty work at the "Tower" Church, Ipswich, in 1866, putting a treble and a tenor to the existing ten, and recasting the present ninth, so as to prevent tuning. Ipswich knows the history of all this work, and it is as needless for me to rehearse it, as to sing the praises of the great twelve, from which I heard a good touch of Grandsire Cinques in December, 1887, when superintending the Cambridge Local Examination.

The sixth and seventh at Beccles were recast by the Cripplegate men in 1871. Two trebles were added by them to Sudbury S. Peter's in 1874, and All Saints' followed suit two years afterwards.

A single bell by Oliver of Wapping hangs in Stowupland bell-cot. I know no more of the make.

In Lavenheath tinkles an old ship's bell, rather curious than antique, bearing the words—

"Back Skieppet ADoLF   Guten
　　　　Bygdt　　　　　　　Stockholm
　i Jacobstad A. X. 1801   af Gerhard Horner."

When the good barque Adolphus, built at Jacobstad, on the east coast of the Gulf of Bothnia, perished, I know not, or how the bell came to Lavenheath. "Guten" may be noted as the Scandinavian for "cast," and compared with the Flemish "ghegoten."

We must now notice a few Suffolk bells by a Suffolk man, John Briant, of Exning, born there in the middle of the last century, and intended for Holy Orders. His love for mechanics and clock-making, however, regulated his destiny, and he developed into bell-founding at Hertford about 1781, when he made the five for Great Thurlow, tenor 13 cwt. In 1800 he cast the old five at Great Waldringfield into six, an achievement which we do not find recorded in his lists. In 1807 and the two following years he recast the tenor at Little Thurlow, added a treble to Gazeley, and recast the third and fourth (apparently Thomas Newman's) at Cowlinge.

For some years he had the benefit of the foremanship of Islip Edmunds, who had served Arnold in the same capacity. An honest, capable, and enthusiastic member of his craft, his advice was sought by the Dean and Chapter of Lincoln when the old "Great Tom" was broken, though at the time he had given up the foundry. His sensible, straightforward correspondence may be read in North and Stahlschmidt's *Church Bells of Hertfordshire*,* and the course of events abundantly justified his counsel. It is painful to record that he fell into difficulties through his unselfishness, and ended his days as a pensioner in the Spencer Almshouses at Hertford, in 1829, not living to witness the completion of the New "Tom o' Lincoln" in 1834.

The great Leicester foundry of the Newcombes and Wattses, though claiming, as it seems, East Anglian, origin by the free use of Brasyer's Norwich shield, did not touch Suffolk; but Joseph Eayre of S. Neot's, who for his part claimed business

* Pp. 57, &c.

descent from Watts, has left his mark at Haverhill, when he recast the fourth in 1765. His foreman, Thomas Osborn, and his cousin, Edward Arnold, continued the foundry for a little time, but soon separated, the former going to Downham Market. From the latter we have a little ring of five at Whepstead (1774), and a recast or two. Towards the end of the century Arnold brought the foundry back to Leicester, and was succeeded by Robert Taylor, one of whose sons, John, with his elder brother William, after working at Oxford, and in Devonshire and Cornwall, finally took up his quarters at Loughborough in 1840. Their first Suffolk work to be noted is the turning of the "Tower" eight into ten in 1845.

When I was a boy, disliking much the noise in Worlington tower, I got up a subscription, and the Taylors recast the fourth and added a treble there.

Ten years afterwards they put the Mildenhall folk into possession of a tuneable six, and nine years after that recast the three for Herringswell, after the fire at that interesting little church. Then 1879 saw the octave completed at Stradbroke, during the incumbency of the present Bishop of Liverpool, and in 1884 filial and fraternal affection moved the members of the well-known family of Garrett of Leiston to do the same work for their parish church. A peculiarity of St. Neot's work used to be the heavy clapping of 1, 4, 6, 8. I know not whether this is still observed. The effect would be manifest.

From the St. Neot's foundry arose that at Downham Market. Thomas Osborn, son of Richard Osborn, joiner of that town, baptized 1741, had been foreman to Joseph Eayre, and for a while partner with Arnold. About 1778 they dissolved partnership, and Osborn returned to his native place, where he conducted an extensive business. For a short time he was in partnership with Robert Patrick of Whitechapel (from whom by himself we have Holbrook third, 1783); but the bulk of his work bears no name but his own.

He made between sixty and seventy bells in our county, the earliest being Great Barton third, in 1779, and the latest, Little Glemham treble and Woodbridge eight, twenty years afterwards.

His work is generally held in good repute, and his *chef d'œuvre* is the fine ten in the Norman tower at Bury, in D, tenor 30 cwt.* He died in December, 1806, and lies in Downham Market Churchyard. For the last six years of his life his name seldom occurs, his grandson, William Dobson, managing the foundry. Suffolk has but two bells of this time, Coney Weston bell, 1802, and Hadleigh fifth, 1806. Afterwards Dobson cast between thirty and forty of our bells, none of more note than the treble and second at Lavenham in 1811, a little five for Brandon in 1815, and the Horningsheath (Horringer) six in 1818. His work is very variable, from the excellent peal at Diss to the not excellent peal at S. Nicholas, Liverpool. After a while he fell into difficulties. Thomas Mears of Whitechapel purchased his business in 1833. He went to London, was made a brother of the Charterhouse, when he died and was buried in 1842.†

From Birmingham we have six at Christ Church, Lowestoft, by Messrs. Blews and Son, and a bell at Newbourne by Carr.

The Redenhall foundry, under my friends Moore, Holmes, and Mackenzie, were not so successful in Suffolk as in Norfolk. They have given us a bell at Holton S. Peter's, 1881, and six at Weybread, their first effort in 1879. I much admire the tone of some of their individual bells, and wish that Weybread may some day experience Walter of Odyngton's "cos et lima," so as to "tell the tale" as prettily as Winterton tells it, or as Thorpe would tell it if it had a tower stout enough to carry the eight made for it. As to their work at Southwold, the pity was that they attempted to do anything with such a queer, though interesting, crew as the present tenants of that glorious tower.

Winterton was occupied by a very "scratch" five, and my counsel to my friends was to attempt nothing with splicing, but send them all to the boiler. The result has been very good, only the Wintertonians would have six out of metal that sufficed for five. Let Southwold take the same course. London, Loughborough, Birmingham—any one of them will do the work,

* Note from Robert Carr. Weight from Dobson's list.
† *L'Estrange's Church Bells of Norfolk*, p. 49.

but let the whole eight know the power of the furnace, and if means do not suffice, have a fairly heavy six, and leave it to the future to put on the trebles. Cutting down is often an irreparable evil.

My story ends where I took it up in 1848, at Mildenhall. After the many vicissitudes already related, the parishioners determined to have a peal of eight worthy of their church, in commemoration of the Jubilee year of Queen Victoria's reign.

Happily they were induced not to top a light six with two trebles, but to "top and tail" with a treble and tenor, flattening by a semitone the old fourth, now the fifth, which being a rather thick bell, from Loughborough, stood the operation well. Mr. Lawson, the representative of Mears and Stainbank, of Whitechapel, undertook the work, and carried it out admirably.

The detail will be found under the head of that parish.

I cannot close this work without an expression of thankfulness to Him from whom all mercies come, for the continuance, amongst varied scenes of labour, of the will and power to persevere in what seemed once an impossible task. So many friends have helped me that I cannot thank them individually. Not a few, indeed, have left this world, and of those that remain I have lost sight of many in the labours of forty years. But none the less do I cherish an affectionate recollection, so far as memory will extend, of my kind helpers.

Long may dear old "sely" Suffolk resound at all appointed times with the solemn and yet cheery music of the "peaceful bells," which

"Still upon the hallowed day,
Convoke the swains to praise and pray!"

INSCRIPTIONS

ON

The Church Bells of Suffolk.

1. **ACTON** *All Saints.* 5 Bells.
    1 John Thornton made me 1716.
    2 Miles Graye made me 1659. Nicholas Kerington.
    3 Miles Graye made me 1663.
    4 Tho. Gardiner fecit 1747.
    5 Miles Graye made me 1685. God save the King.
    "Great bells iiij." Return of 1553.
    Davy, Aug. 18th, 1826, notes the date of the 2nd as 1679, and the name "Kennington"; also the 5th as 1684. 2, 3, 4 chipped.

2. **AKENHAM** *S. Mary.* 1 Bell.
    Bell. John Darbie made me 1678. (45 in.)
    3 in 1553.
    Davy, 9 Sept., 1827, did not go up to it.

3. **ALDEBURGH** *SS. Peter and Paul.* 6 Bells.
    1 Cast by John Warner and Son, London, 1885.
    Rev. H. Thompson, B.A., Vicar.
    J. Harvey } Churchwardens.
    N. F. Hele }
    Hung by G. Day and Son, Eye.
    2 Lester and Pack of London fecit 1764.
    3 Anno Domini 1622. W. I. B.
    4 Recast by John Warner and Sons, London, 1884.
    Rev. H. Thompson, B.A., Vicar.
    J. Harvey } Churchwardens.
    N. F. Hele }
    Hung by G. Day and Son, Eye.
    5 Lester and Pack of London fecit 1764.
    Jn°. Wynter and Samuel Aldrick Ch. Wardens.
    6 Thomas Mears of London fecit 1820.
    Clock-bell. 1812.
    "Great bells iiij. Sancts Bells j." Return of 1553. Old 4 by J. Darbie.

INSCRIPTIONS.   157

In Davy's MS. 2 and 3, then 1 and 2, are reversed, and the bell recast in 1884 has the same inscription as the present 3rd. The old tenor was inscribed "Miles Graye made me 1653."
No mention of bells in certif. of iij Nov. 1547.

4. ALDERTON *S. Andrew.*   1 Bell.
    Bell.   Tho. Gardiner Sudbury fecit 1740.
No mention of bells in certif. of iij Nov. 1547.
"Great bells iij." Return of 1553.
Davy notes the steeple about half down, 9 June, 1830.

5. ALDHAM *S. Mary.*   1 Bell.
    Bell.   ▽ 65 thrice.
    ✚ 67.   Sancta ☐ Maria ☐ Ora ☐ Pro ☐ Nobis.
"Great bells iij." Return of 1553.
"One" Davy, 19 Aug., 1825. Faculty for sale of two, 1759.

6. ALDRINGHAM *S. Andrew.*   1 Bell.
    Bell.   Thomas Mears Founder London. 1842.
Diameter 18¼ in.
"One" Davy, 1808.
From *Eastern Counties' Collectanea*, p. 239, we know that there were three in 1687, when Bishop Lloyd granted a faculty for the sale of two. These were probably those alluded to in the words:—"All ornamēts playt and belles belongyng to owr Cherche ar fore to sell." Certif. iiij Nov., 1547. 5 in 1553. A. cum Thorpe.

7. ALKINSTON *S. John Baptist.*
Ecclesia destructa.
No return in 1553.

8. ALPHETON *SS. Peter and Paul.*   2 Bells.
    1 Roberd O Gvrney made me 1667.
    2 Robard O Gvrney made me 1667.

The mark between the names is a flower with eight petals.
Two heavier bells are said to have disappeared in the early part of the eighteenth century. Traces of them still remain.
"Alton, Great bellis ij." Return of 1553.
Davy, Aug. 16, 1831, "2 bells."

9. AMPTON *S. Peter.*   4 Bells.
    1 Presented by the Honorable Clara E. C. Paley, 1888.
       On a medallion below, John Taylor & Co., Loughborough.
    2 Johannes Draper me fecit 1608.
    3 ☐ 6 thrice.
    ✚ 47. SANCTA : MARRETA : ORA PRO : NOBIS : THOMAS : FECIT.
    4 ☐ 6 thrice.
    ✚ 7. ☐ SANCTE ☐ ANDREA ☐ ORA ☐ PRO ☐ NOBIS ☐ DERBY.

See pp. 12, 41. The occurrence of fig. 6 on a Norwich and a London bell in the same tower is remarkable. The "second" mentioned on p. 41 has become the third.
"Great bells iij." Return of 1553.
"Three bells and a clock," Davy.

10. ASHBOCKING *All Saints.* 2 Bells.
  1 Miles Graye made me 1615.
  2 1584 ☐ 85 five times.
2 in 1553.
Davy, 7 May, 1824, notes 1 "Blank," and the old tenor "Thos. Gardiner made me 1745."
Terrier, 13 May, 1806. "Item, three bells with their frames."

11. ASHBY *S. Mary.* 1 Bell.
  Bell. No inscription.
"Great bells ij." Return of 1553.
No bells. Davy.

12. ASHFIELD, GREAT, *All Saints.* Tenor A♭, c. 11 cwt.
  5 Bells.
  1 Tho. Newman fecit 1735. Thomas Rice Churchwarden. Pull on, brave boys, I am metal to the backbone, but will be hanged before I'll crack.
  2 Thomas Newman of Norwich made me 1745.
  3 John Draper made me 1631.
  4 ▽ 65 thrice.
    ✠ Sum Rofa Pulfata Mundi Maria Vocata.
  5 ▽ 65 thrice.
    ✠ Meritis Edmundi Simus A Crimine Mundi.
"Great bells iiij." Return of 1553.
Davy, 6 July, 1843, no notes.

13. ASHFIELD, LITTLE, *S. Mary.* 2 Bells.
  1 W. M. Moss Churchwarden. 1825.
    T. Mears of London fecit.
  2 Charoli Framlingham Militis 1568.
He was resident at Crow's Hill, Debenham, in 1542. His sole heiress was married to Sir Charles Gawdy of Debenham.
This seems to be the "Ashefeld," of which Wyllm Seme and Wyllm Roger were C. W. iij Nov., 1547, when they made return, "We have styll remaynyng a peyer of Shalys and iij Bells." Same return in 1553.
"The church has long been down . . . part of the steeple still remains, and it is a picturesque object. A small bell hangs near the ground in a latticed shed, at the east end of the chancel." Davy. See Thorpe next Ashfield, whence the larger bell came.

14. ASPALL. 1 Bell.
  Bell. No inscription.
2 in 1553.
Davy, 7 Nov., 1815, "2 bells."

15. ASSINGTON *S. Edmund.* 4 Bells.
  1 Miles Graye made me 1671.
  2 illegible.
  3 ✠ HOC : SIGNVM : SERVA : XPE : MARIA : THOMA.
  4 ✠ Milfi de celis habeo nomen Gabrielis. Weight said to be 19 cwt., diameter 43 in.
See p. 10 for 3. 4 belongs to the group on pp. 34, 35.
"Great bells iiij." Return of 1553.
Davy, Oct. 2, 1828. "The steeple is a square tower, containing 5 bells, but I could not get up."

16. ATHELINGTON S. *Peter*. 3 Bells.

1 ✝ : AVE GRACIA PLENA DNSTECV.
2 ✝ : OMAGDALENA : DUC : NOS : AD GAUDIA PLENA.
3 ✝ SCE BARTHOLOMEE SALVE ME.

See pp. 61—63.
"Alyngton, Great bells iij." Return of 1553.
Davy, 25 Nov. 1813, notes 3 small bells.
The musical notes are E. D. C. Teste Rev. H. W. Thornton.

17. BACTON S. *Mary*. Tenor G$\sharp$. 5 Bells.

1 Charles Newman made me 1699.
2, 5 Thomas Mears Founder London 1841.
   Rev^d. E. B. Barker, Rector.
   Edward Cooper } Churchwardens.
   William Kerry }
3 ▽ 65 thrice.
 ✝ Sancta ☐ Maria ☐ Ora ☐ Pro ☐ Nobis.
4 Pack and Chapman of London fecit 1772.

4 in 1553. 2 and 5 flattened by turning.
Davy, 21 July, 1831, " 5 bells."

18. BADINGHAM S. *John Baptist*. 5 Bells.

1 Anno Domini 1630.
2 Anno Domini 1624.
   A B
   W
3 Anno Domini 1624.
   A B
   W
4 Thomas Gardiner made me 1710.
5 Anno Domini 1624.
   ▽ 50.

No mention of bells in certif. of iij Nov., 1547.
4 in 1553.
Two of them noted correctly by Davy, 27 May, 1806.
One recast by Warner in 1889.

19. BADLEY S. *Mary*. 3 Bells.

1 68 + 68 sancte : augustine ora pro nobis.
2 + John Goldsmith fecit 1702. W. R. S^t. Maria.
3 Ex dono Elebth Pooley + John Goldsmith fecit 1702.
   S^t. Margaret.

Cross on 1 identical with that at Radwinter. This bell has no crown-staple.
3 in 1553.
Davy, 15 June, 1827, imperfectly reports as above.

20. BADWELL ASH S. *Mary*. Tenor F$\sharp$. 5 Bells.

1, 2, 4 John Draper made me 1630.
3 John Darbie made me 1664.
5 ▽ 50 thrice. (Diameter 41¼ in.)
 + 61 Munere Baptiste ☐ 62 Benedictus Sit Chorus Iste.

"Ashefeld p'va. Great bells iiij." Return of 1553.
"Five," Martin; and Davy, 6 July, 1843.

21. **BARDWELL** *SS. Peter and Paul.* 6 Bells.
1 Tho. Gardiner Svdbvry fecit 1719.
2 Pack & Chapman of London fecit 1770.
3 William Eaton Churchwarden 1820.
4 Thomas Spinluf & Charles Phillips C.W. T. Newman fecit 1733.
5 Tho. Newman fecit 173-. Roger Cooke, Robert Bvgg. C.W.
6 John Brett Churchwarden. Thos. Osborn Downham fecit 1780.

"Great bells iiij." Return of 1553.
"6," Davy, July 26, 1832.

22. **BARHAM** *S. Mary.* Diameter of tenor 40½ in. 4 Bells.
1 John Darbie made me 1683. S. D.
2 Miles Graye made me 1641.
3 Charles Newman made me 1702. Francis Weckes C.W.
4 De Bvri Santi Edmondi Stefanvs. Tonni me fecit W. L. 1587.

Left blank in 1553 report. Probably 3, as the numbers fall short of the total by 4, of which Darmsden may reckon for 1.
Davy, 31 May, 1827, gives obviously wrong dates for 1 and 2, which he also crosses.

23. **BARKING** *S. Mary.* 5 Bells.
1 John Darbie made me 1659.
Frances Theobald Esq.
2 John Darbie made me 1659.
Thomas Roberts Bvgg Mvdd.
3 Miles Graye made me 16-4.
4 ▽ 9 thrice.
+ 13 Ḥɑc En Conclabe Gabriel Ṇunc Pange Suabe.
5 ▽ 8 thrice.
+ 12 Piotrge Prece Pia Quos Conboro Sancta Maria.

See p. 17. Needham-in Barking.
No return of bells in certif of 1547. 4 in 1553.
So Davy, 16 June, 1827, though, like ourselves, he cannot read the date on 3. 1, 4, 5 cracked.

24. **BARNARDISTON** *All Saints.* Tenor 37 in. 5 Bells.
1 Milo Graie me fecit.
2 Milo Graie me fecit per nun.
3 ▽ 25 + 22 ▽ 26.
Sancta Maria Magdalena Ora Pro Nobis.
4 Henry Pleasant made mee 1692.
5 ☐ OMNES : SANCTI : DEI : ORATE : PRO : NOBIS.

See pp. 8, 24.
"Great bells iiij." Return of 1553.
. No notes. Davy.

25. **BARNBY** *S. John Baptist.* 1 Bell.
    Bell. ▽ 52 thrice. 𝕵𝖔𝖍. 𝕶𝖎𝖕𝖎𝖓𝖌.
    ✠ 61 𝕴𝖓 𝕸𝖚𝖑𝖙𝖎𝖘 𝕬𝖓𝖓𝖎𝖘 ☐ 62 𝕽𝖊𝖘𝖔𝖓𝖊𝖙 𝕮𝖆𝖒𝖕̄𝖆 𝕵𝖔𝖇𝖎𝖘.
    "Great bells iij." Return of 1553.

26. **BARNHAM** *S. Gregory.* 4 Bells.
    1 John Darbie made me 1664.
    2, 4 Tho. Gardiner Sudbury fecit 1735.
    3 John Draper made me 1623.
    "Great bells iij." Return of 1553.

27. **BARNHAM** *S. Martin.*
    Ecclesia destructa.
    "Great bells iij. Sancts Bells j." Return of 1553.
    In 1639 the Rectories of S. Gregory and S. Martin were consolidated, and the services directed to be performed in them alternatively. In 1682, there was an order for the sale of S. Martin's bells, and S. Gregory's was made the sole Church. Registr. Nor.

28. **BARNINGHAM** *S. Andrew.* 3 Bells.
    1 ▽ 52 thrice.
    ✠ 61 𝕼𝖚𝖊𝖘𝖚𝖒𝖚𝖘 𝕬𝖓𝖉𝖗𝖊𝖆 ☐ 62 𝕱𝖆𝖒𝖚𝖑𝖔𝖗𝖚𝖒 𝕾𝖚𝖘𝖈𝖎𝖕𝖊 𝕴𝖔𝖙𝖆.
    2 ▽ 52 thrice.
    ✠ 61 𝕱𝖑𝖔𝖘 𝕾𝖔𝖈𝖑𝖊𝖙 𝕾𝖊̄𝖙𝖘 ☐ 62 𝕾𝖊𝖒𝖕𝖊𝖗 𝕹𝖎𝖈𝖍𝖔𝖑𝖓𝖚𝖘 𝕴𝖓 𝕬𝖑𝖙𝖎𝖘.
    3 Tho. Gardiner Sudbury fecit 1722.
    "Great bells iij." Returns of 1553.
    The old treble 𝕭𝖔𝖓𝖆 𝕶𝖊𝖕𝖊𝖓𝖉𝖊 𝕻𝖎𝖆 𝕶𝖔𝖌𝖔 𝕸𝖆𝖌𝖉𝖆𝖑𝖊𝖓𝖆 𝕸𝖆𝖗𝖎𝖆. T. Martin's notes.
    Davy, 26 Aug. 1832, "3 bells."
    Tenor G according to Sperling.

29. **BARROW** *All Saints.* 5 Bells.
    1 T. Osborn Downham fecit 1786.
    2 John Darbie made me 1662.
    3 T. Osborn fecit 1786.
    4 John Darbie made me 1662. Robert Hayward C.W.
    5 John Darbie made me 1662. John Daynes.

30. **BARSHAM** *Holy Trinity.* In D. Diam. 27½ in. 1 Bell.
    Bell 𝕶𝕷 𝖓𝖔 𝖒 ☐ 62 ▽ 51.
    "Great Bells iij. Sancts Bells j." Return of 1553.
    Davy mistook KL for RD. He did not see that the inscription is a portion of the alphabet. June 2, 1808. Pits now for three.

31. **BARTON, GREAT,** *Holy Innocents.* 5 Bells.
    1 Tho. Gardiner Sudbury fecit 1731.
    2, 4, 5 John Draper made me 1619.
    3 Tho⁵. Osborn Downham Norfolk fecit 1779.
    So Davy.
    "Great bells iiij." Return of 1553.

32. **BARTON MILLS** *S. Mary.* 3 Bells.
    1 ▽ 66 thrice.
    ☐ 67 𝕾𝖆𝖓𝖈𝖙𝖆 ☐ 𝕭𝖆𝖗𝖇𝖆𝖗𝖆 ☐ 𝖔𝖗𝖆 ☐ 𝖕𝖗𝖔 ☐ 𝕹𝖔𝖇𝖎𝖘.
    2 Johanes Draper me fecit 1608.

V

162   THE CHURCH BELLS OF SUFFOLK.

3 ▽ 65 thrice.
+ 67 §ancte ☐ Anbria ☐ Apostoli ☐ ora ☐ pro ☐
  Nobis.
"Great bells iij. Sancts Bells j." Return of 1553.
T. Martin (no date) notes 3.
Inscriptions incorrectly given by Davy, 21 Aug., 1829.

33. BATTISFORD *S. Mary.*   1 Bell.
Bell. John Darbie made me 1666.   D. P. C.W.
3 in 1553.
Davy, June 18, 1827, could not examine it.

34. BAWDSEY *S. Mary.* ·   1 Bell.
Bell. W. I. B.   Anno Domini 1622.
No return of bells in certif. of iij Nov., 1547. "Great bells iij." Return of 1553.
"One bell which I did not venture to approach." Davy, 9 June, 1830.

35. BAYLHAM *S. Peter.*   Tenor G.   Diam. 41 in.   5 Bells.
1 Cast by John Warner & Sons London 1865.
2, 3, 4 Miles Graye made me 1636.
5 Rev¹. Henry Asplin, Ambros Brown & Sam¹. Southgate
  Ch: Wardens.   Miles Stollery.
  Pack & Chapman of London fecit 1772.
3 in 1553.
Davy, 11 May, 1824, notes the old treble the same as 2, 3, 4, and the 3rd fallen out of its frame.

36. BEALINGS, GREAT, *S. Mary.*   4 Bells.
3, 4 Miles Graye made me 1626.
2 John Stephens made me 1720.   Henry York, Churchwarden.
1 Pack & Chapman of London fecit 1772.
  Robᵗ. York Ch. Warden.
"Great bells ij." Return of 1553. Robert Godewyne, 1457, left 6/- towards a new bell. Davy, 4 Aug., 1810, crosses 1 and 2. T. Martin, 1750, notes 3 bells.

37. BEALINGS, LITTLE, *All Saints.*   2 Bells.
1 John Darbie made me 1677.   John Rose.
2 + 67 §ancta ☐ Maria ☐ Ora ☐ Pro ☐ Nobis.
No return of bells in certif. of 1547. "Great bells iij." Return of 1553.
T. Martin, 1750, notes 3 bells.
Davy. 4 Aug., 1810, notes an intermediate ✠ martir Barbara, &c.
Terrier, 21 Apr., 1834, 3 bells.

38. BECCLES *S. Michael.*   Tenor in B.   10 and Priest's bell.
1 Lester & Pack of London fecit Edwᵈ. Brooks Portreve
  1762.
2, 4 Lester & Pack of London fecit 1762.
3 Thomas Mears of London fecit 1804.
5 Our voices shall with joyfull sound
  Make Hills & Valleys echo round.
  Lester & Pack of London fecit 1762.

INSCRIPTIONS.

6, 7 Cast by John Warner & Sons, London, Royal Arms Patent, 1871.
C. F. Parker }
R. C. Houghton } Churchwardens.
8, 9 [inscriptions entirely covered by an iron band].
10 ☖ O Quam dulces sonas. Domini properemus ad cedes (*sic*) ☖ W^m. Clark & Robt. Margerom Ch. Wardens, Lester & Pack of London fecit 1762.
Priest's bell, 1766.

No return of bells in certif. of iiij Nov., 1547. "Great bells iij. Sancts Bells j." Return of 1553.
East Anglian, N. S. II., 241, 269.
"Eight tuneable bells"! Davy, Oct. 24, 1824, and May 27, 1825.
5 and 8 recast by Warner, 1889. Now a fair peal, though 4 and 9 are cracked. See p. 149.

39. BEDFIELD *S. Nicholas*.   5 Bells.
1 Miles Graye made me 1637.
  Symond Jefrey Peter Aldreg.
2 The Rev^d. Charles Scolding M.A. Rector, William Warner Ch. Warden.
  R. Phelps fecit 1731.
3 ✠ 67 ⁑ ancta ☐ 𝔐aria ☐ ☉ra ☐ ℣ro ☐ 𝔑obis.
4 T. Osborn Downham fecit 1790.
  Saml. Frewer Church Warden.
5 Pack & Chapman London fecit 1774.
  John Pritty Ch. Warden.

4 in 1553.
"Five," Davy, 23 July, 1808.
Terrier, 1753, gives 5 bells.
In 1839, Davy says, "The steeple now contains 4 bells." This is incomprehensible.

40. BEDINGFIELD *S. Mary*.   1 Bell.
Bell. ▽ 52 thrice.
✠ 61 ℭucfumus 𝔄ndrea ☐ 62 𝔉amulorum 𝔖ufcipe 𝔙ota.

No return of bells in certif. of 1547. 3 in 1553.
Martin notes 3, 21 Nov., 1734. Faculty for sale of one of three, 1760.
Terrier, 23 June, 1794, gives 2.

41. BELSTEAD *S. Mary*.   1 Bell.
Bell. John Darbie made me 1664.

"Belstead pva. gregory Crevn^r (?) & Roberte lynde chvrchwardēs one bell solde ffor xxx*s*. which was broke v yers past which is & shalbe Inployed to the reperacn of chvrch roffe & the palyng of the chvrchyerd." Certif. of 1547.
1 in 1553 and Sanctus bell.
Davy by mistake notes "Gardiner" for "Darbie."

42. BELTON *All Saints*.   1 Bell.
Bell. John Darbie made me 1664.

"Great bells iij." Return of 1553.
Faculty granted in 1690 to sell the smaller bell in order to hang the other. Weight 6 cwt. 2 qrs. Weighed at Yarmouth Crane, at the time of rebuilding the tower, by direction of the Rev^d. T. G. F. Howes, Rector.

43 BENACRE S. *Michael*.   1 Bell.
Bell. G. G. W. F. 𝕮𝖍𝖚𝖗𝖈𝖍𝖜𝖆𝖗𝖉𝖊𝖓𝖘 𝕬𝖓𝖓𝖔 𝕯𝖔𝖒𝖎𝖓𝖎 1622.
4 in 1553.
Davy gives this inscription imperfectly, 17 June, 1817.

44. BENHALL S. *Mary*.   6 Bells.
1 T. Mears London. 1842.
2, 3 John Brend made me 1639.
4 James Grimsbye John Bvlling Churchwardens 1639 J. B.
5 ▽ 50 thrice.
 + 6 1 𝖂𝖆𝖈 𝕴𝖓 𝕮𝖔𝖓𝖈𝖑𝖆𝖇𝖊 ☐ 6 2 𝕲𝖆𝖇𝖗𝖎𝖊𝖑 𝕹𝖚𝖓𝖈 𝕻𝖆𝖓𝖌𝖊 𝕾𝖚𝖆𝖛𝖊.
6 Richard Brown John Baldry C. W. 1723.
No return of bells in certif. of 3 Nov., 1547. "Great bells iij." Return of 1553.
Tenor by Gardiner, diameter 36¼ in., weight 7 cwt. Davy gives the five without the treble as here, with "Thomas" for "James," as Grimsbye's christian name.

45. BENTLEY S. *Mary*.   1 Bell.
Bell. Charles Newman made me 1696.
2 in 1553. "One bell," Davy.

46. BERGHOLT, EAST, S. *Mary*.   5 and Priest's bell.
1 Cast by John Warner & Son, London, 1887. Jubilee bell. Hung by G. Day and Son, Eye.
2 ▽ 26 + 22 ▽ 25 𝖂𝖊𝖈𝖈𝖊 𝕲𝖆𝖇𝖗𝖎𝖊𝖑𝖎𝖘 𝕾𝖔𝖓𝖆𝖙 𝖂𝖊𝖈 𝕮𝖆𝖒𝖕𝖆𝖓𝖆
   𝕱𝖎𝖉𝖊𝖑𝖎𝖘.
3 : SVM : ROSA : PVLSATA : MONDI : MARIA
    VOCATA.
    RICARDVS BOWLER : ME : FECIT 1601.
    ISAAC MECHCHEL
    JOHN BRETON CHVRCHWARDENS.
4 Christopher . Hodson . made . me . 1688 . .
   John . Leach . John . Peake . Chvrch . Wardens . . . .
5 John Stephens fecit 1727. Walter Gvllifer, Thomas
      Broven Churchwardens (sic).
Priest's bell. Richardvs Bowler fecit 1591.
No return of bells in certif. of 1547.
5 and Sance bell in 1553.
The treble, which weighed 8 cwt., now weighs 4 cwt.
On the 4th dots denote coins, obv. and rev. of crown of Charles II., &c.
Cut in each side of the pit for the Tenor in the frame "1691. IT IE."
The old treble bore Ricardvs Bowler me fecit 1601 . . . (three impressions of coins, indistinct).
Davy's account mainly agrees with this.
This extract has been kindly copied from the Parish Book by Archdeacon Woolley:—A note what the great bell wayed when it went to Berre, and what it now wayeth this 24th of December, 1621.
It wayed, before it went to Berre, in the Churchyard, 26 hundred and 56 lbs.; it was broken in pieces and wayed agayne at Berre, and found 27 hundred and 24.
It weyeth now at home, 25 c. and 32 lb. at one end of the beame, and at the other end 26 c. and 09; the odes being 89 lb., which being divided, is 44 lb. and half.

The bell now wayeth five and twenty hundred seventy-five pound and half. The bellfounders ware to be allowed for wag £40, and to account the bell at 26 c. and 96 lb.

And it now wayeth 25 c. and 76 and half. So they have in mettell, which they must allow, one hundred twenty five poundes, at eight pence the lb., which makes in money, four pounds, a dozen shillings, eight pence. They are to have for setting the bell, taking it at Barfould (*i.e*, Bergholt) and delivering it there agayne, building a —— and so to kep hur one hole year, nine pounds ten shillings.

Remayne to them four pounds eighteen shillings and fourpence, which is paid to Andrew Gerne, of Berre Seynt Edmundes, by the appoyntment of the Mʳ. Workman, John Draper, of Thetford, Charles Bromey, with others.

47. BEYTON *All Saints.*   1 Bell.
    Bell. John Draper made me 1627.

" Payton, Great bells iij." Return of 1553.
" One," Davy.
T. Martin (c. 1719) notes four bells.

48. BILDESTON *S. Mary.*   6 Bells.
    1 I ▽ 19 D + 22 𝔖𝔞𝔫𝔠𝔱𝔢 𝔗𝔬𝔪𝔞 𝔒𝔯𝔞 𝔓𝔯𝔬 𝔑𝔬𝔟𝔦𝔰.
    2 No inscription.
    3 Miles Graye made me 1683.
    4 ▽ 50 thrice.
    + 61 𝔖𝔲𝔟𝔟𝔢𝔫𝔦𝔞𝔱 𝔇𝔦𝔤𝔫𝔞 ☐ 62 𝔇𝔬𝔫𝔞𝔫𝔱𝔦𝔟𝔲𝔰 𝔓𝔞𝔫𝔢 𝔎𝔞𝔱𝔢𝔯𝔦𝔫𝔞.
    5 Thomas Farrow Joseph Prockter Churchwardens 1704.
    6 Thomas Gardiner Sudbury fecit 1718.

" Bylston, Great bells iiij." Return of 1553.
" Six," Davy, 24 Oct., 1826.

49. BLAKENHAM, GREAT, *S. Mary.*   2 Bells.
    1 ▽ 51 thrice.
    + 61 ℭ𝔢𝔩𝔢𝔰𝔱𝔦 𝔐𝔞𝔫𝔫𝔞 ☐ 62 𝔗𝔲𝔞 𝔓𝔯𝔬𝔩𝔢𝔰 𝔉𝔩𝔬𝔰 ℭ𝔦𝔟𝔢𝔱 𝔄𝔫𝔫𝔞.
    2 ▽ 51 thrice.
    + 61 𝔖𝔲𝔟𝔢𝔫𝔦𝔞𝔱 𝔇𝔦𝔤𝔫𝔞 ☐ 62 𝔇𝔬𝔫𝔞𝔫𝔱𝔦𝔟𝔲𝔰 𝔓𝔞𝔫𝔢 𝔎𝔞𝔱𝔢𝔯𝔦𝔫𝔞.

3 in 1553.
" Two," Davy, 11 May, 1824.

50. BLAKENHAM, LITTLE, *S. Mary.*   2 Bells.
    1, 2 John Darbie made me 1660.

3 in 1553.
Davy, 18 May, 1829, " Two which I did not examine."

51. BLAXHALL *S. Peter.*   5 Bells.
    1, 2, 3 John Brend made me 1655.
    4 Recast by John Warner & Sons, London, 1881. (Royal Arms) Patent.
    A. N. Bates, M.A. Rector.
    James Toller   } Churchwardens.
    George Rope }
    5 Omnis Sonvs Lavdet Dominvm 1655.

No return of bells in certif. of 1547. " Great bells iiij," 1553.
The old fourth like the first three, Davy.

52. BLUNDESTON *S. Mary.*   2 Bells.
    1 T. B. 1661.
    2 E. T. 1675.

No return of bells in certif. of 1547. "Blomston, Great bells iij." Return of 1553.
In Davy's time there were three, one not hung.

53. BLYTHBURGH *Holy Trinity*. 1 Bell.
Bell. James Edbere ☐ 82 1608 (arabesque).
I..
J.M.

No return of bells in certif. of iiij Nov., 1547. Legacies—Joh. Greyfe, 1442, towards covering the bell-tower, and Hen. Tool, 1470, 20 marks for a great bell. 5 in 1553. "Formerly 5." Davy, 12 Aug., 1806, "In the belfry below, however, stands another small one, on which is SCE PETRE SALVA ME."

54. BLYTHFORD *All Saints*. 1 Bell.
Bell. Thomas Newman made me 1711.

3 in 1553, doubly returned.
Davy notes one, but refers to Martin, who gives three.

55. BOTESDALE. 1 Bell.
Bell. John Draper made me 16 . .

A Chantry, with an inscription :—
"Orate p. aiabs Johis Shribe et —— uxoris eius."
No return in 1553.

56. BOULGE *S. Michael*. 1 Bell.
Bell. No inscription.

"Bowge, Great bells iij." Return of 1553.
No return of bells in certif. of iiij Nov., 1547.
"The steeple is a small and low square tower of red brick, ... and contains one bell, which has no inscription on it. The clerk informed me that there were some years ago 3 bells, but that 2 were sold for repairs." Davy, 27 May, 1823.

57. BOXFORD *S. Mary*. Tenor Diam. 52 in. 8 Bells.
1 Tho : . s Gardiner Svdbvry me fecit 1714.
2 Sancte Necolae Ora pro Nobis ▽ 26 + 22 ▽ 25.
3 Tho. Gardiner Sudbury fecit 1754.
4 Charles Newman made me 1688.
5 T. Osborn fecit 1790. Isaac Strutt, Hugh Green C[h]. Wardens.
6 [A border].
+ 49 SVM KATERINA ☐ 48 SEMPER ☐ 46 VIRGO ☐ 48 DEO DIGNA.
7 ▽ 31 ☐ 38 + 41 Intonat & Celis Vot Campane Gabirelis (sic).
8 Hæc Campana Beatæ Trinitatis Sacra Fiat. John Thornton Sudbury fecit 1718.

"Great bells v, Sancts bells j." Return of 1553. Cannons of 7 gone. Davy, Oct. 2 and 3, 1828. Noted imperfectly, but in accordance with this.

58. BOXTEAD *All Saints*. 2 Bells.
1 No inscription.
2 T. Newman made me. A. Golding & S. Spalding C.W. 1738.

"Great bells iiij." Return of 1553.
Davy, 18 Aug., 1831, "Two bells."

INSCRIPTIONS.   167

59. BOYTON *S. Andrew.*   1 Bell.
Bell.   John Darbie made me 1679.
"Great bells iij." Return of 1553.
Davy (22 Jan., 1818), mistakes the date for 1692.

60. BRADFIELD [Combust] *All Saints.*   3 Bells.
  1 Mears & Stainbank Founders London.
     Bartholomew Young Church Warden 1693.
  2 Recast 1869, Arthur Young Warden.
     □ 34 □ 33 □ 35 □ 32.
     + 15 𝕾𝖆𝖓𝖈𝖙𝖆 𝕸𝖆𝖗𝖎𝖆 𝕸𝖆𝖌𝖉𝖆𝖑𝖊𝖓𝖆 𝕺𝖗𝖆 𝕻𝖗𝖔 𝕹𝖔𝖇𝖎𝖘.
  3 □ 81 Thomas □ 82 Cheese made me 1630.
"Great bells iij." Return of 1553. Notes F$\sharp$, E, D$\sharp$.
"The steeple is down, but in the roof at the west end of the Isle are hung 3 bells, but I could not get to them." Davy. Diameter of Tenor 25½ in.

61. BRADFIELD *S. Clare.*   Tenor. Diam. 37½ in.   3 Bells.
  1 ▽ 66 thrice.
     + 𝕾𝖆𝖓𝖈𝖙𝖆 □ 68 𝕸𝖆𝖗𝖎𝖆 □ 68 𝕺𝖗𝖆 □ 68 𝕻𝖗𝖔 □ 68 𝕹𝖔𝖇𝖎𝖘.
  2 Richard Ottewell Ch. Warden. W. & T. Mears, late Lester, Pack, & Chapman of London fecit 1787.
  3 Charles Newman made mee 1699.
"Great bells iij." Return of 1553.
"2 bells," Davy. Notes C$\sharp$, A$\sharp$, G$\sharp$.

62. BRADFIELD *S. George.* Tenor. Diam. 37½ in.   5 Bells.
  1 H. P. made me 1695.
  2 ♛ R O G ♛ 1668.
  3 Robard ♛ Gvrney made ♛ me 1668.
  4 Uriah Woodard & W^m. Smith Ch. Wardens. Lester & Pack of London fecit 1764.
  5 R. A. Wardens. Henry Pleasant made me 1695.
"Great bells iij." Return of 1553.
So Davy, only mistaking "Robard" on 3 for "Richard." He notes 60 steps in the tower staircase. 1 cracked, notes of the others C$\sharp$, B, A$\sharp$, G$\sharp$.

63. BRADLEY, GREAT, *S. Mary.*   3 Bells.
  1 No inscription.
  2 □ 81 De □ 82 Bvri □ 82 Santi □ 82 Edmondi □ 82 Stefanvs □ 88 Tonni □ 82 me fecit □ 82 W. L. □ 81 1576.
  3 □ 𝕽𝕴𝕮𝕬𝕽𝕯 : 𝕯𝕰 𝖁𝖁𝖄𝕸𝕭𝕴𝕾 : 𝕸𝕰 : 𝕱𝕰𝕮𝕴𝕿.
See p. 10.
The treble probably a very old bell. C. Deedes.
"Great bells iij." Return of 1553.
No notes, Davy.

64. BRADLEY, LITTLE, *All Saints.*   1 Bell.
Bell.   ♛ R. G. ♛ 1652.
"Great bells iij." Return of 1553.
No notes, Davy.

65. BRADWELL *S. Nicholas.*   3 Bells.
  1 ▽ 50 thrice.
     + 61 𝕸𝖆𝖊 𝕴𝖓 𝕮𝖔𝖓𝖈𝖑𝖆𝖇𝖊 □ 62 𝕲𝖆𝖇𝖗𝖎𝖊𝖑 𝕹𝖚𝖈 ɫ 𝖆𝖌𝖊 𝕾𝖚𝖆𝖇·.

168   THE CHURCH BELLS OF SUFFOLK.

 2 ▽ 50 thrice.
 ✛ 47 𝔓𝔢𝔱𝔯𝔲𝔰 𝔄𝔡 𝔈𝔱𝔢𝔯𝔫𝔢 ☐ 62 𝔇𝔲𝔠𝔞𝔱 𝔑𝔬𝔰 𝔓𝔞𝔰𝔠𝔲𝔞 𝔙𝔦𝔱𝔢.
 3 ▽ 50 thrice.
 ✛ 𝔟𝔦𝔩𝔦 ☐ 48 𝔦𝔨𝔩𝔪 𝔦𝔨𝔩𝔪 𝔯𝔰𝔱𝔦 no mbt.
"Great bells iiij." Return of 1553.
1 and 2 maiden, 3 a little flattened.

66. BRAISEWORTH S. Mary.   1 Bell.
Bell. Cast by John Warner & Sons, London, 1879.
1606, recast 1879.
R. M. Bingley, Rector.
W. Allen.   }
C. Schofield } Churchwardens.
Hung by G. Day & Son, Eye.

1 in 1553.
Davy, 22 April, 1819, "John Draper made me 1606."

67. BRAMFIELD S. Andrew. Tenor F♯.   5 Bells.
 1, 2 AB ▽ 52 ▽ 86.
 W
 𝔄nno 𝔇omini 1621.
 3 𝔖𝔞𝔫𝔠𝔱𝔞 𝔐𝔞𝔯𝔤𝔞𝔯𝔢𝔱𝔞 𝔒𝔯𝔞 𝔓𝔯𝔬 𝔑𝔬𝔟𝔦𝔰 ▽ 25 ✛ 22 ▽ 26.
 4 𝔖𝔦𝔱 𝔑𝔬𝔪𝔢𝔫 𝔇𝔬𝔪𝔦𝔫𝔦 𝔅𝔢𝔫𝔢𝔡𝔦𝔠𝔱𝔲𝔪 ▽ 25 ✛ 22 ▽ 26.
   ✿ ✿ ✿ ✿ ✿
 5 𝔉𝔫𝔱𝔬𝔫𝔞𝔱 𝔈𝔠𝔠𝔩𝔦𝔰 𝔚𝔬𝔯 𝔠𝔞𝔪𝔭𝔞𝔫𝔞 𝔐𝔦𝔠𝔥𝔞𝔢𝔩𝔦𝔰.
 ▽ 25 ✛ 22 ▽ 26.

So Davy, 23 May, 1806, with one or two involuntary variations. No return of bells in cert. of iiij Nov., 1547. 4 in 1553. The first five of a six. Bells re-opened after hanging, April 17th, 1890.

68. BRAMFORD S. Stephen. Tenor G. Diam. 41 in. 6 Bells.
 1 Thomas Mears & Son of London fecit 1805.
 2, 3, 4, 5, 6 Miles Graye made me 1632.
"Great bells iiij." Return of 1553.
Davy, 10 June, 1828, calls the treble the 2nd, and dates the 5th 1636.

69. BRAMPTON S. Peter. Tenor B♭. Bells in tune. 5 Bells.
 1 John Darbie made me 1668.
 2 Anno Domini 1612. W. B.
 3, 4 ▽ 86 AB ▽ 52.
 W
 anno d͞n͞i 1612.
 5 ▽ 51 thrice.
 ✛ 61 𝔑𝔬𝔟𝔦𝔰 𝔖𝔬𝔩𝔞𝔪𝔢𝔫 𝔒𝔢𝔩𝔬𝔯𝔲𝔪 ☐ 62 𝔇𝔢𝔱 𝔇𝔢𝔲𝔰 𝔄𝔪𝔢𝔫.
4 in 1553.
So Davy, 2 June, 1808.

70. BRANDESTON All Saints.   6 Bells.
 1, 4 Recast at the expense of the parish.
    Lester and Pack of London fecit 1768.
 2 The gift of H. Stebbing, Esqre, Mrs. A. Rivett, Widow,
    and other benefactors, obtained by John Revett
    Gent. 1709.
    R. Phelps made me.

3 Miles Graye made me 1637.
5 Recast at the expense of John Revett,
Lester and Pack of London fecit 1768.
6 This bell was recast at the expense of John Revett 1768.
R. P. F. E.
(two impressions of the arms of Revett.)

No return of bells in certif. of iij Nov., 1547. "Great bells iiij." Return of 1553. AB
Hawes notes 1 as 2 here. 2 W Anno Dom. 1600. 3 In ﬀultis Annis, &c. 4 Sancta Bartholma (sic) ora pro nobis, and dates the tenor 1710. He speaks also of a purchase of bells from Little Ashfield. On woodwork of 4, "T. D. Tho⁵. Packard made me 1670," as at Raveningham, *teste* G. Day.

71. BRANDON SS. *Peter and Paul.* Tenor in A, 16 cwt.
6 Bells.
1 John Warner & Sons, London, 1870.
2 These five bells were cast by William Dobson 1815.
3 Prosperity to the town of Brandon 1815.
4 Give no offence to the Church. W^m. Dobson fecit 1815.
5 William Dobson Downham Norfolk founder 1815.
6 Rev^d. W^m. Parson Rector, Thos. Willett and Robt. Smith Churchwardens 1815.

"Great bells iiij." Return of 1553.
1 recast from the old 2nd at Wangford, q.v.
Five noted by Davy, 22 Aug., 1829.
These were cast out of an old three inscribed—
1 + Hae In Conclave Gabriel Nunc Pange Suabe.
2 + Sum Rosa Pulsata Mundi Maria Vocata.
3 + In Honore [Sancti Marie et Sancti Katerine Virginis (sic)]   Ex infor. J. H. Sperling.

72. BRANTHAM *S. Michael.*   1 Bell.
Bell. Miles Graye made me 1651.
So Davy. 1 in 1553.

73. BREDFIELD *S. Andrew.*   4 Bells.
1 Richard Phelps made me 1735.
2   F C.
W. M. G. F. D. P. I. H. 1622.
3 Thomas Gardiner made me 1715.
4 ▽ 51 thrice.
+ 61 Petrus Ad Eterne ☐ 62 Ducat ﬂos Pascua Vite.

No return of bells in certif. of iij Nov., 1547. "Great bells iij." Return of 1553. Davy notes 4. "W. M. L. F. L. F. I. H. 1592."

74. BRETTENHAM *S. Mary.* Diameter of Tenor 27 in.
3 Bells.
1 H. Pleasant made me Reginald Sayer Warden.
2 Thomas Cheese James Edbere me fecit 1623.
3 ☐ 82 Prais ☐ 82 God ☐ 82 1574 ☐ 82 W. L.

"Brentham, Great bells iij." Return of 1553. T. Martin, 31 May, 1737, 3 bells.

75. BRICETT, GREAT, *S. Mary and S. Laurence.*   2 Bells.
1 Georgius Williams, Coll. Regal. Soc.
Jesuit Anno MDCCCXXXIX.
2 In honore Sanctæ Trinitatis. Anno MDCCCXXXIX.

Very small. 3 in 1553. Davy, Oct. 23rd, 1826, visited this place. He notes, March 28th, 1843, on the authority of Rev. C. P. Parker of Kingshall, "One bell Ex Honore Sancte Trinitatis." Martin had noted Trinitate. It weighed 10 cwt. according to Terrier, 1834.

76. BRICETT, LITTLE.
Ecclesia destructa. No return in 1553.

77. BRIGHTWELL *S. John Baptist.*   1 Bell.
Bell. For Brighwell (sic) in Suffolcke Feb 5. 1657.

"Great bells ij." Return of 1553. T. Martin, Sept., 1725, One in a little tower.

78. BROCKFORD.
Ecclesia destructa. No return in 1553.

79. BROCKLEY *S. Andrew.*   3 Bells.
1 ☐ 21 ▽ 20 ✛ **Vox Augustini Sonet In Aure Dei.**
2 ☐ 21 ▽ 19 ✛ 22 **Cristus Perpetue Det Nobis Gaudia Vite.**
3 ☐ 21 ▽ 20 ✛ **Sit Nomen Domini Benedictum.**

"Great bells j." Return of 1553. See p. 94. No notes by Davy.

80. BROME *S. Mary.* In B♭, not in tune.   5 Bells.
1, 2, 3, 4 Thomas Newman of Norwich made me 1737.
5 Thomas Newman fecit. S. Newstead, P. Rodwell C. W. 1737.

So Davy, 17 June, 1809. 3 in 1553.

81. BROMESWELL *S. Edmund.* Notes D♭ and B.   2 Bells.
1 Jhesus ben ic gheyoten van Cornelis Waghevens int iaer ons Heeren MCCCCXXX.
o o o o
2 ☐ IR : HONORE : SANCTE : PAVLI.

No return of bells in certif. of iij Nov., 1547. "Great bells iij." Re. of 1553. 1 Clear but not melodious, unchipped. 2 Slightly flattened. P. 75. According to Davy (12 Sept., 1807,) there was another, inscribed "Miles Graye made me 1618." The other inscriptions agree with these. The missing bell was the smallest of the three. It fell, was broken, and sold.

82. BRUISYARD *S. Peter.*   1 Bell.
Bell. Cast by John Warner & Son, London, 1867. (Royal Arms) Patent.

No return of bells in cert. of iij. Nov., 1547. "Great bells iij." Return of 1553.
Davy notes 3, 1 R. Phelps made me. Richard Brown, gent., Church-warden, 1732. 2 **Anno Dni** 1610. 3 **Pac En Conclabe**, &c.

83. BRUNDISH *S. Laurence.*   AB   3 Bells.
1 ANNO DOMINI 1606. T G. W T.B.

2 ☉ 52 thrice.
✠ 6: **Dulcis Cisto Melis** ▢ 6: **Campana Voor Michia.**
3 ☉ 50 thrice.
✠ 6: **Surfumus Rubora** ▢ 6: **Famulorum Sulcipe Vota**

T G probably = Thomas Glemham. Pays for 3. 4 in 1553. Terrier, 1 June, 1791, and Davy, 16 June, 1809, give 5 bells.

84. BUCKLESHAM *S. Mary.*   1 Bell.
Bell. Miles Graye made me 1623.
"Great bells iiij." Return of 1553. Davy, 23 Feb., 1825, reports it inaccessible.
Terrier, 3 May, 1845 "One bell in weight about 500 pounds." Diameter 30 in.

85. BUNGAY *S. Mary.*   8 Bells.
1, 2, 3, 4, 5, 6 T. Mears of London fecit 1820.
7, 8 T. Mears of London fecit 1820. Richard Mann, John Reynolds Churchwardens. Chas. Brightly, Richd. Smith, Robt. Butcher, Robert Camell, M. R. Kingsbury, Thomas Hunt, Jas. Sheppard.

No return of bells in certif. of iiij Nov., 1547. "Great bells v. Sancts Bells j." Return of 1553.
No notes by Davy. From a MS. of W. Adams, and notes of Rev. T. Bewicke, I am able to compare the past and present peals.

	Past cwt.	qrs.	lbs.	Present cwt.	qrs.	lbs.	
1718, probably by	1 4	3	18 5	2	5	One, probably 3, was
Stophens	2 5	0	19 5	2	22	an AVE bell. Most of
Long cracked	3 6	0	18 6	2	14	these others seem to have
Bad, long cracked	4 7	0	17 6	3	21	been by Gilpin, 1700. 5
Inscribed—							was brought from S. Peter
Ros Cœum, &c.	5 7	2	24 8	2	21	Mancroft, Norwich. The
Good, cast 1761	6 10	0	11 10	0	21	six were first rung in 1702.
Fine bell	7 13	2	1 10	3	21	See pp. 56, 130.
,, in E. Split 1817	8 18	1	19 16	1	4	
Total	73	0	15 70	3	17	

86. BUNGAY *Holy Trinity.*   1 Bell.
☉ 51 thrice.
✠ 6: **Sec Margareta** ▢ 6: **Nobis Per Munera Leta.**

So Davy, May 14th, 1825.
No return in 1553, the church having been partially burnt not long before. A fine bell cast in 1566, apparently by John Brend, sen., was sold by the parish in 1755 for £82 7s. 6d. The present bell was bought second-hand in 1759. The detail in 1566 contains "Itm gyvin to his (J. B.'s) wife in Rewarde xijd. Itm gyven then to his manservant and unto his mayde in reward vijd," a remnant of guild-privilege.

87. BURES *S. Mary.* Tenor. Diameter 50 in.   6 Bells.
1 T. Mears of London fecit.
2, 3 R. Phelps fecit 1734.
4 John Brend made me 1658.
5 Thomas Mears Founder London 1840.
Revd. Arthur Hanbury Vicar.

Grimmand Wood   John Garrand   } Church-
                John Boggis   } wardens.

6 T. Mears of London fecit 1826.
John Garrard } Churchwardens.
John Boggis }

Davy, Oct. 2, 1828, 3 not noted. 5 "The Rev^d. Philip Gurdon, M.A., Vicar, W^m. Ambrose, John Harvey Church Wardens. Richard Phelps made me 1734."
"Great Bells v. Sancts Bells j." Return of 1553.

88. BURGATE *S. Mary*. 5 Bells.
1 Thos. Gardiner Norwich fecit 1746.
2 1746.
3 Thomas Sturt John Draper made me 1624.
4 Pack & Chapman of London fecit 1772.
5 Thomas Gardiner Sudbury fecit 1732.

5 in 1553. Martin and Davy note five.

89. BURGH *S. Botolph*. Tenor. Diameter 36½ in. 5 Bells.
1 Chapman & Mears of London fecerunt 1782.
2 John Stephens fecit 1718.
3 John Stephens made me 1718.
4 John Stephens Bell Founder of Norwich made us 5. 1718.
5 John Stephens fecit. 1718.
John Votier Rector John Page Churchwarden.

"Great bells iiij." Return of 1553.

90. BURGH CASTLE *S. Peter*. 3 Bells.
1 Thomas Newman cast me new
In 1732.
John Pitcearn Rector.
2 Thomas Killett, Churchwarden, George Harris Over Seer. 1732.
3 John Darbie made me 1663.

"Great bells iij." Return of 1553.

91. BURSTALL *S. Mary*. 3 Bells.
1, 2, 3 John Thornton Sudbury fecit 1718.

3 in 1553. Three bells, Davy.

91a. BURY S. EDMUND'S, *The Abbey*.
The Great Bell Tower at the Abbey.

"The plan of the new building" (of the latter part of the eleventh century), says Mr. John Gage, in *Archæologia*, xxiii., "bore a near resemblance to Ely Minster, and both had, at the west end, a high tower between lower lateral towers." It was not till the time of Samson of Tottington, tenth Abbot, elected in 1180, that the work was finished. Jocelin of Brakelond, in his well-known Chronicle, records the collection of stones and gravel (*sabulum*), made for the purpose by Samson, while he was subsacrist, and the alleged pecuniary assistance afforded by certain burgesses. The passage is well worth reading. In *Notes and Queries*, Sixth Series, i. 303, it is recorded from the Register of Abbot Curteys, that one of the towers fell in 1210, and another, probably the bell-tower, in 1430, "tum propter quercuum magnas et horas (sic) missas in opus lapideum, et conjunctas operi ligneo in quo pendebant campanæ, tum propter inordinatam et immoderatam earundem pulsationem," fortunately after the people had left the church.

The ruin seems not to have been total, for the lead, bells, and some part of the walls were subsequently taken down. Next year the east side of the tower gave way, and was followed by the north wall in 1432.

The mason's contract for reconstruction is given at length by Mr. Gage, together with a list of legacies towards the work, one as late as 1500.

Writing in 1830, he says, "The flinty fragments of a south pier of the tower have escaped the hand of destruction, and together with the flint work of the western façade, which is a mass of deformity, point out to us the spot where the Bell Tower once stood."

Professor Thorold Rogers's note on the weights of the bells in "Bury Hospital" (*N. and Q*, Sixth Series, i. 193), is exceedingly perplexing.

92. BURY S. EDMUND'S *S. James.*   10 Bells.

1, 2, 3, 4, 5 T. Osborn Fecit 1785.
6, 8 T. Osborn, Downham, Fecit 1785.
7 Cum Voco Venite T. Osborn Fecit 1785.
9 Our voices shall in concert ring
   In honour both to God and King
   T. Osborn Fecit 1785.
10 Percute Dulce Cano Bury St Edm^d.
   St James' Parish. Zephaniah Ostler,
   Robt. Carss Church Wardens. T. Osborn Fecit. 1785.

"Great bells v." 1553. Formerly 3 in N. aisle. 1, De Bvri Santi Edmondi Stefanvs Tonni me fecit 1580. Deo Patrie et Proximo; 2, R. G. 1664; 3 Sit Nomen Domini Benedictum ▽ 20 □ 21 +.

93. BURY S. EDMUND'S *S. John Evangelist.*   1 Bell.

Bell. Thomas Mears, Founder, London, 1841.

94. BURY S. EDMUND'S *S. Mary.*   8 Bells.

1, 2, 6 R. Phelps Londini Fecit 1734.
3 T. Osborn Fecit 1785.
4 Anno Domini 1627 AB
                    W
5 R. Phelps Londini Me Fecit 1734.
7 Matthias Wright and Simon Buchanan, Church Wardens
   1776. Pack & Chapman of London Fecit.
8 Mr. Richard Rayment & Mr. Robert Singleton Church
   Wardens. Anno Domini 1734. Richard Phelps
   of London Bellfounder made these eight bells.

"Great bells vj." Ret. 1553. Tenor recast at Bury, 1696, L'E., p. 66.

95. BURY S. EDMUND'S *S. Peter.*   1 Bell.

Bell. T. Mears, Founder, London, 1858.

96. BUTLEY *S. John Baptist.*   1 Bell.

Bell. Eternis Annis Refonet Campana Johannis ▽ 9 coin.

So Davy. No return of bells in certif. of iij Nov., 1547. "Great bells iij." Ret. of 1553. Hawes notes one smaller, inscribed Sancte Petre ora pro nobis.

174 THE CHURCH BELLS OF SUFFOLK.

97. BUXHALL *S. Mary.* 5 Bells.
   1, 2 John Draper made me 1632.
   R. M. & T. N. Wardens.
   3 John Draper made me 1635.
   4 John Griggs C. W. Charles Newman made mee 1698.
   5 Gregory Copinger, Tho. Fuller C. W.
   Tho. Gardiner Sudbury fecit 1739.
   4 in 1553. Davy (June 13th, 1827), notes 5 bells, but the door locked.

98. BUXLOW *S. Peter.*
Ecclesia destructa. 2 in 1553.

99. CAMPSEY ASH *S. John Baptist.* 4 Bells.
   1 I. B. Anno Domini 1615.
   2 Tho. Gardiner fecit me 1714.
   3 Thomas Gardiner Sudbury fecit 1729.
   4 Ricardus Bowler me fecit 1601
   No mention of bells in certif. of iij Nov., 1547. "Great bells iiij." Return of 1553.
   So Davy, 20 April, 1819. Hawes notes the old 2nd, 𝔇ulcis 𝔇isto ꜰetelis 𝔇ampana 𝔇oror 𝔇ichaelis, and the 3rd, R. G. Anno Domini 1583. Martin also notes 𝔇ulcis, &c.

100. CAPEL *S. Andrew.*
Ecclesia destructa. No return in 1553.

101. CAPEL *S. Mary.* 5 Bells.
   1, 2 T. Mears of London fecit 1829.
   Rev^d. Joseph Tweed Rector.
   Cooper Brooke Esqr., Churchwarden.
   3 John Darbie made me 1683. W. O. I. T.
   4 Miles Graye made me 1624.
   5 OF YOVR CHERITE PRAY FOR THE WELFARE OF GREGORY PASCAL.
   5 and Sance bell in 1553. See p. 77.
   Davy was quite beaten by the tenor, which he gives:—DAIW SIN SONGA CNA LAOSNP NONI FO DRAFIEW ROA YARP. He leaves 4 blank, notes 4 as 3, 3 as 2, and gives 1, 𝔇irgomaria ora pria pronobis. Possibly the inscription was one known in the West of England + Entercede 𝔇ia 𝔇ro 𝔇obis 𝔇irgo 𝔇aria.

102. CARLTON *S. Peter.* Tenor. Diam. 31½ in. 4 Bells.
   1, 2, 3, 4 ☐ 81 Thomas ☐ 82 Andrew ☐ 82 me ☐ 82 fecit ☐ 82 1598.
   2 has no fleur-de lis between "me" and fecit.
   Davy, 29 May, 1806, gives 1528, not recognizing the peculiar form of the 9. 3 in 1553.

103. CARLTON COLVILLE *S. Peter.* Tenor. Diam. 45¾ in.
   5 Bells.
   1 Anno Domini 1608. W. B.
   2 John Brend made me 1637.
   3 Anno Domini 1634.
   ▽ 50.

4 Anno Domini 1634.
5 ☐ Omnis Sonvs lavdet Dominom.
Anno Domini 1634.
▽ 50.
No return of bells in certif. of iiij Nov., 1547. "Great bells iiij. Sancts bells j." Return of 1553.
So Davy, save that he gives 1634 as the date of the second.

104. CAVENDISH *S. Mary.* Tenor 12 cwt. 6 Bells.
1 I mean to make it understood
Although I'm little yet I'm good.
Mears London fecit 1779.
2 If you have a judicious ear
You'l own my voice is sweet & clear.
Mears London fecit 1779.
3 Music is medicine to the mind.
Mears London fecit 1779.
4 Peace & good neighbourhood.
Mears and London fecit 1779.
5 Our voices shall in consort ring
In honour both to God & King.
Mears London fecit 1779.
6 Cast by John Warner & Sons, London, 1869.
Royal Arms Patent.
"Great bells v." Return of 1553.
Davy, Nov. 9th, 1805, 6. "T. Osborn Downham Norfolk fecit 1786." al. sim.

105. CAVENHAM *S. Andrew.* 3 Bells.
1 William Dobson founder Downham Norfolk 1831.
2, 3 John Darbie made me 1676.
"Great bells iij." Return of 1553.
T. Martin (12 Nov., 1755), and Davy (20 Aug., 1829), note 3 bells.

106. CHARSFIELD *S. Peter.* 5 Bells.
1 Sic Sacheverellvs [ore melos] immortali olli [ecclesiæ defensori h] anc dicat [Gvlielmvs] Leman de Cher [sfield Eques 1710. R. Phelps].
2 ▽ 50 thrice.
+ 61 𝔚𝔢𝔢 𝔉𝔦𝔱 𝔖𝔠𝔬𝔯𝔲𝔪 ☐ 62 𝔠𝔞𝔪𝔭̄𝔞 𝔏𝔞𝔲𝔡𝔢 𝔅𝔬𝔫𝔬𝔯𝔲𝔪.
3 ☐ 81 James Edbere (arabesque) ☐ 82 1068 (for 1608).
4 ▽ 50 thrice.
+ 61 𝔇𝔲𝔩𝔠𝔦𝔰 𝔖𝔦𝔰𝔱𝔬 𝔐𝔢𝔩𝔦𝔰 ☐ 62 𝔠𝔞𝔪𝔭̄𝔞 𝔙𝔬𝔠𝔬𝔯 𝔐𝔦𝔠𝔥𝔞𝔢𝔩𝔦𝔰.
5 ▽ 65 thrice.
+ 𝔖𝔞𝔫𝔠𝔱𝔞 ☐ 𝔐𝔞𝔯𝔦𝔞 ☐ 𝔒𝔯𝔞 ☐ 𝔓𝔯𝔬 ☐ 𝔑𝔬𝔟𝔦𝔰.
No return of bells in certif. of iij Nov., 1547. "Great bells iiij." Return of 1553.
The inscription on the treble restored from Carthew's MSS., who notes the rest like these, and refers to a legacy (1454) for the tower.
The Sacheverell inscription was evidently intended as a protest against the prominent part taken by Bp. Trimnell in the House of Lords, 1710.

107. CHATTISHAM *S. Mary and All Saints.* 1 Bell.
Bell. Miles Graye made me 1621.
No return of bells in certif. of 1547. 3 in 1553. "Three bells," Davy.

176   THE CHURCH BELLS OF SUFFOLK.

108. CHEDBURGH *All Saints.*   1 Bell.
  Bell. T. Osborn fecit 1797. Edward Drew Church warden.
"Great bells ij." Return of 1553. No note, Davy.

109. CHEDISTON *S. Mary.*   3 Bells.
 1 Tho. Gardiner fecit 1718. R. M. C.W.
 2 W. C. J. S.
  John Brend made me 1640.
 3 ☐ 81 Filius ☐ 82 Virginis ☐ 82 Marie ☐ 82 Dat ☐ 82 Nobis ☐ 82 Gaudia ☐ 82 Vite. ☐ 82 De ☐ 82 Bvri ☐ 82 Santi ☐ 82 Edmondi ☐ 82 Stefanvs ☐ 82 Tonni ☐ 82 me ☐ 82 fecit ☐ 82 1572. (Cracked.)
No return of bells in certif. iiij Nov., 1547. 3 in 1553.
Davy, 25 May, 1807, notes as above.

110. CHELMONDISTON *S. Andrew.*   1 Bell.
  Bell. John Darbie made me 1663.
"We have sold also an old broken bell to the valew of xxis. viijd. The trew s'tificat of Rychard Dylley and Wyllam Camper," C. W. 1547.
1 in 1553. "One bell." Davy.

111. CHELSWORTH *All Saints.*   1 Bell.
  Bell. Lester & Pack, 1763.
"Great bells iiij." Return of 1553.
Davy, 26 Oct., 1826, notes no inscription.

112. CHEVINGTON *All Saints.* Tenor in F. Bells in tune.
  5 Bells.
 1 John Draper made me 1620.
 2 C. & G. Mears, founders, London, 1848.
  W^m. Rayner Rolfe ⎫
  W^m. Jennison ⎬ Churchwardens.
  Elizabeth White, John White, Francis White.
 3 Lester & Pack of London fecit 1760.
 4 ✚ John Sparrow Ambros Ray C.W.[s]
  Tho. Gardiner fecit 1737.
 5 Benj. Downs Church Warden.
  Thos. Osborn, Downham, fecit 1780.
"Great bells iiij." Return of 1553.
Davy notes 5 bells, but no inscriptions.

113. CHILLESFORD *S. Peter.*   1 Bell.
  Bell. ▽ 66 thrice.
  ✚ Sancta ☐ Maria ☐ Ora ☐ Pro ☐ Nobis.
So Davy.
"Great bells iij." Return of 1553. Pits for three, this probably the treble.

114. CHILTON *S. Mary.* Diam. 32 in.   1 Bell.
  Bell. Miles Graye made me 1658.
So Davy, Sept. 13th, 1827. "Great bells ij." Return of 1553.

115. CLARE *SS. Peter and Paul.* Tenor c. 28 cwt. Diam. 54 in.
8 and Clock bell.
1 Given by voluntary subscription 1781.
Mears fecit.
2 T. Mears of London fecit 1829.
3 Miles Graye made me 1640.
and a shield, *party per pale, a griffin* (?) *passant.*
4 Whilst thus we join in chearful sound
Let Love and Loyalty abound.
Pack & Chapman of London fecit 1779.
5 Miles Graye made me 1661.
6 john dier made me 1579.

7 O 17 Conserba O 17 ☿ O 17 Trinitas O 17 Campanam
O 17 Estam.
8 John Kenyon Vic. William Wade C. W. I. L.
Charles Newman made mee 1693.
Clock bell. Tho. Gardiner fecit 1726.
"Great bells v. Sancts Bells j." Return of 1553.
Davy nearly as above, with a mistake or two. The 7th very much worn.
See p. 17, and *East Anglian*, I., 28, for notes by Mr. J. B. Armstead.

116. CLAYDON *S. Peter.* 1 Bell.
Bell. John Darbie made me 1676.
So Davy, 15 Sept., 1827. 3 in 1553.

117. CLOPTON *S. Mary.* Tenor. Diam. 43½ in. 6 Bells.
1, 2, 3, 4, 5 W. & T. Mears, late Lester, Pack, & Chapman
of London fecit 1788.
6 This peal cast in the year 1788 by unanimous consent of
the parishioners; by recasting the five old bells and
adding this tenor made them a peal of six.
W. & T. Mears, late Lester, Pack, & Chapman of London fecit 1788.

The C.W. sold a "payre of challes," of which they made verdict at Ipswich 28 Sept., 1547, "ffrome yt day we haue neyther sold alyenatyd nor pledged neyther ornamˢ jewells plate nor bellys." iiij Nov., 1547.
"Great bells iiij." Return of 1553.

118. COCKFIELD *S. Peter.* 6 Bells.
1 Laus Deo 1843.
Thomas Mears fecit Londini.
2 Charles Newman made mee 1700.
3 Charles Newman made me 1699. G. H. H. T.
4 Miles Graye made me 1656.
5 ☐ 81 James ☐ 82 Edbvry ☐ 82 1608.
6 John Jowars Robᵗ. Debenham C.W.
Tho. Gardiner fecit 1721 Num. 126.
Date on 5 "1098" by mistake. See p. 95.
"Great bells v." Return of 1553.
Davy notes " T. Martin's notes taken in 1735."

X

119. CODDENHAM *S. Mary.* Tenor c. 15 cwt. 8 Bells.
1 Theodore Ecclestone, Esqr, 1742. Thomas Lester made me.
Although I am but small
I will be heard above you all.
T. P.   A. F. C. (incised).
2 Thomas Lester made me 1742. The: Ecclestone.
3 Theodore Ecclestone. Thomas Lester made us all, 1740.
4 The Rev^d. John Longe, Vicar, John Fox, James Brook Ch. Wardens.
Thomas Mears & Son of London fecit 1806.
5, 6 Recast by John Warner & Son, London, 1878.
These bells are for the honour of God & the use of His Church.
Rev^d. Robert Longe, Vicar of Coddenham.
Walter Chapman } Church
Frederick Gull   } Wardens.
7 Thomas Lester made us all 1740.
8 ......:..................................
(filed off)...................... 1742.
Thomas Lester of London made us all.
Clock bell, 1808.
"Great bells iiij." Return of 1553.
Davy, 7 May, 1824, notes all as Lester's, save 4.
Theodore Ecclestone, Esq., was owner of the Crowfield Hall Estate, which was purchased in the year, 1764 by Arthur Middleton, Esq., Governor of S. Carolina, and grandfather of the late Sir W. F. F. Middleton, Bart.

120. COMBS *S. Mary.* Tenor E. Diam. 46¼ in.   4 Bells.
1 John Darbie made me 1662. R. B.
2 Miles Graye made me 1619.
3 ▽ 51 thrice.
☐ 49 𝔉𝔩𝔬𝔰 𝔓𝔯𝔢𝔠𝔢 𝔅𝔞𝔭𝔱𝔦𝔰𝔱𝔢 ☐ 62 𝔖𝔞𝔩𝔟𝔢𝔫𝔱 𝔗𝔲𝔞 𝔙𝔲𝔩𝔫𝔢𝔯𝔞 𝔛𝔭𝔢.
4 John Draper made me 1627.
4 in 1553. Davy notes 5 bells, one broken. Weights, according to Terrier of 1770, 15, 18, 21, and 24 cwt.

121. COOKLEY *S. Michael.*   3 Bells.
1 Ricardvs Bowler me fecit 1598.
2 Thomas Gardiner fecit 1728.
3 𝔄𝔫𝔫𝔬 𝔇𝔬𝔪𝔦𝔫𝔦 1593 W. B.
So Davy, 26 June, 1806.
Thomas Haywarde and Wyllam Sparke certify iiij Nov., 1547, that they have sold "neither plate, joyells, bells." 3 in 1553.

122. COPDOCK *S. Peter.*   5 Bells.
1, 2 Miles Graye made me 1614.
3 Miles Graye made me 1615.
4 John Darbie made me 1677.
5 John Darbie made me 1679.
No return of bells in certif. of iij Nov., 1547. 3 in 1553.
Davy calls the third the treble, otherwise there is no difference.

INSCRIPTIONS.   179

123. CORNARD, GREAT, *S. Andrew.*   Tenor.   Diam. 37 in.
5 Bells.
1 John Thornton made me 1708.
2 Buxton Vnderwood Jef. Poter Warden 1708.
3 Miles Graye made me 1664.
4 Cternis Annis Resonet Campana Jobis ▽ 11 + ▽ 9 twice.
5 John Thornton made me 1708.

The cross on 4 is No. 27 in North's *Church Bells of Bedfordshire.*
" Great bells iiij."   Return of 1553.
Davy, Sept. 12, 1827.   2 " Binxton ... Josef."   3 " 1616 " al. sim.

124. CORNARD, LITTLE, *All Saints.*   Tenor.   Diam. 33 in.
5 Bells.
1 Thornton and Waylet made me 1712.
2, 3 Henry Pleasant made me March 1707.
4 + Ricardvs Bowler me fecit 1597.
5 + IHS NAZARENVS REX IVDEORVM. +

So Davy, Sept. 12, 1827.   The crosses on 5 are Austen Bracker's, *Cambridgeshire*, No. 71, but probably come from an earlier hand.   The letters are rich.   " Great bells iij."   Return of 1553.
In 1581 there were at least two bells, as the Parish account has a charge of xj*d.* for " a Bald'ycke for one of or Belles."

125. CORTON *S. Bartholomew.*   1 Bell.
Bell.   C. & G. Mears, founders, London, 1847.
No return of bells in certif. of iiij Nov., 1547.   " Great bells iiij."   Return of 1553.
The parish in 1697 got a faculty for selling a piece of a bell for hanging a bell in the porch and other expenses.
The old bell bore the Norwich mark (erm.) and the inscription, B. R. Anno Domini 1626.   It used to hang in a frame of timber over the porch, but in 1768 was removed to its present position in the tower.   See Davy's MS.   Suckling says B. R.

126. COTTON *S. Andrew.*   5 Bells.
1, 2 Thomas Lester of London made me 1746.
3 John Draper made me 1627.   Thomas Barthroope
   Robert Rose Wardens A. M. T. E.
4 ▽ 50 thrice.
 + 61 Celesti Manna ☐ 62 Tua Proles Flos Cibet Anna.
5 ▽ 50 thrice.
 + 61 Flos Thome Meritis ☐ 62 Mereamur Gaudia Lucis.

3 cracked.   4 in 1553.   Martin, 16 Dec., 1724, notes 4.
" Five," Davy, 21 July, 1831.

127. COVE, NORTH, *S. Botolph.*   3 Bells.
1 Thomas Gardiner Norwich fecit 1750.
2 Anno Domini 1628.
          AB
          W
3 Tho. Gardiner Norwich fecit 1750.
  Tho. Horth C. W.

" Great bells iij."   Return of 1553.
Davy notes the date on 2 1618 instead of 1628, June 19, 1817.

128. COVE, SOUTH. *S. Laurence.* 1 Bell.
Bell ⛉ 52 thrice.
+ 61 𝔓etrus 𝔄b 𝔈terne ☐ 62 𝔇ucat 𝔉los 𝔓ascua 𝔙ite.

So Martin, 28 June, 1750. " The rest of or Jowells as bells plate and other ornaments remayneth in the Costodye of the Township. " Certif. of James Hanse and Roger Spicer, 1547." 3 in 1553.
Terrier rendered 18 May, 1827, " by computation 500 lbs. weight."

129. COVEHITHE *S. Andrew.* 5 Bells.
1 No inscription.
2   A B
       W
       𝔄nno 𝔇omini 1616
3 𝔄nno 𝔇omini 1626.
   ⛉ 51.
4 ⛉ 50 thrice.
+ 61 𝔓etrus 𝔄b 𝔈terne ☐ 62 𝔇ucat 𝔉los 𝔓ascua 𝔙ite.
5 ⛉ 50 thrice.
+ 61 𝔖um 𝔎osa 𝔓ulsata ☐ 62 𝔐undi 𝔐aria 𝔙ocata.

So Davy, 17 June, 1817, save 1628 on 3rd.
" Northalys," certif., 1547, no sale of bells. 5 in 1553. Well-toned bells.

130. COWLINGE *S. Margaret.* Tenor. Diam. 39 in.
                                              5 Bells.
1, 2 Thomas Newman made me. Ex dono F. Dickins, Esqr., 1734.
3, 4 John Briant Hertford fecit 1809.
5 T. Newman made me. Stephen Phillips & John Fenton, C. Wardens.
" Great bells iij. Sancts bells j." Return of 1553.

131. CRANSFORD *S. Peter.* 3 Bells.
1 W. B. Anno Domini 1594.
2 ⛉ 52 thrice.
+ 47 𝔚ee 𝔉it 𝔖coru ☐ 𝔒ampa 𝔏aude 𝔙onorum.
3 Recast by John Warner & Sons, London, 1878. Hung by G. Day & Son, Eye.
Mrs. Borrett ⎫
Mrs. Pooley ⎪
G. T. Borrett ⎬ Donors.
T. P. Borrett ⎭
G. F. Pooley, M.A., C. C. C. C., Rector of Cransford.
J. Dring ⎫
J. Flory ⎬ Churchwardens.

" Great bells iij." Return of 1553.
The old tenor was inscribed, 𝔈n 𝔐ultis 𝔄nnis, &c., and bore the same marks as the 2nd. The rhyme-stop is not engraved, I think. Not in tune.

132. CRATFIELD *S. Mary.* Tenor a very good bell.
                                         6 and Clock bell.
1 Chapman & Mears of London fecerunt 1781.
2 John Smyth of Norwod and Henry Fiske Chvrchwardens.
Ao Do 1593   W. B.

3 ▽ 50 ▽ 86   AB
                W
    𝕬nno 𝕯omini 1618.
4 Cratfeld. Henry Topsel, R. T. Año Dni 1585.
5 ☐ If with my fellowes I doe agree
    Then listen to our harmony.
    ᵃW. D. G. S Chvrchwardens. W. B. 1618.
6 ☐ 48 Per me fideles invocantur ad preces.
    1637. J. B.
    Clock bell + 47 𝕭irginis 𝕰gregie + 47 𝕾ocor 𝕮ampana
        𝕸arie 𝕻rep 𝕱or 𝕮he 𝕾ole 𝕺f 𝖂illiam 𝕬leps.
So Davy, 22 May, 1807, with one or two involuntary variations. No return of bells in certif. of Symond Smyth and John Bateman, C. W., iiij Nov., 1547. The battlement to the tower was then built by the sale of "a peyer of Chalys a peyer of Sensors and a Crosse, the pᵣce xxli." 4 and a Sance bell in 1553.
The Clock bell has a staple for a tongue, and is worn internally. See pp. 41, 103.
Some of the capitals on the 2nd are of the Norwich mediæval type, like Nos. 54, etc., and the A is quite peculiar.

133. CREETING *All Saints*.
Ecclesia destructa.
"Great bells iij." Return of 1553.
T. Martin, Sept., 1732, "3 Bells (old ones)."

134. CREETING *S. Mary*. Diam. 39 in.   1 Bell.
Bell. Thomas Gardiner fecit 1727.
"Great bells iij." Return of 1553.
Davy, 13 June, 1827, "One bell which I did not examine." Hung in a chestnut frame and wheel, diam. of latter 7 ft. On the wheel is "Thomas Sharman, Churchwarden, 1...... FF (letters chipped off) 1733."

135. CREETING *S. Olave*.
Ecclesia destructa. No return in 1553.   *

136. CREETING *S. Peter*. Tenor. Diam. 27 in. 3 Bells.
    1 Ricardvs Bowler me fecit 1600.
    2 Thomas Gardiner Sudbury fecit 1726.
    3 Johannes Drivervs T C. me fecit 1618.
"West cretynge. Great bells iij. Sancts bells j." Return of 1553.
Notes, probably by Tom Martin, 26 Sept., 1732, record "3 modern bells."
Davy, June 15, 1827, apparently by mistake notes only two, inaccessible. Treble cracked.

137. CRETINGHAM *S. Peter*.   5 Bells.
    1 John Darbie made me 1661. T. C.
    2 John Darbie made me 1661. H. C.
    3 ▽ thrice.
      + 𝖂er 𝕱il 𝕾coru ☐ Campā 𝕷aude 𝕭onoru.
    4 ▽ thrice.
      + 𝕮elesti 𝕸aana ☐ 𝕮ua 𝕻roles 𝕱los 𝕮ibet 𝕬nna.

---
* William Dowsing and Gregorie Smith.

5 ▽ thrice.
   ✠ Subveniat Digna ☐ Donantibus Hanc Katerina.
No return of bells in certif. of iij Nov., 1547. "Great bells iiij." Return of 1553. 3, 4, 5 Norwich bells. Shield 50, Cross 61, Rhyme-stop 62, I feel tolerably sure.

138. CROWFIELD *All Saints.*   1 Bell.
Bell. Robt. Catlin fecit 1740.

From Davy, 12 May, 1824. 1 in 1553.

139. CULFORD *S. Mary.*   1 Bell.
Bell. Thomas Newman made me 1704

"Great bells iij." Return of 1553. Davy, 18 Aug., 1829, "one bell."

140. CULPHO *S. Botolph.*   1 Bell.
Bell. Miles Graye made me 1641 (cracked).

"Cvlsfo...Great bells ij." Return of 1553.

141. DALHAM *S. Mary.*   5 Bells.
1 Thomas Gardiner Sudbury fecit 1755.
2 SIR MARTIN STUTHILDE ▽ (Stuteville). *Per pale, arg. and sa. a saltire engrailed ermine and ermines.*
    I am the second in degree
    And will in tune and time agree.
    John Draper made me 1627.
3 SIR MARTIN STUTHILDE ▽ his arms.
    I am the third and you shall her
    Me beare my part, and sound most cleere.
    John Draper made me 1627.
4 Sir Jas. Affleck Bart., and Jeremiah Moore Churchwardens. Chas. D. M. Drake Rector.
    This bell was recast by Wm. Dobson, Downham, Norfolk, A.D. 1832.
5 ▽ 50 thrice.
    ✠ 61 Sum Rosa Pulsata ☐ 62 Mundi Maria Vocata.

Sir M. S. died suddenly while smoking at the Bell at Thetford. See Rous's Diary. See also Gawdy MSS., p. 116. His daughter Anne married James de Grey of Merton, who died in 1665.
"Great bells iiij." Return of 1553. Davy could not get the key.

142. DALLINGHOO *S. Mary.* Tenor G. Diam. 37 in.
                                                              4 Bells.
1 C.
    W. M. L. F. L. F. H. M. 1592.
2 Richard Phelps made me 1732.
3 ▽ 50 thrice.
    ✠ 61 Petrus Ab Eterne ☐ 62 Ducat Nos Pascua Vite.
4 Thomas Gardiner made me 1715.

"Great bells iiij." Return of 1553. Hawes says "3 by Miles Graye, 5 formerly," and Martin, 1745, says 3.

143. DARMSDEN *S. Andrew.*   1 Bell.
   Bell. John Goldsmith fecit 1710. Santa Maria.
No return of bells in certif. of iij Nov., 1547, probably 1. Left blank in 1553. Davy, 14 Sept., 1827, "One bell ... no ladder."

144. DARSHAM *All Saints.*   4 Bells.
   1 John Brend made mee 1656.
   2, 4 John Brend made me 1656.
   3 ▽ 65 thrice.
   + Sanctt (sic) Oponia Ora Pro Nobis.
The churche reves of Darsham, John Reve and Robt. Backler, Ao. 1547, certify to the sale of "j peyer of handbells for the pṛce of ijs. iiijd." 3 in 1553. Davy, 3 June, 1808, gets the numbers wrong, and reads Thoma on the Tenor. Oponia is for Apollonia. See *Cambridgeshire*, p. 126.
First four of a five in G, all maiden, in tune.

145. DEBACH *All Saints.* In F. Diam. 23½ in.   1 Bell.
   Bell. No inscription.
No return of bells in certif. of iiij Nov., 1547. "Debedge...Great bells ij." Return of 1553. Davy (27 May, 1823), found it inaccessible.

146. DEBENHAM *S. Mary.* Tenor 1 ton, in E. Diam. 44 in.
    8 Bells.
   1, 3, 6 Lester & Pack of London fecit 1761.
   2 Lester & Pack fecit 1761.
   4 Lester & Pack of London fecit. Thos. Kersey 1761.
   5 Thos. Mears of London fecit 1793.
   7 Lester & Pack of London fecit. Edwd. Davie & Jno.
       Orford Ch. Wardens 1761.
   8 In Wedlock's bands all ye who join
       With hands your hearts unite
       So shall our tuneful tongues combine
       To laud the nuptial rite.
   [The Revd. Mr. Jas. Clubb Vicar: The Revd. Mr. Robert
       Leman Curate, *engraved*].
So Davy substantially, but without a date to 4, and 1795 on 5.
"Gret bells v." Return of 1553.

147. DENHAM *S. John Baptist.*   1 Bell.
   Bell. 1614. I. D.
3 in 1553. Davy, 16 June, 1809, notes one bell. See p. 109.

148. DENHAM *S. Mary.* In F. Diam. 21 in.   1 Bell.
   Bell. No inscription.
"Great bells ij." Return of 1553. Long-waisted, and apparently old.

149. DENNINGTON *S. Mary* (fine bells).   5 Bells.
   1 ▽ 52 thrice.
   + Sancta Maria Ora Pro Nobis.
   2 + 47 Fac Margareta □ 48 Nobis Hec Munera Leta.
   3 + Sancta Thoma Ora Pro Nobis.
   4 Anno Domini 1628. W. I. B. Omnis Sonvs Lavdet
       Dominvm.

5 1666 Anno Orbis incendio redempti vrbis peremptæ.
Gvil. Bell T. P. Vicarius.
John Darbie made me.

5 and a Sance bell in 1553.
So Davy and Jermyn, Aug. 5, 1806. Gillingwater, 10 May, 1798, notes 5. Terrier, 3 July, 1753, "Five large bells, the Tenor of 25 cwt., the other proportionable."

Much curious matter in parish accounts. The bell-frame is athwart the tower, which has been built around it. Part of the capstan forms a beam.

150. DENSTON *S. Nicholas*. 2 Bells.

1 ▽ 65 thrice.
+ Sancta ☐ Maria ☐ Ora ☐ Pro ☐ Nobis.
2 ▽ 65 thrice.
+ Sancte ☐ Petre ☐ Ora ☐ Pro ☐ Nobis.

"Denarston...Great bells iij." Return of 1553.
No notes. Davy. Mr. Deedes notes these as 1 and 3 of a trio, as the middle pit is vacant. The usual failure has of course resulted from an attempt to cut the crack out of 2.

151. DEPDEN *S. Mary*. Tenor. Diam. 36 in. 3 Bells.

1 ▽ 65 thrice.
+ 67 Sancte ☐ [Nico]lae ☐ Ora ☐ Pro ☐ Nobis.
2 ▽ 65 thrice.
+ 67 Sancta ☐ Anna ☐ Ora ☐ Pro ☐ Nobis.
3 Ric ardvs Bowler me fecit 1600.
(A band between each word, and six Elizabeth coins on the sound-bow.)

"Debden...Great bells iij." Return of 1553.
No notes. Davy. Notes C, A$\sharp$, and A.

152. DRINKSTONE *All Saints*. Tenor. Diam. 39 in.
6 Bells.

1 Pack & Chapman of London fecit 1771. Henry Plume Church Warden.
2 Henry Pleasant made me 1696. F. P.
3, 5 Mears & Stainbank, founders, London, 1869.
4 Henry Pleasant made me 1696.
6 Reginald Sayer, Tho. Cocksedge C.W. Henry Pleasant made me 1695.

"Great bells iiij. Sancts Bells j." Return of 1553.
Davy notes 3 and 5 like the rest, but "P. C." for "F. P." Tenor cracked. Notes of the others F, D$\sharp$, C$\sharp$, C, A$\sharp$.

153. DUNNINGWORTH *S. Mary*.

Ecclesia destructa. No return in 1553. The church was standing and in use in the year 1561. Davy.

154. DUNWICH *All Saints*.

Ecclesia destructa. See extracts from Gardiner, 1734. No mention of bells in certif. of iiij Nov., 1547. 3 in 1553.

"The steeple appears in tolerable repair: I remember a man who had occupied a farm at Yoxford, and whose name was Parker, being convicted and transported for stealing, I think, one of the bells and some of the lead." Davy, 24 Oct., 1839.

INSCRIPTIONS.   185

155. DUNWICH *S. James.* c. 5 cwt.   1 Bell.
Bell. T. Mears of London fecit 1832.
Coeval with the church, given by Frederick Barne, Esq.

156. DUNWICH *S. John Baptist.*
Ecclesia destructa.
No return of bells in certif. of iiij Nov., 1547. 3 in 1553.

157. DUNWICH *S. Leonard.*
Ecclesia destructa. No return in 1553.

158. DUNWICH *S. Martin.*
Ecclesia destructa. No return in 1553.

159. DUNWICH *S. Nicholas.*
Ecclesia destructa. No return in 1553.

160. DUNWICH *S. Peter.*
Ecclesia destructa.
No return of bells in certif. of iij Nov., 1547. 3 in 1553.

161. EASTON *All Saints.*   5 Bells.
 1 Thomas Gardiner Sudbury fecit 1731.
 2 T. Osborn fecit 1791.
   Rev. Loder Allen, Rector. Joseph Rust Ch. Warden.
 3 Miles Graie made me 1627. I. E.
 4 + MISSVS VERO PIE GABRIEL BERT LETA
     MARIE.
 5 Recast by John Warner & Sons, London, 1884.
   This bell was cast and the peal rehung at the expense of
     the Duke of Hamilton, A.D., 1884.
   Hung by G. Day & Son, Eye.
"Great bells iiij." Return of 1553.
No return of bells in certif. of iiij Nov., 1547.
The places are still visible in the under-chamber where the beams were built in. The old tenor, like the 4th, was of the "Burlingham" type, inscribed + SPES NOSTRA SALVS NOSTRA O BEATA TRINITAS. It bore shield No. 64.

162. EASTON BAVENTS *S. Margaret.*
Ecclesia destructa. 3 in 1553, either in this Church or the next.

163. EASTON BAVENTS *S. Nicholas.*
Ecclesia destructa. See No. 162.

164. EDWARDSTONE *S. Mary.*   6 Bells.
 1 Mr. Cook and Nvtting C W. 1709.
 2 Tvned by W^m. Cvlpeck 1710.
 3 Miles Graye made me 1640.
 4 Miles Graye made me 1641.
 5 Miles Graye made me 1663.
 6 About ty second Cvlpeck is wrett
   Becavse the fovnder wanted wett
   Thair jvdgments ware bvt bad at last
   Or elce this bell I never had cast.
       Tho. Gardiner.

Y

See p. 142. "Great bells iiij." Return of 1553.
Davy, May 21, 1829, leaves out "tuned by" on 2. 4 "1663." He could not read the Tenor.

165. ELEIGH, BRENT, *S. Mary.* 3 Bells.
  1 ☐ 81 Thomas Cheese ☐ 82 made me 1629.
  2 ☐ 81 Thomas ☐ 82 Cheese made me 1632.
  3 (arabesque) Jeams ☐ 81 Edbvry ☐ 82 1612.

"Brondylly...Great bells iij." Return of 1553.
Davy, Oct. 25, 1826, " 1, 1632," al. sim.

166. ELEIGH, MONKS, *S. Peter.* 6 Bells.
  1 T. Osborn fecit 1790.
  2 Miles Graye made me M 1638.
  3 Miles Graye made me M 1637.
  4 ▽ 65 thrice.
  + 67 Ora ☐ 68 Laurenti ☐ 68 Bona ☐ 68 Campana ☐ 68 Paci.
  5 ☐ ASSYMPTA : EST : MARIA : IN : CELVM.
  6 Miles Graye made me M. 1638.

See p. 10. "Mounksylle...Great bells iiij." Returns of 1553.
Davy, Oct. 25, 1826. Imperfect, but accordant notes. "31 May, 1737. There were only 5 bells."

167. ELLOUGH *All Saints.* Tenor. Diam. 32 in. 3 Bells.
  1 ☐ AVE : MARIA : GRACIA : PLENA : DOMINVS : TECVM.
  2 The Rev^d. Robt. Lemon Rector. John Warne Ch. Warden 1763. Lester & Pack of London fecit.
  3 Anno Domini 1597.

See p. 74. So in substance, Davy, June 1, 1808.
"Great bells iiij." Return of 1553.

168. ELMHAM, SOUTH, *All Saints.* Note C. 1 Bell.
Bell. Anno Domini 1603.

"Pōchia omn Scōr in Sowthe elmehm...Great bells iiij." Return of 1553.
Here were three bells till about 60 years ago. It is said that two were sold to Southwold, where there was recasting and addition in 1828. The following note is from the Churchwardens' book :—
"C^r. By Cash of M^r. Burgess for 2 Bells.
  W^t. 10 cwt. 1 qr. 3 lbs. at 6½d.   £31 3 5
D^r. Allowed Mr. Burgess for Tare and Tret in the
  weight of Bells   8 1
      Geo. Durrant Churchwarden."
That this is true there can be little doubt, for Davy records 3 bells, " 1 Laudes (for laudet) Deo in ...... 2 Anno Domini 1603. 3 ... ora pro ..."
Now the Southwold 6th bears, "En Heplih and in Vo Laudes Deo," which Davy may well be excused for not deciphering. This was, according to him, the largest of the three.

169. ELMHAM, SOUTH, *S. George.* 5 Bells.
  1 J Taylor & Son, Founders, Loughborough, 1844.
    J. Hurry, Norwich, Agent.
  2 anno domini 1610 AB
    W

3 ▽ 64.
+ AVE : MAR̨IA : GR̨ACIA : PLENA : DN̄S :
  TECV̆.
4 ▽ 51 thrice.
+ 61 ﬂos Tɦome Ṁerritis □ 62 Ṁereamur Gaubia Lucis.
5 John Brend made me 1635.
See p. 61. "Sandcroft in Sowtvilla...Great bells iiij." Return of 1553.
Davy notes four, which he did not venture to inspect.

170. ELMHAM, SOUTH, *S. James.* Tenor. Diam. 31¾ in. in C♯.
                                                           4 Bells.
  1 R. B. 1662.
  2 Thomas Newman made mee 1707. Joseph Barber C.W.
  3 + JOHAṄṄES : BR̨OVN : ME : FECIT : BIER̨I.
  4 Anno Domini 1581. I. B.
Bells not in tune. See p. 74. R, B. for Ralph Brend.
No sale of bells in certif. of 1547. "Great bells iij. Sancts j." Return
of 1553. Davy dates 2 1704, crosses 3 and 4, and could not read
JOHAṄṄES on 3.

171. ELMHAM, SOUTH, *S. Margaret.*   5 Bells.
  1, 2, 3 John Brend made me 1657.
  4 Anno Domini 1627.
    A B
     W
  5 ▽ 51 thrice.
    Anno Domini 1596. W. B.
So Davy, save that he reads "1586" for 1596.
"Great bells iiij." Return of 1553.

172. ELMHAM, SOUTH, *S. Michael.* A good clear bell.
                                                           1 Bell.
  Bell. C. & G. Mears, founders, London, 1847.
"Great bells iij." Return of 1553. "Only 1 bell," Davy.

173. ELMHAM, SOUTH, *S. Nicholas.*
Ecclesia destructa. "Great bells iiij. Sancts Bells j." Return of 1553.
"The church is now entirely demolished." Davy.

174. ELMHAM, SOUTH, *S. Peter.* Tenor. Diam. 34½ in.
                                     Note Bb.   3 Bells.
  1 ▽ 9 four times.
  2 ▽ 11 four times.
  + 15 Johannes O 16 Cristi O 16 Care O 16 Dignare
    O 16 Pro O 16 Nobis O 16 Orare.
  3 ▽ 8 four times.
  + 15 Sum O 16 Gabriel O 16 Fata O 16 Marie. O 16
    Sum O 16 Comitata.
See p. 17. Well-toned bells.
No sale of bells in certif. of 1547. "Great bells iij." Return of 1553.
(The same three hung in the tower in 1889.)

175. ELMSETT *S. Peter.* Notes C and A♯   2 Bells.
  1 Thomas + Gardiner + Sudbury + fecit + 1726 (two
    coins).

2 Miles Graye made me 1636.
Pits for two others, which are said to be in Stowmarket tower. "Great bells iiij." Return of 1553. Davy by mistake, 20 May, 1829, " 1 Bell."

176. ELMSWELL *S. John Evangelist.* Tenor. Diam. 40½ in.
5 Bells.
1 Robard Gvrney ♊ made me ♛ 1670. W. M. T. F.
2 De ☐ 82 Bvri ☐ 82 Santi ☐ 82 Edmondi ☐ 82 Stefanvs ☐ 82 Tonni ☐ 82 me ☐ 82 fecit ☐ 82 WL ☐ 81 1582 ☐ 81.
3 ▽ 65 thrice.
✠ 𝕾anctɛ ☐ 𝕰bmunbɛ ☐ 𝕺ra ☐ 𝕻ro ☐ 𝕹obis.
4 John Darbie made me 1677.
5 𝕵ohn 𝕯rapɛr made me 1616 (cracked).
"Great bells iij." Return of 1553.
Davy, 11 June, 1827, imperfect notes, but correct as far as they go.

177. ELVEDEN *S. Andrew.* 1 Bell.
Bell. John Darbie made me 1664.
"Elvedene...Great bells iij." Return of 1553.
Davy, 24 Aug., 1829, notes one bell, but gives Ringers' Rules, dated Sept. 19, 1707, showing that there was at that time a ring of bells in this tower, copied by Jermyn, 1817.

178. ENDGATE *S. Mary.*
Ecclesia destructa. "Ingate. Great bells iij." Return of 1553.
Church taken down 1577. Bells, lead, etc., sold for £76 18 4, which was given to Dunwich on account of losses sustained there. See W. J. A. in *East Suffolk Gazette*, Aug. 9, 1887.

179. ERISWELL *S. Laurence.*
Ecclesia destructa. No return in 1553.

180. ERISWELL *S. Peter.* 3 Bells.
1, 2 Thos. Osborn founder 1795. John Spark Church Warden.
3 Tho. Gardiner made me 1743.
So Davy, 21 Aug., 1828. "Great bells vj." Return of 1553.

181. ERWARTON *S. Mary.* 1 Bell.
Bell. C. Newman made me 1700. R. Sporll. W. Fisher C. W.
So Davy. 1 and Sance bell in 1553.

182. EUSTON *S. Genevieve.* 5 Bells.
1, 2, 3 Henricvs Pleasant me fecit 1701.
4 Thomas Gardiner Sudbury fecit 1730.
5 Domini Thome Hanmeri Baronetti.
Anno Domini 1701. H. P.
"Great bells iij. Sancts bells j." Return of 1553.
Davy, 4 July, 1843, "Five."

183. EXNING *S. Martin.* 5 and Clock bell.
1, 2, 3, 4 John Draper made me 1623.

INSCRIPTIONS.

5 C. & G. Mears, founders, London, 1845.
William Fyson   } Church Wardens.
John Dobede   }
Clock bell. T. Mears of London fecit.
W^m. Fyson   } Church Wardens 1831.
Thos. Bryant   }
Late the gift of Francis Shepherd Esqr., 1723.
"Eyenyng Halfe Hundred:—Eyenyng...Great bells iiij. Sancts Bells j." Return of 1553.

184. EYE *SS. Peter and Paul.* 8 Bells.
1 Ex dono Gulielmi Brampton generosi Anno Domini 1721.
2 Pack & Chapman of London fecerunt. Simon Cook Churchwarden 1779.
3 Thomas Rust oppidi Præfecto J. Stephens made us 3 1721.
4 Let us rejoice our King restord.
Saml. Gowing Danl Sewell C^h. Wardens.
T. Osborn fecit 1789.
5 O God continue thy tender mercies to the King.
Danl. Sewell Saml. Gowing, C^h. Wardens.
T. Osborn fecit 1789.
6, 8, Miles Graye made me 1640.
7 ▽ 51 thrice.
✠ 61 Dona Repende Pia ☐ 62 Rogo Magdalena Maria.

So Davy, 17 and 18 June, 1809. 5 and a Sance bell in 1553.
Sperling notes the tenor as in E♭, 24 cwt.
Comparison of dimensions of 7th and Tenor:—

	7		8	
	ft.	in.	ft.	in.
Height in full	3	0¼	2	10½
„ to shoulder ...	2	6¼	2	6
Diam. lip	3	6¼	4	0
Circum at inscription ...	6	4	6	11½

Eye Town Hall possesses an old bell without inscription, but apparently from London, c. 1350. Till the last century it used to hang in a spire which formerly surmounted Eye tower. Very likely the original Sance bell.

185. EYKE *All Saints.* 3 Bells.
1 No inscription.
2 Henry Pleasant made me 1706.
3 ▽ 55 thrice.
✠ Sancta ☐ Maria ☐ Ora ☐ Pro ☐ Nobis.

So Davy, 12 Sept. 1807. Martin (no date) notes 5.
From Hawes :—1.
2 Henry Pleasant made me 1706.
3 Sancta —— Ora Pro Nobis.
4 En Multis, &c.
5 Miles Graye made me 1630.
"Great bells iiij. Sancts bells j." Returns of 1553. Faculty for selling two bells in Davy.

186. FAKENHAM, GREAT, *S. Peter.* Tenor A♯. c. 8 cwt.
3 Bells.

1 + sancta : maria : ora : pro : nobis.
2 De Bvri Santi Edmondi Stefanvs Tonni me fecit 1572.
3 R. G. 1667.
"Great bells iij." Returns of 1553. Davy, no notes.

187. FAKENHAM, LITTLE, S. *Andrew.*
Ecclesia destructa. No return in 1553.

188. FALKENHAM S. *Ethelbert.*   4 Bells.
1, 2 John Darbie made me 1666.
3, 4 Tho. Gardiner Sudbury fecit 1728.
So Davy, 15 July, 1829. No return of bells in certif. of iiij Nov., 1547.
"Great bells iiij." Return of 1553.

189. FARNHAM S. *Mary.*   2 Bells.
1 T. S.   T. P.   1590.
2 Anno Domini 1631.
♱ 50.
So Davy. Diameters 2ft. 2in., 2ft. 3⅛in. No clappers.
"Great bells iij." Return of 1553.

190. FELIXSTOWE SS. *Peter and Paul.*   1 Bell.
Bell. Miles Graye made me 1627.
"ffylstowe. Great bells j." Return of 1553. Davy, 15 July, 1829, 1 Bell.

191. FELSHAM S. *Peter.* Tenor. Diam. 45¼ in. in F.
6 Bells.
1 Robard ♛ Gvrney made me ♛ 1668.
2, 4 Miles Graye made me M. 1638.
3 ♱ 65 thrice.
+ 67 Sancta ☐ Anna ☐ Ora ☐ Pro ☐ Nobis.
5 John Warner and Sons, London, 1887.
6 Miles Graye made me M. 1639.
"ffeltham...Great bells iiij." Re. of 1553. Davy, "6 bells and a clock."
The old 5th bore ♱ 51 thrice, with + 61, ☐ 62, and Dona Repende, &c.

192. FINBOROUGH, GREAT, S. *Andrew.* Very small.
1 Bell.
Bell. Josephus Carter me fecit ☐ 1609.

3 in 1553. Notes, probably by Martin, 15 April, 1756, record three bells; the Terrier of 1784 mentions but one. The tower fell in 1819; Davy, June 13 and 14, 1827, names a single bell hanging in a cupola.

193. FINBOROUGH, LITTLE, S. *Bartholomew.*   1 Bell.
Bell. No inscription.

2 in 1553. Davy, June 14, 1827, notes a single bell within the roof of the nave, at the west end, and that the steeple was standing within the memory of some of the present inhabitants.

194. FINNINGHAM S. *Bartholomew.*   3 Bells.
1 Thomas Lester & Thos. Pack fecit 1754.
2 ♱ 50 thrice.
+ 61 Virginis Egregie ☐ 62 Vocor Campana Marie.

3. No inscription.
3 in 1553. Davy, 22 July, 1838, notes 3.
The third apparently a very old bell, with long barrel, sharp shoulder, no beadings, and light cannons.

195. FLEMPTON *S. Catherine.*   1 Bell.
           Bell. Percute Dulce Cano. T. Osborn fecit 1786.
"Great Bells iij." Return of 1553. Tom Martin, c. 1724, notes "The steeple half down, three bells." See Davy's further notes.

196. FLIXTON *S. Andrew.*
Ecclesia destructa. No return in 1553.

197. FLIXTON *S. Mary.*   1 Bell.
           Bell. No inscription.
No return of bells in certif. dated iiij Nov., 1547. "ffyxon...Great bells iiij." Return of 1553.
The late Rev^d. H. Warren, Vicar, informed me that there were three bells formerly, the inscriptions on the other two being
     ✠ 𝕸𝖎𝖘𝖘𝖚𝖘 𝖁𝖊𝖗𝖔 𝖕𝖎𝖊 𝕲𝖆𝖇𝖗𝖎𝖊𝖑 𝖋𝖊𝖗𝖙 𝖑𝖊𝖙𝖆 𝕸𝖆𝖗𝖎𝖊, and
     ✠ 𝕼𝖚𝖊𝖘𝖚𝖒𝖚𝖘 𝕬𝖓𝖉𝖗𝖊𝖆 𝖋𝖆𝖒𝖚𝖑𝖔𝖗𝖚𝖒 𝕾𝖚𝖘𝖈𝖎𝖕𝖊 𝖁𝖔𝖙𝖆.
Davy's account is intended to agree with this. Here the late Sir R. Shafto Adair placed a large Dish-bell bearing twice the arms and motto of his family, and inscribed, 𝖁𝖊𝖓𝖎𝖙𝖊 𝖊𝖝𝖇𝖑𝖙𝖊𝖒𝖇𝖘 𝕯𝖔𝖒𝖎𝖓𝖔. 𝕸𝖊𝖆𝖗𝖘 𝖒𝖊 𝖋𝖊𝖈𝖎𝖙 MDCCCLVII. It was struck on the outside with a large hammer, and emitted a somewhat broken, booming sound, very effective at a distance. After some years' use it became cracked, and was sold to help to buy an organ.

198. FLOWTON *S. Mary.*   1 Bell.
           Bell. No inscription.
3 in 1553.

199. FORDLEY *Holy Trinity.*
Ecclesia destructa. 3 in 1553.

200. FORNHAM *All Saints.*   4 Bells.
     1, 2 John Draper made me 1623.
     3 ▽ 50 thrice.
     ✠ 61 𝖂𝖆𝖈 𝕴𝖓 𝕮𝖔𝖓𝖈𝖑𝖆𝖛𝖊 ☐ 62 𝕲𝖆𝖇𝖗𝖎𝖊𝖑 𝕹𝖚𝖓𝖈 𝕻𝖆𝖓𝖌𝖊 𝕾𝖚𝖆𝖛𝖊.
     4 John Draper made me 1624.
"Great bells iij." Return of 1553. Davy has mistaken "Draper" for "Darbie," and put a century on the dates.

201. FORNHAM *S. Genevieve.*
Ecclesia destructa. "ffornham Genofefye...Great bells ij." Return of 1553. "Three bells." Martin?

202. FORNHAM *S. Martin.*   6 Bells.
     1, 2, 3, 4, 5, 6 C. & G. Mears, Founders, London, 1844.
"Great bells iij." Return of 1553.
Three bells noted by Davy, but no inscriptions.

203. FOXHALL *All Saints.*
Ecclesia destructa. "ffoxhall. Chalice one, wayinge vijoz. q^r. Great bells ns (= nescio)."

204. FRAMLINGHAM *S. Michael.*

1 John Stephens of Norwich made me 1718.
2 John Stephens fecit 1718. Prosperity to all my benefactors.
3 John Stephens made me 1720.
4 ▽ 50 thrice.
   + 61 𝔚ac 𝔦n 𝔠oclabe ☐ 62 𝔊abriel 𝔑ūc 𝔓ange 𝔖uabe.
5 ▽ 50 thrice.
   + 61 𝔙irginis 𝔈gregie ☐ 62 𝔙ocor 𝔠ampna 𝔐arie.
6 Omnis Sonvs lavdet Dominvm Anno Domini 1583.
7 Anno Domini 1622. W. I. B.
8 Per me fideles convocantur ad preces I. S. 1718. Thomas Mvlliner Moses Bvry C. W.

No return of bells in certif. of iij Nov., 1547. "Great bells v. Sancts bells j." Return of 1553. 7th a bad bell.
Many bequests "novo Campanili," from 1497—1534, by Christiana Durrant, Margery Spinke, Tho Skimming, Rob, Maggs, Joan Trusse, Joh. Botson de Saxsted, &c.
In 1657 a sixth bell was bought, probably of John Brend, partly by contribution, partly by the sale of timber. Mr. Alexander, a Town feoffee, gave £10. This is the second or third eight in the county, Horham being the first, and Bungay S. Mary's old eight completed in the same year with Framlingham.

205. FRAMSDEN *S. Mary.* Tenor 16 cwt.   8 Bells.

1 and 2 Gift of R^t Honourable Wilbraham Earl of Dysart, 1814. T. Mears of London fecit.
3 Willm. Dobson, Downham, 1809.
4 No inscription.
5 Sir Lionel Tollemache, Earl of Dysart, Baron of Huntingtower Bart and K^t. of the most ancient order of the Thistle, who died March 10th, 1770, recast these bells to complete the peal.
Pack & Chapman of London fecit 1770.
6 Henry Pleasant made me 1706.
7 T. Mears of London fecit 1815.
8 Sir Lionel Tollemache, Earl of Dysart, Baron of Huntingtower Bart and K^t of the most ancient order of the Thistle, who died March 10th, 1770, left by will this bell.
Pack & Chapman of London fecit 1772.

No return of bells in certif. of iij Nov., 1547. "Great bells iiij." Return of 1553. Davy records 3 as bearing the same inscription as 5: and 7, "Renovata Senectus in florem redeat. John Robers, A.M., Vicar, John Revell, Ch. Warden, 1740."

206. FRECKENHAM *S. Andrew.*   5 Bells.

1 William Dobson Fecit Downham Norfolk 1809.
2, 3 John Draper made mee 1623.
4 The Rev^d. H. Bates Rector W^m. Westrop and W^m. Mainprice Churchwardens 1809.
5 T. Osborn fecit 1792.

"ffrakenham...Great bells iiij. Sancts Bells j." Return of 1553. The same inscriptions, but allotted to wrong bells by Davy, 21 Aug., 1829.

207. FRESSINGFIELD SS. *Peter and Paul.*   8 Bells.
    1, 2 T. Mears of London fecit 1819.
    3 Thomas Newman made me 1741.
    4 Mr. T. Sancroft & P. James C. W. 1741.
       T. Newman made me.
    5 George Mears, founder, London, 1866.
    6, 7 Thomas Mears of London fecit 1817.
    8 ▽ 50 thrice.
    + 42 𝔖corum 𝔐eritis ☐ 48 𝔓angamus 𝔒antica 𝔏audis.

See pp. 43, 83. 7 a little flat.
No return of bells in certif. of iij Nov., 1547. 4 and a Sance bell in 1553. Jermyn and Davy were here, 14 Oct., 1806. They note 3 and 4 as they are now, 5 like 4 (as it was at my visit, 19 March, 1862), 6, 𝔇ona 𝔑ependc, &c., and 7, Omnis Sonus laudet Dominum 1632. I. B. On the crown I. A. R. A. See Gillingwater's extract for the opening of the complete eight.

The 5th, which ringers think inferior to its predecessor, was recast after an accident while William Riches was ringing in a course of 720.
There seemed to be no cause for the sudden cracking of the bell, so W. R. tells us.

208. FRESTON *S. Peter.*
    Bell. Ricardvs Bowler me fecit 1600.

No return of bells in certif. of 1547. 3 in 1553. A good bell.
Davy, by mistake, 1660.
L'Estrange, p. 65, mistakes this parish for Friston.
The Visitation Records of the Archdeaconry of Suffolk (1674) mention an order for a new bell to be provided in place of an old one, which had been sold. This order was repeated in 1675. In 1689 "the great bell" is mentioned.

209. FRISTON *S. Mary.*   3 Bells.
    1 Johannes Drivervs me fecit 1614.
    2 ▽ 50 thrice.
    + 𝔔uesumus 𝔄ndrea ☐ 62 𝔉amulorum 𝔖uscipe 𝔙ota.
    3 No inscription.

So Davy. "Great bells iij." Return of 1553.

210. FRITTON *S. Edmund.*   1 Bell.
    Bell. M. Sydnor Esquier. 1598.
"ffreton...Great bells ij." Return of 1553.
In Reeve's Historical Collection two bells are mentioned.

211. FROSTENDEN *All Saints.*   3 Bells.
    1 + CAMPANA : OMNIVM : SANCTORVM
       (cracked).
    2 John Brend made me 1639. (Note B.)
    3 ☐ : O : UGO : BBARA : PRO : NOBIS : DEVEXORA : (Note A).

So Davy, 3 Sept., 1837. Treble probably an early London bell. Tenor bears "Burlingham" lettering. See p. 60.
No return of bells in certif. of iiij Nov., 1547. 3 in 1553.

212. GAZELEY *All Saints.* Weight 10 cwt. 6 Bells.
    1 A grateful strain boys let us sing
      To praise the name of Messrs. King
      Wedge, Cornell, Norman, Hynes, and Fyson,
      Death, Barnes, Staples, also Wilson,
      By whose kind and generous aid
      I(leader of this peal) was made.
      John Briant fecit A.D. 1808.
    2 Pack & Chapman of London Fecit 1775.
    3 Whilst thus we join in chearful sound
      May Love and Loyalty abound
          Pack & Chapman of London Fecit 1775
    4 Ye ringers all that prize
      Your health and happiness
      Be sober merry wise
      And you'll the same possess.
          Pack & Chapman of London Fecit 1775.
    5 In Wedlock's bands all ye who join
      With hands your hearts unite
      So shall our tuneful tongues combine
      To laud the nuptial rite.
          Pack & Chapman of London Fecit 1775.
    6 William Brewster and Rich^d. Hynes Churchwardens 1775. Pack & Chapman of London Fecit.
"Great bells v." Return of 1553. No note. Davy.

213. GEDDING. 2 Bells.
    De Bvri Santi Edmondi.
    1 Stefanus Tonni me fecit 1572.
    2 De Bvri Santi Edmondi Stefanus Tonni me fecit 1572.
      Omnia Iovam lavdent animantia.
No return in 1553. "2 bells and a small Pully." Davy.

214. GIPPING. 1 Bell.
    Bell. Charles Tyrell, Esq., Patron.
    Recast Anno Dom: 1812. Gipping Chapel.
1 in 1553.

215. GISLEHAM *Holy Trinity.* Diams. 28 & 34 in. 2 Bells.
    1, 2 Anno Domini 1627 AB
                   W
  So Davy. No return of bells in certif. of iiij Nov., 1547. "Great bells iij." Return of 1553.

216. GISLINGHAM *S. Mary.* In E., in tune. Tenor. Diam 45¼ in.
                                                      6 Bells.
    1 Cast by William Dobson of Downham Norfolk 1814.
    2, 3, 4 Miles Graye made me 1641.
    5 John Darbie made me 1671.
    6 John Darbie made me 1671. G. S. C.W.
4 in 1553. Fine-toned bells.

217. GLEMHAM, GREAT, *All Saints*.   5 Bells.
1 ▽ 52 thrice.
+ 61 ⱭⱭⱤⱻ Ⱡⱡⱡit Ʃcorum ▢ 62 Campā Ɽaudƒ Ʋonorum.
2 Thomas Gardiner fecit 1722.
3 ▽ 52 thrice.
+ 61 ⱩⱭunƒrƒ Ʋaptistƒ ▢ 62 Ʋƒnƒdictus Ʃit Ⱪhorus Ɇstƒ.
4 Anno Domini 1599.
5 + 14 ▽ 23 + 14 Ʃum Ʀofa Ɽulfata ⱭⱭundi ⱭⱭaria Ʋocata.

So Davy. No return of bells in certif. of iij Nov., 1547. "Great bells v." Return of 1553.

218. GLEMHAM, LITTLE, *S. Andrew*. Tenor. Diam. 44 in.
                                           F♯.   3 Bells.
1 Thomas Osborn Downham Norfolk fecit 1799. John Cottingham Churchwarden.
2 De Byri Santi Edmondi Stefanvs Tonni me fecit 1574.
3 Little Glemham November 1749. Cast by Thomas Lester of London.

So Davy. No return of bells in certif. of iij Nov., 1547. "Great bells iij." Return of 1553.

219. GLEMSFORD *S. Mary*.   6 Bells.
1 Thos. Mears of London fecit 1830.
2, 3 Miles Graye made me 1659.
4 Tho. Gardiner Sudbury fecit 1754.
5 Thos. Mears of London fecit 1830.
Rev. Wm. Butts, Rector.
Rev. E. D. Butts, Curate.
Ambrose Jefferys ⎫
Charles Bigg   ⎬ Churchwardens.
6 Charles Newman made mee 1686.
William Stanby ⎫ Churchwardens.
John Tomson   ⎭

Davy, Aug. 18, 1831. No notes. "Great bells v." Return of 1553.
Nov. 16, 1698, "Wm. Tamplin for hanging the tenor and mending the other bells, 9/6." P. Acc.

220. GORLESTON *S. Andrew*.   6 Bells.
1, 2, 3, 4, 5 Mears & Stainbank, founders, London, 1873.
6 Mears & Stainbank, founders, London, 1873.
    This peal of bells dedicated to the honor and glory of God and the use of the parish church of St. Andrew's Gorleston by Miriam Chevallier Roberts born at Southtown in that parish A.D. 1853.

The old 4 were thus inscribed :—
1 ▽ 50 AB ▽ 86.
  W
1619. Dame Chamberlin Xpofer Poope.
2 (see p. 42) + I AM : MAD : IN : YE WORCHEPE : OF YE : CROS.
+ SANCTE : NYCHOLAE : ORA : PRO : NOBIS.

3 Anthony Taylor, W^m. Cross Ch.Wardens 1763. Lester & Pack of London fecit.
4 ▽ 50 AB ▽ 86.
W
John Belton, Dame Chamberlin, Xpofer Poope, Churchwardens 1619.

"iiij Nov., 1547. Certif. of Erasmus ffox and and Barnard Sudbrū Chyrchewardens ther. We s^rtefye that the towneshypp have sold one Crosse of sulu^r and one sens^r of sylu^r to the value and sma of xiiijli iiijs. yerys sence. The whyche xiiijli is bestowyd vppon a newe bellfframe to the bells and a new Battylment to the stepull for iiij yerys paste."
"Great bells iiij. Sancts bells j." Return of 1553.

When I was here in 1866 I found only the two smaller of the four whole, being the 2nd and 4th of a six. The treble and third were sold c. 1845 to assist in pewing the church.

221. GOSBECK *S. Mary.* 1 Bell.
Bell. Recast by J. Taylor & Co., Loughborough, 1879. The Rev^d. F. S. Barry Rector.
W. Mayhew, Churchwarden.

3 in 1553. Davy, 8 May, 1824. One bell inscribed—
Sancta Maria ora pro nobis.

222. GROTON *S. Bartholomew.* Tenor. Diam. 40¼ in. Weight 10 cwt. 3 qrs. 11 lbs. 5 Bells.
1 John Darbie made me 1676.
2 Lester & Pack of London fecit 1764.
  Rich^d. Lifton & Geo Mumford C^hWardens W^m. Dawson.
3 ▽ 25 + 22 ▽ 26 Sancte Katerina Ora Pro Nobis.
4 ✠ 38 ▽ 31 + Sit Nomen Domini Benedictum.
5 Lester & Pack of London fecit 1763.
  Geo Mumford & Rich^d. Lifton Ch.Wardens.
"Great bells iiij. Sancts bells j." Return of 1553.

223. GRUNDISBURGH *S. Mary.* Tenor. Diam. 38½.
6 Bells.
1 T. Mears. of London fecit 1830.
  Rev^d. D^r. Ramsden Rector.
  James Hayward Churchwarden.
  Saml. Cutting Subscriber.
2 John Darbie made me 1665.
  William Yorke C. W.
3 Pack & Chapman of London fecerunt 1779.
  James Johnson Churchwarden.
4 John Darbie made me 1665.
5 G. Mears & Co., London, 1864.
6 Miles Graye made me 1628.

T. Martin, 1725, notes "John Darbie made me 1665 upon 4th bell lying at the West end of the Church, upon the least but one
William   W
Yorke   C
upon the biggest Sr William Bloys Knight. Another broken bell run at the same time lies in a Vestry or inclosed place at the West end of the South Isle."

224. GUNTON *S. Peter.*
No Bell.
No return in 1553. None in Robert Reeve's time.
"We neu^r sold no other ymplemens (but plate) nat for y* xx^{ti} yers past.
Certif. of Henry Heyham and Henry Blocke, C.W. iij Nov., 1547."

225. HACHESTON *All Saints.*
1 [Inscription wholly obscured by iron band].
2, 4 Ihon Darbie made me 1683.
3 ▽ 50 thrice.
+ 61 𝕭ulcis 𝕮ifto 𝕸elis □ 62 𝕮ampa 𝖁ocor 𝕸iebis.
5 ▽ 51.
   1582. S. G. Rector. H. F. C.W.
Four bells are returned under "Parham Haston" in 1553.
Hawes notes the treble as "Richard Phelps made me 1712," and the tenor as SG. RBCT RR RE CR HR. SH BR HT GT MW HI PH 1589.
Davy, Oct. 24, 1817, adds "Anno."

226. HADLEIGH *S. Mary.* Tenor 28 cwt. Diam. 52¼ in.
                                                            8 and Clock bell.
1, 2 Miles Graye made me 1678.
3 Miles Graye made me 1679.
4 + 89 ▽ 31 + 37 𝕾it 𝕹omen 𝕯omini 𝕭enedictum.
5 The Rev. D^r. Drummond Rector.
   J. B. Leake and Thos. Sallows Churchwardens 1806.

Fig. 89.

6 The Very Rev. H. B. Knox Rector.
   J. Rand W. Grimwade Churchwardens.
   C. & G. Mears, founders, London, 1856.
7 The Rev. D^r. Thos. Drake, Rector. Samuel Hyell
   Edward Sallows Ch. Wardens. T. Osborn fecit 1788.
8 Miles Graye made me 1680.
   Clock bell. AVE 𝕸ARIA GRACIA PLENA
   (backwards).
"Great bells vj." Return of 1553.
Davy, 5 and 6 Nov., notes 5, Johannes Thornton fecit 1719. In Multis Annis Resonet Campana Johannis, and 6, 𝕾um 𝕽osa 𝕻ulsata 𝕸undi 𝕸aria 𝖁ocata. al. sim.

227. HALESWORTH *S. Mary.* Tenor in C.
8 and Clock bell.
1, 2 Pack & Chapman of London fecit 1770.
3 Lester & Pack of London fecit 1759.
4 ▽ 65 thrice.
+ 67 𝔖𝔞𝔫𝔠𝔱𝔢 ☐ 68 𝔗𝔥𝔬𝔪𝔞 ☐ 68 𝔒𝔯𝔞 ☐ 68 𝔓𝔯𝔬 ☐ 68 𝔑𝔬𝔟𝔦𝔰.
5 RICHARD WELTON AND DANIEL BARNE CHVRCH WARDENS IVLII 1625 WIB
6 ▽ 65 thrice.
+ 67 ☐ 68 𝔍𝔬𝔥𝔞𝔫𝔫𝔢𝔰 ☐ 68 𝔠𝔥𝔯𝔦𝔰𝔱𝔦 ☐ 68 𝔠𝔞𝔯𝔢 ☐ 68 𝔇𝔦𝔤𝔫𝔞𝔯𝔢 ☐ 68 𝔭𝔯𝔬 ☐ 68 𝔑𝔬𝔟𝔦𝔰 ☐ 𝔬𝔯𝔞𝔯𝔢.
7 ▽ 86 AB ▽ 50.
W
𝔄𝔫𝔫𝔬 𝔇𝔬𝔪𝔦𝔫𝔦 1611.
8 𝔑𝔢𝔴 𝔕𝔢𝔭𝔞𝔦𝔯𝔢𝔡 𝔅𝔶 𝔕𝔬𝔤𝔢𝔯 𝔚𝔬𝔬𝔡𝔰 𝔈𝔯𝔞𝔰𝔪𝔲𝔰 𝔐𝔬𝔰𝔰 𝔠𝔥𝔲𝔯𝔠𝔥 𝔚𝔞𝔯𝔡𝔢𝔫𝔰 𝔍𝔞𝔣𝔢𝔯𝔶 𝔅𝔞𝔯𝔢𝔱𝔱 𝔤𝔞𝔟𝔢 𝔪𝔢. WIB.
Clock bell. T. Mears London fecit 1826.

Davy, 1806, agrees with this. No return of bells in certif. of 1547. 5 and a Sance bell 1553. 7th, inconceivably honeycombed, lasts by a miracle.

228. HARGRAVE *S. Edmund.* Tenor in A. 3 Bells.
1 ♛ Thomas Cheese ☐ 82 James ☐ 82 Edbere 1622.
2 T. Mears of London fecit 1841.
Elizabeth White, Sarah White.
3 ☐ 81 Anno ☐ 82 : ☐ 82 Regni ☐ 82 Regine ☐ 81 Elizabeth. De Bvri Santi Edmondi Stefanvs Tonni me fecit.
☐ 81 Anno ☐ 82 Domini ☐ 82 1566.
"Great bells iij." Return of 1553. "3 bells," Davy. The treble has been over-flattened.

229. HARKSTEAD *S. Mary.* 5 Bells.
3, 4 Miles Graye made me 1611.
1, 2 Thomas Gardiner fecit 1722.
5 Thomas Gardiner Sudbury fecit 1722.
So Davy. 3 in 1553.

230. HARLESTON *S. Augustine.* Diam. 16¾ in. Note D.
1 Bell.
Bell. J. Warner & Sons, London.
(Royal Arms) Patent.
Recast 1862. Rev^d. C. Perry Rector. James Matthew Churchwarden.

2 in 1553. Davy, June 13th, 1827, notes a small bell in a cupola, inaccessible.

231. HARTEST *All Saints.* Tenor. Diam. 38½ in. 11 cwt.
5 Bells.
1, 2, 3, 4 John Darbie made me 1661.
5 John Darbie made me 1661. William Coppinge Richard Mirrld (sic) C.W.
"Great bells iiij." Return of 1553. Davy, Aug. 17, 1831, "5 Bells."

INSCRIPTIONS.   199

232. HASKETON *S. Andrew.* Tenor. Diam. 36½ in. Note A.
5 Bells.
1, 3, 4, 5 Miles Graye made me 1628.
2 T. Mears of London fecit 1832. Samuel Randale,
   Churchwarden.
1, 3, 4, 5 also bear the arms of Nath. Atherold, ob. 1678. No return of bells in certif. of 1547. "Wodbridge haston...Great bells iiij." Return of 1553.

233. HAUGHLEY *S. Mary.* Tenor. Diam. 45 in., in F. Weight
1 ton.   5 Bells.
1 Virorum ⁝ sumptus ⁝ nostrorum ⁝ sunt ⁝ Haughley.
Recast in memory of E. Ebdon Surgeon for 43 years a resident of this Parish.
E. E. Ward Vicar, S. J. Harrison } Churchwardens
                   S. S. Baker   }   1885.
J. Smyth, G. Reed 1702 HP
Recast by John Warner & Son, London.
2, 3, 4, 5 Stefanvs ▢ 82 Tonni ▢ 82 me ▢ 82 Fecit ▢ 82 WL ▢ 82 1572.
▢ 81 De ▢ 82 Buri ▢ 82 Santi ▢ 82 Edmondi ▢ 82.
∪ 81 Sumptus ▢ 82 Nostrorum ▢ 82 Sunt ▢ 82 Haughlue ▢ 82 Virorum.
So Davy. 4 and a Sance bell in 1553.

234. HAVERHILL *S. Mary.*   5 Bells.
1, 3 John Darbie made me 1669.
2 John Darbie made me 1685.
4 Joseph Eayre St. Neots 1765. John Godfrey and Abel Bull Churchwardens.
5 Tho. Newman of Norwich made mee.
W. Wilshere & S. Bridge C.W. 1729.
"Great bells iiij. Sancts bells j." Return of 1553. No notes. Davy.

235. HAWKEDON *S. Mary.*   5 Bells.
1, 2, 3, 5 Miles Graye made me 1683.
4 Samuel Sparrow William Pettit Church Wardens. J. S. fecit 1721.
So Davy. "Great bells iiij." Return of 1553.

236. HAWSTEAD *All Saints.*   3 and a Sance bell.
1 + 15 ∪ 9 𝕰𝖙𝖊𝖗𝖓𝖎𝖘 𝕬𝖓𝖓𝖎𝖘 𝕽𝖊𝖋𝖔𝖓𝖊𝖙 𝕮𝖆𝖒𝖕𝖆𝖓𝖆 𝕴𝖔𝖍𝖆𝖓𝖓𝖎𝖘.
2, 3 Henry Pleasant made me 1696. Thomas Cason C.W.
Sance Bell. No inscription.
"Halstede...Great bells j." Return of 1553. The engraving of the Sance bell, fig. 78, is taken from the chancel, and the bell hangs at the south end of the Rood-screen. See p. 82.
The Whitechapel foundry cast five bells, tenor 9 cwt., for Hardwick House in this parish at some time in the last 100 years.

237. HAZLEWOOD.
Ecclesia destructa. "Great bells iij." Return of 1553.

238. HELMINGHAM S. *Mary*. Tenor. Diam. 49 in., in D.
Weight 19¾ cwt. 8 Bells.
1, 2, 3, 4, 5, 6 T. Mears of London Fecit 1815.
7 1815.
8 The Peal of Eight Bells were the gift of the Right Hon[ble], the Earl of Dysart. Anno Domini 1815.
' T. Mears of London Fecit.

Davy, 5 Aug., 1806, left spaces for inscription on 6 bells, but alas ! did not write them in. T. Martin (no date) notes 5. Old Tenor, Lionell Tallmach Esq. De Bvri S[d]. Edm. 1562. Stephanvs Tonni me fecit. Davy. See Henley. 4 in 1553.

239. HEMINGSTONE S. *Gregory*. Tenor. Diam. 45in.
3 Bells.
1 Charles Newman made me 1686.
2 ☉ 6s.
+ 𝕾ancta ☐ 𝔐aria ☐ Ora ☐ Pro ☐ 𝔑obis.
3 ☉ 6s.
+ 𝕮ell ☐ 𝔇et ☐ 𝔐unus ☐ 𝔒ui ☐ 𝔑egnat ☐ 𝔈t ☐ 𝔙nus.

So Davy, 8 May, 1824, imperfectly, crossing 1 and 2. 3 in 1553.

240. HEMLEY *All Saints*. 1 Bell.
Bell. Tho. Gardiner Sudbury fecit 1714.

So Davy, 21 May, 1811, save 1715.
No return in certif. of 1547. "Great bells iij." Return of 1553.

241. HENGRAVE S. *John*. 1 Bell.
Bell. 1796.

"Great bells iij." Return of 1553.
" No bells, except a small one for the clock." Davy.

242. HENHAM.
Ecclesia destructa. No return in 1553.

243. HENLEY S. *Peter*. Tenor 9 cwt. 5 Bells.
1 Thomas Mears & Son of London fecit 1809.
2 John Darbie made me 1658.
Rafve Meadowe } gave this bell.
Willyam Meadowe
3 Lionellus Tolmach Comes de Dysart hunc de novo fundi C. 1736.
4 6s thrice.
+ 𝕾ancta ☐ 𝔐aria ☐ Ora ☐ Pro ☐ 𝔑obis.
5 ☉ 6s thrice.
+ 𝕾ancte ☐ 𝔗oma ☐ Ora ☐ Pro ☐ 𝔑obis.

Davy, 9 May, 1824, "The Clerk told me this (now the 3rd) came from Helmingham." 4 in 1553.
The old tenor was by Gardiner, 1729, and weighed 10 cwt. 1 qr. 25 lbs., without the crown staple. From this the present treble is supposed to be made. The old 3rd by Miles Graye, 1617, was exchanged for a bell at Helmingham, c. 1870. In 1730 £22 12s. was paid to a Sudbury founder, no doubt Gardiner, for casting a bell and carriage.

244. HENSTEAD *S. Mary.* 1 Bell.
Bell. No inscription.
So Davy, 31 Aug., 1809. "One," Martin, 1750.
3 and a Sance bell in 1553.

245. HEPWORTH *S. Peter.* Tenor. Diam. 35 in, in A.
5 Bells.
1, 2, 3 Tho. Gardiner Sudbury fecit 1726.
4 Robt. Nunn Churchwarden. William Dobson 1825.
5 ▽ 50 thrice.
+ 𝔓etrus 𝔄d 𝔈terne ▢ 62 𝔇ucat 𝔉los 𝔓ascua 𝔙ite.
Impressions of coins and medals on 1, 2, 3. "Great bells iij." Return of 1553. 4 "Thomas Draper the younger made me 1593," says Davy, 6 Jan., 1810, otherwise as above.

246. HERRINGFLEET *S. Margaret.* 2 Bells.
1 1837.
2 AB ▽ 86 ▽ 52.
W
𝔄nno 𝔇omini 1611.
"Heryngsheath...Great bells iij." Return of 1553. We find from Reeve's Historical Collection that there were three bells, one inscribed + 𝔔uesumus 𝔄ndrea. 𝔉amulorum 𝔖uscipe 𝔙ota, and another + 𝔇ulcis 𝔈isto 𝔉letis. 𝔈ampana 𝔙ocor 𝔐ichaelis.

247. HERRINGSWELL *S. Ethelbert.* Tenor in B♭, all tuned by turning. 3 Bells.
1, 2, 3 I. Taylor & Co., Founders, Loughborough, 1869.
"Great bells iij." Return of 1553.
The original treble, 𝔉ac 𝔐argareta 𝔑obis 𝔚ec 𝔐unera 𝔏eta 𝔈x dono roberti dou (T. Martin). Recast 1741, inscribed John Pond C.W. 1741. Tho. Newman made me. 2 ▢ 𝔚ec 𝔉it ≈coru ▢ 𝔈ampa 𝔏aude 𝔅onoru. 3 ▢ 𝔖ac 𝔈n 𝔈onclabe ▢ 𝔊abriel 𝔉lunc 𝔓ange ≈uabe.
These three bells seen by me early in 1849 bore the usual Norwich marks. Davy reports these so, 22 Aug., 1828. Martin notes 3 in 1755, so that the 𝔉ac 𝔐argareta must have come from earlier notes.

248. HESSETT *S. Ethelbert* (fine bells). 5 Bells.
1, 2 Robert Midson John Vacher Churchwardens.
John Stephens made me 1724.
3 T. Osborn Founder 1787.
4 John Stephens Bell-founder of Norwich made me 1724.
5 John Stephens made me 1724.
So Davy. "Great bells iiij." Return of 1553.
See notes in Canon Cooke's *History of Hessett*, in the proceedings of the Suffolk Institute of Archæology, vol. iv., No. 6, pp. 330, 331.

249. HEVENINGHAM *S. Margaret.* Tenor 9 cwt. 5 Bells.
1 Tho. Osborn fecit 1797. Percute dulce cano.
2 T. Osborn Downham fecit 1797.
3 T. Osborn fecit 1797. Cum voco Venite.
4 T. Osborn fecit 1797.
5 Thos. Osborn fecit 1797. Long live King George the Third.

No return of bells in certif. of 1547. 4 in 1553.
Extract from Terrier rendered 24 May, 1784, "also four bells with frames, the least thought to weigh 7 cwt., the 2nd 9 cwt., the 3rd 11 cwt., and the 4th about 15 cwt." One of the present five is cracked in the shoulder.

250. HIGHAM *S. Stephen.*   1 Bell.
    Bell. Cast by John Warner & Sons, London, 1861. Presented by Joseph Gurney Barclay Esqr., Higham, 1861.

251. HIGHAM *S. Mary.* Tenor 8 cwt.   6 Bells.
    1 Thomas Mears, Founder, London 1842. The gift of A. C. Reeve, Esq.
    2 John Darbie made me 1675.
    3 William Mears of London fecit 1781. John Stubbin Churchwarden.
    4 John Darbie made me 1663.
    5 + 43 ▽ 23 𝔖𝔞𝔫𝔠𝔱𝔞 𝔉𝔦𝔡𝔢𝔰 𝔒𝔯𝔞 𝔓𝔯𝔬 𝔑𝔬𝔟𝔦𝔰.
    6 John Darbie made me 1675. John Partridge C. W.

So Davy, only transposing 2 and 3. See p. 23.
No return of bells in certif. of 1547. 4 in 1553. On the battlement of the steeple "J. S. W. M. 1786."
The late Vicar, the Rev. A. C. Reeve, died early in 1889. He was instituted in 1835.

252. HINDERCLAY *S. Mary.* Tenor. Diam. 39¼ in., in G.
                                                  c. 13 cwt.   6 Bells.
    1 Cum voco venite. T. Osborn Downham fecit 1790.
    2 Thomas Gardiner Sudbury fecit 1716.
    3 ▽ 65 thrice.
    + 𝔰𝔞𝔫𝔠𝔱𝔞 : 𝔠𝔞𝔱𝔢𝔯𝔦𝔫𝔞 : 𝔬𝔯𝔞 : 𝔭𝔯𝔬𝔫𝔬𝔟𝔦𝔰.
    4 I. D. and A. G. made me 1621.
    5 Thomas Gardiner Sudbury fecit 1734.
    6 ▽ 50 thrice.
    + 61 𝔑𝔬𝔰 𝔗𝔥𝔬𝔪𝔢 𝔐𝔢𝔯𝔦𝔱𝔦𝔰 ☐ 62 𝔐𝔢𝔯𝔢𝔞𝔪𝔲𝔯 𝔊𝔞𝔲𝔡𝔦𝔞 𝔏𝔲𝔠𝔦𝔰. 𝔍𝔬𝔥𝔢𝔰 𝔖𝔞𝔪𝔣𝔬𝔫.

"Great bells iij." Return of 1553. Davy's notes on the Pitcher, 19 June, 1844. Sperling says, "Tenor G, 14 cwt."

253. HINTLESHAM *S. Nicholas.* Tenor. Diameter 37 in., about
                                                             8½ cwt.   5 Bells.
    1, 5 John Darbie made me 1678.
    2 John Darbie made me 1677.
    3 John Darbie made me 1678. S. H. C.W.
    4 Thomas Gardiner Sudbury me fecit 1722.
So Davy. 2 in 1553.

254. HITCHAM *All Saints.* Tenor 8 cwt.   6 Bells.
    1, 2 Thomas Mears of London, Founder, 1837.
    3 William Powell } Churchwardens.
       W^m. Everett
    4 Henry Pleasant made me 1697.
    William Powell } Wardens.
    W^m. Everett

5 Thomas ₰ Gardiner Sudbury fecit 1755.
I Fieldgate } C. W.
R. Kemball }
6 Thomas Gardiner fecit 1744.
I. Fieldgate } C. W.
I. King   }
"Great bells iiij." Return of 1553.
T. Martin, 6 July, 1741, notes 6. Davy, 24 Oct., 1826, 5.

255. HOLBROOK *All Saints*.   5 Bells.
1 Pack & Chapman of London Fecit 1775.
Thomas Green & Jn°. Clark Ch. Wardens.
2 William Dobson Founder Downham Norfolk 1807.
3 Robert Patrick of London Founder 1783.
Thoˢ. Green Churchwarden.
4 John Darbie made me 1661.
5 Thomas Gardiner Sudbury fecit 1722.
No return of bells in certif. of 1547. 4 in 1553.
"Five bells, the oldest founded 1661." Davy.

256. HOLLESLEY *All Saints*.   3 Bells.
1 Anno Domini 1620.
2 ▽ 65 thrice.
+ 𝔖ancta 𝔐aria 𝔒ra 𝔓ro 𝔑obis.
3 Per me fidelis invocantur ad preces. Anno 1620.
"Great bells liij." Return of 1553.
There was another bell, with a large hole in the upper part of it, probably the treble, at Davy's visit, 14 Sept., 1824, inscribed, " Miles Graye made me 1637," otherwise his record agrees with this, save that he kindly corrects "fidelis" to "fideles."

257. HOLTON *S. Mary*. Notes B, B♭, A♭.   3 Bells.
1 ▽ 65 thrice.
+ 𝔖ancte ☐ 68 𝔓aule ☐ 68 𝔒ra ☐ 68 𝔓ro ☐ 68 𝔑obis.
2 John Darbie made me 1674. R. T. C.W.
3 ▽ 65 thrice.
+ 67 𝔄be ☐ 68 𝔐aria ☐ 68 𝔊acia (sic) ☐ 68 𝔓lena ☐ 68 𝔇ominus ☐ 68 𝔗ecum.

3 in 1553.

258. HOLTON *S. Peter*.   1 Bell.
Bell. Three marks, "M. H. M. 1881" (by Moore, Holmes and Mackenzie.)

2 in 1553. "One bell." Davy.

259. HOMERSFIELD *S. Mary*. 2 & 3 out of tune.   3 Bells.
1 ▽ 86 AB ▽ 52.
W
𝔄nno 𝔇omini 1619.
2 ▽ 52 thrice.
+ 61 𝔉ac 𝔐argareta ☐ 62 𝔑obis 𝔇ec 𝔐uneca 𝔏eta.
3 ▽ 50 thrice.
+ 61 𝔓ac 𝔌n 𝔒onclabe ☐ 62 𝔊abriel 𝔑unc 𝔓ange 𝔖uabe.
"Humᵣsfelde in Sowthelma...Great bells iij." Return of 1553.
Davy notes three bells, but could not get the key. May 18, 1830.

260. HONINGTON *All Saints.* Tenor A, c. 8 cwt. 3 Bells.
1 No inscription.
2 ☩ 50 thrice.
✠ 61 Ave Maria Gracia Plena ☐ 62 Dns Tecum.
3 John Draper made me 1600.
"Great bells iij." Return of 1553. Davy, 25 July, 1832, " 2 bells.'

261. HOO *SS. Andrew and Eustachius.* 1 Bell.
Bell. No inscription (very small, cracked).
No return of bells in certif. of 1547, or in 1553.
Davy, Apr. 21, 1819, notes it as inaccessible.

262. HOPTON *All Saints.* Tenor in F♯, c. 13 cwt. 6 Bells.
1 William Dobson Downham Norfolk fecit 1807.
2 John Draper made me 1629.
3, 4, 5 John Draper made me 1630.
6 John Draper made me 1626.
"Great bells iij." Return of 1553. Davy, 27 July, 1824, omits date on 2. al. sim. Sperling (1860) says, " Tenor F♯, 13 cwt."

263. HOPTON *S. Margaret.* 1 Bell.
Bell. T. Mears of London fecit 1815.
No return of bells in certif. of iij Nov., 1547. "Great bells iij." Return of 1553. Three bells mentioned in Reeve's Historical Collection.

264. HORHAM *S. Mary.* Tenor in B♭, out of tune. 8 Bells.
1 John ☐ Clvb 1673 ☐ Horham.
☩ ✠
2 John Clvb Horham 1672.
☩ ✠
3 John Clvb Horham 1672.
☩ ✠
4 John Clovb [Clerke] 1658.
5 Johanes Draper me fecit 1605.
6, 7 John Darbie made me 1663. John Clovbe Rector of Horham and Athelington.
8 Anno Domini 1568 (1568 also scratched in the mould).
4 in 1553. Davy, 16 July, 1809, notes these nearly so, except the tenor. They are the earliest octave, apparently, in the county. The Terrier, 13 Dec., 1672, notes " Eight bells, with frames, ropes, etc."
John Clubb, Rector, left in 1693, 6s. 8d. to be given to the poor on Plough Monday. His arms are on 1, 2, 3. Lettering of these puzzling.

265. HORNINGSHEATH *S. Leonard.* 6 Bells.
1 William Dobson Founder 1818.
2 Peace and good neighbourhood.
3 William Dobson Downham Norfolk Fecit 1818.
4 These Six Bells were given by Arthur Brooks Esq[r]., 1818.
5 W[m]. Bacon Wigson Esq[r]. and Thomas Gardiner Churchwardens 1818.
6 The gift of Arthur Brooks Esq[r]. The Rev[d]. Henry Hasted, M.A. Rector.
"Great bells iiij." Return of 1553. Tom Martin, c. 1724, notes, " Steeple lowered. 3 bells." Davy in 1834 by mistake records only 5 bells.

266. **HOXNE** SS. *Peter and Paul.* 5 Bells.
   1 John Darbie made me 1676. E. W. A. G. J. H. S. L.
   2 Omnis Sonus laudet Dominum. 1655 J. B.
     ꭒ (arms of Thruston, engraved on the bell).
   3 + John Goldsmith fecit 1711 Gabriel J. L. R. W. C. W.
     T. P.
   4 ꭒ 50 𝔒𝔯𝔞𝔱𝔢 ꭒ 50 𝔭𝔯𝔬 𝔞𝔦𝔞 ꭒ 50 𝔑𝔦𝔠𝔞𝔯𝔡𝔦 𝔖𝔪𝔦𝔱𝔥.
     ☐ 62 𝔍𝔩𝔬𝔰 𝔗𝔥𝔬𝔪𝔢 𝔐𝔢𝔯𝔦𝔱𝔦𝔰 ☐ 61 𝔐𝔢𝔯𝔢𝔞𝔪𝔲𝔯 𝔊𝔞𝔲𝔡𝔦𝔞 𝔏𝔲𝔠𝔦𝔰.
   5 ☐ 47 𝔍𝔣𝔞𝔠 𝔍𝔐𝔞𝔯𝔤𝔞𝔯𝔢𝔱𝔞 ☐ 48 𝔑𝔬𝔟𝔦𝔰 𝔚𝔢𝔢 𝔐𝔲𝔫𝔢𝔯𝔞 𝔗𝔢𝔱𝔞.

5 and a Sance bell in 1553. See Thorpe Abbot's, L'Estrange, p. 223.
Martin (without date) notes "upon one cast some years ago was this,
𝔋𝔞𝔠 𝔦𝔫 𝔠𝔬𝔫𝔠𝔩𝔞𝔳𝔢 𝔊𝔞𝔟𝔯𝔦𝔢𝔩 𝔑𝔲𝔫𝔠 𝔭𝔞𝔫𝔤𝔢 𝔖𝔲𝔞𝔳𝔢." This was almost certainly
the present 3rd. He gives wrongly 𝔅𝔯𝔬𝔴𝔫𝔢 for 𝔖𝔪𝔦𝔱𝔥 on the 4th. See his
note. Gillingwater, 20 Aug., 1799, says, "The 6th bell being split was sold
about 50 years ago, and the money applied towards seating and repairing
the church." In witness whereof the present five are in note the first five of
a six.
   N.B. At Thorpe Abbot's are two bells:—
     1 John Darbie made me 1678.
     2 John Goldsmith fecit 1712. Mr. John Caton Ch. Wd. Mr.
        S!. Stañard.
T. R. E. iij belles. One said to have been sold to Hoxne.
East Anglian, I., 108, for repair of Clock (1521) in Bishop's Palace.

267. **HULVER.**
Ecclesia destructa.

268. **HUNDON** *All Saints.* Tenor. Diam. 3 ft. 10 in. 6 Bells.
   1 Thos. Osborn Downham Norfolk Founder 1796.
   2 Charles Newman made mee 1701.
   3 Thomas Gardiner Sudbury Fecit 1726.
   4 T. Osborn Fecit Downham Norfolk 1801.
   5 Thomas Mears Founder London 1841.
   6 John Thornton Sudbury Made me 1720.
     Henry Teverson } Chh. Wds.
     John Hills   }
"Great bells v." Return of 1553. No notes, Davy.

269. **HUNSTON** *S. Michael.* 3 Bells.
   1 Pack & Chapman of London fecit. John Rust C. W.
   2 J. D. made me 1614.
   3 Johannes Driverys me fecit 1617.
"Great bells iij." Return of 1553. Davy, 6 July, 1843, "three bells."

270. **HUNTINGFIELD** *S. Mary.* Tenor cracked. 5 Bells.
   1 Thomas ꭒ Gardiner ☐ fecit 1722.
   2 Thomas Gardiner fecit 1720.
   3, 4, 5 Tho. Gardiner fecit 1720.
No return of bells in certif. of 1547. 3 in 1553.
Davy, 1 Aug., 1806, gives no inscriptions. Frame very bad now.

271. **ICKLINGHAM** *All Saints.* 3 Bells.
   1 ꭒ 8 thrice.
     ☐ 61 𝔙𝔦𝔯𝔤𝔦𝔫𝔦𝔰 𝔈𝔤𝔯𝔢𝔤𝔦𝔢 ☐ 61 𝔙𝔬𝔠𝔬𝔯 𝔆𝔞𝔪𝔭𝔞𝔫𝔞 𝔐𝔞𝔯𝔦𝔢.

2 ☉ 51 thrice.
☐ 47 **Quesumus Andrea** ☐ 48 **Famulorum Suscipe Vota.**
3 Johanes Draper me fecit 1608.
"Great Bells iij. Sancts Bells j." Return of 1553.

272. ICKLINGHAM S. *James*. 1 Bell.
Bell. No inscription.
"Great bells iij." Return of 1553. Davy, 20 Aug., 1829, notes one bell.

273. ICKWORTH S. *Mary*. 1 Bell.
Bell. Tho: Gardiner he me did cast
I'll sing his praise unto the last. 1711.
"Great bells iij." Return of 1553. No mention of bells by Davy.

274. IKEN S. *Botolph*. 4 Bells.
1 ☉ 26 ☐ 22 ☉ 25 **Sancte Thoma Ora Pro Nobis.**
2 **Mor Augustini Sonct En Aure Dei.**
☉ 26 ☐ 22 ☉ 25
3 ☉ 26 ☐ 22 ☉ 25 **Sancta Katerina Ora Pro Nobis.**
✠ ✠ ✠ ✠
4 **Sancte Iacobe Ora Pro Nobis** ☉ 29.
No return of bells in certif. of 1547. "Great bells iiij." Return of 1553.
So Davy, save that he could not read No. 2. See pp. 25, 33. 2 should have been mentioned with 1 and 3.

275. ILKETSHALL S. *Andrew* (before the fire, Sept., 1889).
4 Bells.
1, 2, 3 **Anno Domini** 1623.
AB
W
4 Ricardvs Bowler me fecit 1598.
So Davy, March 16th, 1810. "Great bells iij." Return of 1553.
In 1547 John Emerys and John Chevez C.W. return that "Robert Skytte wth the consent of thole Towne did sell one payre of chalyes v yeres agone to the sum of iiij m^rcs x*d*." which was bestowed about one bell, also "that Roger Walker and Rychard Warner did selle one payre of chalyes this last yeare to the S̄m̄e of xxxvs. whereof we have bestowed vpō a great belle xxjs."
The date on the tenor and one of the other bells remained unmelted. The metal, when run out, yielded 14 cwt., enough for recasting the two larger bells. Old tenor B. Diam. 34 in. 1 and 2 cracked in the crown.

276. ILKETSHALL S. *John Baptist*. 1 Bell.
Bell : ☐ : SANCTE : PETRE : ORA : PRO : ME :
"Great bells ij. Sancts bells j." Return of 1553.
"One small bell," Davy, March 16, 1810.

277. ILKETSHALL S. *Laurence*. 2 Bells.
1 1619. W. B.
2 Anno D̄n̄i 1619. W. B.
"Great bells iij." Return of 1553. So in substance, Davy, Mar. 16, 1810.

278. ILKETSHALL S. *Margaret*. 3 Bells.
1 ☉ 8 thrice.
☐ 12 **Sum Rosa Pulsata Mundi Katerina Vocata.**

2 ♄ 8 thrice.
☐ 12 **Dulcis Sisto Mells Campana Vocor Gabrielis**.
3 ♄ 50 thrice.
☐ 61 **Munere Baptiste** ☐ 62 **Benedictus Sit Chorus Iste**.
"Great bells iij. Sancts bells j." Return of 1553.
Treble cracked, 2 and 3 poor tinny bells. Tenor in F, a little sharp. Inaccessible to Davy, May 20, 1830.

279. INGHAM S. *Bartholomew*. Tenor F♯. Diam. 41¾ in.
5 Bells.
1, 2, 3, 4, 5 G. Mears, founder, London.
Offered at the Church at Ingham in memory of her Ancestors by Frances Wakeham, June, 1860.
The old bell was inscribed, ♄ 9 + ♄ 9 **Hec Noba Campana Margareta Est Nominata**. See p. 17.
"Great bells iij." Return of 1553. Davy, 25 Aug., 1829, "Only one bell."

280. IPSWICH *All Saints*. 1 Bell.
Bell. No inscription.

281. IPSWICH S. *Clement*. Tenor F♯. Diam. 43 in. 6 Bells.
1, 2, 3, 4, 5, 6 John Darbie made me 1680.
So Davy, 19 May, 1811.
"Itm bells in the Stepyll iiij." Return of 1553. See *East Anglian*, N. S. III., 204, etc., January, 1890.

282. IPSWICH S. *Helen*. 2 Bells.
1 Me Made Graye Miles 1621.
2 + 67 **Sancta** ☐ **Maria** ☐ **Ora** ☐ **Pro Nobis**.
"Seynt Ellyns...Impms bells in the Stepyll iij." Return of 1553.
Davy, 19 May, 1811, notes a third bell, like the present 2nd.

283. IPSWICH S. *Laurence*. Tenor F. Diam. 43½ in. 5 Bells.
1 ♄ 66 thrice.
+ 67 **Sancta** ☐ **Maria** ☐ **Ora** ☐ **Pro** ☐ **Nobis**.
2 ♄ 32 ☐ 22 **Sancta Katerina Ora Pro Nobis**.
3 ♄ 50 thrice.
☐ 61 **Sonitus Egidii** ☐ 62 **Ascendit Ad Culmina Celi**.
4 ♄ 50 thrice.
☐ 61 **Flos Thome Meritis** ☐ 62 **Mereamur Gaudia Lucis**.
5 ♄ 50 thrice.
☐ 61 **Sum Rosa Pulsata** ☐ 62 **Mundi Maria Vocata**.
So Davy, 20 May, 1811. See his note for legacies to the steeple.
"Bells we have sold non." Certif. of parishioners, 1547. "Itm in the Stepyll bells v Wheruppon gothe the Chymes. Itm Sanctus bell." Return of 1553. Tower engraved in the *Building News*, Dec. 29, 1882.

284. IPSWICH S. *Margaret*. Tenor F. Diam. 44 in. 6 Bells.
1, 3, 4, 5 Miles Graye made me 1630.
2 Robertus Richmond.
Miles Graye made me 1630.
6 Miles Graye made me 1630.
The living to the church, the dead unto the grave,
Thats my onely calling and propertie I have.
No return of bells in certif. of 1547. "Itm bells in the stepyll iiij." Return of 1553. Davy, 31 Aug., 1825, "six."

285. **IPSWICH** *S. Mary-at-Elms.* Tenor G. Diam. 36 in.
1, 3, 5 John Darbie made me 1660. 5 Bells.
2 ✠ ✠ ♆ 23.
4 Miles Graye made me 1613.
"Itm̄ bells in the stepyll iiij. Itm̄ Sanctus bell j." Return of 1553.
Davy, 21 Aug., 1821, notes 1 and 4 as here, gives 1662 as the date of the tenor, crosses 2 and 3, the former of which he calls "plain."

286. **IPSWICH** *S. Mary-at-Quay.* Tenor A. Diam. 33 in.
6 Bells.
1 T. G. fecit 1732. Mr. Henry Bowell C.W.
2, 3, 6 John Darbie made me 1662.
4 Miles Graye made me 1613.
5 Pack & Chapman London fecit 1775.
"Itm̄ Sanctus bell i. Itm̄ bells in the stepyll iv." Return of 1553.
Davy, 11 June, 1811, notes 2 and 3 as dated 1663.

287. **IPSWICH** *S. Mary Stoke.* 2 Bells.
1 No inscription.
2 Miles Graye me made 1615.
"Itm̄ bells in the stepyll iiij." Return of 1553. Another removed 1887, which Davy, 2 Aug., 1824, notes "plain."

288. **IPSWICH** *S. Mary le Tower.* Tenor D♭, 32 cwt. Diam. 58 in.
12 Bells.
1 ✠ **Cantate Domino Cantico Nobo** ✠ 1866.
2 John Taylor & Son, Loughborough, Founders, July 15th, 1845.
3 George Taylor Joselyn & Edwin Brook Churchwardens 1844.
4 Christopher Hodson made me 1688. R. M. T. S
5 ✠ **Laudate Dominum En Cymbalis Benesonantibus** ✠ 1866.
6, 8, 10 John Darbie made me 1671.
7 Miles Graye made me 1607.
9 ✠ **En Resono Reparata Maria Decora Vocata** ✠
Cast by John Warner & Sons, London, 1866.
11 Miles Graye made me 1610.
12 ✠ **Tripler Persona Trinitas Nunc Gaudia Dona.**
Cast by John Warner & Sons, London, 1861.
No return of bells in certif. of 1547. 5 and a Sanctus bell in 1553.
Davy, 2 Aug., 1810, notes 1, 3, 4, 5, 7, 8 (the present 4, 6, 7, 8, 10, and 11) as here. The old 2nd (present 5th) was like the old treble, and Warner in 1866 repeated the inscription on the old 6th (present 9th), dated 1707. The recasting saved any tuning.

289. **IPSWICH** *S. Matthew.* Tenor G. Diam. 39 in. 5 Bells.
1, 2, 5 Pack & Chapman of London fecit 1772.
3 ♆ 65 thrice.
✠ Sancta ▢ Katerina ▢ Ora ▢ Pro ▢ Nobis.
4 Miles Graie made me 1605.
So Davy, 17 June, 1824. No return of bells in certif. of 1547.
"Itm̄ bells in the stepyll iiij. Itm̄ Sanctus bell. Return of 1553.
In 1583, £4 4s. 2d. was paid for casting a bell and overweight, and 5s. 4d. for carrying it to Bury. In 1606 the brass of the 3rd cost 6d. for carrying to Colchester and back, and Myles Graye received £4 2s. 6d. for casting the 2nd. There are some more curious items.

INSCRIPTIONS.

290. IPSWICH *S. Nicholas.* Tenor G. Diam. 39 in. 5 Bells.
    1, 3 H. P. 1706. W Tweedy E. Syer C^{wm}.
    2 Miles Graye made me 1630.
    4 Henry Pleasant have at last
      Made us as good as can be cast. 1706.
    5 H. P. 1706. Marlburio duce castra cano vastata inimicis.
So Davy, 30 June, 1826. No return of bells in certif. of 1547.
"Itm̄ bells in the stepyll iiij. Itm̄ Sanctus bell." Return of 1553.
It is supposed that a Church dedicated to All Saints once stood on the site of S. Nicholas. See p. 141.

291. IPSWICH *S. Peter.* Tenor G$^{\sharp}$. Diam. 34½ in. 6 Bells.
    1 John Darbie made me 1682.
    2 Thos. Gardiner Sudbury Fecit 1733.
    3 No inscription
    4 John Darbie made me 1683.
      George Maciery Moreto. ?
    5 T. Rainbird, W. Goodrich C.W^s. T. G. Fecit 1735.
    6 Miles Graye made me 1630.
"Itm̄ bells in the Stepyll iiij." Return of 1553.
Davy, 15 June, 1811, assigns these inscriptions thus :—
    1 nowhere   4 to 3
    2 to 1   5 to 4
    3 to 2   6 to 5, and calls the tenor
"John Catchpole C.W. Charles Newman made me 1701."

292. IPSWICH *S. Stephen.* Tenor B.   3 Bells.
    1 ▽ 11 thrice.
      + 𝔙𝔬𝔯 𝔄𝔲𝔤𝔲𝔰𝔱𝔦𝔫𝔦 𝔖𝔬𝔫𝔢𝔱 𝔈𝔫 𝔄𝔲𝔯𝔢 𝔇𝔢𝔦.
    2 ▽ 11 thrice.
      + 𝔈𝔯𝔦𝔰𝔱𝔲𝔰 𝔓𝔢𝔯𝔭𝔢𝔱𝔲𝔢 𝔇𝔢𝔱 𝔑𝔬𝔟𝔦𝔰 𝔊𝔞𝔲𝔡𝔦𝔞 𝔙𝔦𝔱𝔢.
    3 Miles Graye made me 1630.
No return of bells in certif. of 1547. "Itm̄ bells in the Stepyll iiij."
Return of 1553. Davy, 3 Aug., 1810, "3 Bells." See p. 17.

293. IPSWICH *Holy Trinity.*   1 Bell.
    Bell. Thomas Gardiner Norwich fecit 1751.
Church about the beginning of the century.

294. IXWORTH *S. Mary.* Tenor E, c. 18 cwt.   6 Bells.
    1 John Darbie made me 1682. Sim: Boldero, Tho.
      Clark ChvrchWardens.
    2, 3 John Darbie made me 1665.
    4 ▽ 65 thrice.
      + 𝔖𝔞𝔫𝔠𝔱𝔞 ☐ 𝔐𝔞𝔯𝔦𝔞 ☐ 𝔒𝔯𝔞 ☐ 𝔓𝔯𝔬 ☐ 𝔑𝔬𝔟𝔦𝔰.
    5 ▽ 50 thrice.
      + 61 𝔑𝔬𝔰 𝔗𝔥𝔬𝔪𝔢 𝔐𝔢𝔯𝔦𝔱𝔦𝔰 ☐ 62 𝔐𝔢𝔯𝔢𝔞𝔪𝔲𝔯 𝔊𝔞𝔲𝔡𝔦𝔞 𝔏𝔲𝔠𝔦𝔰.
    6 Roger Boldero Gent & Thos. Garnham Ch. Wardens.
      Lester & Pack of London fecit 1766.

"Yxford...Great bells v. Sancts Bells j." Return of 1553.
Davy, 24 July, 1832, gives no bell notes, but an interesting inscription from the tower. The tower bears the name of "Master Robert Schot, Abot" (of Bury). He was a native of Ixworth, and the date is c. 1470. See pp. 55, 69, 123, 125.

295. KEDINGTON *SS. Peter and Paul.*   5 and Clock bell.
1 Thomas Mears, Founder, London, 1838.
2 Tho. Gardiner Sudbury fecit 1743.
3, 4, 5 John Darbie made me 1673.
Clock bell. 1779.
"Great bells iiij." Return of 1553. No notes, Davy. See p. 124.

296. KELSALE *S. Peter.*   8 Bells.
1, 2 T. Mears of London fecit 1831.
3 John Darbie made me 1681.
4 J. Peele me fecit. E. H. Burssor Churchwarden 1708.
5 T. Mears London fecit 1830.
6 S. Newton, J. Peele fecit. E. Hobart, E. H. Burssor, John Brothers, Ralph Eade Churchwardens 1708.
7 ▽ 50 thrice.
☐ 61 𝕯ona 𝕽epende 𝕻ia ☐ 62 𝕽ogo 𝕸agdalena 𝕸aria.
8 John Darbie made me 1681. Philip Eade, A. E. feoffees, Ralph Eade, Churchwarden, William Wright, M. W. C. E.

No return of bells in certif. of 1547. 4 and a Sance bell in 1553. 6 and 7 noted so by Davy, 29 May, 1806. I am not quite sure of the 7th marks. See pp. 58, 124, 146.

297. KENTFORD *S. Mary.*   3 Bells.
1, 2 Thomas Newman of Norwich made mee 1735.
3 T. Newman made me. R. Norman & T. Mullinger
C. W. 1735.
"Great bells iij." Return of 1553. Three bells. Davy. See p. 138.

298. KENTON *All Saints.*   2 Bells.
1 Miles Graye made me 1613
2 Miles Graye made me 1630.
"Great bells iij." Return of 1553. Davy, 10 Nov., 1815, notes two bells.
See pp. 117, 118.

299. KERSEY *S. Mary.* Tenor F. Diam. 42 in.   6 Bells.
1, 2 Thomas Gardiner Sudbury fecit 1716.
3 ☐ 81 1576 ☐ 82 De ☐ 82 Bvri ☐ 82 Santi ☐ 82 Edmondi ☐ 82 Stefanvs ☐ 82 Tonni ☐ 82 me ☐ 82 fecit ☐ 82 W L.
4 Christopher Hodson made me 1689.
John Fellget Edward Lapeg Church Wardens.
5 Stephen Kembell John Hodson made me 1662. W. H. Rodger Clarke Church Warden.
6 Samuel Sampson Church Warden I say
Caused me to be made by Colchester Graye M. 1638.
Clock bell. Thomas Gardiner Sudbury fecit 1716.
So with one or two involuntary variations, Davy. Clock bell from him, 19 Aug., 1825. "Carsseye...Great bells v." Return of 1553. See pp. 96, 118, 132, 143.

300. KESGRAVE *All Saints.*   1 Bell.
Bell. ✠ 𝕾ancta 𝕸aria 𝕺ra 𝕻ro 𝕹obis ▽ 29.
"Great bells iij." Return of 1553.
Davy. Note on Sir Samuel Barnardiston's generosity. See p. 33.

INSCRIPTIONS.   211

301. KESSINGLAND *S. Edmund.*   Tenor E.   5 Bells.
    1 Anno Domini 1617. WIB
    2 Thomas Newman made me 1711.
      Thomas Jealous C. W.
    3 Tho'mas Newman made me 1728.
      Thomas Brown, C. Warden.
    4 Mears & Stainbank, Founders, London, 1866.
    5 J. S. Crowfoot Churchwarden.   R. Manthorp Overseer
      1813.   T. Mears of London fecit.

No return of bells in certif. of 1547. "Great bells iiij. Sancts bells j."
Return of 1553. The old fourth was merely dated 1615, and the old tenor was inscribed, "Thomas Newman made me 1728. Thomas Brown C.W. John Jenner." Davy, who gives 1615 as the date of the treble. Tower, 93 feet high, a fine sea-mark. See pp. 114, 137.

302. KETTLEBASTON *S. Mary.*   3 Bells.
    1 John Darbie made me 1663.
    2 Steven Barton John Jenings Churchwardens 1699.
    3 ☐ 81 1567 ☐ 82 De ☐ 82 Bvri ☐ 82 Santi ☐ 82 Edmondi ☐ 82 Stefanvs ☐ 82 Tonni ☐ 82 me ☐ 82 fecit.

"Great bells iij." Return of 1553.
Davy, by mistake, 27 August, 1826, 2 Bells. See pp. 96, 123, 136.

303. KETTLEBURGH *S. Andrew.*   3 Bells.
    1 Samuel Thompson, D.D., Rector. Robert Sparrow Gent.
      Robert Salmon, Ch.W. R. P. fec. 1711.
    2 ✠ 𝔖𝔞𝔫𝔠𝔱𝔞 ☐ 𝔐𝔞𝔯𝔦𝔞 ☐ 𝔒𝔯𝔞 ☐ 𝔓𝔯𝔬 ☐ 𝔑𝔬𝔟𝔦𝔰.
    3 AP RG WW PA F.R. WP SRSNGLBI FTP. O 1592

So Davy, 3 Oct., 1805. "Great bells iij." Return of 1553. See pp. 102, 148.

304. KIRKLEY *S. Peter.*   1 Bell.
    Bell. ∪ 52 thrice.
    ✠ 61 𝔇𝔲𝔩𝔠𝔦𝔰 𝔖𝔦𝔰𝔱𝔬 𝔐𝔢𝔩𝔦𝔰 ☐ 62 ℭ𝔞𝔪𝔭𝔞 𝔙𝔬𝔠𝔬𝔯 𝔐𝔦𝔠𝔥𝔦𝔰.

So Davy. No return of bells in certif. of 1547. "Great bells iiij." Return of 1553. See p. 55.

305. KIRTON *S. Mary.*   1 Bell.
    Bell. No inscription.

"Great bells iij." Return of 1553. Davy, 15 July, 1829, 1 Bell.
In C, not a modern bell, and possibly an old one, with high crown. Diameter 28 in. C. H. H.

306. KNETTISHALL *All Saints.*   3 Bells.
    1 Tho. Gardiner Sudbury fecit 1720.
    2 John Draper made me 1628.
    3 John Draper made me 1609.

"Great bells iij." Return of 1553. Davy, 7 July, 1843, no notes. See pp. 111, 112, 144.

307. KNODDISHALL *S. Laurence.*   1 Bell.
    Bell. W. I. B. Anno Domini 1622.

So Davy, 1 Aug., 1808. 3 in 1553. No return in 1553. Terrier of 1725 names three bells. Terrier of 1806 names one bell. See p. 114.

308. LACKFORD *S. Laurence.* 1 Bell.
Bell. Thomas Newman of Norwich made me 1735
"Great bells iij." Return of 1553. One bell. Davy. See p. 138.

309. LAKENHEATH *S. Mary.* 5 Bells.
1 Thomas Mears, Founder, London, 1841.
2 Sancta Katerina ora pro nobis $+$ 21 ☉ 20 $+$
3 Cristus perpetue Dei nobis Gaudia Cite $+$ 21 ☉ 20 $+$
4 John Parsley Vicar. Charles Newman made me 1697.
5 John Darbie made me 1676. Thomas Denton James
Parlet Churchwardens.
Clock Bell.—auc ☐ maria ◇ Gratia.
"Great bells iiij." Return of 1553. Davy, 28 Aug., 1829, notes 5 bells.
See pp. 21, 111.

310. LANGHAM *S. Mary.* 2 Bells.
Two small modern bells, about the size of a school-bell.
"Great bells ij. Sancts Bells j." Return in 1553.
Davy, 7 July, 1843, "one bell."

311. LAVENHAM *SS. Peter and Paul.* Tenor. C. 23 cwt.
8 Bells.
1, 2 William Dobson, Founder, 1811.
3 Henry Pleasant made me 1702.
4 Ricardus Bowler me fecit 1603
Jacobus Fuller et Antonius Hormesby Guardiani ecclesie
de Lavenham.
5 Henry Pleasant made me 1703.
6 Ricardus Bowler me fecit 1603.
Hic mevs vsvs erit popvlvm vocare (four dwarfs and
other devices).
7 C. & G. Mears, Founders, London.
Richard Johnson, M.A., Rector. James Knight Jennings, M.A., Curate.
George Mumford } Churchwardens.
Robert Howard }
Thomas Turner, Woolstapler. Charles King, Shoemaker, 1846.
8 Miles Graye made me 1625.

Davy, Aug. 14 and 15, 1826, omits "Hic, etc., on 6." al. sim. Long and interesting note. The old 7th "Henry Pleasant made me 1702." The Whitechapel men were rightly proud of their new seventh. She had to be flattened, however. The tenor (see p. 117) is a very noted bell. John Carr when he first heard her, said, "She came in with such a noble sound that she vibrated a perfect octave." Others have observed the absence of overtones. Some consider that she varies with the weather. Mr. H. A. O. Mackenzie has kindly allowed me the sight of the vertical section. The peculiarity seems to be thinness, especially at the crown. "Great bells v. Sancts bells j." Return in 1553. See Dr. Howard's *Vis. of Suffolk*, pp. 170, etc.

312. LAVENHEATH *S. Matthew.* 1 Bell.
Bell. Back Skieppet ADoLF   Guten
Bygdt   Stockholm
i Jacobstad. A X 1801   af Gerhard Horner.
See p. 151.

Fig. 90.

313. LAWSHALL *All Saints.* 6 Bells.
  1, 2, 3, 4, 5 Thomas Newman of Norwich made me 1735.
  6 T. Mears of London fecit 1828.
Davy, Aug. 16, 1831, "contains 5 bells, which I did not visit."
"Great bells iiij. Sancts bells j." Return in 1553.

314. LAXFIELD *All Saints* (good). 6 Bells.
  1 Lester & Pack of London fecit 1760.
  2, 4 Cast by John Warner & Sons, 1873.
  W^m. Bloomfield } Church Wardens.
  W^m. Aldridge } George Day hung me.
  Rev^d. J. Dallas Vicar.
  3 ▽ 65 thrice.
  + 67 Sancta ☐ Maria ☐ Oro (sic) ☐ Pro ☐ Nobis.
  5 : ☐ DIUINŪ : AUNXILIV (sic) : MANEAT : SEM-
    PER : NŌBISCV.
  6 Thomas Mears of London fecit 1804.
No return of bells in certif. of 1547. 5 and a Sance bell in 1553.
Davy, 22 May, 1807, notes the old 2nd, En Multis Annis Resonrt Campana
Jobis, and the old 3rd, Sancta Maria Ora Pro Nobis, and the rest as here.
The tenor has a crack, which Day has stopped by boring a hole. This noble
tower (fig. 90) bears the arms of Wingfield and Fitz-Lewes in pale. See
pp. 62, 69.

315. LAYHAM *S. Andrew.* 1 Bell.
  Bell. ▽ 50 twice ▽ 86.
  + 61 Dona Repende Pia ☐ 62 Rogo Magdalena Maria.
"Great bells iiij." Return in 1553.
T. Martin, 17 Aug., 1717, 4 Bells. Davy, 18 Aug., 1825, only one bell.
See p. 58.

316. LEISTON *S. Margaret.* 8 Bells.
  1, 2 J Taylor & Company B.F. Added by F. Garrett in
    remembrance of his partner and brother, who died
    30th July, 1884.
    Vicar, B. W. Raven.
    Churchwardens, F. Sherwood, W. H. Borrett.
  3 John Taylor & Son, Loughborough, 1854.
  4, 6 John Brend made me 1640.
  5, 8 J Taylor & Co., Bell-founders, Loughborough, 1884.
    Dedicated by affectionate children to the memory of
    Elizabeth Garrett, who died the 30th of March, 1884.
    Vicar, B. W. Raven, C. W. F. Sherwood, W. H. Borrett.
  7 John Darbie made me 1674 James Reeve John Wool-
    nough C. W.
The old treble also by Brend 1640.
Terrier, 1806, 1 c. 5 cwt.; 2, 7 cwt.; 3 c. 9 cwt.; 4, 12 cwt.; 5, 15 cwt.
No return of bells in certif. of 1547. 3 in 1553. See pp. 124, 153.

317. LETHERINGHAM *S. Mary.* 1 Bell.
  Bell. De Buri Santi Edmondi Stefanvs Tonni me fecit
    1572 W. L.
"Great bells iiij." Return in 1553.
Davy gives the date 1579 (21 April, 1819). See p. 96.

318. LEVINGTON *S. Peter.*   3 Bells.
1 Sit ℕomen Domini Benedictum ▽ 31 + + 37.
2 ☐ ЄЛ ☐ ORD ☐ ARO ☐ AIRAM ☐ ATCNAS.
3 ☐ 81 De ☐ 82 Bvri ☐ 82 Santi ☐ 82 Edmondi ☐ 82 Stefanvs ☐ 82 Tonni ☐ 82 me ☐ 82 fecit ☐ 81 WI.. ☐ 81 1581.

So Davy, 3 Aug., 1810. "Great bells iiij." Return in 1553. They hang from N. to S. 1, 3, 2. Levington second is of the same type as Capel S. Mary tenor. The stop is not engraved, as far as I know. See pp. 35, 77.

319. LIDGATE *S. Mary.*   5 Bells.
     1, 2 John Draper made me 1625.
     3 Charles Newman made mee 1698.
     4 John Draper and Andrew Gurny made me 1625.
     5 W. S. T. T. C.W. Tho. Gardiner Fecit 1721.

Five bells, Davy. "Great bells iiij. Sancts bells j." Return in 1553. See pp. 112, 136, 144.

320. LINDSEY *S. Peter.*   1 Bell.
     Bell. Inscription unknown.

"Great bells iiij." Return of 1553. Davy, 19 Aug., 1825, 4 Bells. The tower fell in 1836, when three of the four were sold.

321. LINSTEAD, GREAT, *S. Peter.*   1 Bell.
     Bell. ▽ 52 thrice.
     + 61 Virginis Egregie ☐ 62 Vocor Campana Marie.

2 in 1553. Davy, 31 May, 1833, "Only one small bell." Terrier, 7 June, 1806, no mention of a bell. See p. 54.

322. LINSTEAD, LITTLE, *S. Margaret.*   1 Bell.
     Bell. 1789.

2 in 1553. Davy, 7 Jan., 1810, "a single bell." See his note.

323. LIVERMERE, GREAT, *S. Peter.* Tenor 5 cwt.   5 Bells.
     1, 2, 3, 4 Lester & Pack of London Fecit 1762.
     5 Simon Mothersole Farmer & Simon Mothersole Bricklayer Ch.Wardens 1762.
     Lester & Pack of London Fecit.

Davy notes this as recorded on the north wall of the Church. "Great bells iij." Return of 1553. See p. 149.

324. LIVERMERE LITTLE, *SS. Peter and Paul.*   1 Bell.
     Bell. Charles Newman made mee 1697.

"Great bells iij." Return of 1553. Davy, 26 Aug., 1829, "Only 1 bell."

325. LOUND *S. John Baptist.*   3 Bells.
     1, 2 Tho. Newman of Norwich made mee 1730.
     3 Tho. Newman of Norwich made mee 1730.
     John Kett and William Ellis C. W.

"One bell hanging and two splitt ones standing in the belfry." Reeve's Historical Collection. He adds in a parenthesis, "3 new bells."
"iiij^{or} Nouembr An^o. R. R. Edwardi p^rmo Lounde. A newe ertyficat maid by ye church Wardens of lownde Thomas Jaxe and Rob^rt Candlar. Itm y^t we haue sold a bell for ye some of iiij*li*.

Itm for ye yottyng of a bell   ...   .   xl*s*."
"Great bells ij." Return of 1553. See p. 137.

326. LOWDHAM.
Ecclesia destructa. No return in 1553.

327. LOWESTOFT *Christ Church.*   6 Bells.
  1. W. Blews & Sons, Birmingham.
     Eleanor Strong
        1876.
  2 W. Blews & Sons, Founders, 1875.
  3, 4 W. Blews & Sons, Birmingham, 1875.
  5 W. Blews & Sons, Birmingham, 1875.
     Charles Hebert, D.D., Vicar.
     E. J. Barnes } Churchwardens.
     R. S. Barnes }
  6 W. Blews & Sons, Founders, Birmingham, 1875.
  + Voce mea viva depello cuncta nociva.
See p. 154.

328. LOWESTOFT *S. John Evangelist.*   1 Bell.
  Bell. 1855.

329. LOWESTOFT *S. Margaret.*   1 Bell.
  Bell. I tell all that doth me see
      That Newman of Norwich new cast mee 1730.
      G. Durrant, C. W.

"Spire. Square Tower. 1 Bell. 5 formerly. 4 of them stole or perhaps taken away during the time of the Commonwealth." Reeve's Historical Collection.

"iiij° Nouember A°. D^m. 1547.
Leystoft. The certyficate of Jamys Jeto^r. Antony Jeto^r. Robert Aleyn and Roberd Hudschyd Cherchewardens there" makes no mention of bells. "Great bells iiij. Sancts bells j." Return of 1553. See p. 132.

330. LOWESTOFT *S. Peter.*   1 Bell.
  Bell. No inscription.
Small and modern.

331. MARLESFORD *S. Andrew.*   4 Bells.
  1 ▽ 52 thrice.
  + 61 𝔈𝔫 𝔐𝔲𝔩𝔱𝔦𝔰 𝔄𝔫𝔫𝔦𝔰 ☐ 62 𝔑𝔢𝔣𝔬𝔫𝔢𝔱 𝔈𝔞𝔪𝔭𝔞 𝔍𝔬𝔥𝔦𝔰.
  2 Anno Domini 1615.
    𝔈 𝔭   𝔈 𝔙   mp
  3 Anno Domini 1615.
    ℜ p   𝔈 𝔙.
  4 ▽ 50 thrice.
  + 61 𝔐𝔲𝔫𝔢𝔯𝔢 𝔅𝔞𝔭𝔱𝔦𝔰𝔱𝔢 ☐ 62 𝔅𝔢𝔫𝔢𝔡𝔦𝔠𝔱𝔲𝔰 𝔖𝔦𝔱 𝔈𝔥𝔬𝔯𝔲𝔰 𝔈𝔰𝔱𝔢.

So Davy, nearly. "Mr. Edwd. Williams, Rector, has built a place for the Saint's bell."

iij° Nouember A° D^m 1547. Certif. of Tho. Bayman and John Nuttall C. W. makes no mention of bells. "Great bells iiij." Return of 1553. See p. 59.

332. MARTLESHAM *S. Mary.*   3 Bells.
  1 ▽ 52 thrice.
  + 61 𝔐𝔦𝔰𝔰𝔲𝔰 𝔡𝔢 𝔈𝔢𝔩𝔦𝔰 ☐ 62 𝔚𝔞𝔟𝔠𝔬 𝔑𝔬𝔪𝔢𝔫 𝔊𝔞𝔟𝔯𝔦𝔢𝔩𝔦𝔰.
  3 ▽ 51 thrice.

+ 61 ꬶac ꬶargareta ☐ 62 ꬶobis ꬶec ꬶunera ꬶeta.
3 Miles Graye made me 1631.
1547, certificate of ——— and — Syluerne C. W. of Martellesham makes no mention of bells. See pp. 53, 57, 118.
"Great bells iij." Return of 1553.

333. MELFORD, LONG, *Holy Trinity*.   8 Bells.
1 T. Lester made me.
2, 3 Thomas Mears of London, founder, 1833.
Rev^d. Edward Cobbold, M.A., Rector.
Richard Almack, F.S.A., Sir Hyde Parker, Churchwardens.
4, 7 Thomas Lester made me 1744.
5 C. & G. Mears, Founders, London, 1845.
Rev^d. Edwd. Cobbold, Rector.
George John Coe Robert Harris Esq. Churchwardens.
6 Abram Oakes Rector.
Giles Jarmin & Joseph Middleditch Churchwardens 1744.
Thomas Lester of London made us all.
John Williams of Stonham Aspal hung us all.
8 Cast by John Warner & Sons, London, 1865.
Rev^d. William Wallace Rector.
D. Mills } Churchwardens.
H. Cooper }
W. Downs hung me.

Davy, Aug. 16—18, 1826, 8. "Abraham Oaks Rector, Giles Jarmin Joseph Middleditch Churchwardens 1764. The end crown (sic) the work. Thomas Lester of London made us all." 2, 3, 5, as 4 and 7. Long and interesting note. When Dr. Warren, Rector, was ejected "as he returned home, one of the party beat a frying-pan before him, crying. 'This is your Saints bell.'" For an account of Dr. Warren see C. Deedes's Dr. Bisbie's MS. collections in *Suffolk Archæology*, 1889. Peal in *East Anglian*, 2nd S I., 322. "Great bells v. Sancts bells j." Return of 1553. Weight of the old tenor, 16 cwt., Mears and Stainbank, 31 Jan., 1888. See pp. 97, 149.

334. MELFORD, LONG, *S. Catharine's* (Mission Room).
Bell. Miles Graye made me, 1672.
This bell used to hang on the top of the tower. It was sold about 1868, and repurchased by the Rector, the Rev. C. J. Martyn, for the Mission Room. See p. 134.

335. MELLIS *S. Mary*.   1 Bell.
Bell. Miles Graye made me 1626.

4 in 1553. Martin, 18 Jan., 172⁵/₆, notes 5 bells. Bought from Thwaite c. 1846. Davy, 23 April, 1819, notes this inscription as on the Thwaite bell. C. W. accounts are interesting.

336. MELLS *S. Margaret*.
Ecclesia destructa. No return in 1553. A small towerless Norman building.

337. MELTON *S. Andrew*.   3 Bells.
1 Miles Graye made me 1618.
2 ▽ 51 thrice.
+ ꬶac In Coelaue ☐ 62 ꬶabriel ꬶue ꬶange ꬶuabe.

3 ▽ 51 thrice.
  ╋ 𝕹os 𝕮home 𝕸eritis ☐ 62 𝕸erranuue 𝕮aubia 𝕷uci·.
4 ▽ 51 thrice.
  ╋ 61 𝕯ona 𝕽epenbe 𝖁ia ☐ 62 𝕽ogo 𝕸agbalena 𝕸aria.

So Davy, 12 Sept., 1807. (1 in old church, 2, 3, 4 in new.) iij Nov., 1547, certif. of Roger Truston and John Chamberleyn, C.W. makes no mention of bells. "Great bells iiij." Return of 1553. See pp. 53, 55, 58, 117.

338. MENDHAM *All Saints*. 6 Bells.

1, 2 Tho. Gardiner Norwich fecit 1748.
3 Anno Domini 1628 W. I. B.
4 Tho. Lines C.W.   Tho. Gardiner Norwich fecit 1748.
5 ▽ 86 ▽ 50. AB
           W
  Anno Domini 1623.
6 Cook Freston Esq. Willm. Rant Esq.
  Tho. Gardiner fecit 1748.

4 in 1553. Davy, 21 June, 1839, notes 6 bells. See pp. 114, 145.

339. MENDLESHAM *S. Mary*. 5 Bells.

1 Ultima tuba fui sonitu non ultima vita magna ubi magnanimo Frederico optimo nuptialia. 1612. AB
2 ▽ 50 thrice.   W
  ╋ 61 𝕯ulcis 𝕮isto 𝕸elis ☐ 62 𝕮ampa 𝖁ocor 𝕸ichis.
3 ▽ 50 thrice.
  ╋ 61 𝖁etrus 𝕬b 𝕮terne ☐ 62 𝕯ucat 𝕹os 𝖁ascua 𝖁ite.
4 John Darbie made me 1669.
5 ☐ 81 De ☐ 82 Bvri ☐ 82 Santi ☐ 82 Edmondi ☐ 82 Stefanys ☐ 82 Tonni ☐ 82 me ☐ 82 fecit ☐ 82 1575.
  Clock bell ▽ 52.

4 in 1553. Martin and Davy 5. See pp. 55, 56, 96.

340. METFIELD *S. John Baptist*. 3 Bells.

1 Anno Domini 1568 I. B.
2 Mr. John Franclin and Mr. Charles Watson Churchwardens 1647.
3 ▽ 50 ▽ 86 twice.
  ╋ 61 𝕸unere 𝕭aptiste ☐ 62 𝕭enedictus 𝕾it 𝕮horus 𝕰ste.

Davy, 7 Jan., 1810, gives "Richard" as Mr. Watson's christian name, and crosses 1 and 2. Anno Dñi 1547. Metffilde. Certif. of John hybarde and Nycholas Gooche C.W. makes no mention of bells. 4 and a Sance bell in 1553. See p. 59.

341. METTINGHAM *All Saints*. 4 Bells.

1 ▽ 52 thrice.
  anno Domini 1612.
2 John Stephens fecit 1722. Beniamin Culham Church Warden.
3 No inscription. (A pretty border.)
4 No inscription. (A rough old bell.)

So in substance, Davy, Aug. 18, 1814. "Great bells iiij." Return of 1553. The *compoti* of the College founded here by Sir John de Norwich contain notices of bells.

342. MICKFIELD *S. Andrew.* 3 Bells.
    1 T. Mears of London fecit 1816.
    2 Miles Graye made me 1626.
    3 Tho. Gardiner Sudbury E. F. F. C. 1716.
From Davy, 14 April, 1828. No sale of bells in 1547 certif. 3 in 1553.

343. MIDDLETON *Holy Trinity.* 5 Bells.
    1, 3 Pack & Chapman London fecit 1779.
    2, 4 John Darbie made me 1670.
    5 Pack & Chapman London fecit 1779.
      In Wedlock's bands all ye who join
      With hands your hearts unite
      So shall our tuneful tongues combine
      To laud the nuptial rite.
So Davy, 23 Sept., 1805. 4 in 1553. No sale of bells in 1547 certif. Terrier of 1678, no mention.
    ,,   1753, " five bells in good tune."
    ,,   1820   ,,   ,,

344. MILDEN *S. Peter.* 1 Bell.
    Bell. Mears, Founder, London, 1860.
" Myldyng...Great bells iij." Return of 1553.
Noted inaccessible by Davy, Oct. 25, 1836.

345. MILDENHALL *S. Andrew.* Tenor in E, c. 18 cwt.
        8 Bells.
    1, 8 Mears and Stainbank, founders, London.
      V. R.
      Jubilee
      1887.
    2 John Darbie made me 1676. IT DP RS RC IW.
    3, 4 Thomas Newman cast me new in 1732, Norwich.
    5 I TAYLOR AND CO. LOVGHBOROVGH C. F.
      YOVNGMAN E CHAPMAN A PEACHEY.
      1860.
    6 + 21 ▽ 20 + En Multis Annis Refonet Campana Johahnis.
    7 IOHN TAYLOR AND CO LOVGHBOROVGH
      IAMES READ AND CHARLES OWERS 1860.
" Myldenaelye...Great bells iiij. Sancts Bells j." Return of 1553.
Davy, 21 Aug., 1829, notes 6 bells. See pp. 21, 46-50, 83, 124, 137, 138, 145, 153, 155.

The frame was clearly made for five bells, but the difficulties about the tenor, to which reference has been made, which were not solved in 1530, seem to have been waiting solution in 1553, when there were only four bells in the tower. I regard the old fourth of the six hanging in the tower when I went up in 1848, inscribed + 21 ▽ 19 + Nomen Magdalene Campana Gerit Melodie, as the treble of these. The present 5th was recast from it. It weighed 7½ cwt. Thus the present 6th would have been the 2nd, a missing bell, from which perhaps John Darbie made the treble (with loss of metal) in 1676, would have been the 3rd, and the bell from which the old tenor before 1860 was made would have been the 4th. This old tenor weighed close on 15 cwt., and was inscribed " Jos. Arthy, Tho. Casburn, C. W. Tho. Gardiner, Norwich, fecit, 1751." Whether there ever was before the Jubilee a larger bell than this I cannot say. Henry Poulter of Worlington used to quote his father to the effect that the Isleham tenor, see *Cambs.*, was brought from Mildenhall because the tower was not strong enough for it. Before 1860 there was on the top of the tower a Clock bell, weighing 4¼ cwt., inscribed, " Thomas Newman of Norwich made me, 1744."

346. MONEWDEN *S. Mary.* 3 Bells.
1 De Bvri Santi Edmondi Stefanus Tonni me fecit 1586
    W. L. ☐ 81.
2 Miles Graye made me 1637.
3 WM RB GS O S E B U R + PT PS MH AI MR^cM
    O 1592 O TK FB

So Harvey's MS , p. 606. iij Nov., 1547. Moneden. Certif. of John Malster and John haryson C.W. makes no mention of bells.
" Monedele...Great bells iij." Return of 1553. See p. 96.

347. MOULTON *S. Peter.* Tenor 6 cwt. 5 Bells.
1, 3 Chapman & Mears of London Fecerunt 1782.
2 Chapman & Mears of London Fecerunt 1783.
4 Chapman & Mears of London Fecerunt 1784.
5 Chapman & Mears of London Fecerunt 1783.
    Messrs. Abr^m. Cawston & T. Poole ChWardens.
" Mowton...Great bells iij. Sancts bells j." Return of 1553.

348. MUTFORD *S. Andrew.* 3 Bells.
1 John.Brend made mee 1638.
2 Anno Domini 1615. W. B.
3 John Brend made me 1636.
"Great bells iij." Return of 1553.
Eastern Counties' Collectanea, p. 240. Davy records three.

349. NACTON *S. Martin.* 2 Bells.
1 Miles Graye made me 1625.
2 John Darbie made me 1662.

So T. Martin, Sept , 1725, save date of 2, which he gives 1666 or 1660.
" Great bells ij." Return of 1553.

350. NAUGHTON *S. Mary.* 1 Bell.
Bell. ☐ 81 Johannes ☐ 82 Drivervs + C me fecit 1618.

So Davy, 14 Sept., 1827, noting also an " old treble Miles Graye made me 1672 (?), and an old second, Thomas Andrew me fecit 1522 or 99 (sic)." (1599. J. J. R.) "Great bells iij." Return of 1553. See pp. 102, 110.

351. NAYLAND *S. Stephen.* 6 and Clock bell.
1 W^m. Dobson, Downham, Norfolk fecit 1810.
2 Henry Pleasant made me 1698.
3 John Murrell, Will. Infield C.W. I.G. 1733. E.G.
4 Messrs. Samuel Alston & Isaac Nicholson Church-
        Wardens 1789. W. & T. Mears Late Lester & Pack
        of London fecit.
5 Miles Graye made me 1636.
6 James Edbvrie of Bury made my fellowes and mee.
    ∪ 1605 ☐. Both marks contain curious monograms.
    Clock bell. 1764.

" Great bells iiij. Sancts bells j." Return of 1553. Tenor omitted on p. 109. Davy, Sept. 30 and Oct., 1828," Six bells which I did not examine."

INSCRIPTIONS. 221

352. NEDGING *S. Mary.*   2 Bells.
1 ☐ 81 Thomas ☐ 82 Andrew ☐ 82 me ☐ 82 fecit ☐ 82 1598.
2 ▽ 8 thrice.
✠ 𝕴𝖔𝖍𝖆𝖓𝖊𝖘 O 16 𝕮𝖗𝖎𝖘𝖙𝖎 O 16 𝕮𝖆𝖗𝖊 O 16 𝕯𝖎𝖌𝖓𝖆𝖗𝖊 O 16 𝕻𝖗𝖔 O 16 𝕹𝖔𝖇𝖎𝖘 O 16 𝕺𝖗𝖆𝖗𝖊.
" Great bells iij." Return of 1553. See pp. 17, 102.

353. NEEDHAM MARKET *S. John Baptist.*   1 Bell.
Bell. By Private gift 1886. S. Maude M.A. Vicar.
C. Cooper Churchwarden.
See Barking. The return for 1553 is for " Nedham in Barkynge."

354. NETTLESTEAD *S. Mary.*   1 Bell.
Bell. Miles Graye made me 1618.
3 in 1553. Davy, 18 May, 1829, notes two inaccessible.

355. NEWBOURNE *S. Mary.*   1 Bell.
Bell. Miles Graye 1621 me made.
C. Carr 1885 me remade.
Davy. Terrier, 1780, "about six hundred." No sale of bells in 1547 certif. "Great bells ij." Return of 1553.

356. NEWMARKET *S. Mary.*   5 and Clock bell.
1, 4 John Draper made me 1619.
2, 3 ☐ 81 De Buri Santi Edmondi Stefanus Tonni me fecit W. L. 1580.
5 Tho. Gardiner and Tho. Newman Fecit 1719. W. Sandiver W. Headley, C. W.
Clock Bell. John Thornton Sudbury Fecit 1718.
So Davy, 21 Aug., 1828. He notes the tenor as not hung.
"Eycenyng Halfe Hundred...Newmarkett...Great bells iij. Sancts bells j." Return of 1553. See pp. 96, 111, 138.

357. NEWTON, OLD, *S. Mary.*   5 Bells.
1, 3, 4 John Darbie made me 1663. TH RP
2 William Dobson Founder 1810.
5 John Darbie made me 1663. Thomas Hoggar R. P. C. W.
3 in 1553. See p. 123.

358. NEWTON-NEXT-SUDBURY *All Saints.*   5 Bells.
1, 2, 3, 4 Cast by John Warner & Sons, London, 1872. (Royal Arms) Patent.
5 Miles Graye made me 1664.
Thomas Dearesle.
"Great bells iiij." Return of 1553.
Davy, Sept. 13, 1827, "Contains three bells:—1 Thomas Kearsle Miles Graye made mec 1685. I. W. 2 Miles Graye made me 1658. 3 Miles Graye made me 1685." He is wrong. See p. 133.

359. NORTON *S. Andrew.* Tenor c. 13 cwt.   4 Bells.
1 Illegible, broken.
2 John Darbie made me 1674. Richard Clarke C. W.

3 John Draper made me 1628.
4 John Draper made me 1635.
"Great bells iij." Return of 1553.
T. Martin, 26 May, 1757, "Four bells." Mentioned by mistake on p. 151.

360. NOWTON *S. Peter.*   6 Bells.
     1, 2, 3, 4, 5 T. Mears of London fecit 1829.
     6 T. Mears of London fecit 1829. This peal of six bells was given by O. R. Okes Esqr. Henry Ja^s. Okes Esqr. & the Rev^d. Auston Okes.

"Nolton...Great bells iij." Return of 1553.
T. Martin, 26 Aug., 1749, notes 4 bells. Davy, Aug. 27, 1829, speaks of the present bells as "all cast and hung in the present year, the gift of Mr. Oakes. The belfry is locked up." See p. 151.

361. OAKLEY, GREAT, *S. Nicholas.*   5 Bells.
     1 John Goldsmith Fecit 1711 S. Margaret. Mr. I. K. C.W.
     2 John Goldsmith Fecit 1711.
     3 William Dobson, Founder, Downham, Norfolk, 1828.
     4 ◊ 15 Sum O 16 Rosa O 16 Pulsata O 16 Mundi O 16 Katerina O 16 Vocata.
     5 John Goldsmith Fecit 1711. Mr. John Kett, Mr. Brown Turner Church Wardens.

3 in 1553. Martin, 5. See pp. 14, 176.

362. OAKLEY, LITTLE, *S. Peter.*
Ecclesia destructa. No return in 1553.

363. OCCOLD *S. Michael.*   5 Bells.
     1, 2, 5 John Brend made me 1653.
     3 Charles Newman made mee 1698.
     4 William Dobson, Downham, Norfolk, Founder, 1824.

4 in 1553. Davy, 18 June, 1809, notes the old 4th like 1, 2, 5. See p. 136.

364. OFFTON *S. Mary.*   5 Bells.
     1 Thos. Gardiner Sudbury Fecit 1735.
     2, 4 Henry Pleasant made me 1700.
     3 ✠ Sancta ☐ Maria ☐ Ora ☐ Pro ☐ Nobis.
     4 John Darbie made me 1667.

So Davy, 19 May, 1829. A curious extract from Mr. Parker of Ringshall.
4 in 1553. See pp. 69, 123, 140, 144.

365. ONEHOUSE *S. John Baptist.*   2 Bells.
     1 R ☐ G 1673 ☐
     2 ☐ 81 1604 James ☐ 82 Edbery ☐ 82.

No return in 1553. Tom Martin, 16 April, 1756, "Good Fryday," notes, "Round steeple, two bells." Davy, 13 June, 1827, records the same number, inaccessible, or to use his own words, "the way up seemed by no means convenient, or perhaps safe." See pp. 109, 132.

366. ORFORD *S. Bartholomew.*   5 Bells.
     1 Miles Graye made me M 1639.
     2 Henry ▽ Pleasant ▽ made ▽ me ▽ 1694. John Cragg. W. A.

INSCRIPTIONS.   223

3, 4 John Darbie made me 1679.
5 Tho. Gardiner Sudbury fecit 1739.   J. Harris C. E.
   Ellis C. W.
S⁊ Davy.   No sale of bells in certif. of 1547.   "Great bells iiij."   Return
of 1553.   See pp. 118, 124, 140, 145.

367. OTTLEY *S. Mary.*   6 Bells.
   1 Cast by John Warner & Son, London, 1878.
     Henry & Catherine Woolner gave me August 8th, 1877.
     H. Wilkinson, M.A., Rector.
     G. F. W. Meadows   } Church
     T. King   } Wardens.
   2 R. Phelps made me 1728.   Mr. Bartholomew Russell
     Donor.
   3 ▽ 65 thrice.
     + 𝔖ancta ☐ 𝔎aterina ☐ 𝔒ra ☐ 𝔓ro ☐ 𝔑obis.
   4 ▽ 50 thrice.
     + 𝔋ac 𝔈u 𝔈onclabe ☐ 62 𝔈abriel 𝔑ūc 𝔓ange 𝔖uabe.
   5 ▽ 50 thrice.
     + 𝔉los 𝔗home 𝔐eritis ☐ 62 𝔐ereamur 𝔈audia 𝔏ucis.
   6 De Buri Santi Edmondi Stefanus Tonni me Fecit W. L.
     1576.
Davy.   Terrier, 1794, 5.   "Great bells iiij."   Return of 1553.   See pp.
53, 55, 67, 96.

368. OULTON *S. Michael.*   5 Bells.
   1 Edw. Tooke made me 1676.
   2 Edw. Tooke made me 1677.
   3, 4 ▽ 50 ▽ 86 AB
        W
     𝔄nno 𝔇omini 1618.
   5 ▽ 50 ▽ 86 AB
        W
     𝔒mnis 𝔖onus 𝔏audet 𝔇ominum 1618 G ℭ 𝔗 𝔅
"Great Bells iij."   Return of 1553.   See pp. 114, 132.

369. OUSDEN *S. Peter.*   5 Bells.
   1 Lester & Pack of London Fecit 1758.   *T. M. & R. B.*
     6 = 1 = 0.
   2 Lester & Pack of London Fecit 1758.   *T. M. & R. B.*
     7 = 0 = 20.
   3 Lester & Pack of London Fecit 1758.   *T. M. & R. B.*
     8 = 1 = 12.
   4 Lester & Pack of London Fecit 1758.   *T. M. & R. B.*
     10 = 2 = 26.
   5 Lester & Pack of London Fecit 1758.   *This peal of bells
     was the gift of Thoʳ. Moseley Esqʳ & The Rev. R.
     Bethell.*   14 = 1 = 10.
"Great bells iij."   Return of 1553.   See p. 149.

370. PAKEFIELD *All Saint and S. Margaret.*   4 Bells.
   1 Thomas Gardiner Norwich fecit 1749.
   2 AB ▽ 86 ▽ 50.
     W

𝔖𝔢𝔠𝔲𝔫𝔡𝔲𝔰 𝔓𝔢𝔯𝔤𝔯𝔞𝔱𝔲𝔰 1618.
3 𝔄𝔫𝔫𝔬 𝔇𝔬𝔪𝔦𝔫𝔦 1621.
4 Thomas Newman at Norwich made me 1728.
Davy records five. No sale of bells in certif. of 1547. "Great bells iij."
Return of 1553. See pp. 114, 137, 145.

371. PAKENHAM *S. Mary.*   5 Bells.
  1 Mears & Stainbank, founders, London. C. W. Jones Vicar, G. W. Mathew T. Thornhill Jun. Churchwardens 1872.
  2 John Draper made me 1626.
  3 Lester & Pack of London fecit 1760.
  4 G. Mears & Co., Founders, London, 1862.
    Good Will to Man.
    C. W. Jones Vicar, Robt. Stedman G. W. Mathew Churchwardens.
  5 G. Mears & Co., Founders, London, 1862.
    Glory to God.
    C. W. Jones Vicar, Robt. Stedman G. W. Mathew Churchwardens.
No notes by Davy. See p. 112.

372. PALGRAVE *S. Peter.*   6 Bells.
  1 Gloria Deo in excellsis (sic) W. Plampin Gen^t. 1737.
  2, 3, 4, 5 Gloria Deo in Excelsis W. Plampin Gen^t. 1737.
  6 I tell all that doth me se
    that Newman of Norwich new cast me 1737.
So Davy, 4 June, 1810. 3 in 1553. Sperling (c. 1860), "Tenor G$\sharp$."
See p. 123.

373. PARHAM *S. Mary.*   3 Bells.
  1 ☐ ueni : sponsa : mea : ad : oᵲtum : meum.
  2 ☐ assumpta : est : maria : in : celum.
  3 W. I. B. Anno Domini 1623.
So Davy. No sale of bells in certif. of Nov., 1547. "Great bells iij."
Return of 1553. See Cant. v. 1, vulg.

374. PEASENHALL *S. Michael.*   5 Bells.
  1, 4 Mears & Stainbank, Founders, London, 1876.
  2 Henry Pleasant made me 1691.
  3 ▽ 51 thrice.
    + 61 𝔔𝔲𝔢𝔰𝔲𝔪𝔲𝔰 𝔄𝔫𝔡𝔯𝔢𝔞 ☐ 62 𝔉𝔞𝔪𝔲𝔩𝔬𝔯𝔲𝔪 𝔖𝔲𝔰𝔠𝔦𝔭𝔢 𝔙𝔬𝔱𝔞.
  5 ▽ 9 thrice.
    + 13 𝔖𝔲𝔪 𝔕𝔬𝔰𝔞 𝔓𝔲𝔩𝔰𝔞𝔱𝔞 𝔐𝔲𝔫𝔡𝔦 𝔎𝔞𝔱𝔢𝔯𝔦𝔫𝔞 𝔙𝔬𝔠𝔞𝔱𝔞.
4 and a Sance bell in 1553. Davy, June 11, 1806, calls 3 "4," notes a 𝔓𝔞𝔠 𝔈𝔫 𝔒𝔬𝔫𝔠𝔩𝔞𝔟𝔢... for 3, old treble and present 2nd, " Henry Pleasant made me 1694." al. sim. W^{ts} from Terrier.
No sale of bells in certif. of Nov., 1547. See pp. 17, 56, 140.

375. PETISTREE *SS. Peter and Paul.*   6 Bells.
  1 John Taylor & Sons, Founders, Loughb^o, 1848.
  2 One bell recast unto three at the expense of Richard Brook Esqr of Petistree Lodge A.D. 1848. Jo. Taylor & Son fecit.

3 John Taylor & Son, Founders, Loughborough, A.D. 1848.
4 ▽ 8 thrice.
+ 12 €ternis Annis Resonet Campana Johannis.
5 ▽ 8 thrice.
+ 12 Me Clamante Jhesu Maneat Bethleem Sine Iesu.
6 ▽ 8 thrice.
+ 61 Jungere Nos Xpo ☐ 62 Student Nicholaus In Alto.

Pytestre. Certif. of 1547 records no sale of bells. "Petystre. Great bells iiij." Return of 1553.

At Davy's visit (6 June, 1806), the inscription on the old tenor, no doubt a grand bell, was "De Bvri Santi Edmondi Stefanvs Tonni me fecit 1576." See pp. 17, 58.

376. PETTAUGH S. *Catherine*.   1 Bell.
Bell. ▽ 51 thrice.
+ 61 Quesumus Andrea ☐ 62 Famulorum Suscipe Vota.

"Pettawe, iii Nov., 1547. The certyficate of Thomas Mallyng and ffraunces pyrson Cherchewardens th(ere) ffyrst we p'sent that Robert orwell and Lacy Lord that tyme beyng Cherchewardens hathe sold a peyer of Shalys p'ce-xls.
Whereof
We did bestowyd vpon the cherche in ladyng the seid xls. And y^t remayn styll a peyer of Shalys and iiij bells. "Great bells iiij." Return of 1553.

There were three bells at Davy's visit. That which remains seems to have been the tenor. The others were inscribed. John Darbie made me 1662, and Missus Vero Pie Gabriel Fert Leta Marie. See pp. 53, 57.

377. PLAYFORD S. *Mary*.   2 Bells.
1 ▽ 50 thrice.
+ 61 Hac In Conclave ☐ 62 Gabriel Nūc Pange Suave.
2 ▽ 50 thrice
+ 61 Jungere Nos Xpo ☐ 62 Student Nicholaus In Alto

Terrier, 1784. "Three bells, two of them by Computation about 18 cwt. The third on the ground, having been broken time out of mind, by computation about 12 cwt."

Terrier, 1801. "Two bells, by computation about 18 cwt."

Certif. of 1547 imperfect, but apparently no mention of sale of bells. "Great bells iij." Return of 1553. See pp. 53, 58.

378. POLSTEAD S. *Mary*. Tenor, c. 10 cwt.   6 Bells.
1, 2, 3, 4, 5 T. Mears of London fecit 1825.
6 T. Mears of London fecit 1825.
Rev^d. John Whitmore, Rector.
John Corder } Churchwardens.
Isaac Strutt

"Great bells iiij. Sancts bells j." Return of 1553. No date to any visit by Davy. Formerly 5 heavier bells. Present tenor 12 cwt. A tuneful ring.

379. POSLINGFORD S. *Mary*.   5 Bells.
1, 2, 3 Robard Gurney made me 1668.
4 Tho. Gardiner Sudbury me fecit 1725.
5 Peter Hawkes made me 1613.

"Great bells iiij." Return of 1553. See pp. 109, 132, 144.

380. PRESTON S. *Mary*.   6 Bells.
1, 2 Tho. Gardiner Sudbury fecit 1744.

3 Tho. Norden Roger C. W. Tho. G. fecit 1744.
4 Miles Graye me fecit 1640.
5 Henry Pleasant made me 1702.
6 Henry Pleasant made me 1704.

"Great bells iiij." Return of 1553. Davy, Aug. 15, 1826, puts 3 for 1· al. sim. See pp. 119, 140. The surname to Roger is Coe, as it appears from the parish book (1743), when a cracked treble and a sound tenor were ordered to be cast into three small bells, at a cost not exceeding £7.

381. RAMSHOLT *All Saints.* 1 Bell.
Bell. John Darbie made me 1679.

"Great bells ij." Return of 1553.
"The steeple is round and has but one bell." May, 1726, T. Martin (?) In 1747 the top of the steeple was blown down, and now the tower has no roof, and is much dilapidated. See p. 124.

382. RATTLESDEN *S. Nicholas.* 5 Bells.
1, 2 Tho. Gardiner Sudbury fecit 1754.
3 Robart Bumstead John Drake Church Wardens 1754.
4 Tho. Gardiner he did us cast
   Wee will sound his praise to the last.
5 Henry Westley John Jewers Churchwardens. T. Osborn fecit 1789.

"Great bells iiij." Return of 1553.
Davy notes 1, 3 as 1, 2, 2 as 5, 4 as 3, and 5 as 3. See p. 145.

383. RAYDON *S. Mary.* 1 Bell.
Bell. Cast by John Warner & Sons, London, 18—.

3 in 1553. Davy records the inscription on the old bell, Sancte Barnabe (sic) Ora pro nobis.

384. REDE *All Saints.* 3 Bells.
1 ☐ 81 De ☐ 82 Bvri ☐ 82 Santi ☐ 82 Edmondi ☐ 82 Stefanvs ☐ 82 Tonni ☐ 82 me ☐ 82 fecit ☐ 82 W L ☐ 82 1578.
2 ☐ 81 De ☐ 82 Bvri ☐ 82 Santi ☐ 82 Edmondi ☐ 82 Stefanvs ☐ 82 Tonni ☐ 82 me ☐ 82 fecit ☐ 82 W L ☐ 81 1586.
3 John ☐ 81 Dry ☐ 82 Ver ☐ 81 me fe cet ☐ 81 1602.

"Great bells iij." Return of 1553.
Tom Martin, March 12, 1724, says, "Steeple above half down, 3 bells." Davy, by mistake, Aug. 25, 1831, speaks of 2 bells. See pp. 96, 109.

385. REDGRAVE *S. Mary.* 6 Bells.
1 T. Osborn fecit 1785.
2, 3, 4, 5 Thomas Newman of Norwich made me 1736.
6 John Munns & John Goldsmith C. W. Thomas Newman of Norwich made me 1736.

3 in 1553. T. Martin notes, In Sept., 1736, the five bells were taken out of Redgrave steeple, in order to be new (run or) cast. The tenor had a piece broken out of the top of it, and this circumscription: Chas. Newman made me 1691. Goldsmith Ch W. On the other 4: Chas. Newman made mee 1691, in capitals. Sperling (1860) says, "Tenor G$\sharp$, 9 cwt." See pp. 138, 145.

386. REDISHAM, GREAT, *S. Peter.* 1 Bell.
Bell. No inscription.

Suckling notes a split bell dated 1621. "The steeple has been long down. But one bell hangs at the west end, in a frame on the ground. It bears inscription, Anno Domini 1621." Davy, June 2, 1808 (?)
" Great bells ij." Return of 1553.

387. REDISHAM, LITTLE, *S. James.*
Ecclesia destructa. No return in 1553.

388. REDLINGFIELD *S. Andrew.* 1 Bell.
Bell. No inscription.

3 in 1553. So Davy, 5 Dec., 1817.
Martin (without date) notes three modern bells hanging in a wooden frame.

389. RENDHAM *S. Michael.* 5 Bells.
1 T. Mears of London fecit 1831.
2 Inscription entirely covered with an iron band. Date of stock 1794.
3 ▽ 65 thrice.
+ 𝔙irgo ☐ Coronata ☐ Duc ☐ Nos ☐ Ad ☐ Regna Beata.
4 N. S.   T. H.   E. I.
Anno Domini 1622. WIB.
5 Thomas Mears of London fecit 1802.

Davy gives the 2nd "Edmond Palmer, John Blinco Churchwardens. R. Phelps fecit, 1729."
Jonathan Grimwood of Rendham went up to see the tenor cast, and flung seven half-crowns into the metal, to which some are said to attribute the good tone of the bell. Tenor c. 13 cwt.
"for ye ornaments and ye Bells we haue solde non as we wull answere." Certif. of Rob. Thurston and Edm. ffeavyear. C.W. 1547. "Great bells iiij." Return of 1553. See pp. 69, 91, 114.

390. RENDLESHAM *S. Gregory.* 3 Bells.
1 Tho. Gardiner Sudbury me fecit 1714.
2 Thomas Gardiner made me 1713.
3 Miles Graye made me 1630.

Pits for five. The usual coins and marks on 1 and 2. Bells in C♯, C, and B, with diameters 27½ in., 29½ in., and 31½ in. Certif. of 1547 records no sale of bells. "Great bells iij." Return of 1553. See p. 143.

391. REYDON *S. Margaret.* 1 Bell.
Bell. ▽ 50 thrice.
+ 61 𝔔ue In Conclabe ☐ 62 Gabriel Nunc Pange Suabe.

3 in 1553. "formerly 4 if not 5," Davy, Aug. 19, 1814. See p. 53.

392. RICKINGHALL INFERIOR *S. Mary.* 3 Bells.
1 + SCE : JACOBE : INTERCEDE : PRO : ME
2 I. D.   1630.
3 No inscription.

"Great bells iij. Sancts bells j." Return of 1553.
Davy, 6 Jan., 1810, "3 bells." See pp. 62, 112.

393. RICKINGHALL SUPERIOR *S. Mary.* 6 Bells.
  1 Jonathan Steggal George Porter C.Wardens. In a scroll
    " E. Taylor and Son ffounders Loughborough " 1850.
  2, 3, 4, 5 John Goldsmith fecit 1712.
  6 Mr. George Elmy & Mr. Henry Freeman C. W. 1741.
    Tho. Newman made me.
  4 in 1553. See pp. 138, 146.

394. RINGSFIELD *All Saints.* 2 Bells.
  1 John Stephens made mee 1726.
  2 ♅ 50 thrice.
    Donvm Clem. Gooch et Rob. Shelford 1610.
"Great bells ij. Sancts Bells j." Return of 1553. Pits for four.
Davy notes 3, June 2, 1808. See pp. 113, 139.

395. RINGSHALL *S. Catherine.* 2 Bells.
  1 R. Phelps Londini fecit 1737.
  2 + 24 ♅ 23 + 43 Sancta Katerina Ora Pro Nobis.
3 in 1553. So Mr. Parker, who does not condescend to note 1. See pp. 23, 148.

396. RISBY *S. Giles.* 3 Bells.
  1 ♅ 51 thrice.
    + 61 Virginis Egregie ▢ 62 Vocor Campana Marie.
  2 JOHN DRAPER MADE ME 1617.
  3 ♅ 65 thrice.
    + 67 Meritis ▢ 68 Edmundi ▢ 68 Simus ▢ 68 A ▢
    Crimine ▢ 68 Mundi.
"Great bells iij." Return of 1553. "3 bells," Davy. See pp. 54, 69, 111.

397. RISHANGLES *S. Margaret.* 3 Bells.
  1 ♅ 52 thrice.
    + Wee Fit Scorum ▢ 62 Campa Laude Bonorum
  2 ♅ 51 thrice.
    + 61 Celesti Manna ▢ 62 Tua Proles Nos Cibet Anna.
  3 ♅ 51 thrice.
    + 61 Meritis Edmundi ▢ 62 Simus A Crimine Mundi.
3 in 1553. So Davy with involuntary variations from Martin. 4 Dec., 1817. See pp. 54, 58.

398. ROUGHAM *S. Mary.* 5 Bells.
  1 John Darbie made me 1661. William Maning C.W.
  2 John Darbie made me 1661.
  3 ♅ 9 thrice.
    + 13 Sum Rosa Pulsata Mundi Maria Vocata.
  4 John Darbie made me 1678.
  5 John Martin Church Warden. Thos. Osborn fecit 1790.
    Venite Exultemus.
"Great bells iiij." Return of 1553.
Davy notes five bells, but no inscriptions.

399. RUMBURGH *S. Michael.* 5 Bells.
  1, 4 Anno Domini 1624 WIB.
  2 R S I T Churchwardens. Anno Domini 1624 WIB.

3 Tho. Gardiner Sudbury fecit 1728.
5 The Revnd. Lombe Althills (sic) Perp. Curate. John Briant Hertford fecit 1823. C. Reynolds.
3 and a Sance bell in 1553. "Old treble T. B. 1660." Davy, 16 May, 1806. See pp. 7, 114.

400. RUSHBROOKE S. Nicholas. 3 Bells.
1 Thomas Newman of Norwich made me 1733.
2 ☐ 81 Andrew Gvrny made me 1636.
3 Thomas Newman made mee 1711.

"Square steeple, 3 bells, and Dr. Needen says, modern ones." Davy. See p. 112.

401. RUSHMERE S. Andrew. 6 Bells.
1, 2 John Darbie made me 1675.
3 ☉ 26 + 22 ☉ 25 Sancte Botolfe Ora Pro Nobis.
4 ☉ 26 + 22 ☉ 25 Vor Augufilni Sonet En Aure Dei.
5 ☉ 26 + 22 ☉ 25 Sancta Katarina Ora Pro Nobis.
6 Mears & Stainbank, Founders, London, 1885.
Ad gloriam Dei et in memoriam Sancti Andreae, Apostoli et Martyris, dedicata. Gulielmus Wigston, Vicarius, Alfredus Meller, Gulielmus Dawson, Sacrorum Custodes.

"Great bells iiij." Return of 1553. Davy, 4 Aug., 1810.

402. RUSHMERE S. Michael. 2 Bells.
1 ☉ 52 thrice.
En Vilet and En too Laudes Deo.
2 ☉ 64 thrice.
+ : SCA : BARBARA : PRO : ME : DEVM : EXORA.

"Great bells iij." Return of 1553. See p. 59.

403. SANTON DOWNHAM S. Mary. 1 Bell.
Bell. Robard Gvrney made me 1663.

"Great bells ij." Return of 1553.
Davy, 24 Aug., 1829, notes one bell. See p. 132.

404. SAPISTON S. Andrew. 4 Bells.
1 John Draper made me 1628. The gift of Thomas Mannynge.
2 Thomas Newman of Norwich made me 1730.
3 Thomas Draper 1591.
4 ☉ 51 thrice.
+ 61 Flos Thome Merilis ☐ 62 Mereamur Gaudia Lucis.

"Great bells iiij." Return of 1553. Davy, 25 July, 1832, "four bells." See pp. 56, 100, 112, 137.

405. SAXHAM, GREAT, S. Andrew. 3 Bells.
1 T. Osborn 1787.
2 T. Osborn fecit 1787.
3 Thomas Mears of London, founder, 1836.

"Great bells iij." Return of 1553. The old tenor was inscribed, "Fred. Evered, Ch. Warden, 1787." Davy, Aug. 19, 1828.

230   THE CHURCH BELLS OF SUFFOLK.

406. SAXHAM, LITTLE, *S. Nicholas.*   3 Bells.
1 ▽ 51 thrice.
+ 61 𝔄𝔟𝔢 𝔐𝔞𝔯𝔦𝔞 𝔊𝔯𝔞𝔱𝔦𝔞 𝔓𝔩𝔢𝔫𝔞 ☐ 62 𝔇𝔬𝔪𝔦𝔫𝔲𝔰 𝔗𝔢𝔠𝔲𝔪.
2 ▽ 51 thrice.
+ 61 𝔐𝔦𝔣𝔣𝔲𝔰 𝔇𝔢 𝔈𝔢𝔩𝔦𝔰 ☐ 62 𝔓𝔞𝔟𝔢𝔬 𝔑𝔬𝔪𝔢𝔫 𝔊𝔞𝔟𝔯𝔦𝔢𝔩𝔦𝔰.
3 Thomas Cheese made me 1603. SB
"Great bells iij." Return of 1553. Davy transposes 1 and 2, and omits S. B. on the tenor. See pp. 52, 53, 109.

407. SAXMUNDHAM *S. John Baptist.*   6 Bells.
1 Cast by John Warner & Sons, London. Presented by Mrs. Ann Crampin. Hung by G. Day & Son, Eye, 1880.
2 Anno Domini 1609. W. B.
3 : + : sancta : margareta : ora : pro nobis.
4 + O 𝔖ancte 𝔍acobe 𝔒ra 𝔓ro 𝔑obis.
5 ☐ 34, ☐ 35, ☐ 32, ☐ 33.
+ O 𝔖ancta 𝔐argareta 𝔒ra 𝔓ro 𝔑obis.
6 1762. Lester & Pack of London fecit. *J^{no}. Eade & Ja^t. Last Ch. Wardens.*
Davy gives 1602 as the date of the 2nd.
"Great bells v. Sancts bells j." Return of 1553. See pp 35, 113.

408. SAXSTEAD *All Saints.*   1 Bell.
Bell. John Darbie made me 1678.
3 in 1553. Martin, 15 June, 1735, notes 3. No notes in Davy. Hawes and Loder, p. 324, give a 2nd, "Anno I. P. I. A. 1589, and a 3rd, 𝔙𝔦𝔯𝔤𝔦𝔫𝔦𝔰 𝔈𝔤𝔯𝔢𝔤𝔦𝔢 𝔙𝔬𝔠𝔬𝔯 𝔈𝔞𝔪𝔭𝔞𝔫𝔞 𝔐𝔞𝔯𝔦𝔢." See p. 124.

409. SEMER *All Saints.*   3 Bells.
1 ☐ 81 Thomas ☐ 82 Cheese me fecit 1621.
2 ▽ 52 thrice.
+ 61 𝔐𝔢𝔯𝔦𝔱𝔦𝔰 𝔈𝔡𝔪𝔲𝔫𝔡𝔦 ☐ 62 𝔖𝔦𝔪𝔲𝔰 𝔄 𝔈𝔯𝔦𝔪𝔦𝔫𝔢 𝔐𝔲𝔫𝔡𝔦.
3 ☐ 81 Johannes ☐ 82 Me fecit TC Me fecit 1618.
So Davy, 26 Oct., 1826. "Great bells iij." Return of 1553. See pp. 58, 110.

410. SHADINGFIELD *S. John Baptist.*   1 Bell.
Bell. James ☐ 81 Edbere ☐ 82 1608 (arabesque).
"Great bells iij." Return of 1553. "1 Bell," Davy, 2 June, 1808. See p. 109.

411. SHELLAND.   1 Bell.
Bell. H. P. }
W. 333 } cut in the shoulder.
☐ 81 Thomas ☐ 82 Cheese me fecit 1624.
Davy, June 13, 1827, notes one in a cupola, inaccessible. 4 in 1553.

412. SHELLEY *All Saints.* Tenor. Diam. 39 in.   5 Bells.
1 John Darbie made me 1663.
Samvell Kerridge Esqvire gave me.
2 Miles Graye made me 1629.
3 ▽ 65 thrice.
+ sancta O ana (sic) O ora O pro O nobis

4 ▽ 65 thrice.
✠ sancta : maria : ora : pro : nobis.
5 John Hodson made me 1662. This bell was given by Samvell Kerredge Esqvier W. H. C (W?)
☐ ▽ O (the first a fleur-de-lis, the last a medallion, probably intended for Charles II.)

·3 in 1553. Davy transposes 4 and 5. See pp. 69, 118, 123, 132. These are never rung. They have a wondrous system of "clocking."

413. SHIMPLING *S. George.*   5 Bells.
1, 4 Thomas Newman made me 1735.
2, 3 Thomas Newman of Norwich made me 1735.
5 Thomas Mears, London, 1843.

"Great bells iij." Return of 1553.
Davy, "Four bells 1734, five bells 1831." See p. 138.

414. SHIPMEADOW *S. Bartholomew.*   1 Bell.
Bell. John Brend made me 1640.

"Great bells iij. Sancts bells j." Return of 1553. "Only one bell," notes, 6 June, 1769, in Davy's MSS. See p 115.

415. SHOTLEY *S. Mary.*   1 Bell.
Bell. John Darbie made me 1686. W. D. R. F. Sʳ. Henry Felton : Baronett ▽ (Felton).

So Davy, 1823. But under "MS. notes by Sir J. Blois, p. 180," there is "Ric. Bowler on the bells." 4 in 1553. See p. 125.

416. SHOTTISHAM *S. Margaret.*   1 Bell.
Bell. ▽ 65 thrice.
✠ 67 Sancta ☐ Maria ☐ Ora ☐ Pro ☐ Nobis.

"Great bells iij." Return of 1553. "One bell," Davy, 12 Oct., 1818. See p. 69.

417. SIBTON *S. Peter.*   5 Bells.
1 Thomas Mears, founder, London, 1848.
2 John Darbie made me 1670.
3 ▽ 9 thrice.
✠ En Multis Annis Refonet Campana Johannis.
4 ▽ 52 thrice.
✠ 61 Petrus Ab Eterne ☐ 62 Ducat flos Pascua Vite.
5 Henry Pleasant made me 1694. Edmund Rickit Warding.

Dec. 6, 1805, Davy notes the old treble, "John Darbie made me 1681. W. R." Dec. 1805, dates the 2nd 1673, and gives Eternis on the 3rd for En Multis. No sale of bells recorded in certif. of 1547. 4 in 1553. See pp. 17, 56, 123, 140.

418. SIZEWELL *S. Nicholas.*
Ecclesia destructa. No return in 1553.

419. SNAPE *S. John Baptist.*   3 Bells.
1 John Wehincopp. 1674.
2 N. H. O. I. 476 W C. P. O. C. N. I. H. I. W.
3 Tho. Gardiner fecit. 1713. R. H. I. K.

From Davy, June 12, 1806. No sale of bells in certif. of 1547. "Great bells iij." Return of 1553. The date of 2 is probably 1576.

420. SOHAM, EARL, *S. Mary.* 5 Bells.
1 Miles Graie made me 1610.
2 ▽ 50 thrice.
   + 61 ⓠuesumus 𝔄nbrea ☐ 62 𝔉amulorum 𝔖uscipe 𝔙ota.
3 John Darbie made me 1663. R. D. H. B. W. S.
4 ▽ 50 thrice.
   + 61 𝔓etrus 𝔄d 𝔈terne ☐ 62 𝔇ucat 𝔑os 𝔓ascua 𝔙ite.
5 John Darbie made me 1663 R D H B W S.

Hawes crosses 1 and 3, and gives a wrong date for 5. The old windlass remains.
On the buttresses of the tower is the following hexametrical quatrain, in stone and cut flint:—

  𝔑anlphus 𝔒obytt bōa mariā cotulit isti
  𝔈cclie sacte cui presit gracia cristi

  𝔒ampailis eiu' thomas 𝔈boa fuit autor
  𝔔ui' et ——— simul optimus auxiliator.

I regret to leave a word unread.
The wills of Radulph Cubytt of Norwich, and Thomas Edwarde of Congham, in the first half of the reign of Henry VIII., have reference to Earl Soham, and they seem to be the persons indicated in the inscription.
No sale of bells in certif. of 1547. " Some comits Great bells iiij." Return of 1553. See pp. 56, 57, 117, 123.

421. SOHAM, MONK, *S. Peter.* Tenor G. Diam. 40¾ in.
                 5 Bells.
1 Miles Graye made me 1631.
2 Post nullas renovata sodales. Reverendus Vir Gulielmus Ray A.M. Rector. Thomas Martin & Laurentius Spinny Ecclesie Guardiani. R. Phelps London fecit 1734.
3 ▽ 50 thrice.
   + 61 𝔇ulcis 𝔖isto 𝔐elis ☐ 62 𝔒ampā 𝔙ocor 𝔐ichaelis.
4 ▽ 51 thrice.
   + 61 𝔓etrus 𝔄d 𝔈terne ☐ 62 𝔇ucat 𝔑os 𝔓ascua 𝔙ite.
5 John Darbie made me 1661. John Aldrich Robart Rous.

So Davy, 30 April, 1828. 4 in 1553.
No bells in 1547 certif. mentioned as sold. See pp. 55, 56, 118, 122, 148.

422. SOMERLEYTON *S. Mary.* Tenor G. 6 Bells.
1 J. Taylor & Co., Founders, 1872.
2 S^r. Richard Allen Baronet 1700 I B O 88
3 ☐ 47 𝔄𝔙𝔈 ☐ 48 𝔘𝔦𝔕𝔊𝔒 ☐ 48 𝔘𝔦𝔕𝔊𝔦𝔑𝔘𝔐 ☐ 48 𝔐𝔄𝔗𝔈𝔕 ☐ 48 𝔦𝔥𝔲 ☐ 48 𝔛𝔓𝔦.
4 ▽ 51 thrice.
   + 61 𝔙irginis 𝔈gregie ☐ 62 𝔙ocor 𝔒ampana 𝔐arie.
5 ▽ 51 thrice.
   + 61 𝔥ac 𝔦n 𝔒onclabe ☐ 62 𝔊abriel 𝔑unc 𝔓ange 𝔖uabe.
6 William Ayton C.W. Thomas Newman made me 1706.

"Great bells iij." Return of 1553. Re-opened Oct. 7, 1872. See pp. 41, 53, 54, 147.

INSCRIPTIONS. 233

423. SOMERSHAM *S. Mary.*　　　　　　　　2 Bells.
　　1 John Darbie made me 1662.
　　2 Miles Graye made me 1626.
3 in 1553. Davy, 18 May, 1829, notes an old treble like the present 2nd. See pp. 118, 123.

424. SOMERTON *S Margaret.*　　　　　　　4 Bells.
　　1 De Bvri Santi Edmondi. Stefanvs Tonni me fecit W. L. 1578.
　　2, 3 De Bvri Santi Edmondi Stefanvs Tonni me fecit 1573.
　　4 Miles Graye made me 1681.
"Great bells iiij." Return of 1553.
Davy, March 23rd, 1814, calls 1, 2; and 2, 1; 3, 4; and 4, 3." See pp. 96, 134.

425. SOTHERTON *S. Andrew.*　　　　　　　1 Bell.
　　Bell. Thomas Mears, Founder, London, 1842. T. F.
So Davy, June 1, 1808. Terrier rendered 24 June, 1794, "One small bell with the frame, weighing about ¾ cwt."
Certif. of iiij Nov., 1547, by Thomas Davy and John Noone.
　　"Itm for a broken hande bell　　...　　...　viij*d*."
No bell returned in 1553.

426. SOTTERLEY *S. Margaret.*　　　　　　2 Bells.
　　1 Thomas Gardiner fecit 1717.
　　2 : + : SANCTA : MARGARETA : ORA : PRO NOBIS.
So Davy, 1 June, 1808. No sale of bells in certif. of 1547. "Great bells iij." Return of 1553. See p. 62.

427. SOUTHOLT *S. Margaret.*　　　　　　　1 Bell.
　　Bell. John Darbie made me 1677.
4 in 1553. Davy, 3 May, 1837, "One small bell." See p. 124.

428. SOUTHTOWN *S. Mary.*　　　　　　　　1 Bell.
　　Bell. 1831 (the year of Consecration).

429. SOUTHWOLD *S. Edmund.*　　8 and old Clock bell.
　　1, 2 No inscription.
　　3 William Dobson Downham Norfolk fecit 1820.
　　4, 5 John Darbie made me 1668.
　　　　R. I. T. S. Chvrch Wardens. T. P. T. N. Baylifes.
　　6 En Ueglth ▽ 52 and En Elo Laudes Deo.
　　7 ▽ 50 thrice.
　　　　+ 61 Subbeniat Digna ☐ 62 Donatibus Hanc Katerina.
　　8 Honble. & Revd. A. Rous, Vicar, J. Sutherland, P. Edwards, Bailiffs, E. Freeman Ch. Warden, 1828.
　　Bell attached to old "Jack o' th' Clock." No inscription.
5 and a Sance bell in 1553. 1 and 2 cast not many years ago by Moore, Holmes and Mackenzie. See extract from Gardiner's MS. 6 and another bought from South Elmham All Saints. See No. 168, p. 186.
Davy, 12 Aug., 1806. "5 bells hung, and one standing on the ground," on which he did not note the inscrn. Old Tenor En ꝰultis...
"A litill syluyr belle" was sold in 1547 by Thomas Jentylman and Willm Wright, C. W.

2E

The treble, from which the present 3rd was cast, was of the same make as the present 4th and 5th, and that which occupied the place of the present 6th, according to Davy, bore no inscription. Gardiner notes Katherine and John as the Christian names of K. Tylls (1470) and Joh. Cawnteler (1471) who left 5 marks each "ad facturam unius Campanæ."

T. P. T. N. are apparently the initials of Thomas Postle and Thomas Nunn, Bailiffs in 1671 and 1662 respectively. Those of 1667 and 1668 bore other initials. Tokens of Postle's are mentioned in Golding, p. 67. See pp. 57, 59, 123, 154.

430. SPEXHALL *S. Peter*. 1 Bell.

∪ 52 thrice.

+ 61 𝔇𝔲𝔩𝔠𝔦𝔰 𝔖𝔦𝔰𝔱𝔬 𝔐𝔢𝔩𝔦𝔰 ☐ 62 𝔈𝔞𝔪𝔭𝔞̄ 𝔙𝔬𝔠𝔬𝔯 𝔐𝔦𝔠𝔥𝔦̄𝔰.

3 in 1553. Davy, June 3rd, 1808. "3 bells formerly hung in a shed in the yard, but in 1771 a faculty was obtained to sell 2 of them to repair the church. The other hangs in a cupola at the west end of the nave."

Terrier rendered June, 1791. "Also one Bell hanging in a new erected Cupola." See p. 55.

431. SPROUGHTON *All Saints*. 5 Bells.

1, 2, 4 John Darbie made me 1658.
3 Thomas Mears of London fecit 1813.
5   O
     I
     T
  O H O
     O

So Davy, who merely notes the tenor blank.
No sale of bells recorded in certif. of 1547. 3 in 1553. See pp. 80, 122.

432. STANNINGFIELD *S. Nicholas*. 3 Bells.

1 Robard ⁂ Gvrney ⁎ made ⚜ me 1664.
2 ∪ 51 thrice.

+ 61 𝔄𝔟𝔢 𝔊𝔯𝔞𝔠𝔦𝔞 𝔓𝔩𝔢𝔫𝔞 ☐ 62 𝔇𝔬𝔪𝔦𝔫𝔲𝔰 𝔗𝔢𝔠𝔲𝔪.

3 ☐ 81 De ☐ 82 Bvri ☐ 82 Santi ☐ 82 Edmondi ☐ 82 Stefanvs ☐ 82 Tonni ☐ 82 me ☐ 82 fecit ☐ 82 ☐ 81 1567.

"Great bells iij." Return of 1553. So Davy, with slight variations. See pp. 52, 96, 192.

433. STANSFIELD *All Saints*. 5 Bells.

1, 2, 3, 4, 5 Miles Graye made me 1652.
"Great bells iij." Return of 1553. See p. 121.

434. STANSTEAD *S. James*. 6 Bells.

1, 2 T. Mears of London fecit 1830.
3, 4 Miles Graye made me 1662.
5 ☐ 74 𝔖𝔞𝔫𝔠𝔱𝔞 ☐ 75 𝔱𝔯𝔦𝔫𝔦𝔱𝔞𝔰 ☐ 76 𝔲𝔫𝔲𝔰 ☐ 75 𝔇𝔢𝔲𝔰 ☐ 76 𝔪𝔦𝔰𝔢𝔯𝔢𝔯𝔢 ☐ 75 𝔫𝔬𝔟𝔦𝔰.

1544	
	73 stephene tonne me fecit.

6 Pack & Chapman of London fecit 1775.

"Great bellys iij." Return of 1553. Davy, Aug. 18, 1831, "Six bells." See pp. 79, 133.

435. STANTON *All Saints.* Tenor G. Diam. 39¼ in. 4 Bells.
  1 ▽ 65 thrice.
    ✠ : sancta : maria : ora : pro : nobis.
  2 ▽ 65 thrice.
    + 67 ☉ martir ☐ 68 Barbara ☐ 68 Prome ☐ 68 Deum
      ☐ 68 Erora ☐ 68.
  3 ▽ 65 thrice.
    + 67 Osibus ☐ 68 Celi ☐ 68 Fac ☐ 68 Barbara ☐ 68
      Cremina (sic) ☐ 68 Deli.
  4 ☐ 81 Anno ☐ 82 : ☐ 82 Regni ☐ 82 Reginae-Elizabeth
      ☐ 82 De Bvri Santi Edmondi Stefanvs Tonni me
      fecit ☐ 81 Anno ☐ 82 Domini ☐ 82 1560.
"Great bells iij." Return of 1553.
Davy, 5 Jan., 1810, notes the inscription on treble defaced. See pp. 69, 95.

436. STANTON *S. John Baptist.* Tenor G. Diam. 37 in.
                                                                                     4 Bells.
  1, 2 John Darbie made me 1680.
  3 No inscription.
  4 John Darbie made me 1680. I W S B CW's.
"Great bells iij." Return of 1553. Davy, 5 Jan., 1810, as this. See p. 124.

437. STERNFIELD *S. Mary Magdalene.*   4 Bells.
  1 John Brend made me 1659.
  2 John Darbie made me 1681. I. B.
  3 Thomas Gardiner Sudbury fecit 1716.
  4 De Bvri Santi Edmondi. Stefanvs Tonni me fecit 1573.
"Great bells iij." Return of 1553. From Davy, June 12, 1806.

438. STOKE ASH *All Saints.*   4 Bells.
  1 William Dobson, founder, Downham, Norfolk.
  2 No inscription.
  3 ▽ 65 thrice.
    + Sancta ☐ Anna ☐ Ora ☐ Pro ☐ Nobis.
  4 + Credo ☐ En Deum Omni ☐ potentem.
4 in 1553. Davy, 23 April, 1819, notes the treble as AVE MARIA GRACIA PLENA, the third Sancta Maria Ora Pro Nobis.
These two dedications had been recorded by T. Martin, c. 1719. See p. 69.

439. STOKE-BY-CLARE *S. Michael.*   6 and Clock bell.
  1, 3 T. Osborn fecit 1786. Cum voco venite.
  2 T. Osborn Downham Norfolk fecit 1786.
  4 Mors vincet omnia. T. Osborn fecit 1786.
  5, 6 Joseph Harrison Daniel Pannell Churchwardens.
    Thos. Osborn founder Downham Norfolk 1786.
  Clock bell + 77 furge : mane : farbire : deo.
"Great bells v." Return of 1553. See p. 79.

440. STOKE-BY-NAYLAND *S. Mary.*   6 and Clock bell.
  1 Thomas Gardiner fecit 1725.
  2 John . Hollon . Samuel . Bigsbe . C.W's. 1725.

236   THE CHURCH BELLS OF SUFFOLK.

3 + 89 In Multis Annis Refonet Campana Johannis +

O Jobes froft alias thorn

4 + ORA : MENTE : PIA : PRO : NOBIS : VIRGO : MARIA : AMEN :

5 Joseph Holles . 1699. Thomas Williams . 1699. H. Pleasant made me.

6 Reverend Joshua Rowley Minister Henry Cook Ed. Cook Churchwardens 1811. Thomas Mears.

Clock bell. No inscription, apparently.

"Great bells v." Return of 1553. Davy, Sept. 29 and 30, 1828. "12 bells which I omitted to visit." This is remarkable. J. J. R.

The capital lettering on the fourth is unknown to me; but the initial cross looks like an enlargement of No. 47.

After the dissertation was printed, my friend, Mr. Justice Clarence, of Colombo, Ceylon, went to see Giffard Hall, in this parish, formerly the residence of the Mannock family. Here over the gateway he found a small bell, scarce 18 in. high, bearing a coin or two, and the inscription, Sancte Hugo Ora Pro Nobis. There were no marks, but the lettering is Culverden's, see pp. 37, etc. It is remarkable that his Lincolnshire proclivities show themselves here in a dedication to the well-known Bishop of Lincoln.

441. STONHAM ASPALL *S. Lambert.* Tenor E. 24 cwt.
10 Bells.

1, 2, 4 T. Mears of London fecit 1826.

3 T. Mears of London fecit 1826. Danl. Wade aged 80 years. W^m. Last, Two of the Parish Ringers.

5 Pack & Chapman of London fecit 1770. W^m. Banyard & Saml. Davie Ch: Wardens.

6 T. Mears of London fecit 1826. Job Roper John Blomfield.

7 T. Mears of London fecit 1826. Rev^d. Thos. Methold Rector. W^m. Taylor & Saml. Ford Churchwardens.

8 Thomas Lester made me 1746.

9 In this tower hung 5 bells the tenor weighing 10 hun: 2 qrs. 0 lb. In the year 1742 they were taken down & with ye addition of 3 tons 10 hun: of mettle were recast into ten att ye expence of Theodore Ecclestone Esqre of Crowfield Hall, aged 27 years. He gave also a new frame att ye same time, 1742. Thos. Lester made us all.

10 Theodore Eccleston Esqr. gave me 1742. Thomas Lester of London made me 1745. John Williams hanged me. The end crowns the work.

So Davy, 12 May, 1824.

1, 2 Theodore Ecclestone Esq. 1742.

3 Tho. Lester of London made me.
At proper times my voice I'll raise
Unto my Benefactor's praise.
Theodore Ecclestone Esqr. 1712.

No mention of bells in certif. of iij Nov., 1547. 4 in 1553. See p. 149.

442. STONHAM EARL *S. Mary.*   Tenor G♯. Diam. 38 in.
5 Bells.
1 Henry Pleasant made me 1706.
2 Thomas Gardiner Sudbury fecit 1727.
3 ▽ 50 thrice.
   ✛ 61 𝔔uefumus 𝔄nbrea ☐ 62 𝔉amulorum 𝔖ufcipe 𝔙ota.
4 ▽ 50 thrice.
   ✛ 61 𝔙irginis 𝔈gregie ☐ 62 𝔙ocor Campa 𝔐arie.
5 Candler Bird Ch: Warden. T. Osborn Downham fecit
   1781. Percute dulce cano.
So Davy imperfectly, 28 March, 1811. 4 in 1553. See pp. 54, 57, 140, 144.

443. STONHAM, LITTLE, *S. Mary.*   5 Bells.
1 T. Mears of London fecit 1817.
2 T. Mears of London fecit 1816.
3 Miles Graye made me 1617 V.
4 ▽ 65 thrice.
   ✛ 𝔙irgo Corna 𝔇uc 𝔉los 𝔄d Regna.
5 R. Phelps fecit 1729.
4 in 1553. T. Martin notes 5 bells.
   3 𝔖ancta 𝔐aria ora pro nobis.
   4 𝔙irgo Coronata duc nos ad regna beata.
   5 𝔖ancta 𝔐aterina ora pro nobis.
Davy, 26 Oct., 1829, notes 5 inaccessible. See pp. 67, 117.

444. STOVEN *S. Margaret.*   1 Bell.
Bell. 1759.
So Davy, 13 June, 1808. 2 in 1553.

445. STOW WEST *S. Mary.* Tenor. Diam. 42¾ in. 6 Bells.
1 C. AND G. MEARS LONDON 1849. PRAISE
   YE THE LORD.
2, 6 John Draper made me 1631.
3, 4 John Draper made me 1629.
5 John Darbie made me 1674.
"Great bells iiij." Return of 1553.
Davy, 19 Aug., 1829. "5 bells which I did not visit." See pp. 112, 124.

446. STOWLANGTOFT *S. George.*   4 Bells.
1 John Draper made me 1631.
2 J. D. 1614.
3 ▽ 51 thrice.
   ✛ 61 𝔖ubbeniat 𝔙ingna ☐ 62 𝔇onantibus 𝔓anc 𝔎aterina.
4 For the service of God. Cast at the expense of Henry
  Wilson Esq. 1856. Taylor and Son, Founders,
  Loughborough.
"Great bells iij." Return of 1553.
Davy, 6 July, 1843. "4 bells," apparently quoting T. Martin. See pp.
57, 109, 112.

447. STOWMARKET *SS. Peter and Mary.* Tenor D, c. 24 cwt.
Diam. 51¼ in.   8 Bells.
1 William Dobson, Downham, Norfolk, Founder, 1810.
2 Tho: Osborn fecit 1791.

3 John Darbie made me 1691.
Thomas : Godard MP. John : Keeble : Richard : Osbvrnd :
4 + 22 ▽ 20 Sit Nomen Domini Benedictum.
5 Charles Newman made mee 1699.
6 T. Mears of London fecit 1823.
7 John Darbie made me 1672.
8 Miles Graye made me 1622.
Clock bell + AVE MARIA GRACIA PLENA.
Probably the old Sance bell.

5 and a Sance bell in 1553. Davy transposes 2 and 3. The inscription on the former he records as Adoremus unum Deum in Trinitate fideliter. On 2 he mistakes "Tho" for "John," gives both Darbie's bells wrong dates, and changes the names on 3. See pp. 21, 118, 123, 125, 136.

448. STOWUPLAND *Holy Trinity.* 1 Bell.
Bell. Oliver, Wapping, London. Revd. A. G. H. Hollingsworth.
Boby
G. R. Freeman } Churchwardens.
In Nomine SS. Trinitatis 1843.
See p. 151.

449. STRADBROKE *All Saints.* Tenor E♭, c. 22 cwt.
8 Bells.
1 I Taylor & Co., Founders, Loughborough, 1879. Awake thou that sleepest.
2 I. Taylor & Co., Founders, Loughborough, 1879. Hallelujah.
3 John Borrett Donor. Charles Newman made mee 1697. I. ▽ B. I. ▽ B. (arms of Borrett).
4 Miles Graye made me 1613.
5 + Miles ☐ Graye ☐ 87 made ☐ me ☐ 87 1622.
6 Fili Dei vivi miserere nobis 1567 I. B.
7 Nvmen inest nvmers. John Darbie made me 1683. Thomes Aldous, Joseph Gibbs, C. W.

8 + 44 ▽ 25 + 14 Ecce Gabrielis Sonat Hec Campana
Fidelis.

The figure "6" on the sixth is inverted, and looks like a "9." 5 and a Sance bell in 1553. Davy, 16 Oct., 1806, "6 bells." See pp. 25, 102, 117, 118, 125, 136.

450. STRADISHALL *S. Margaret.* 5 Bells.
1 Tho. Gardiner Sudbury fecit 1743.
John Yale Rector, Tho⁵. Flack & Thos. Cook C.W.
2 Edwᵈ. Arnold St. Neots fecit 1775.
3 De Bvri Santi Edmondi Stefanvs Tonni me fecit 1570.
4 Miles Graye made me 1646.
5 THOMAS DRAPER MADE ME 1593 ☐ 83.

"Great bells iiij." Return of 1553. "Five bells and a clock." Davy. See pp. 96, 101, 119, 145.

451. STRATFORD *S. Andrew.*   3 Bells.
    1, 2 Cast by John Warner & Sons, London, 1870.
    3 Recast by John Warner & Sons, London, 1885.
    Rev. E. Hall, M.A., Rector, S. Plant, Churchwarden.
    Hung by George Day & Son, Eye.
"Great bells iij." Return of 1553.
Old Tenor ▽ 65 thrice.
✠ 𝕾𝖆𝖓𝖈𝖙𝖆 ☐ 𝖁𝖆𝖗 ☐ 𝖁𝖆𝖗 ☐ 𝕬 ☐ 𝕺𝖗𝖆 ☐ 𝖕𝖗𝖔 ☐ 𝖓𝖔𝖇𝖎𝖘." See p. 67.
This was the original treble. The others were inscribed, 𝕾𝖆𝖓𝖈𝖙𝖆 𝕸𝖆𝖗𝖎𝖆 𝕺𝖗𝖆 𝖕𝖗𝖔 𝖓𝖔𝖇𝖎𝖘, and 𝕾𝖙𝖊𝖗𝖎𝖙𝖎𝖘 𝕰𝖉𝖒𝖚𝖓𝖉𝖎, &c.

452. STRATFORD *S. Mary.*   5 Bells.
    1 Rector Ecclesiam restoravit
      Campanam Sextam me donavit
      Cum gratiis Dominum adoravit
        H. G. Anno 1879.
      I. Taylor & Co., Founders, Loughborough.
    2 Thomas Gardiner fecit 1745.
      John Sacker, John Cooper, C.W.
    3 Thomas Gardiner fecit 1723.
    4 ✠ 43 ✠ 37 𝕴𝖓 𝕸𝖚𝖑𝖙𝖎𝖘 𝕬𝖓𝖓𝖎𝖘 𝕽𝖊𝖋𝖔𝖓𝖊𝖙 𝕮𝖆𝖒𝖕𝖆𝖓𝖆 𝕵𝖔𝖍𝖆𝖓𝖓𝖎𝖘.
    5 ✠ Richardvs Bowler me fecit 1589.
    6 ☉ ☉ ✠ 𝕾𝖆𝖓𝖈𝖙𝖊 ☉ 𝕲𝖗𝖊𝖌𝖔𝖗𝖎 ☉ 𝕺𝖗𝖆 ☉ 𝖕𝖗𝖔 ☉ 𝖓𝖔𝖇𝖎𝖘
      ▽ 45
So Davy. "Great bells iiij." Return of 1553. See pp. 37, 104, 145.

453. STRATTON *S. Peter.*
Ecclesia destructa. No return in 1553.

454. STURSTON *All Saints.*   4 Bells.
    1 No inscription.
    2 John Draper made me 1627.
    3 C. & G. Mears, Founders, London.
      Walter Chenery, Rector.
      Osborn Tippell, Churchwarden, 1853.
    4 C. & G. Mears, Founders, London, 1857.

    4 in 1553. Davy, 16 Oct., 1806, notes the old 3rd, ❀ 𝖒𝖆𝖙𝖊𝖗 𝕯𝖊𝖎 𝖒𝖊𝖒𝖊𝖓𝖙𝖔 𝖒𝖊𝖎, and the old tenor, James Edbere me fecit 1603. R. B. W. S. E. D. The old 3rd belonged to the "Burlingham" group, as recorded in L'Estrange's *Church Bells of Norfolk*, p. 80. Messrs. Mears and Stainbank note that 1, 3, and 4 were supplied by them in 1847, and the latter two since recast.
Peal first of 5 bells, tenor 8 cwt.; now of 4, tenor 4 cwt. 3 qrs. 4 lbs. Diameter of treble 21¼ in., of tenor 32 in. See p. 112.

455. STUTTON *S. Peter.*   5 Bells.
    1, 4, 5 Miles Graye made me 1684.
    2 Charles Newman made mee 1692.
    3 Henry Pleasant made me 1706.

So Davy. 3 in 1553. See p. 134, where "first three" is an error; also pp. 135, 140.

456. SUDBOURNE *All Saints.*   1 Bell.
      Bell. John Darbie made me 1674.
"Great bells iiij." Return of 1553. No notes in Davy. Diam. 3 ft. 3 in. See p. 124.

457. SUDBURY *All Saints.* Tenor D♭, c. 30 cwt.
8 and Clock bell.
1 Cast by John Warner & Sons, London, 1876.
  In memory of Charles Badham M.A. 27 years Vicar of this Parish. Died April, 1874.
2 Cast by John Warner & Sons, London, 1876.
  Presented by Elliston Allen.
3 George Dashwood Esq. John Crystall Wardens.
  H. P. 1701.
4 Miles Graye made me 1671.
5 ▽ 65 thrice.
6 + 67 𝕾𝖆𝖓𝖈𝖙𝖆 ☐ 𝕶𝖆𝖙𝖊𝖗𝖎𝖓𝖆 ☐ 𝕺𝖗𝖆 ☐ 𝕻𝖗𝖔 ☐ 𝕹𝖔𝖇𝖎𝖘.
  + 91 + 41 𝕾𝖚𝖒 𝕽𝖔𝖘𝖆 𝕻𝖚𝖑𝖘𝖆𝖙𝖆 𝕸𝖚𝖓𝖉𝖎 𝕸𝖆𝖗𝖎𝖆 𝖁𝖔𝖈𝖆𝖙𝖆.
7 ▽ 65 thrice.
  + 67 𝕾𝖙𝖊𝖑𝖑𝖆 ☐ 𝕸𝖆𝖗𝖎𝖆 ☐ 𝕸𝖆𝖗𝖎𝖘 ☐ 𝕾𝖚𝖈𝖈𝖚𝖗𝖗𖊹 ☐ 𝕭𝖎𝖋𝖋𝖎𝖒𝖆 ☐ 𝕹𝖔𝖇𝖎𝖘.
8 Cast by John Warner & Sons, London.
  I toll the Funeral knell
  I ring the Festal Day
  I mark the fleeting hours
  And chime the Church to pray.
    Cast 1576.
    Recast 1875.
  Revd. A. H. Arden, Vicar.
  H. S. Pratt } Churchwardens.
  A. Archer   }
  Clock bell. No inscription.

"Great bells iij. Sancts bells j." Return of 1553. Davy notes no date, reverses 6 and 7. Tenor as in Badham's notes. al. sim.
The tenor was by S. Tonni of Bury, 1576, inscribed, "Filius Virginis Marie dat nobis gaudia vite." Badham. The crosses on the 6th are in lozenges, instead of octagon, our blocks being according to the form at Gloucester Cathedral and S. Alban's. See pp. 140, 151.

Fig. 91.

INSCRIPTIONS.

458. SUDBURY *S. Bartholomew.*
Ecclesia destructa. No return in 1553.

459. SUDBURY *S. Gregory.* Tenor F, 16 cwt.   8 Bells.
1, 2, 3, 4, 5, 6 T. Mears of London fecit 1821.
7 Mears of London fecit 1821.
H. W. Wilkinson, Minister.
A. Dacon, W^m. Jones, Churchwardens.
8 Pack Chapman of London fecit 1774.
Ye Ringers all that prize
Your health and happiness
Be sober, merry wise
And you'll the same possess.
"Great bells v. Sancts bells j." Return of 1553. See p. 151.

460. SUDBURY *S. Peter.* Tenor E♭. Diam. 49 in.   23 cwt.
                                                           8 Bells.
1, 2 Cast by John Warner & Sons, London, 1874.
3 John Darbie made me 1662.
4 ☐ 81 ⋮ James ⋮ Edbvrie (arabesque) 1605.
   RB IS RS IW RE RB TB RB WB IC EC
5 + ☡ 31 + 37 Șit Ꞥomen Ꝺomini Ꞵenedictum.
6 + ☡ 31 + 36 Ꞵn Ꝺultis Ꞥnnis Ꞥefonet Ꞓampana
   Ꞥobannis.
7 Miles Graye made me 1641.
8 + 15 ☡ 31 + Ꞥntonat Ꞓ Ꞓelis Ꞟoy Ꞓampane Ꝺichaelis.
"Great bells v." Return of 1553. Davy, no date. The lower 6 correctly though imperfectly given. The beauty of these capitals is extraordinary. See pp. 35, 109, 119, 123, 151.

461. SUTTON *All Saints.*   1 Bell.
   Bell. Robert Hvrnard Tho. Gardiner fecit 1713.
"Great bells iiij." Return of 1553. "The steeple is down. One small bell hangs in the roof." Davy, 12 Oct., 1818. Order for sale of a bell, 1692. *Eastern Counties' Collectanea*, p. 240.

462. SWEFFLING *S. Mary.*   6 Bells.
1 Cast by John Warner & Son, London, 1887.
Jubilee bell. Rev^d. R. Peek, M.A., Rector.
Hung by G. Day & Son, Eye.
2 T. Mears of London fecit 1831.
3 Tho. Gardiner fecit 1718.
4 Thomas Mears & Son of London fecit.
5, 6 Thomas Gardiner Benhall fecit. 1716.
"Swestlyng...Great bells iij." Return of 1553. No notes in Davy. See p. 143.

463. SWILLAND *S. Mary.*   1 Bell.
   Bell. + AVE MARIA GRACIA PLENA DOM-
          INVS TECVM.
So Davy imperfectly, 28 May, 1827. 3 in 1553. See p. 61.

2F

464. SYLEHAM *S. Mary.* 3 Bells.
1 John Darbie made me 1676.
2 John Goldsmith made me 1708. S^t. Margaret's.
3 + 61 ꜰʟᴏs Ƭ𝔥𝔬𝔪𝔢 𝔐𝔢𝔯𝔦𝔱𝔦𝔰 ☐ 62 𝔐𝔢𝔠𝔠𝔞𝔪𝔲𝔯 𝔊𝔞𝔲𝔡𝔦𝔞 𝔏𝔲𝔠𝔦𝔰.
So Davy nearly, 13 Oct., 1805. 3 in 1553. See pp. 56, 124. 2 omitted from Goldsmith's list, p. 145.

465. TANNINGTON *S. Ethelbert.* 5 Bells.
1, 2, 4 John Darbie made me 1662.
3 John Darbie made me 1662. Thomas Dade Esqvire.
5 John Darbie made me 1662.
William Dade Esq, John Jeffrey, W.K. C.W.

3 in 1553. Davy, 23 July, 1808, crosses 3 and 5. 2 and 4 are maidens, the others chipped. On each stock is G. Day, Eye, 1866.
A William Dade of Tannington married Mary Wingfield of the Crowfield branch. She died in 1624. No sale of bells in certif. of 1547.

466. TATTINGSTONE *S. Mary.* 5 Bells.
1, 2, 3 John Darbie made me 1661.
4 Thos. Mears of London fecit 1795.
5 Ransomes & Sims made me 1853.

The inscription on the old tenor is noted by Davy as 1, 2, 3.
No sale of bells in certif. of 1547. 4 in 1553. See p. 146.

467. THEBERTON *S. Peter.* 5 Bells.
1, 2, 3, 4, 5 Mears & Stainbank, Founders, London, 1875.
Facti Sumus In Honorem Domini.

"One in 1553.
1, 2] E. I. D. 1614.
3 John Darbie made me 1663.
4 Nos sumus instructi ad laudem Domini 1594 (Arms, France and England) E. R." Davy, Oct. 8, 1806. (He says I. A. on 1, 2, but of course he means I. E.) Diameters, 2 ft. 2¾ in.; 2 ft. 4 in.; 2 ft. 5¼ in.; 2 ft. 7⅜ in.; 2 ft. 10 in. Weights, 4 cwt. 0 qrs. 12 lbs.; 4 cwt. 1 qr.; 4 cwt. 3 qrs. 21 lbs.; 5 cwt. 2 qrs. 19 lbs.; 7 cwt. 0 qrs. 11 lbs. See p. 110.

468. THELNETHAM *S. Nicholas.* 5 Bells
1 T. L. made me 1748.
2 T L 1748.
3 Thomas Lester of London fecit 1748.
4 John Draper made me 1603 : ☐ 83.
5 Thomas Gardiner Sudbury fecit 1729.

"ffeltham...Great bells iiij." Return of 1553. Davy, 27 July, 1824. 5, 1722. al. sim. Sperling says, "Tenor A, 8¾ cwt." See pp. 111, 144, 149.

469. THETFORD *S. Mary.* 6 Bells.
1 Lester & Pack of London fecit 1765.
2 John Draper made me 1615.
3 Thomas Lester & Thos. Pack of London made me 1753.
4 Thomas Gardiner Sudbury fecit 1725.
5 John Darbie made me 1664 IT
Orsburne Clarke Burrage Martine CW.
6 Sa Maria John Goldsmith fecit 1711.
Isaac Fawkes Churchwarden. Sa Maria.

No Suffolk return in 1553. Davy, 26 July, 1824, notes 6 bells. See pp. 111, 123, 144, 146.

470. THORINGTON S. *Peter*. 1 Bell.
   Bell. (A pentacle) ✠ambell—Owen ☐ ✠ade ☐ ✠e
   ☐ for ☐ wansted. 1596.
So Davy, Aug. 17, 1806. The Terrier, 19 June, 1801, says, "weighing about 1 cwt"!
Aº. 1547 Thoringhtonne. Thes be the peells yᵗ hathe been solde wᵗⁱⁿ the pishe of Thoryngton in Suff. Itm sold by the holle pysche ij bells for the pʳce of vj. iiij. iiij. One in 1553. See p. 104.

471. THORNDON *All Saints*. Tenor F. 6 Bells.
   1 C. & G. Mears, founders, London, 1856.
   2, 3, 4 John Darbie made me 1667.
   5 John Darbie made me 1667. Isaac Wellvm Gent. C.W.
   6 En mea campana qvam belle sonas Ex parte donvm
      Isaaci Wellvm Rectoris 1671. John Darbie made.
4 in 1553. Davy, 18 June, 1809, notes the old treble, Isaac Wellvm Gent: Ch: Warden I. D. 1669. See his note. See p. 123.

472. THORNHAM, GREAT, S. *Mary*. 5 Bells.
   1, 2 Charles Newman made mee 1701.
   3 ▽ 65 thrice.
   ✠ Sancta ☐ Maria ☐ Ora ☐ Pro ☐ Nobis.
   4 Charles Newman made mee 1701. John Goveh C.W.
   5 ▽ 50 thrice.
   ✠ 61 Nos Thome Meritis ☐ 62 Mereamur Gaudia Lucis.
4 in 1553. Davy, 22 April, 1819, calls 5 4, and omits John Goveh. See pp. 56, 136.

473. THORNHAM, LITTLE, S. *Mary*. 1 Bell.
   Bell. Thomas Newmman (sic) of Norwich made me
      1727.
3 in 1553. Davy, 22 April, 1829. "Charles . . 1707." See p. 137.

474. THORPE-BY-ALDRINGHAM S. *Mary*.
Ecclesia destructa. No return in 1553.

475. THORPE-BY-ASHFIELD S. *Peter*.
Ecclesia destructa. "Grete bells iij." Return of 1553.
"The steeple contains only one bell, thus inscribed, 1 Charoli Framlingham Militis 1592." Davy. Vid. Little Ashfield, No. 13.

476. THORPE-BY-IXWORTH *All Saints*. 1 Bell.
   Bell. Edmund Whaites Ihon Howlet Church Wardens.
      John Stephens fecit 1723.
"Yexforthe Thorpe...Great bells ij." Return of 1553.
Davy, 25 July, 1832, "One bell in a cupola." See p. 139.

477. THORPE MORIEUX S. *Mary*. 3 Bells.
   1 Thomas Cheese made me 1632.
   2 ☐ 81 Thomas ☐ 82 Cheese made me 1629.
   3 J. Thornton made me 1713.
      R. Santy I. Burton CWds.
"Thorpe Moresse...Great bells iij." Return of 1553. See p. 110.
Martin, 5 July, 1741, by mistake says that they are modern ones.

244   THE CHURCH BELLS OF SUFFOLK.

478. THRANDESTON *S. Margaret.*   5 Bells.
1 John Brend made me 1654.
2 ℧ 50 thrice.
+ 61 ꝼac 𝔐argareta ☐ 62 𝔑obis 𝔙ec 𝔐uncra 𝔏eta.
3 Miles Graie made me 1608.
4 George Clay Esq. and Osborn Roper Churchwardens 1813.
5 Christopher Graye made me 1678.

4 in 1553. Davy, 17 June, 1809, crosses 2 and 3, and records 4. Katherin Chittocke John Brend made me 1650. Sperling (c. 1860), "Tenor G." See pp. 57, 117, 121, 134.

479. THURLESTON *S. Botolph.*
Ecclesia destructa. No return in 1553.

480. THURLOW, GREAT, *All Saints.*   5 Bells.
1, 3 Miles Graye made me 1660.
2 Recast by I. Taylor & Co., Founders, Loughborough, 1880.
4 C. & G. Mears, founders, London. This bell recast at the expence of Lady Harland, Lady of the Manor of Great Thurlow, 1849.
5 A. Gardner & W. Eagle, C.W.
John Briant Hertford fecit 1781.
Clock bell. Thos. Mears of London fecit 1794.

"Great bells iiij. Sancts bells j." Return of 1553. "Five bells," Davy. See p. 121.

481. THURLOW, LITTLE, *S. Peter.*   5 Bells.
1, 2, 3, 4 John Draper made me 1621.
5 T. Crick Rector, W. Burch C.W. John Briant Hertford fecit, 1807.

"Great bells iiij." Return of 1553. "Five bells," Davy. See p. 112. For "Great" read "Little."

482. THURSTON *S. Peter.*   5 Bells.
1, 2 John Draper and Andrew Gvrny made me 1630.
3, 5 Thomas Newman made me 1714.
4 Charles Newman made mee 1699.

"Great bells iiij." Return of 1553. Davy notes "3 bells." See pp. 112, 136.

483. THWAITE *S. George.*   1 Bell.
Bell. No inscription. New when the church was restored in 1846.

3 in 1553. The old bell, inscribed "Miles Graye made me 1626," was sold to Mellis c. 1846. See No. 335.

484. TIMWORTH *S. Andrew.*   4 Bells.
1, 2 John Darbie made me 1675.
3 Charles Newman made mee 1698.
4 John Draper made me 1626.

"Great bells iij." Return of 1553. "4 bells," Davy. See pp. 112, 124, 136.

INSCRIPTIONS. 245

485. TOSTOCK *S. Andrew.* 4 Bells.
1 No inscription.
2 ☉ 66 + fanct cpctre ora pro nobis.
3 + 67 Sancta Maria ora pro nobis ☉ 65.
4 1671 ☬ R Ā G ☬
"Great bells iiij." Returns of 1553.
Davy calls the tenor "blank," but notes two inscriptions as 2 and 3.

486. TRIMLEY *S. Martin.* 1 Bell.
Bell. No inscription.
"Great bells j." Return of 1553. From Davy, 16 July, 1829, "very small."

487. TRIMLEY *S. Mary.* 1 Bell.
Bell. Lionellus Tolmach comes de Dysart hanc de novo fundi C. 1736. (Coronet and crest of Tollemache.) (Arms of Tollemache.)
Davy, 16 July, 1829, inaccessible. No sale of bells recorded in certif. of 1549. "Great bells iiij." Return of 1553. See p. 148.

488. TROSTON *S. Mary.* Tenor, Diam. 28¾ in. Wt. 6 cwt.
6 Bells.
1, 2, 3 Robert Stainbank, Founder, London, 1868.
4 + Stefanus Tonni de Buri Sante Edmonde me fecit 1567.
Recast by Robert Stainbank, London, 1868.
5 + Subveniat Dingna. Donantibus Hanc Katerina.
Recast by Robert Stainbank, London, 1868.
6 + Dona Repende Pia. Rogo Magdalena Maria.
Recast by Robert Stainbank, London, 1868.
So T. Martin. Davy says, "with 2 bells"!
"Great bells iij." Return of 1553. See p. 151.
These inscriptions were reproduced from the old bells. I saw them in Jan., 1859. The 2nd and tenor bore shield No. 51 thrice each; and the usual cross and rhyme stop, Nos. 61 and 62. The treble bore Tonni's usual marks, Nos. 81 and 82.

489. TUDDENHAM *S. Martin.* 5 Bells.
1 John Darbie made me 1685 R. C.
2, 3, 4, 5 John Darbie made me 1665.
"Great bells iij." Return of 1553. T. Martin, 23 April, 1725, 5. See p. 125.

490. TUDDENHAM *S. Mary.* 5 Bells.
1 R. G. 1672.
2 R. G. 1666.
3 Thomas Draper made me 1591.
4 ☉ 65 thrice.
+ Sancta ☐ Anna ☐ ora ☐ pro Nobis.
5 John Darbie made me 1675. William Baker C.W.
So Davy with a mistake or two, 22 Aug., 1828.
"Great bells iiij." Return of 1553. See pp. 69, 100, 124, 132.

491. TUNSTALL *S. Michael.* 6 Bells.
1 This bell was added to the former five by the subscription of the Rector and parishioners 1823.

2 T. Mears of London 1814.
3, 5 T. Mears of London fecit 1814.
4 T. Mears of London fecit 1832.
6 Rev. Jos. Gerrard Ferrand Rector.
T. Flatt C^h. Warden.
W^m. Dobson fecit 1823.
" Great bells iiij." Return of 1553. The old six.
" 1, 2, 3, 4, 5 Anno Domini 1721.
6 George Cutting, Joseph Green, Churchwardens. John Stephens made me 1720." Davy.

492. UBBESTON *S. Peter.* The larger cracked.   2 Bells.
1 Sancta Anna Ora Pro Nobis O ∪ 45.
2 De Bvri Santi Edmondi ☐ 82 Stefanvs ☐ 82 Tonni ☐ me ☐ 82 fecit ☐ 81 1573 ☐ 81.
So Davy, 1 Aug., 1806, save that he dates 2 1567. Terrier, 16 June, 1801, "Three bells, one of which is cracked." 3 in 1553. Pits for three. See pp. 37, 96.

493. UFFORD *S. Mary.* Tenor F.   6 Bells.
1 John Taylor & Son, Founders, Loughborough, 1848.
2 ∪ 52 thrice.
+ 61 Ane Margareta ☐ 62 Nobis Vice Muncra Leta.
3 John Darbie made me 1686.
4 + 14 Sum O 16 Rosa O 16 Pulsata O 16 Mundi O 16 Maria O 16 Vocata.
5 Thos. Simpson Gent. Churchwarden.
T. Osborn founder Downham Norfolk 1798.
6 ∪ 50 thrice.
+ 61 En Multis Annis ☐ 62 Resonet Campā Lobis.
No sale of bells recorded in certif. of 1547. "Great bells v." Return of 1553. The old treble was inscribed "Rev^d. Jacob Chilton, D.D., Rector, John Hill C.Warden 1727." Davy, 7 June, 1806. The rest of his account mainly agrees with the above. See pp. 17, 57, 59, 125.

494. UGGESHALL *S. Mary.* In B♭.   1 Bell.
Bell. ∪ 52 thrice.
+ 61 Hac In Conclabe ☐ 62 Gabriel Nunc Pange Suabe.
So Davy, 3 Sept., 1807. "There were formerly more bells, which were sold for the repairs of the church" (Mr. Sheriffe, R. 1786—1842). 3 in 1553. Pits for three, this probably being the old 2nd. The other two are said to have been taken to Stoven and Sotherton. At the base of the unfinished tower is the following inscription:—Orate p'o auimab: Lobis jewle et marioue ur' eius, with two shields bearing emblems said to be those of a Free Mason and a Mark Mason. See p. 53.

495. WALBERSWICK *S. Andrew.*   1 Bell.
Bell. Lester & Pack of London fecit 1767.
Diam. 2 ft. o½ in., badly cracked in three or four places across the crown. Davy, 22 June, 1809, "1 Bell." Terrier, 8 June, 1791, "One bell with a frame, weight about three hundred."
See Ellacombe's *Church Bells of Gloucestershire, Supplement,* p. 150, and extracts from Gardiner's *Dunwich.* No sale of bells recorded in certif. of 1547. 2 and a Sance bell in 1553.

INSCRIPTIONS.

496. WALDINGFIELD, GREAT, *S. Laurence.* Tenor F♯.
Diam. 42 in.   6 Bells.
1 Canite Jovæ Laudes novo Carmine.
John Briant Hartford fecit An: Dom: 1800.
2 Omnes incolæ audite. John Briant Hartford fecit 1800.
3 Sit Nomen Domini Benedictum.
John Briant Hartford fecit An: Dom: 1800.
4 Cast by John Warner & Sons, London, 1876.
E. W. Downs & Son, Glemsford, hung me.
5 Supremis Locis Jovam laudate. John Briant Hartford fecit An: Dom: 1800.
6 Adeste. Rev^{nd}. Thomas Royce Rector, John Lott & Ed. Prior C: W: Adeste. John Briant Hartford fecit An: Dom: 1800.
"Great Bells iiij." Return of 1553.
Davy, Aug. 18, 1826. 4 "John Briant Hartford fecit 1800. Laudate Deum" (tympanis?)
Entry in the Vestry book that 5 old bells were recast into 6 in 1800. See p. 152.

497. WALDINGFIELD, LITTLE, *S. Laurence.* Tenor F♯.
Diam. 40 in.   6 Bells.
1, 4 T. Osborn fecit 1785.
2 Jeames ☐ 81 Edbere ☐ 82 1612 (arabesque).
3 Jeames (arabesque) Edbury ☐ 81 1612 ☐ 82.
5 Miles Graye made me 1617.
So Davy, Sept. 10, 1827. "Great bells iij." Return of 1553.

498. WALDRINGFIELD *All Saints.*   1 Bell.
Bell. Stephen Brame Churchwarden T. G. 1714.
"Great bells iij." Return of 1553. Davy, 21 May, 1811, gives 2, 3, 4, Thomas Gardiner Sudbury me fecit 1714, but on 2 Jan., 1824, notes but one bell left. See p. 143.

499. WALPOLE *S. Mary.*   1 Bell.
Bell. 1786.
So Davy, 26 June, 1806. T. Martin, 13 Sept., 1760, "They tell me there was once a good steeple with 5 Bells." 3 in 1553.

500. WALSHAM-LE-WILLOWS *S. Mary.*   6 Bells.
1 Charles Newman made mee 1700.
2, 3 Charles Newman made mee 1699. Johannes Hunt Esq.
4 ☐ 81 De Bvri Santi Edmondi Stefanvs Tonni me fecit 1576.
5, 6 Thomas Newman made me 1704. John Hunt Esq.
"Great bells iiij." Return of 1553. Davy, 7 July, 1843, "6 Bells." See pp. 96, 136, 137.

501. WALTON *S. Mary.*   1 Bell.
Bell. + SANCTE JOHANNES ORA PRO NOBIS.
Davy, 15 July, 1829, SANCTA JOHANNIS.
"The steeple . . . has long been down." No sale of bells recorded in certif. of 1547. "Great bells ij." Return of 1553.

502. WANGFORD *S. Denis.* 1 Bell.
Bell. Robard ⁕ Gvrney made me 1668.
"Waynforde...Great bells iij." Return of 1553. Davy, 23 Aug., 1829, notes "one small bell." There were certainly two, for I found two not very small ones in 1849, and no one would have brought in a bell in the interim. The larger of these two weighed 11 cwt., and bore $+$ 24 ▽ 23 $+$ 24 𝕾𝖎𝖙 𝕹𝖔𝖒𝖊𝖓 𝕯𝖔𝖒𝖎𝖓𝖎 𝕭𝖊𝖓𝖊𝖉𝖎𝖈𝖙𝖚𝖒. It was taken down in 1871, and weighed before being recast into the present Brandon treble. That lamented ringer and campanologist, the late Rev. A Sutton, Rector of West Toft, gave me the weight. Pits for three. See pp. 24, 132, 169.

503. WANGFORD *S. Peter.* Tenor in G. 5 Bells.
1 𝕬𝖓𝖓𝖔 𝕯𝖔𝖒𝖎𝖓𝖎 1624 WIB.
2 Cast by John Warner and Sons, London, 1863. (Royal Arms) Patent.
3 John Darbie made me 1668.
4 John Stephens made mee 1721. John Sayer Church Warden.
5 𝕬𝖓𝖓𝖔 𝕯𝖔𝖒𝖎𝖓𝖎 1625 AB
  W

Davy, 3 Sept., 1807, notes the old 2nd of the same date as the 4th. Terrier, 1827, 5. No sale of bells recorded in certif. of 1547. 4 in 1553. See pp. 114, 123, 139.

504. WANTISDEN *S. John Baptist.* 1 Bell.
Bell. Pack & Chapman of London fecit 1773.
So Davy, July 31, 1810. "Great bells iij." Return of 1553.

505. WASHBROOK *S. Mary.* Diam. 39½ in. 1 Bell.
Bell. ▽ 23 $+$ 𝕴𝖓 𝕸𝖚𝖑𝖙𝖎𝖘 𝕬𝖓𝖓𝖎𝖘 𝕽𝖊𝖘𝖔𝖓𝖊𝖙 𝕮𝖆𝖒𝖕𝖆𝖓𝖆 𝕵𝖔𝖍𝖆𝖓𝖓𝖎𝖘.
3 in 1553. Davy was unable to reach this bell in 1824. See p. 23.

506. WATTISFIELD *S. Margaret.* 5 Bells.
1, 2, 3, 5 John Darbie made me 1685.
4 .WL TD IN ☐ 84 THE ☐ 84 ℞AYNE ☐ 84
OB ☐ 84 QVENE ☐ 84 ELSE ☐ 84 BETH ☐ 84
BIS ☐ 84 XIII ☐ 84.
"Great bells iij." Return of 1553. Davy, 6 Jan., 1810, as this. Sperling (1860), "Tenor G♯." See pp. 98—100, 125.

507. WATTISHAM *S. Nicholas.* 2 Bells.
1 John Gardiner Church Warden T G fecit 1719.
2 ▽ 66 thrice.
$+$ 67 𝕾𝖆𝖓𝖈𝖙𝖆 ☐ 68 𝕸𝖆𝖗𝖎𝖆 ☐ 68 𝕸𝖆𝖌𝖉𝖆𝖑𝖊𝖓𝖆 ☐ 68 𝕺𝖗𝖆 ☐ 68 𝕻𝖗𝖔 ☐ 68 𝕹𝖔𝖇𝖎𝖘.
So Davy, 24 Oct., 1826. "Great bells iiij." Return of 1553. See p. 69.

508. WELNETHAM, GREAT, *S. Thomas.* 1 Bell.
Bell. H. P. made 1695. R. G. Churchwarden.
"Great bells ij." Return of 1553. "The steeple is down, but on the roof, at the west end of the nave hangs 1 small bell." Davy. See p. 140.

INSCRIPTIONS. 249

509. WELNETHAM, LITTLE, *S. Mary Magdalene.* Tenor G.
Diam. 33½ in.   3 Bells.
1 ☐ me : margarete : campanam : dicite : lete o
2 ˙R. B. IT IE ? 1614 ID.
3 R. ✠ G. ⚜ 1671 ✠ O
"Burlingham" lettering on treble, but Austen Bracker's cross. *Cambs.*, No. 71.
"Great bells iij." Return of 1553. "2 bells," Davy. See pp. 62, 132.

510. WENHAM, GREAT, *S. John.*   3 Bells.
1, 2 No inscription.
3 Richardus Bowler me fecit 1592.
So Davy. No sale of bells recorded in certif. of 1547. 3 in 1553. See p. 104.

511. WENHAM, LITTLE, *All Saints.*   1 Bell.
Bell. Thomas Gardiner Sudbury me fecit 1714.
3 in 1553. "In the steeple there is but one bell, inscribed 'John Club Rector of Horham 1672.'" Davy. See Horham, No. 264. See p. 143.

512. WENHASTON *S. Peter.* Tenor C♯. Diam. c. 40 in.
6 Bells.
1, 2 Jnº. Ellis & Robᵗ. Tallant Ch.Wardens.
W. & T. Mears, late Lester, Pack & Chapman, London fecit 1787.
3 T. Mears of London fecit 1823.
4 ▽ 65 thrice.
✠ sancta ☐ Anna ☐ Ora ☐ Pro ☐ nobis.
5 Lester & Pack of London fecit 1767.
6 ▽ 51 thrice.
✠ 61 Quesumus Andrea ☐ 62 famulorum Suscipe Vota.
So Davy, 3 June, 1808. Old 3rd, "Wᵐ. Fiske, John Fiske, Anno Domini 1629." A clean little ring.
No sale of bells recorded in certif. of 1547. 4 and a Sancts bell in 1553.

513. WESTERFIELD *S. Mary.*   3 Bells.
1 M thrice ▽ 9.
2 Mor Augustini Sonet In Aure Dei ▽ 9.
3 C. & G. Mears, founders, London, 1852.
"Itm̄ bells in the Stepyll iij." Return of 1553, with the Ipswich churches.
Davy, 7 Aug., 1829, "3 inaccessible." See p. 17.

514. WESTHALL *S. Mary.* Tenor is a rather sharp F, slightly flattened, vibrates a minor third.   5 Bells.
1, 4 Anno Domini 1616 AB
W
2 C. & G. Mears, founders, London, 1875.
3 No inscription.
5 Omnis Sonus Laudet Dominum.
Anno Domini 1626 AB
W
So Davy, 2 June, 1808. Old 2nd, "John Darbie made me 1678."
4 in 1553. On the screen, S. Antony's pig with a crotal. See p. 114.

2G

515. **WESTHORPE** S. *Margaret.* 5 Bells.
 1, 2 John Osborne Gent. Simon Hunt Churchwardens.
 1702. H. P.
 3 Tho. Gardiner Norwich fecit 1740.
 4 ☥ 65 thrice.
 ✠ Sancta ☐ 68 Maria ☐ 68 roa (sic) ☐ 68 Pronobis.
 5 William Grimwood and Jeremiah Hayward Churchwardens 1808.

4 in 1553. Davy, 22 July, 1831, 5. See pp. 140, 145.

516. **WESTLETON** S. *Peter.* 1 Bell.
 Bell. C. & G. Mears, founders, London, 1849.
 S. A. Woods, jun. Esqr } Churchwardens.
 R. Girling, Esqr

Davy, 22 June, 1809. Sancta Maria ora pro nobis. See his note.
No sale of bells recorded in certif. of 1547. 3 in 1553.

517. **WESTLEY** S. *Mary.* 1 Bell.
 Bell. Thomas Mears of London fecit 1803.

"Great bells iij." Return of 1553. Davy, Aug. 18, 1828, notes it as inaccessible. The present church was built in 1836.

518. **WESTON** S. *Peter.* 3 Bells.
 1 ✠ : DOMINUS : SIT : ADIUTOR : MEUS :
 2 ✠ SCE : PETRE : PRO : ME : DEU : INTERCEDE :
 3 ✠ MISSUS : UERO : PIE : GABRIEL : HERT : LETA : MARIE.

So Davy, 1 June, 1808. "Great bells iij. Sawnce bells j." Return of 1553. See p. 63.

519. **WESTON, CONEY,** S. *Mary.* 1 Bell.
 Bell. John Barnes Rector, John Alderton Thomas Lanchester Church Wardens. Coney Weston, Suffolk, 1802.

"Great bells iij. Sancts Bells j." Return of 1553. A bell sold in 1690. *Eastern Counties' Collectanea*, p. 240. T. Martin noted one bell inscribed, Hac In Conclave Gabriel Auc Pange Suabe.
The tower fell in 1690.

520. **WESTON MARKET** S. *Mary.* 5 Bells.
 1 Thomas Gardiner Sudbury me fecit 1712.
 2 ☥ 66 thrice.
 ✠ Sancte Andrea Apostoli Ora Pro Nobis.
 3 ☥ 50 thrice.
 ✠ Nos Socict Sanctis ☐ Semper Nicholaus In Altis.
 4 ☐ M ☐ I ☐ S ☐ E ☐ R ☐ I ☐ S ☐ M ☐
    I ☐ S ☐ E ☐ R ☐ E ☐ R ☐ E ☐
 5 Charles King, Thomus (sic) Peck Churchwardens.
 John Stephens made mee 1725.

"Great bells iiij." Return of 1553. Tenor according to Sperling 18 cwt. Davy, 27 July, 1824. He noted 2, erased ... ora pro nobis ; 3, erased ; 4, chipped off ; 5, " Stephenson " for " Stephens," of course wrong. Sperling, in 1860, noted a defaced inscription on single letters with a leopard's head and a fleur-de-lis alternately separating them. My own notes, however, show an initial cross, No. 47; and the pot No. 46, at the end of ᛰISEᛰIS. The leopard's head is probably No. 48. There has been barbarous mutilation in this tower. See pp. 41, 58, 69, 143.

521. WETHERDEN *S. Mary*. 5 Bells.
    1, 2 Miles Graye made me 1673.
    3 Mears & Stainbank, Founders, London, 1886.
       C. J. Goodhart Rector.
       S. W. Hunt
       P. C. N. Peddar } Churchwardens.
    4 T. Osborn Downham fecit 1786.
    5 Ralph Rouse Warden. Henry Pleasant made me 1703.

4 in 1553. Old 3 as 1 and 2, says Davy. See p. 140.

522. WETHERINGSETT *All Saints*. Tenor. Diam. 43½ in.
    5 Bells.
    1 John Darbie made me 1660.
    2 John Draper made me 1636.
    3 G. Mears & Co., Founders, London, 1864.
    4 Wᵐ. Dobson, Founder, 1824. William Grimwade & John Cobbald Churchwardens.
    5 Lester & Pack of London fecit. Jaˢ. Keen & Thoˢ. Edwards Ch. Wardens 1765.

3 in 1553. Davy, 23 May, 1828, crosses 2 and 3, and notes the inscription on the bell recast in 1864, **Cɛli ðɛt munus qui rɛgnat Crinus ɛt Ꙋnus.** See pp. 112, 122.

523. WEYBREAD *S. Andrew*. 6 Bells.
    1, 2, 3, 4, 5, 6 ▽ (Moore, Holmes and Mackenzie).

See also *East Anglian* II., 6.
3 in 1553. The old three noted by me, 12 March, 1862.
    1 No inscription.
    2 ✠ AVE ᛰARIA GRACIA PLENA.
    3 John Brend made me 1651.

So Davy, 13 Oct., 1806. Mr. John Calver says that No. 1, a very rough bell, is said to have been cast in Weybread, that Mr. Robert Bond, Churchwarden, knew this, and that some knew the very field where it had been cast. See pp. 62, 154.

The "greate bell" had a new baldrick in 1599, at a cost of xij*d*. "Brande" the bellfounder received for casting it in 1651, "wᵗʰ some charges spent with him," £3 2*s*. The parish book is full of small items about the bells.

524. WHATFIELD *S. Margaret*. 3 Bells.
    1 Miles Graye made me 1678.
    2 ☐ 81 Omnia ☐ 82 Jovam ☐ 82 lavdent. ☐ 82 animantia ☐ 81 1575. S. T. W. L. T. D.
    3 Miles Graye made me 1634.

So Davy, 26 Oct., 1826. "Great bells iij." Return of 1553. See p. 98.

525. WHEPSTEAD *S. Petronilla*. 5 Bells.
    1, 2, 3, 4, 5 E. Arnold, Sᵗ. Neot's, 1774.

"Great bells j." Return of 1553. Church notes about 1724 (Tom

Martin's). "Church leaded, chancel tyled, steeple lowered. 4 bells." "Five bells." Davy, Aug. 26, 1831.
The old leaden spire is said to have been blown down in the tremendous storm of Sept 3rd, 1658, the night on which Cromwell died. See p. 153.

526. WHERSTEAD *S. Mary*. 3 Bells.
1 John Darbie made me 1675. Richard Goodinge C.W.
2 Miles Graye made me 1622.
3 ▽ 50 thrice.
+ 61 **ꝼloſ Thome ꝳeritis** ☐ 62 **ꝳereamur Gaudia Lucis**.

3 in 1553. Davy notes two bells, but does not give the inscriptions. See pp. 56, 118. R. Gooding was buried 27 Nov., 1682. Zincke's *Wherstead*, p. 9.

527. WHITTON 1 Bell.
Bell. ✠ 72 **abe** ✠ 72 **maria** ✠ 72 **gracia** ✠ 72 **a͠no** ✠ 72 **meece** ✠ 72 **xli**.

1 in 1553. Inscription quite close up to shoulder of bell. Diameter 22¾ inches. Height to shoulder 21 inches. Height to top of cannons 28 inches; square shouldered (Pearson, W.C. 15 May, 1887).
Davy, 9 Sept., 1827, "1 Bell." No sale of bells recorded in certif. of 1547. See p. 74.

528. WICKHAM MARKET *All Saints*. Tenor F. Diam. 41 in.
6 and Clock bell.
1 John Brend made me 1657.
2 The monvment of Gray
   Is past awaie
   In place of it doth stand
   The name of John Brend, 1657.
3 A. D. 1883.
   Gulielmus Thomas Image A.M. Aul : SS : Trin : Cantab: Vicarius. Johannes Cracknell et Gulielmus Nathaniel Whitmore hujus Ecclesiæ custodes.
4 ▽ 65 thrice.
   + 67 **Celi** ☐ 68 **det** ☐ 68 **munus** ☐ 68 **qui** ☐ 68 **regnat** ☐ 68 **et** ☐ 68 **unus**.
5 R C H E S D N A I C R S W C W C I B. 1601.
   RICARDVS BOWLER ME FECIT.
6 Anno Domini 1613 W1B.
Clock bell. Inaccessible.

"Great bells v. Sancts Bells j." Return of 1553.
Davy crosses 5 and 6 and 3 and 4, and records the bell recast in 1883 as inscribed, "John Darbie made me 1672." 4 Nov., 1805.
John Sawer and Tho. Gyrling C.W. of Wykham record no sale of bells in their certif., 1547. It may be Wickham Skeith. 4 honeycombed. The chime-barrel machinery was in the tower in 1873. The Clock bell, now on the outside of the spire, appears to be the old Sance bell. There is an old 30 h^r clock, without nut or screw in it. See pp. 69, 104, 113, 121.

529. WICKHAM SKEITH *S. Andrew*. 6 Bells.
1 Osborn fecit 1780.
2 Thos. Osborn Downham fecit 1780.

3 I D I E 1615 B B
DE QVATVOR QVINQVE INVITO LIVORE
SVPERBO
VT TEMPLA BONA SINT INVIOLATA DEI.
P R N G
 I G
4 John Darbie made me 1669.
5 The Lord to praise
  My voice I raise.
  Thoˢ. Osborn founder 1797:
6 John Draper made me 1627.

4 in 1553. Martin in 1724 could not read the 3rd, and Davy in 1819 only succeeded imperfectly.
The initials on the 3rd (besides I. D. and I. E., which are those of John Driver and James Edbury, of Bury, the founders,) appear to be those of Benjamin Bonden, bapt. 1598, Peter Fryer or Frere, whose son George was baptized in 1597, Nicholas Goddard, bapt. 1591, and John Goddard, who married Anne Fryer, or Frere, in 1584, and was Churchwarden in 1628. Will of Henr. ffryer of Wickham in Ipsw. Registry between 1444 and 1455. The inscription on the 3rd points to resistance by "village Hampdens" to some "little tyrant of their fields." See pp. 110, 112.

530. WICKHAMBROOK *All Saints*. 5 Bells.
1 Miles Graye made me 1641.
2 Charles Newman made mee 1695.
3 William Dobson 1823.
4 Miles Graye made me 1611.
5 John Darbie made me 1663.

"Great bells iiij." Return of 1553. "Five bells," Davy. See pp. 117, 119, 123, 135. The date on the 4th is doubtful.

531. WILBY *S. Mary*. 6 Bells.
1 John + Goldsmith + fecit + 1713 ☐ + ☐
2, 3 Anno Domini 1606. W. B.
4 Robt. Coates Cʰ. Warden. Thoˢ. Osborn Downham
  fecit 1789.
5 Miles Graye made me 1615.
6 ▽ 65 thrice.
  + 67 𝕌irgo ☐ 68 𝕮oronata ☐ 68 𝕭ut ☐ 68 𝕱los ☐
  𝕬d ☐ 68 𝕽egna ☐ 68 𝕭eata.

So Davy, 16 June, 1809. See some quaint lines on xxxviii score of Crown Bob, March xxviii MDCCXXXIV in his note. 4 and a Sance bell in 1553. 3rd cracked, but hardly perceptibly so. See pp. 67, 117, 146.

532. WILLINGHAM *S. Mary*.
Ecclesia destructa. No return in 1553.
The church is alluded to in Davy's MSS. as standing in 1529.

533. WILLISHAM *S. Mary*. 1 Bell.
  Bell. 1777.
2 in 1553. Davy, 19 May, 1829, 1 inaccessible.

534. WINGFIELD *S. Mary*. 6 Bells.
1 Thoˢ. Newman of Norwich made me.
  Mr. Daws C. W. 1742.

254   THE CHURCH BELLS OF SUFFOLK.

    2 AB ▽ 86 ▽ 52
    W.
    𝔒mnis 𝔖onus 𝔏audet 𝔇ominum ifgfe 1598 qay □
    3 Anno Domini 1613 W. B.
    4 Anno Domini 1613 W I B.
    5 Anno Domini 1602 AB
        W.
    6 Anno Domini 1613 AB
        W.

4 and a Sance bell in 1553. Davy, 24 Sept., 1827, crosses 1 and 2 and 4 and 5. See pp. 113, 138.

535. WINSTON *S. Andrew.*   5 Bells.
    1 John Darbie made me 1662 R. M.
    2 John Darbie made me 1662 T D.
    3, 5 Miles Graye made me 1638.
    4 Tho⁵. Gardiner Sudbury fecit 1737.
So Davy, except the initials. "Great bells iiij." Return of 1553. See pp. 118, 123, 144.

536. WISSETT *S. Andrew.*   5 Bells.
    1 T. Mears London fecit 1818.
    2, 3 Thomas Gardiner Benhall fecit 1718.
    4 □ UIRGO □ MARIA.
    5 Tho. Gardiner fecit 1718. Robᵗ. More C.W.
4 in 1553. Davy, 15 May, 1806, notes 2 and 3 as 1 and 2, 4 as 3, 5 as 4, and an old tenor, 𝔣los 𝔗home...
The tenor was clearly recast for a treble. See pp. 11, 143.

537. WISTON *S. Mary.*   3 Bells.
    1 W. L. T. D. 1574. Nicolas Grice Benefacter.
    □ 82 Fear ⚜ God □ 81.
    2 Miles Graye made me 1664.
    3 John Thornton Sudbury fecit 1719.
"Great bells iij." Return of 1553. Davy, Oct. 1, 1828, "A cupola which contains three small bells." See pp. 98, 133, 142.

538. WITHERSDALE *S. Mary Magdalene.*   2 Bells.
    1 W. B.
    2 No inscription.
2 in 1553. "Two" Terriers; and Davy, 10 Jan., 1811. See p. 115.

539. WITHERSFIELD *S. Mary.*   5 Bells.
    1, 3, 5 Robert Taylor, St. Neot's, 1804.
    2 Richard Bowler made me 1603.
    4 John Thornton Sudbury fecit 1718.
"Great bells iiij." Return of 1553. "Five tuneable bells," Davy. See pp. 104, 142.

540. WITNESHAM *S. Mary.*   6 Bells.
    1 Cast by John Warner & Son, London, 1871.
    2 John Darbie made me 1660.
    3 Thomas Gardiner made me 1717.

4 John Darbie made me 1660 C W
5 John Darbie made me 1660.   John Hettridges C. W.
6 John Darbie made me 1660.   Daniel Meadows C. W.
"Great bells iiij." Return of 1553. Davy, 28 May, 1827. See pp. 122, 143, where "tenor" is a mistake for "third."

541. WIXOE *S. Leonard.*   Diam. 28 in.   1 Bell.
Bell.   ▽ 25 O 18 ▽ 26 Sancte Ꞥecolae Ora Ꞥro Ꞥobis
So Davy. "Great bells ij." Return of 1553. See p. 25.

542. WOODBRIDGE *S. John-the-Evangelist.*   1 Bell.
Bell.   Thomas Mears, London, founder, 1843.

543. WOODBRIDGE *S. Mary.*   Tenor 27 cwt.   8 Bells.
1 The Lord to praise my voice I'll raise.
  Tho⁵. Osborn Downham Norfolk Founder 1799.
2 Hear me when I call.
  Tho⁵. Osborn Downham Norfolk Founder 1799.
3 Strike me and I'll sound sweetly.
  Tho⁵. Osborn Downham Norfolk Founder 1799.
4 Peace and good neighbourhood.
  Tho⁵. Osborn Downham Norfolk Founder 1799.
5 Our voices shall with joyful sound
  Make hills and valleys echo round.
  Tho⁵. Osborn Downham Norfolk Founder 1799.
6 In wedlock's bands all ye who join
     With hands your hearts unite
     So shall our tuneful tongues combine
        To laud the nuptial rite.
  Tho⁵. Osborn Downham Norfolk Founder 1799.
7 We to the church the living call
  And to the grave do summon all.
  Tho⁵. Osborn Downham Norfolk Founder 1799.
8 John Hammond, Robert Allen Churchwardens.
  Tho⁵. Osborn Downham Norfolk Founder 1799.

"Great bells v. Sancts bells j." Return of 1553. No sale of bells recorded in certif. of 1547.

An older tower seems to have become ruinous by the beginning of the 15th century. Hawes has collected the following items from old wills:—W. Foder, 1444, 3s. 4d.   Joh. Newport, 1444, £6 13s. 4d. Joh. Allrede, 1448, 20 marks. Joh. Spicer, 1453, £7. Galfr. Kempe, 1450, £7. W. Berard, 1451, 3s. 4d. Walt. Doft, 1448, 40s. Rob. Parterick, 1459, 13s. 4d. Joh. Kemp, 1458, £14. Rob. Barfoot, 40s.

The expression in Foder's will, "Ad fabricationem campanilis cum fuerit inceptum," shows that the work had been already in project, perhaps for some time; "de novo faciend," in others points to the existence of a previous belfry.

By 1612, according to Hawes, the bells were increased from 5 to 6. Towards the end of the seventeenth century these had all been recast. Martin's note (1712) is as follows:

"1 John Darbie made me 1669.
 2 Miles Grey made me 1638.
 3 Miles Grey made me 1638.
 4 Miles Grey made me 1676.
 5 John Darbie made me 1679.
 6 John Darbie made me 1677."

From notes in Davy, taken at the time of the removal of the bells for recasting, Nov. 10, 1798, it appears that "Grey" on 4 is a mistake for "Darbie," and that the date on 5 should have been 1676. The octave was completed by the addition of two trebles, and the old 2nd, which thus became the 4th, recast by Phelps in 1721; but Phelps's new 2nd went to the furnace again at the hands of Pack and Chapman in 1779 The old 3rd, which had become the 5th, had already visited Whitechapel in 1751, during Lester's days.

Mr. Robert Allen, Churchwarden, caused the weights to be taken, with this result :—

	Old Bells. Received.			New Bells. Founders' Weight.			Weighed at Woodbridge.		
	Cwt.	qrs.	lbs.	Cwt.	qrs.	lbs.	Cwt.	qrs.	lbs.
1.	5	1	14	8	1	17	8	1	6
2.	5	1	14	8	0	23	8	0	20
3.	6	1	0	9	0	26	9	0	22
4.	6	3	2	9	2	27	9	2	25
5.	8	1	9	11	1	17	11	1	14
6.	9	3	10	12	2	2	12	2	0
7.	13	0	7	17	3	8	17	3	3
8.	18	2	18	26	3	11	26	3	11

Mr. Osborne's bill for the whole was £376 17s. 6d.

544. WOOLPIT S. Mary. Tenor G♯. Diam. 37¼ in. 6 Bells.

1, 2, 3 C. & G. Mears, founders, London, 1844.
4, 5 John Darbie made me 1658.
6 C. & G. Mears, founders, London, 1855.

Davy seems in this case to have counted from the treble. His notes are:
1 John Darbie made me 1658. Thomas Hudson, K. C. (?)
2 John Draper made me 1616.
3 Sancta Maria Ora Pro Nobis.
4, 5 John Darbie made me, 1658.

"Great bells v." Return of 1553. See p. 122.

545. WOOLVERSTONE S. Michael. 1 Bell.

Bell. C. & G. Mears, founders, London. Recast 1847.

1 in 1553. Davy notes one bell inscribed "Miles Graye made me 1610." East Anglian N. S. III., 112. See pp. 92, 117.

546. WORDWELL All Saints. 1 Bell.

Bell. No inscription.

"Great bells ij." Return of 1553. Davy, 18 Aug., 1829, "A small bell in a cupola, which I could not get to." See p. 2.

547. WORLINGHAM All Saints. Tenor. Diam. 37½ in.
5 Bells.

1 ᙎ 52 ᙎ 86 AB
W.
Anno Domini 1622.
2 Anno Domini 1621. W. A. B.
3 Anno Domini 1608.
4, 5 ᙎ 52 ᙎ 86 AB
W.
Anno Domini 1621.

So Davy, 12 Aug., 1809. "Great bells iij." Return of 1553. No sale of bells recorded in certif. of 1547. See pp. 113, 114.

548. WORLINGHAM S. Peter.

Ecclesia destructa. No return in 1553.

549. WORLINGTON *All Saints.* 5 Bells.

1 Percute dulce cano. THE REV. JAMES GIBSON RECTOR. FREDERIC JOHN CLARK AND JAMES BOOTY CHURCHWARDENS. 1850.

I Taylor and Son Founders Loughboro'.
2 Robard Gvrney made me 1665.
3 John Draper made me 1635.
4 ✠ Omnis : sonus : laudet : DOMINUM
THIS BELL WAS RECAST AND A TREBLE ADDED BY SUBSCRIPTION. 1850.
I Taylor and Son Founders Loughboro.
5 ☐ 1 JOHANNES : GODYNGE : DE : LENNE : ME : FECIT.

"Wrydlynton...Great bells iij." Return of 1553.
Till 1850 there were four (as noted by Davy, 24 Aug., 1829), and the old 3rd was inscribed "I. E. 1614 l. D." These bells are now the first five of a six. See pp. 7, 110, 112, 132, 153.

550. WORLINGWORTH *S. Mary.* Tenor 13 cwt. 6 Bells.

1, 2, 3, 5 Thomas Mears of London fecit 1804.
4 Mears & Stainbank, Founders, London.
   Restaur.
   In Memoriam
  Elizabeth Jesser French
   A.D. 1887.
6 Cast by subscription A.D. 1804.
Patrons: the Duchess of Chandos and Lord Henniker, Emily Lady Henniker.
The Rev[d]. Charles Buckle Rector, Henry Cupper Samuel Wardley Church Wardens. Jn[o]. Jessup a subscriber Treasurer. Thomas Mears of London fecit.

4 in 1553. Davy, 23 July, 1808, notes the 4th as like the rest, as I noted it in 1874.
These lines are on Jessup's tomb (ob. June 19th, 1825, æt. 80):—
"To ringing from his youth he always took delight,
Now his bell has rung and his soul has took its flight ;
We hope to join the choir of heavenly singing
That far excells the harmony of ringing."

The Tenor "Tolled xii Hours año D. 1821 And A Funeral Peal Rang after as a Token of Heartfilt Grief At The Death of Her Majesty Queen Caroline."

551. WORTHAM *SS. Thomas and Mary.* 1 Bell.

Bell. T. Osborn Downham Norfolk fecit 1785. Cum Voco Venite.

3 in 1553.

552. WRATTING, GREAT, *S. Mary.* 1 Bell.

Bell. W. H. 1625.

So Davy. "Great bells iij. Sancts bells j." Return of 1553.
Evidently William Harbert's, for the letters are those of Miles Graye's larger alphabet.

553. WRATTING, LITTLE, *S. Mary.* 1 Bell.
Bell. ☐ 74 sanctorum ☐ 76 more ☐ 75 modo ☐ 76 pulso ☐ 75 laudis ☐ 76 honore.

| 73 Johannes tonne me fecit

"Great bells iij." Return of 1553. One bell. Davy.
Through the kind perseverance of Mr. Deedes this interesting bell has been added to our list. It is in a turret, and was long regarded as inaccessible, and thus has received no notice in the Dissertation. In the medallion under the founder's name is a sitting figure, and on the opposite side of the bell is a design enclosed in a pear-shaped figure, point upwards.

554. WRENTHAM *S. Nicholas.* Tenor G. Bells not in tune.
5 Bells.
1 Thomas Gardiner fecit 1723.
2 (Pentacle) JOHN CLARK MADE THIS BELL 1606.
3 Thomas Gardiner me fecit 1714.
4 Thomas Newman made me. Mr. John Bardwell C.W. 1745.
5 C. & G. Mears, founders, London. Recast 1847. Thomas Girling Esqr. Church Warden.

Davy, 31 Aug., 1809, notes the old tenor, "Anno Domini 1620 I B B." No sale of bells recorded in certif. of 1547. 4 and a Sance bell in 1553. See pp. 108, 138, 143, 144.

555. WYVERSTONE *S. George.* Tenor. Diam. 36 in.
3 Bells.
1 ▽ 52 (Arms of England with C. R.) Henry ▽ Yaxle made me 1674.
2 Tho. Gardiner fecit 1719.
3 ▽ 52 thrice.
+ 61 Petrus Ad Eterne ☐ 62 Ducat Nos Pascua Vite.

So Martin gives the tenor. Davy notes three. 3 in 1553. See p 144.
The shield between "Henry" and "Yaxle" is *Yaxley*, of Yaxley, *erm.*, a chevron *sa.* between three mullets pierced, *gu.* The family appears to have been of great antiquity. Henry Yaxley's bells are very rare, and of poor quality. I think it possible that some of the Horham bells are from him. One by him, bearing the family arms, is at Fritton, Norfolk. From his use of Brasyer's shield it seems that he may have been at work in Norwich. There is here a vacant pit, larger than those occupied.

556. YAXLEY *S. Mary.* 6 Bells.
1 Cast by John Warner & Sons, London, 1857. (Royal Arms) Patent.
2 William Dobson, Founder, Downham, Norfolk, 1828.
3, 4 John Brend made me 1658.
5 ▽ 65 thrice.
+ Virgo ☐ Coronata ☐ Duc ☐ Nos ☐ Ad ☐ Regna ☐ Beata.

6 Thomas Draper made me at Thetford 1594.
Celi solamen nobis det Deus. Amen.

Davy, 17 June, 1809, notes the 2nd split, and the 3rd, *Virgo Coronata Duc Nos ad Regna Beata.*
4 in 1553. On the old treble, T. Lester made me R. Jacob, D. Tripp, 1746. Sperling (c. 1860) "Tenor G." See p. 101.

557. YOXFORD *S. Peter.* 6 Bells.

1, 3, 4, 5 John Brend made me 1655.
2 I. B. made me 1656. Richard Hayle.
6 John Darbie made me 1685. C. R.

So Davy, 17 May, 1806. No sale of bells recorded in certif. of 1547. 3 in 1553. See pp. 121, 125.

Index Nominum.

As the parishes are arranged alphabetically, and under them are frequent references to the Dissertation, there is no necessity for an *Index Locorum*. The Table of Contents renders an *Index Rerum* superfluous.

The names of Bell-founders and County Historians occur so constantly in the list of inscriptions that the Index contains no reference to either, save where they occur in the Dissertation.

A

Name	Page
Adair	191
Adams	130, 171
Affleck	182
Alcock, Bishop	87, 88
Alderton	250
Aldreg	163
Aldrich	232
Aldrick	156
Aldridge	214
Aldous	238
Alexander	192
Aleyn	9, 216
Aleys	44, 181
Allen	147, 168, 185, 232, 240, 255, 256
Allrede	255
Almack	217
Alston	220
Ambrose	172
Andrew	102, 110
Andrews	40, 110
Archer	240
Arden	240
Armstead	177
Arnold	153, 238
Arundel	87
Arthy	219
Aspland	138
Asplin	162
Asteley	101
Atherold	199
Athills, by founder's mistake Althills	229
Ayton	232

B

Name	Page
Backler	183
Badham	141, 240
Baker	199, 245
Baldry	164
Banyard	236
Barber	187
Barclay	202
Bardwell	258
Baret	85, 86
Barett	97, 198
Barfoot	255
Barker	51, 60, 159
Barnardiston	210
Barne	185, 198
Barnes	194, 216, 250
Barrett	97
Barry	196
Barthroope	179
Bartlett	147
Barton	46
Bateman	181
Bates	165, 192
Baxter	41, 43
Bayly	71
Bayman	216
Beacher	97
Becket Thomas à	55, 148
Bell	184
Belle van	76
Belleyettir	8
Belton	8
Belyetere	61
Berard	255
Bernard	67
Bethell	149, 223
Bewicke	171
Bigg	195
Bigsbe	235
Billeyetti	8
Billes Ion	34
Bingley	168
Bird	237
Bisbie	217
Bixby	120
Bixon	148
Blackburn, Lord	46
Blews and Son	154
Blinco	227
Blithe de	14
Blocke	197
Blois	231
Blomefield	22, 60
Blomfield	236
Bloomfield	214
Blower	93
Bloys	196

INDEX NOMINUM.   261

	Page		Page		Page
Boaden	... 253	C		Cooke	... 160, 201
Boby	... 238			Cooper	159, 217, 221, 239
Boggis	171, 172	Cade	... 38	Coote	... 86
Boldero	... 209	Calle	... 48	Copinger	... 174
Bond	... 251	Calver	... 251	Coppinge	... 198
Booty	... 257	Calverley	... 19	Corbet	... 110
Borrett	180, 214, 238	Cambridge, Sir Ralph		Corder	... 225
Botson	... 192	of	... 11	Cornell	... 194
Bowell	... 208	Camell	... 171	Cornwaleys	... 91
Bowler	104, 116, 120	Camper	... 176	Cornwallis	19, 105
Bracker, 62, 179, 248, 249		Candlar	... 215	Cottingham	... 195
Brakelond, Jocelyn de		Carnsewe	... 38	Cotton	... 93
3, 172		Caroline, Queen	... 257	Cracknell	... 252
Brame	... 247	Carr	... 154, 212, 221	Cragg	... 222
Brampton	.. 189	Carss	... 173	Crampin	... 230
Bramston	... 93	Cartare	... 26	Cranmer	... 91
Brasyer, 41—46, 48 (2),		Carter	109, 190	Crevnr	... 163
49—51, 60, 72, 146,		Carthew	148, 175	Crick	... 244
152		Casburn	... 219	Crickmore	... 130
Brend, 102, 103, 110, 113,		Cason	... 199	Cromwell	40, 119, 252
115, 116, 121, 148,		Caster, Van	... 76	Cross	... 196
187		Caton	... 205	Crowfoot	... 211
Brereton	... 127	Catchpole	... 209	Crystall	... 240
Breton	... 164	Catlin	147, 182	Cubytt	... 232
Brett	... 160	Cawnteler	... 234	Culham	... 218
Brewster	... 194	Cawston	... 220	Culpeck	142, 185
Briant	97, 154	Chainley, alias Rainse	105	Culverden, 37, 38, 40, 79,
Bridge	... 199	Chamberleyn	... 218	236
Brightly	... 171	Chamberlin	195, 196	Cupper	... 257
Brook	178, 208, 224	Chandos, Duchess of		Curteys	... 172
Brooke	34, 174	150, 257		Cutting	196, 246
Brooks	162, 204	Channell	... 41		
Bromey	... 165	Chapman	47, 150, 178		
Brothers	... 210	Charles I.	... 122	D	
Broun	43, 74, 187	Charles II.	164, 231		
Brown	162, 164, 170, 211	Charles VI. of France		Dacon	... 241
Broven	... 164	19, 20		Dade	... 242
Bryant	... 189	Chaucer	... 44	Dale	... 90
Buchanan	... 173	Cheese	109, 110	Dallas	... 214
Buckle	... 257	Chenery	... 239	Danby	48, 49, 51, 52
Budaeus	... 84	Chevez	... 206	Danyell, 22, 23, 25, 27,
Bugg	... 160	Chilton	... 246	34, 47
Bull	... 199	Chirche 69, 70, 71, 72, 73		Darbie. 121, 122, 132, 134,
Bulling	... 164	Chittocke	... 244	136
Bullisdon	... 34	Choke	48, 50, 52	Darbye	... 120
Bumstead	... 236	Churton	... 2	Darcye of Cheche,
Banyan	... 121	Clarence	77, 236	Lord	... 91
Burch	... 244	Clark, 27, 163, 203, 209,		Dashwood	... 240
Burford	11, 14	257, 258		Davie	183, 236
Burgess	... 186	Clarke, 104, 108, 109, 210,		Davy	101, 233
Burley de	... 19	221, 242		Dawe, 18, 19, 20, 25, 37,
Burney	129, 130	Clay	... 244	58, 73
Burrage	... 242	Clubb 183, 204, 246, 249		Dawes	... 127
Burssor	... 210	Coates	... 253	Daws	... 253
Burton	... 243	Cobbald	... 251	Dawson	196, 229
Bury	... 192	Cobbold	... 217	Day and Son, 156, 164,
Butcher	... 171	Cobytt	... 232	168, 169, 180, 185,
Butts	... 195	Cocksedge	... 184	214, 230, 239, 241,
Buxton	... 101	Coe	217, 226	242
Byrde	... 72	Cok	... 8	Daynes	... 161
		Coke	22, 106	Dearesle	... 221
		Colmar	... 82	Death	... 194
		Cook 185, 189, 236, 238		Debenham	... 177

	Page		Page		Page
Deedes, 132, 167, 184, 217, 258		F		Glemham	... 171
				Gloucester Sandre de	14
de Grey ...	... 182	Fairfax ...	... 119	Godard ...	... 238
de la Pole	... 44	Farrow ...	... 165	Goddard ...	... 253
Dennaunt	... 93	Fawkes ...	... 242	Godewyne	... 162
Denton ...	... 212	Felix S. ...	... 2	Godfrey ...	... 199
Derby ...	12, 14	Fellget ...	... 210	Godynge ...	7, 8, 257
Derlyngton	... 29	Felton ...	... 231	Golde ...	... 107
d'Ewes ...	... 127	Fenton ...	... 180	Golding ...	165, 234
Deye ...	... 98	Ferrand ...	... 246	Goldsmith	145, 146, 226
Dick ...	... 46	Festus ...	... 84	Goldyngham	... 101
Dickins ...	... 180	ffcavyear ...	91, 227	Gooch ...	... 228
Dier 103, 104, 108, 177		ffoundor 16, 18, 19, 20		Gooche ...	... 218
Dobede ...	... 189	ffox ...	... 196	Goodhart	... 251
Dobson ...	... 154	Ffyncham	... 29	Goodinge	... 252
Doft ...	... 255	Fieldgate	... 203	Goodrich	... 209
Dou ...	... 201	Fisher ...	... 188	Goslin ...	... 150
Downs ...	176, 217, 247	Fiske ...	180, 249	Gowing ...	... 189
Dowsing ...	... 181	Fitzlewes ...	15, 214	Grant-Francis	... 38
Draper, 100, 101, 102, 110, 111, 112, 113, 116		Flack ...	... 238	Graye, 104, 110, 113, 116, 118, 119, 120, 121,
		Flatt ...	... 246	
Drake ... 182, 197, 226		Flory ...	... 180	125, 133, 134, 135,
Drew ...	... 176	Foder ...	... 255	140, 141, 142
Dring ...	... 180	Fogossa ...	... 52	Gregory ...	... 47
Driver ...	109, 110	Foppe ...	... 71	Green 95, 166, 203, 246
Drummond	... 197	Ford ...	... 236	Greene ...	... 120
Dudley ...	... 105	Fox ...	120, 178	Grey ...	... 105
Dulley ...	... 176	Foxe ...	... 40	Greyse ...	... 166
Durrant ... 186, 192, 216		Framlingham 102, 158, 243		Grice ...	... 254
Dyer ...	... 120	Franclin ...	... 218	Griggs ...	... 174
Dysart, E. of, 150, 192, 200, 245		Freeman, 135, 228, 233. 238		Grimsbye	... 164
		French ...	... 257	Grimwade	197, 251
		Freston ...	... 218	Grimwood	227, 250
		Frewer ...	... 163	Guddine ...	... 8
		Frost ...	... 236	Gull ...	... 178
E		Froude ...	... 94	Gullifer ...	... 164
Eade ...	210, 230	Fryer ...	... 253	Gurdon ...	... 172
Eagle ...	... 244	Fuller ...	174, 212	Gurney ...	131, 132
Eaton ...	... 160	Fyson ...	189, 194	Gyrling ...	... 252
Eayre ... 152, 153, 199					
Ebdon ...	... 199				
Ecclestone 149, 178, 236		G		H	
Edbury ...	109, 110				
Eden ...	... 111	Gage ...	172, 173		
Edmund, King	... 62	Gardiner, 138, 140, 142, 143. 145, 184, 204, 233, 234, 246		Hale ...	... 127
Edmunds	... 152			Hall ...	... 239
Edward I.	... 7			Hamilton, Duke of	185
Edward III.	2, 126	Gardner ...	... 241	Hammond	... 255
Edward IV.	... 49	Garnham	... 209	Hamond ...	... 72
Edward VI., 30, 52, 84, 106		Garrard ...	171, 172	Hanbury ...	... 171
		Garrett ...	153, 214	Hanmer ...	... 188
Edwarde ...	... 232	Gawdy ...	158, 182	Hanney ...	... 20
Edwards ...	233, 251	Gellius, Aulus	... 84	Hanse ...	... 180
Ellacombe	... 246	Genney 48, 49, 50, 52, 72		Harbert ...	... 257
Elizabeth, Queen, 38, 80, 99, 235, 248		George II.	... 143	Hardy ...	... 120
		Gerbertus Scholasticus	5	Harington	... 101
Ellis 130, 215, 223, 249		Gerne ...	111, 165	Harland ...	... 244
Elmy ...	... 228	Gibbs ...	... 238	Harleton ...	25, 26
Emerys ...	... 206	Gibson ...	... 257	Harris ...	172, 217, 223
Evered ...	... 229	Gillingwater, 184, 193, 205		Harvey ...	156, 172, 220
Everett ...	... 202	Gilpin ...	... 171	Haryson ...	... 220
Evesham, Walter of	3	Girling ..	250, 258	Hasted ...	... 204
Eyer ...	... 106	Glasscock	... 70	Hawes ...	55, 76

INDEX NOMINUM.

Name	Page
Hawes	169, 173, 174, 181, 189, 197, 230, 232, 255
Hawke	68
Hawkes	109, 225
Hayes	29
Hayle	259
Hayward	161, 196, 250
Haywarde	178
Headley	221
Hebert	216
Hele	156
Henniker	150, 257
Henry I.	88
Henry II.	3
Henry III.	3
Henry V.	20
Henry VIII.	93
Herbert	101
Hettridges	255
Heyham	197
Heylin	36
Hieronymus Magius	84
Hill	107, 246
Hille	23, 24, 26, 47
Hills	205
Hindes	110
Hobart	210
Hodson	121, 132, 133
Hoggar	221
Holdfield	104
Holles	236
Hollingworth	238
Hollon	235
Hollwell	134
Hopton	91
Hormesby	212
Horner	152, 212
Horth	179
Houghton	163
Howard	212
Howes	163
Howlet	243
Hudschyd	216
Hudson	256
Huggan	48
Hugh, S.	236
Humfrey	94
Hunt	171, 247, 250, 251
Hurnard	241
Hurry	186
Hyhard	218
Hyell	197
Hynes	194

I

Name	Page
Image	252
Infield	220
Ingulph	22
Isaacke	97

J

Name	Page
Jacob	259
Jacquemart	89
James II.	134
James	193
Jarmin	217
Jaxe	215
Jealous	211
Jefferys	195
Jeffrey	242
Jefrey	163
Jenings	211
Jenkins	130
Jennings	132, 212
Jennison	176
Jentylman	233
Jermyn	184, 188, 193
Jernegan	91
Jessup	257
Jetur	216
Jewell	111
Jewers	226
Jewle	246
John V. of Portugal	143
John XXII, Pope	87
Johnson	2, 77, 145, 196, 212
Jones	224, 241
Jordan	23, 25, 26, 27, 28, 29, 30, 31, 32, 34, 37, 47, 94
Joselyn	208
Jowars	177
Julius II., Pope	40

K

Name	Page
Kebyll	36
Keeble	238
Keen	251
Kemball	203
Kembell	210
Kemp	255
Kempe	255
Kenyon	177
Kerington	156
Kerredge, Kerridge	230, 231
Kerry	159
Kersey	183
Kett	105, 215, 222
Killett	172
King	194, 203, 212, 223, 250
Kingsbury	171
Knight	142, 147
Knox	197

L

Name	Page
Lacroix	89
Lanchester	250
Land	97, 98, 99, 100
Laj eg	210
Larke	50
Last	230, 236
Latimer, Bishop	106
Laud, Archbishop	111
Lawrence	40, 41
Lawson	155
Leach	164
Leake	197
Leman	148, 175, 183
Lemon	185
le Rous	14
Lester	149, 150
Lester and Pack	27, 149
L'Estrange	8, 60, 63, 73, 111, 113, 116, 134, 141, 154, 193, 205, 239
Lewis	3
Lifton	190
Lines	218
Liverpool, Bishop of	153
Lloyd	157
Lockes	100
Loder	230
Longe	97, 178
Lord	245
Lott	247
Lynam	4
Lynde	163
Lyttleton	48, 50, 52

M

Name	Page
Mackay	46
Mackenzie	211
Mackerell	60
Maddocke	93
Maggs	192
Mainprice	192
Malet	41
Mallyng	225
Malster	220
Manchester, Earl of	115
Maning	228
Mann	171
Mannock	236
Mannynge	229
Manthorpe	211
Marck	89
Margerom	163
Marlborough, Duke of	141, 209
Martin	146, 228, 232
Martyn	217
Mason	86
Mathew	224
Matthew	198
Maude	221
Mayhew	196
Mayo	94

	Page		Page		Page
Meadowe	200	O		Plume	184
Meadows	223, 255			Plowden	52
Mears	150, 151, 154	Oakes	217, 222	Pond	201
Mears and Stainbank	154	Odyngton, Walter of		Poole	220
Mechel	104		3, 4, 5, 6, 154	Pooley	159, 180
Meller	229	Okes	222	Poope	195, 196
Methold	236	Oliver	151, 238	Pope	50
Mevias	106	Orford	183	Porter	228
Michel	39	Orwell	225	Postle	234
Middleditch	217	Osborn	151	Potter	179
Middleton	178	Osborne	250	Potter	41, 43
Midson	201	Osburnd	238	Poulter	219
Mildmay	90	Ostler	173	Powell	202
Millard	93	Ottewell	167	Power	71
Mills	217	Owen, 104, 105, 106, 108,		Pratt	240
Milton	121, 138	243		Preston	40
Mirrld (sic)	198	Owers	219	Prior	247
Moody	149	Oxnedes, John of	2	Pritty	163
Moore	71, 130, 182			Prockter	165
Moore, Holmes and				Pycot	10
Mackenzie, 63, 154,		P		Pye	68
203, 233				Pyrson	225
More	254	Pack	149, 150		
Moreto	209	Pack and Chapman	151		
Morris	39, 75	Packard	169	Q	
Moseley	223	Page	130, 172		
Moss	158	Paley	157	Quivil, Bishop	10
Mothersole	215	Palmer	227		
Moyle	48, 50, 52	Pannell	235		
Mudd	100	Pargeter	94	R	
Mulliner	192	Paris	3		
Mullinger	210	Parker, 3, 106, 163, 170,		Radcliffe	84
Mumford	196, 212	184, 217, 222, 228		Rainbird	209
Munns	226	Parlet	212	Rainse	105
Murrell	220	Parr	105	Ramsden	196
Muskett	91	Parsley	212	Rand	197
		Parson	169	Randale	199
		Parterick	255	Ransomes and Sims	146
N		Partridge	202	Rant	218
		Pascal	77, 174	Raven	214
Needen	229	Pascall	78	Rawlinson	6
Needham	48, 50, 52	Paston	44, 48	Ray	176, 232
Newcombe	152	Patrick	153, 203	Rayment	173
Newman, 29, 135, 136, 137,		Peachey	219	Read	219
139, 141, 152		Peake	164	Reede	199
Newport	255	Pearson	252	Reeve, 193, 197, 201, 202,	
Newstead	177	Peck	250	204, 214, 215, 216	
Newton	147, 210	Peddar	251	Reniger	52
Nicholson	220	Peek	241	Reve 72, 73, 69, 70, 72, 95,	
Noone	93, 233	Peele	147, 210	183	
Norden	226	Perfey	88	Revel	10, 11
Norman	43, 194, 210	Perrers	12	Revell	192
North	37, 91, 108, 152	Perry	198	Revett	168, 169
Northampton, M. of	105	Pettit	199	Reynolds	171, 229
Norwich, Sir John de	218	Peyton	67	Rice	158
Nottingham, Brasiere		Phelps	148	Richard II.	19, 20
de	41	Phillips	160, 180	Riches	193
Nunn	201, 234	Pigot	48, 49, 51, 52, 72	Richmond	207
Nuthall	00	Piicearn	172	Rickit	231
Nuttall	216	Plampin	224	Rider	9
Nutting	185	Plant	239	Riping	161
		Pleasant	140, 141	Ripyng	60
		Plot	20	Riston	8

	Page		Page		Page
Rivett	168	Slater	130	**T**	
Robers	192	Smith, 60, 130, 167. 169,			
Roberts	151, 160, 195	171, 181, 182, 205		Tallant	249
Rodwell	170	Smyth, 68, 97, 99, 180,		Tamplin	195
Rofforde	14	181, 199		Tapsell	103, 104
Roger	158	Sone	93	Taylor	153, 236
Rogers	173	Southgate	162	Teverson	205
Rokewood	3, 88	Southwell	90	Theobald	160
Rolfe	176	Spalding	130, 66	Thomas of Canterbury,	
Romeneye	11	Spark	188	S.	148
Rope	165	Sparke	178	Thompson	40, 156, 211
Ruper	236, 244	Sparrow	176, 199, 211	Thorn	236
Rose	14, 162, 179	Spencer	152	Thornhill	224
Rous	14, 182, 232, 233	Spenser	40	Thornton	140, 142, 159
Rouse	251	Sperling, 161, 169, 189,		Thruston	205
Rouwenhale	20	202, 204, 224, 226,		Thurkill	70
Rowley	236	244, 250, 259		Thurston	91, 227
Royce	247	Spicer	180, 255	Tippell	239
Rufford	14, 15	Spilling	130	Toller	165
Russe	14	Spinke	192	Tollemache	192, 200, 245
Russell	88, 223	Spinluf	160	Tomson	195
Rust	185, 189, 205	Spinny	232	Tonne, 41, 78, 79, 80, 94,	
Rye	19	Sporll	188	95, 97, 98, 100, 102,	
Ryle	153	Stahlschmidt, 8, 10, 11, 12,		109, 258	
Kyon	40	14, 18, 19, 20, 22, 23,		Tony	79
		26, 37, 61, 62, 108,		Tooke	132, 223
		109, 133, 147, 152		Tool	166
S		Stainbank	151	Topsel	103, 104, 181
		Stanard	205	Torry	131
S., H.	67, 68, 69	Stanby	195	Tottington, Samp-	
Sacheverell	148, 175	Stanesby	29	son, de	3, 172
Sacker	239	Stanley	151	Trimnell, Bishop	175
Sallows	197	Staples	194	Tripp	259
Salmon	211	Starlinge	120	Trusse	192
Samson	60, 202	Stebbing	168	Truston	218
Sampson	210	Stedman	127, 128, 130	Turage	252
Sancroft	193	Steggall	228	Turke	29
Sandiver	221	Stephens	139	Turner	212, 222
Santy	243	Sterne	97	Tweed	174
Sawer	252	Stevenson	46	Tweedy	209
Sayer	169, 184, 248	Stollery	162	Tylls	233
Schofield	168	Strickland, Bishop	9	Tymms	85
Schot	209	Strong	216	Tynny	41, 79
Scolding	163	Strutt	166, 225	Tyrrell	194
Scott	11, 97, 148	Strype	91	Tyssen, 34, 37, 49, 62, 77,	
Sekole	122	Stuart	133	79, 98, 109	
Seme	158	Stubbin	202		
Sewell	189	Sturdy	24, 26	**U**	
Shakespeare	38, 89, 105	Sturt	172		
Sharman	181	Stuteville, Stutfilde	182	Udall	127
Sheffield, Lord	105	Stuttesbury	94	Ufford, de	9, 14
Sheldrake	130	Suckling	179, 227	Underhill	15
Shelford	228	Suffolck, W. de.	9, 14	Underwood	179
Shepherd	189	Suffolk, A. de	9		
Sheppard	171	Sudbrū	196		
Sheriffe	246	Sudbury	81	**V**	
Sheringe	101	Suidas	84		
Sherwood	214	Sutherland	233	Vacher	201
Shrive	166	Sutton	41, 248	Venloe, Van	75
Simpson	246	Sydnor	193	Vergil, Polydore	87
Singleton	173	Syer	209	Victoria, Queen	155
Skimming	192	Sylverne	217	Viollet le Duc	4
Skytte	206	Sylvester II., Pope	5	Votier	172

	Page		Page		Page
W		Wentworth, Lord	91	Woolner	223
		West	72	Woolnough	214
Wade	92, 177, 236	Weston, P. de	10, 11	Wray	120
Waghevens	75, 76, 77, 170	Westley	226	Wright	36, 173, 210, 233
Wakeham	151, 207	Westrop	192	Wulfred	2
Waldegrave	91	Whaites	243	Wymbis	167
Walgrave	20	White	91, 176, 198	Wymbish	10
Walker	206	Whitmore	225, 252	Wydmrpole	31
Wallace	217	Whittington	126	Wynter	93
Walsingham, A. de	8	Wigson	204	Wynkfield	156
Ward	199	Wigston	229		
Wardley	252	Wilkinson	223, 241		
Warne	186	Willett	169	**Y**	
Warner	162, 206	Williams,	170, 216, 217,		
Warren	191, 217		236	Yale	238
Washington	94	Wilshere	199	Yare	109
Waters	94	Wilson	194, 237	Yaxle, Vaxley	258
Watson	218	Wimbis	10	York	162
Watts	152, 153	Winchelsey, Arch-		Yorke	196
Waylet	179	bishop	81, 84	Young	167
Waylett	141, 142	Wingfield,	90, 94, 214, 242	Youngman	219
Waynflete, Bishop	18	Wolferston	93		
Wedge	194	Wood	171		
Weekes	160	Woodard	167	**Z**	
Webincopp	231	Woods	198, 250		
Wellum	243	Woolley	164	Zincke	252
Welton	198				

www.ingramcontent.com/pod-product-compliance
Lightning Source LLC
Chambersburg PA
CBHW031327230426
43670CB00006B/265